The Nature of Soviet Power

An Arctic Environmental History

During the twentieth century, the Soviet Union turned the Kola Peninsula in the northwest corner of the country into one of the most populated, industrialized, militarized, and polluted parts of the Arctic. This transformation suggests, above all, that environmental relations fundamentally shaped the Soviet experience. Interactions with the natural world both enabled industrial livelihoods and curtailed socialist promises. Nature itself was a participant in the communist project. Taking a long-term comparative perspective, *The Nature of Soviet Power* sees Soviet environmental history as part of the global pursuit for unending economic growth among modern states. This in-depth exploration of railroad construction, the mining and processing of phosphorus-rich apatite, reindeer herding, nickel and copper smelting, and energy production in the region examines Soviet cultural perceptions of nature, plans for development, lived experiences, and modifications to the physical world. While Soviet power remade nature, nature also remade Soviet power.

Andy Bruno is Assistant Professor in the Department of History and Faculty Associate in Environmental Studies at Northern Illinois University.

Studies in Environment and History

Editors

J. R. McNeill, *Georgetown University*
Edmund P. Russell, *University of Kansas*

Editors Emeritus

Alfred W. Crosby, *University of Texas at Austin*
Donald Worster, *University of Kansas*

Other Books in the Series

Erik Loomis, *Empire of Timber: Labor Unions and the Pacific Northwest Forests*
David A. Bello, *Across Forest, Steppe, and Mountain: Environment, Identity, and Empire in Qing China's Borderlands*
Peter Thorsheim, *Waste into Weapons: Recycling in Britain during the Second World War*
Kieko Matteson, *Forests in Revolutionary France: Conservation, Community, and Conflict, 1669–1848*
George Colpitts, *Pemmican Empire: Food, Trade, and the Last Bison Hunts in the North American Plains, 1780–1882*
Micah Muscolino, *The Ecology of War in China: Henan Province, the Yellow River, and Beyond, 1938–1950*
John Brooke, *Climate Change and the Course of Global History: A Rough Journey*
Emmanuel Kreike, *Environmental Infrastructure in African History: Examining the Myth of Natural Resource Management*
Paul Josephson, Nicolai Dronin, Ruben Mnatsakanian, Aleh Cherp, Dmitry Efremenko, Vladislav Larin, *An Environental History of Russia*
Gregory T. Cushman, *Guano and the Opening of the Pacific World: A Global Ecological History*
Sam White, *Climate of Rebellion in the Early Modern Ottoman Empire*
Alan Mikhail, *Nature and Empire in Ottoman Egypt: An Environmental History*
Edmund Russell, *Evolutionary History: Uniting History and Biology to Understand Life on Earth*
Richard W. Judd, *The Untilled Garden: Natural History and the Spirit of Conservation in America, 1740–1840*
James L. A. Webb, Jr., *Humanity's Burden: A Global History of Malaria*
Frank Uekoetter, *The Green and the Brown: A History of Conservation in Nazi Germany*
Myrna I. Santiago, *The Ecology of Oil: Environment, Labor, and the Mexican Revolution, 1900–1938*
Matthew D. Evenden, *Fish versus Power: An Environmental History of the Fraser River*
Nancy J. Jacobs, *Environment, Power, and Injustice: A South African History*
Adam Rome, *The Bulldozer in the Countryside: Suburban Sprawl and the Rise of American Environmentalism*

Judith Shapiro, *Mao's War Against Nature: Politics and the Environment in Revolutionary China*
Edmund Russell, *War and Nature: Fighting Humans and Insects with Chemicals from World War I to Silent Spring*
Andrew Isenberg, *The Destruction of the Bison: An Environmental History*
Thomas Dunlap, *Nature and the English Diaspora*
Robert B. Marks, *Tigers, Rice, Silk, and Silt: Environment and Economy in Late Imperial South China*
Mark Elvin and Tsui'jung Liu, *Sediments of Time: Environment and Society in Chinese History*
Richard H. Grove, *Green Imperialism: Colonial Expansion, Tropical Island Edens and the Origins of Environmentalism, 1600–1860*
Elinor G.K. Melville, *A Plague of Sheep: Environmental Consequences of the Conquest of Mexico*
J. R. McNeill, *The Mountains of the Mediterranean World: An Environmental History*
Theodore Steinberg, *Nature Incorporated: Industrialization and the Waters of New England*
Timothy Silver, *A New Face on the Countryside: Indians, Colonists, and Slaves in the South Atlantic Forests, 1500–1800*
Michael Williams, *Americans and Their Forests: A Historical Geography*
Donald Worster, *The Ends of the Earth: Perspectives on Modern Environmental History*
Samuel P. Hays, *Beauty, Health, and Permanence: Environmental Politics in the United States, 1955–1985*
Warren Dean, *Brazil and the Struggle for Rubber: A Study in Environmental History*
Robert Harms, *Games Against Nature: An Eco-Cultural History of the Nunu of Equatorial Africa*
Arthur F. McEvoy, *The Fisherman's Problem: Ecology and Law in the California Fisheries, 1850–1980*
Alfred W. Crosby, *Ecological Imperialism: The Biological Expansion of Europe, 900–1900*, Second Edition
Kenneth F. Kiple, *The Caribbean Slave: A Biological History*
Donald Worster, *Nature's Economy: A History of Ecological Ideas*, Second Edition

The Nature of Soviet Power

An Arctic Environmental History

ANDY BRUNO
Northern Illinois University

CAMBRIDGE
UNIVERSITY PRESS

University Printing House, Cambridge CB2 8BS, United Kingdom

One Liberty Plaza, 20th Floor, New York, NY 10006, USA

477 Williamstown Road, Port Melbourne, VIC 3207, Australia

4843/24, 2nd Floor, Ansari Road, Daryaganj, Delhi - 110002, India

79 Anson Road, #06-04/06, Singapore 079906

Cambridge University Press is part of the University of Cambridge.

It furthers the University's mission by disseminating knowledge in the pursuit of education, learning and research at the highest international levels of excellence.

www.cambridge.org
Information on this title: www.cambridge.org/9781316507926

First published 2016
First paperback edition 2017

A catalogue record for this publication is available from the British Library

ISBN 978-1-107-14471-2 Hardback
ISBN 978-1-316-50792-6 Paperback

Contents

Figures

Maps

Tables

Acknowledgments

In one way or another, this book has been with me for over a third of my life. As one would expect from such a long-term project, I have accrued countless debts while working on it. Far too many people have assisted me in the process to mention them all. So let me start by offering a huge "thank you" to everyone who has helped in even the smallest of ways. This book would not be what it is without you.

I began concocting the idea of an in-depth environmental history of a region in the Russian Arctic as an undergraduate at Reed College, even before I knew that the field of environmental history existed. My wonderful professors there did a tremendous amount to start me off on a serious scholarly path. While studying as an MA student at the European University at Saint Petersburg with support from the Fulbright U.S. Student Program, Julia Lajus, Alla Bolotova, Aleksei Kraikovskii, and Daniil Aleksandrov introduced me to many of the classics of environmental history scholarship and taught me about the fascinating history of the Kola Peninsula. Over the years they have gone from being supportive mentors to treasured colleagues.

As a doctoral student at the University of Illinois at Urbana-Champaign, I had the privilege of working with many remarkable Russian historians: professors Mark Steinberg, Diane Koenker, John Randolph, and Eugene Avrutin and graduate students Rebecca Mitchell, Randy Dills, Elana Jakel, Sharyl Corrado, Dmitry Tartakovsky, Christina Varga-Harris, Greg Stroud, Jesse Murray, Steven Jug, Maria Cristina Galmarini, Rachel Koroloff, and Patryk Reid. Mark Steinberg was an astute, attentive, and affable academic adviser at Illinois and has continued to offer valuable advice on this book since I finished my degree. His intellectual enthusiasm, engagement, and critique have done an amazing amount to help me develop as a scholar. Diane Koenker has offered incredibly thoughtful and thorough feedback. I know that her insightful challenges have forced me to make considerable improvements to this work. John Randolph has been a wonderful mentor who has frequently engaged me in deep discussions about Russian and environmental history. While all of my graduate school colleagues have been immensely helpful and supportive, I should single out Rebecca Mitchell for having often gone above and beyond as a friend and flatmate in various corners of the globe. I would also like to thank the late Jane Hedges, who taught me much about how academic publishing works while I was an editorial assistant at *Slavic Review*, and all of the other participants in Illinois's Russian studies *kruzhok* who offered feedback on my work on more than one occasion. Finally, Zsuzsa Gille, Jesse Ribot, Jennifer Monson, the late Don Crummey, and my cohort in the Human Dimensions of Environmental Systems program at Illinois exposed me to many theories of human-nature interaction that have enriched the analysis I offer here.

An International Dissertation Research Fellowship from the Social Science Research Council with funds from the Andrew W. Mellon Foundation supported my main research stint in Russia for this book. During this time, I spent seven months living and working in Murmansk, including through the polar night. Many local scholars and librarians helped make this research possible: Aleksandr Portsel′, Nikolai Voronin, Pavel Fedorov, Aleksei Kiselev, Dmitrii Fokin, Elena Makarova, Valerii Berlin, and Svetlana Salivova. On a later trip to Kirovsk that was funded by the National Science Foundation (NSF ARC 0922651), Yulia Zaika generously arranged an invaluable stay at the Khibiny Scientific-Educational Base of Moscow State University. I have also benefited tremendously from the assistance of scholars, archivists, and librarians elsewhere in Russia, including Moscow, Saint Petersburg, Orenburg, and, most recently, Lake Baikal.

While revising my doctoral dissertation into a book, I spent time at two temporary positions that helped me advance my research and thinking. As a National Science Foundation (NSF ARC 0922651) postdoctoral fellow at Florida State University, I learned a remarkable amount from Ron Doel about how to see things from the perspective of Arctic history. His kindness, enthusiasm, and second-to-none network building set me on the right course as I began to reconceptualize my scholarship. Klaus Gestwa brought me to the University of Tübingen as a visiting scholar of the "Threatened Orders" Collaborative Research Center, which provided me with a fruitful intellectual environment to revise my manuscript and develop future research directions.

In a day and age when too many excellent young scholars have had difficulty finding the permanent academic positions that they deserve, I had the great fortune of being hired by Northern Illinois University directly out of graduate school. NIU has a rich tradition of stellar Russian historians and a top-notch press in the field. The history department there has demonstrated an exemplary commitment to offering a rigorous education at a regional public university. I also came on board just as a new and vibrantly interdisciplinary program in environmental studies was getting off the ground. My colleagues at NIU have warmly mentored me through this stage of my career, offering encouragement, advice, and insightful questions about my work. They kept their ears open too when I have needed to vent about the frustrations of revision. Jim Schmidt, Melissa Lenczewski, Beatrix Hoffman, and Chris McCord have made research funding available to me to complete the manuscript. Additionally, Emma Kuby, Emily McKee, Mark Schuller, Laura Heideman, and Beatrix Hoffman provided extremely helpful feedback on my writing.

Environmental history has gone from a somewhat marginalized subfield to one of the most active and innovative arenas in the historiography of Russia while I have been writing this book. I have had the opportunity to attend numerous workshops and conferences and learn an amazing amount from a generous and collegial cohort of scholars. Far too many individuals deserve acknowledgment for discussing my scholarship with me and offering good ideas for potential directions to take my work. Limiting myself to naming only those who have invited me to participate in focused workshops or to give invited talks, I'd like to express my gratitude to Julia Lajus, Amy Nelson, Jane Costlow, Paul Josephson, Nick Breyfogle, Julia Herzberg, Jon Oldfield, Denis Shaw, Klaus Gestwa, Mark Elie, Andrei Vinogradov, and David Moon. Pey-Yi Chu also reviewed this work as a dissertation and proposed exciting avenues for revision. Participants in the biannual Midwest Russian History Workshop and the Chicagoland and Madison-area Russian History discussion groups have likewise given me valuable advice on my scholarship. Audiences at national and international conferences, the European University at Saint Petersburg, the University of Illinois at Urbana-Champaign, New York University, the University of Chicago, Ohio State University, Florida State University, Northern Illinois University, the University of Tübingen, École des hautes études en sciences sociales, and the Murmansk State Pedagogical University raised many probing and thoughtful questions for me to consider. In the final stages of preparation, the reviewers and editors of the manuscript provided thorough feedback that allowed me to make significant improvements.

Lastly and most significantly, I would like to thank my friends and family who have sustained my mostly good cheer for many years. My parents, Carol Jarema and Dennis Bruno, enabled me to pursue my education and have always supported me emotionally. In the final stages of writing, my dad even gave the whole thing a read and made some great stylistic suggestions. My twin brother, Mike Bruno, has encouraged my pursuit of intellectual inquiry since probably before either of us even understood what that phrase meant. Often my toughest, yet proudest, critic, Mike has refined my thinking about the world in more ways than I can even comprehend. I have also benefited from my large extended family, my warm and gracious in-laws, and the more recent members of my immediate family, including Polly Bruno, Charlie Goins, and Mike Jarema. My daughter, Maya Frohardt-Bruno, has endured living in six different locations during her first three years of life while I've been obsessed with this book. She has done so with delight, affection, and good humor. Her excitement and amazement at the world around her inspires me daily.

I owe the most to Sarah Frohardt-Lane. We began as fellow colleagues in environmental history at graduate school, but soon fell in love. In addition to bringing more happiness to my life than I could ever have anticipated before being together, Sarah has turned me into a much better scholar and teacher. Though I bear all responsibility for what is in this book, her contributions are reflected on every single page. She spent a month in the Arctic with me, read drafts of my writing more times than reasonable, discussed ideas about this project on an almost daily basis, supported and encouraged me through setbacks and difficulties, and done too many other things than can fit in these acknowledgments. Indeed, it would double the length of this book to thank her properly.

Archives and Abbreviations

Note: The following list of archival collections appears in lieu of a bibliography. Readers interested in consulting a full list of cited works should feel free to contact the author.

Archival Collections

Archive of the Russian Academy of Sciences, Moscow (ARAN)
- Fond 544 (Lichnyi fond Akademika A. E. Fersmana)

Bentley Historical Library, Ann Arbor, MI
- Polar Bear Collection. Harry Duink Papers
- *Russia Route Zone A: Murman Railway and Kola Peninsula*. Copy No. 706. Washington, DC: Government Printing Office, 1918

Harvard Project on the Soviet Social System, Widener Library, Harvard University, http://hcl.harvard.edu/collections/hpsss/index.html
- Schedule B, Vol. 3, Case 49 [i.e. 31] (interviewer A.P.)

Kirovsk Branch of the State Archive of the Murmansk Region, Kirovsk (KF GAMO)
- Fond 54 (Kombinat "Severonikel′," 1936–1987)
- Fond 87 (Otdel zdravookhraniia ispolnitel′nogo komiteta Monchegorskogo Soveta narodnykh deputatov Murmanskoi oblasti, 1936–1988)

National Archives and Records Administration, College Park, MD (NARA)
- Record Group 120 (Historical Files of the American Expeditionary Force, North Russia)
- Record Group 182 (War Trade Board, Preliminary Inventory 100, Entry 253 – Correspondence with United States Regarding Shipment of Goods to Murmansk and Vladivostok)

Russian State Archive of Social and Political History, Moscow (RGASPI)
- Fond 17 (Tsentral′nyi komitet KPSS, 1903–1991)

Fond 67 (Severnyi oblastnoi komitet RKP(b), 1918–1919)
Russian State Archive of the Economy, Moscow (RGAE)
Fond 386 (Ministerstvo tsvetnoi metallurgii SSSR, 1965–1989)
Fond 3106 (Glavnoe upravlenie khimicheskoi promyshlennosti (Glavkhimprom) VSNKh SSSR, 1921–1922, 1926–1930)
Fond 4372 (Gosudarstvennyi planovoi komitet Soveta Ministrov SSSR, 1931, 1952, 1960, 1976–1991)
Fond 7793 (Glavnoe upravlenie po nikeliu i olovy Narkomtiazhprom SSSR, 1934–1939)
Fond 9037 (Glavnoe upravlenie nikelevoi i kobal'tnoi promyshlennosti Mintsevmeta, 1939–1957)
State Archive of the Murmansk Region, Murmansk (GAMO)
Fond I-72 (Upravlenie po postroike Murmanskoi zheleznoi dorogi, 1915–1918)
Fond P-152 (Proizvoditel'noe ob"edinenie "Apatit" imeni S. M. Kirova, 1932–1991)
Fond P-359 (Pechengskii raionnyi komitet KP RSFSR, 1946–1991)
Fond P-881 (Kombinat "Pechenganikel'," 1946–1991)
Fond R-163 (Otdel zdravookhraneniia pri ispolnitel'nogo komiteta Murmanskogo okruzhnogo Soveta, 1927–1937)
Fond R-169 (Murmanskii Komitet Severa, 1924–1934)
Fond R-397 (Upolnomochennyi Narodnogo komissarieta putei soobshcheniia SSSR po Murmanskoi zheleznoi dorogi, 1923–1927)
Fond R-459 (Kombinat "Pechenganikel'," 1944–1978)
Fond R-483 (Zheleznodorozhnyi komitet po zagotovke topliva i lesnykh materialov po Murmanskoi zheleznoi dorogi, 1918–1921)
Fond R-488 (Tsentral'nyi prodovol'stvennyi komitet Murmanskoi zheleznoi dorogi, 1917–1918)
Fond R-621 (Upravlenie Murmanskoi zheleznoi dorogi, 1917–1927)
Fond R-773 (Lichnyi fond V. I. Kondrikova, 1929–1936)
Fond R-810 (Murmanskii filial geografo-ekonomicheskoi nauchno-issledovatel'skoi institut Leningradskogo Gosudarstvennogo universiteta, 1919–1953)
Fond R-889 (Kolkhoz "Kransoe Pulozero," 1930, 1940–1960)
Fond R-955 (Murmanskaia olenevodecheskaia opytnaia stantsiia, 1930s–1960s)
Fond R-959 (Nizhne-Tulomskaia gidroelektrostantsiia, 1936–1964)
Fond R-990 (Kol'skoe proizvodstvennoe ob"edinenie energetiki i elektrifikatsii, 1936–1987)

Fond R-1032 (Zhandovskii gorno-obogatitel′noi kombitat, 1960–1969)

State Archive of the Russian Federation, Moscow (GARF)

Fond A-358 (Glavnoe upravlenie okhotnich′ego khoziaistva i zapovednikov pri Sovet Ministrov RSFSR i ego predsestvenniki, 1933–1990)

Fond A-482 (Ministerstvo zdravookhraneniia RSFSR)

Fond 8009 (Ministerstvo zdravookhraneniia SSSR)

Abbreviations for Archival References

ARAN	Archive of the Russian Academy of Sciences
d.	*delo*, file
GARF	State Archive of the Russian Federation
GAMO	State Archive of the Murmansk Region
f.	*fond*, collection
KF GAMO	Kirovsk Branch of the State Archive of the Murmansk Region
l./ll.	*list/listy*, sheet(s)
NARA	National Archives and Records Administration
op.	*opis′*, inventory
RGAE	Russian State Archive of the Economy
RGASPI	Russian State Archive of Social and Political History

Abbreviations for Newspapers, Journals, and Books

EH	*Environmental History*
IAOIRS	*Izvestiia Arkhangel′skogo obshchestva izucheniia Russkogo Severa*
KDF	Petrova, M. D., S. M. Salimova, and T. I. Podgorbunskaia, eds. *Kirovsk v dokumentakh i faktakh, 1920–1945 gg. Khrestomatiia*. Kirovsk: "Apatit-Media" 2006
KhR	*Khibinogorskii rabochii*
KhV	*Khibinskii vestnik*
KK	*Kandalakshskii kommunist*
KMK	*Karelo-Murmanskii krai*
KR	*Kirovskii rabochii*
MR	*Monchegorskii rabochii*
NBM	*Nauka i biznes na Murmane*
PP	*Poliarnaia pravda*

SM	*Sovetskii Murman*
SO	*Sovetskoe olenevodstvo*
SR	*Slavic Review*
SS	*Sovetskii Sever*
VMZhD	*Vestnik Murmanskoi zheleznoi dorogi*
ZhA	*Zhivaia Arktika*

1

Nature and Power in the Soviet North

Northern nature inspired many individuals like Aleksandr Platonovich Engel′gardt. In 1893 Tsar Alexander III promoted this active state official to the post of governor of the Arkhangel′sk province – an enormous territory in the north of Russia that at the time extended from the Ural Mountains in the east to Finland in the west. Soon after the appointment Engel′gardt took a trip to inspect the vast lands now under his tutelage, devoting particular attention to the natural conditions of a special section of his dominion in the far northwestern corner of the country. He saw plenty of economic potential in this region, which, along with the rest of the Russian north, existed "in complete stagnation."[1] Upon his arrival, Engel′gardt intimated that the sparse and forbidding landscape possessed the seeds of its own renovation: "In general a sort of majestic tranquility comes forth, such that it seems that in these shores are hidden forces, only temporarily seized by a deep sleep. But in the mirage of this ancient silence and tranquility, the mind of the traveler already discerns a locomotive rushing here that will awaken the dormant forces all around and enliven this silently sullen and presently unpopulated place."[2] The rush of a locomotive certainly came during the next century as the world's first communist country expanded economic activity in this part of the Arctic to a greater extent than even imaginable to Engel′gardt.

[1] A. P. Engel′gardt, *Russkii sever″: putevyia zapiski* (Saint Petersburg: Izdanie A. S. Suvorina, 1897), 1. An English translation of this book was also published. A. P. Engel′gardt, *A Russian Province in the North*, trans. Henry Cooke (Westminster: Archibald Constable and Company, 1899).

[2] Engel′gardt, *Russkii sever″*, 57.

The northern territory that elicited Engel′gardt's premonition was the Kola Peninsula. With a mix of taiga and tundra ecosystems, the region rests almost entirely north of the Arctic Circle, except for a small portion of its southern Tersk coast. In the interior several small mountain ranges tower over the lowlands, including the Khibiny Mountains and the massifs of Lovozero and Monche. Many fresh water lakes, including the sizable Lake Imandra, dot the landscape and numerous rivers such as the Niva, Tuloma, Ponoi, Iokanga, and Varzuga cross it. Coniferous forests that thin out with altitude and latitude and swamps that rest on poorly draining soils cover much of the terrain. With a polar location the region endures long periods of darkness during the snowy winters and enjoys weeks of perennial light in the brief, but vivacious, summers. Some patches of permafrost exist in the coldest upland areas. Nevertheless, the Gulf Stream current bathes the northern shores of the Kola Peninsula (the Murman coast) with warm waters, generally moderating the climate and leaving many steep rocky inlets with unfrozen bays year-round. While the territory contains less total biomass than most temperate or tropical zones, a wide array of mammals, migratory birds, fish, insects, lichen, coniferous trees, shrubs, and other plants make it their home.

At the dawn of the twentieth century fewer than 10,000 people lived on the Kola Peninsula. They were an increasingly ethnically diverse bunch of Russians, Pomors, Sami, Finns, Norwegians, Komi, and Nenets, who mostly resided in coastal settlements. With limited potential for agricultural cultivation in this environment, fishing and hunting provided the primary means of subsistence for most of the population. Slavic Pomors had temporarily traveled to the Murman coast for summer fishing in the Barents Sea since the Middle Ages. Within the interior of the peninsula, the indigenous Sami lived in highly dispersed settlements and practiced semi-nomadic lifestyles suitable for hunting and herding reindeer. Official state colonization efforts since the 1860s had brought in some new permanent residents, as had the establishment of a new commercial port called Aleksandrovsk in the 1890s and the recent migration of Komi and Nenets reindeer pastoralists. However, at the time the territory remained without any sizable cities, major military installations, or large industrial enterprises.

Less than a hundred years later, the Kola Peninsula had become a very different place. The largely coterminous Murmansk region, which took up some 144,900 square kilometers in area, now administered it. Soviet campaigns to develop the Kola north metamorphosed its natural environment and swelled its human population. Numerous dense cities, industrial enterprises, and military facilities filled the central corridor

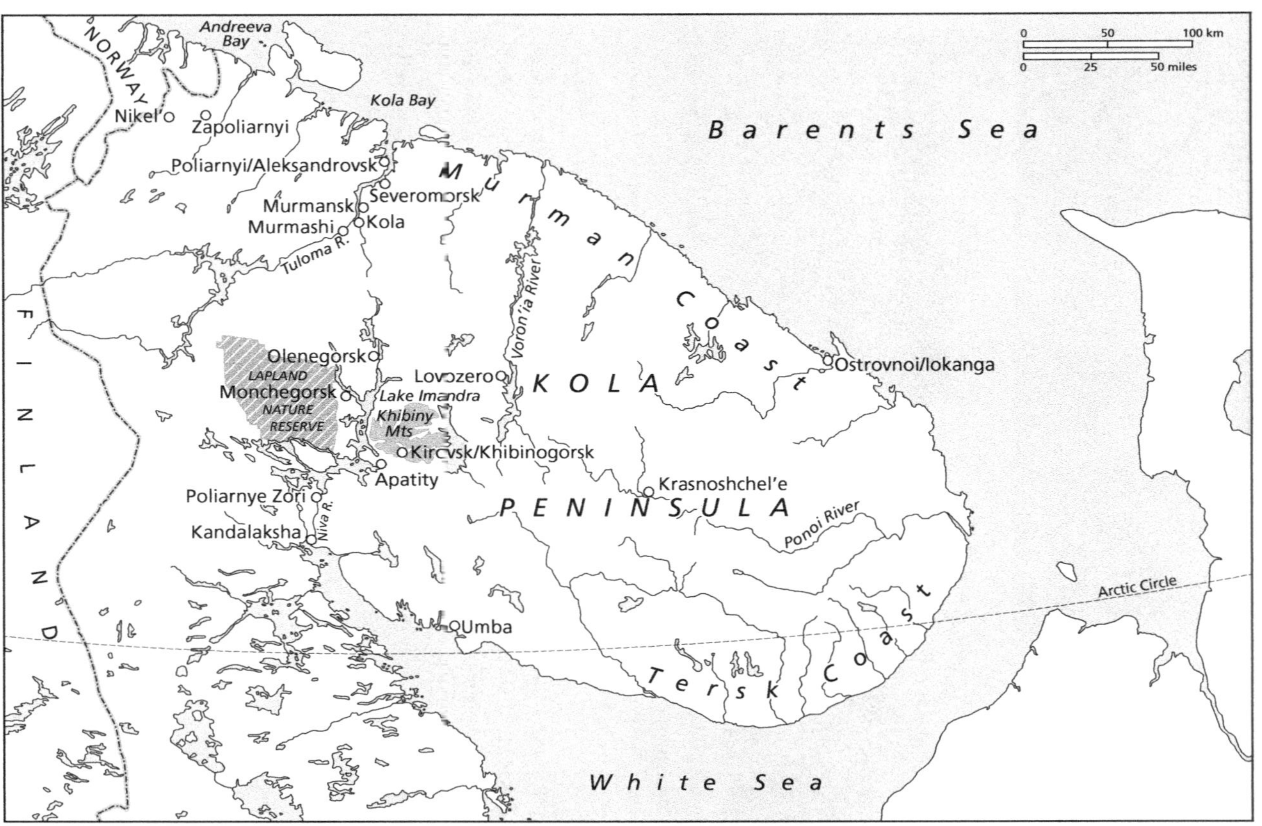

MAP 1. The Kola Peninsula.

FIGURE 1. The Kola Peninsula During Aleksandr Engel′gardt's Trip at the End of the Nineteenth Century.
Source: A. P. Engel′gardt, *Russkii sever″: putevyia zapiski* (Saint Petersburg: Izdanie A. S. Suvorina, 1897), 77.

along Lake Imandra from Kandalaksha on the White Sea to Severomorsk and Murmansk in the Kola Bay. Over a million people made the Murmansk region their home at the beginning of the 1990s. Many had moved there for career opportunities, but others initially arrived as the result of forced relocations. Proportionally, the Sami dwindled to a small minority of the population, while Russians made up an overwhelming majority. By the late Soviet period, huge gashes extended deep into the mined mountains. Some of the forests felled in the first half of the century had begun to recover, but elsewhere a mixture of acid rain and metal emissions denuded enormous zones of vegetation. The tainted chemistry of soils, air, and water killed off aquatic species and threatened human health. Reindeer, which once roamed throughout the territory, were now confined to specified and separate areas for herding and conservation. The impulse to find energy in a place without large supplies of fossil fuels led to the damming and regulation of rivers and lakes and the proliferation of radioactive wastes from a nuclear power plant, atomic submarines, and icebreakers. Overall, Soviet rule had turned the Kola Peninsula into the most populated, industrialized, and militarized section of the global Arctic, as well as one of the most polluted.

FIGURE 2. Murmansk in the Early Twenty-First Century.
Source: Author's photograph.

Why did this distant outpost of the Russian empire become one of the most economically developed and environmentally damaged territories of the north in the twentieth century? What drove the Soviets to build up this piece of the Arctic so extensively? Was Engel′gardt onto something when he wrote that "hidden forces" in the environment could help bring the region to life? How, indeed, did Kola nature affect the Soviet industrial efforts that in turn changed Kola nature? Which ideas about transforming the natural world and practices for doing so did communist leaders borrow from others and which ones did they invent themselves? How can the Soviet experience in the polar north be compared to what occurred elsewhere in the Arctic and what took place in modernizing countries more broadly? Perhaps most importantly, what can be learned about power in the Soviet system as a whole by viewing it through an environmental lens? These questions animate the pages that follow.

Nature as Actor

The Nature of Soviet Power tells the history of economically driven environmental change on the Kola Peninsula. It covers the entire Soviet period (1917–1991), beginning with late imperial Russia and extending into the post-Soviet era. In order to observe varied forms of environmental interaction, I investigate five different industries that burgeoned in the twentieth century: railroad construction, the mining and processing of chemical fertilizers, reindeer husbandry, nickel and copper smelting, and the energy sector. Many characters populate this story: reformist bureaucrats who came of age in tsarist Russia; scientists seeking to benefit the state; upwardly mobile communists who found themselves in perilous positions of authority during the Stalinist terror; regional and central state authorities; coerced laborers who built and worked in an array of industries; different ethnic groups that depended on hunting and herding reindeer; a variety of technical experts who concerned themselves with everything from improving the extraction of mineral ore to limiting the effects of pollution; and elements of the natural environment itself, including animals, rocks, and snow. Taking an all-encompassing approach to environmental history, I examine cultural perceptions of nature, plans for development, lived experiences in an Arctic environment, and modifications to the physical world.

The transformation of this far northern region suggests, above all, that environmental relations fundamentally shaped the Soviet experience. In this book I argue that interactions with the natural world both enabled industrial livelihoods and curtailed socialist promises. Nature itself was a participant in the communist project. Physical, geographical, and ecological features of the Kola north offered opportunities for, accommodated meddling by, and posed resistance to Soviet industrializers. The unfrozen waters of the Kola Bay, the strategic and comparatively accessible location of the peninsula within Russia itself, the geological composition of the earth there, and the region's hydrological properties fostered the rise of certain industrial sectors and naval facilities. At the same time, the darkness of the polar night, the sharp relief of mountain ranges, the behavior of animals, and even the chemical properties of excavated minerals interfered with state schemes and redirected their outcomes in crucial ways.

By revealing the essential role of the natural environment in northern economic development, this study opens a new perspective on Soviet power. Earlier generations of historians saw political power in the USSR in disparate ways. Some classified the Soviet Union as a totalitarian state, others emphasized how the social support underlying Stalinism and the chaos that imbued the communist project laid bare crucial limitations on dictatorial control, and a third group provided a synthesis of these two schools that investigated the imperfect interaction of totalistic ideologies and everyday practices.[3] None of these totalitarian, revisionist, and post-revisionist approaches paid much attention to how the environment influenced what the Soviets accomplished. More recent historians stress the importance of communist culture and ideology for mobilizing Soviet citizens, highlight the impact of international trends and interactions on Soviet trajectories, or bring spatial discourses and practices into assessments of political power.[4] I join these scholars in exploring the

3 The first group notably includes Carl Friedrich and Zbigniew Brzezinski, *Totalitarian Dictatorship and Autocracy*, 2nd edn. (New York: Praeger Publishers, 1966) and Alex Inkeles and Raymond Bauer, *The Soviet Citizen: Daily Life in a Totalitarian Society* (Cambridge, MA: Harvard University Press, 1959). A couple of important works of the second, revisionist, set of scholars are Sheila Fitzpatrick, *Education and Social Mobility in the Soviet Union, 1921–1934* (Cambridge: Cambridge University Press, 1979) and Moshe Lewin, *The Making of the Soviet System: Essays in the Social History of Interwar Russia* (London: Methuen, 1985). Self-consciously post-revisionist works include Stephen Kotkin, *Magnetic Mountain: Stalinism as a Civilization* (Berkeley: University of California Press, 1995) and Jochen Hellbeck, *Revolution on My Mind: Writing a Diary under Stalin* (Cambridge, MA: Harvard University Press, 2006).

4 Renewed stress on communist ideology appears in Igal Halfin, *From Darkness to Light: Class, Consciousness, and Salvation in Revolutionary Russia* (Pittsburgh: University of Pittsburgh Press, 2000); David Priestland, *Stalinism and the Politics of Mobilization: Ideas, Power, and Terror in Inter-war Russia* (Oxford: Oxford University Press, 2007); David Brandenberger, *Propaganda State in Crisis: Soviet Ideology, Indoctrination, and*

ideological, international, and spatial dimensions of power, but also redirect the discussion toward materialist concerns.

This monograph is the first to fully consider alive and inert elements of the natural world as participants in the dramas of Soviet history. Animate and inanimate materials were not just passively acted upon as objects, but also played a role as subjects in this story. I build upon the work of a wide range of theorists who provide examples of how insects, bacteria, organic and inorganic wastes, rivers, precipitation, and animals intrude into histories that have often been interpreted in more classically humanist terms. Such thinkers seek to capture the interactive mix between the natural and non-natural and reveal the potency of neglected materials.[5] For instance, Paul Robbins illustrates the varied ways that the chemical and biological needs of turf grass have manipulated lawn owners' behavior,

Terror under Stalin, 1927–1941 (New Haven: Yale University Press, 2011); and Jan Plamper, *The Stalin Cult: A Study in the Alchemy of Power* (New Haven: Yale University Press, 2012). For the recent attention to international connections in Soviet history, see Katerina Clark, *Moscow, the Fourth Rome: Stalinism, Cosmopolitanism, and the Evolution of Soviet Culture, 1931–1941* (Cambridge, MA: Harvard University Press, 2011); David L. Hoffmann, *Cultivating the Masses: Modern State Practices and Soviet Socialism, 1914–1939* (Ithaca: Cornell University Press, 2011); and Michael David-Fox, *Showcasing the Great Experiment: Cultural Diplomacy and Western Visitors to the Soviet Union, 1921–1941* (Oxford: Oxford University Press, 2012). The spatial turn in Soviet historiography is reflected in Kate Brown, *A Biography of No Place: From Ethnic Borderland to Soviet Heartland* (Cambridge, MA: Harvard University Press, 2005); Nick Baron, *Soviet Karelia: Politics, Planning and Terror in Stalin's Russia, 1920–1939* (London: Routledge, 2007); Nick Baron, "New Spatial Histories of 20th-Century Russia and the Soviet Union: Exploring the Terrain," *Kritika* 9, no. 2 (Spring 2008): 433–447; Mark Bassin, Christopher Ely, and Melissa K. Stockdale, eds., *Space, Place, and Power in Modern Russia: Essays in the New Spatial History* (DeKalb: Northern Illinois University Press, 2010); and Heather D. DeHaan, *Stalinist City Planning: Professionals, Performance, and Power* (Toronto: University of Toronto Press, 2013). For an analysis of the Kola Peninsula from the perspective of spatial history, see Pavel V. Fedorov, "The European Far North of Russia and Its Territorial Constructions in the Sixteenth – Twenty-First Centuries," *Acta Borealia: A Nordic Journal of Circumpolar Studies* 28, no. 2 (2011): 167–182.

5 Tim Ingold, *The Perception of the Environment: Essays in Livelihood, Dwelling, and Skill* (London: Routledge, 2000); Timothy Mitchell, *Rule of Experts: Egypt, Techno-Politics, Modernity* (Berkeley: University of California Press, 2002); Kristin Asdal, "The Problematic Nature of Nature: The Post-Constructivist Challenge to Environmental History," *History and Theory* 42, no. 4 (December 2003): 60–74; Zsuzsa Gille, *From the Cult of Waste to the Trash Heap of History: The Politics of Waste in Socialist and Postsocialist Hungary* (Bloomington: Indiana University Press, 2007); Sverker Sörlin and Paul Warde, "The Problem of the Problem of Environmental History: A Re-reading of the Field," *EH* 12, no. 1 (January 2007): 107–130; Daniel Schneider, *Hybrid Nature: Sewage Treatment and the Contradictions of the Industrial Ecosystem* (Cambridge, MA: The MIT Press, 2011); and Richard Peet, Paul Robbins, and Michael J. Watts, eds., *Global Political Ecology* (London: Routledge, 2011).

while Jane Bennett highlights the vitality of metals, fish oils, electricity, and foods as vibrant matter that contributes to contemporary politics.[6] Scholars of state-socialist countries, however, have been slow to move from taking "nature as proxy" to investigating "nature as actor," as sociologist Zsuzsa Gille has encouraged them to do.[7] Beyond analyzing the physical and biological features of the Kola landscape as simply victims, impediments, valuable objects, or stand-ins for other questions, I show here how they responded to state manipulation in sometimes surprising and unanticipated ways, thereby shaping the Soviet system itself.

To do this, I treat Soviet power as part of an assemblage. In Bruno Latour's rendering, an assemblage includes an eclectic grouping of ostensibly social and natural actors into transitory, but potent, collectivities.[8] Out of necessity, central and regional communist leaders shared power not only with a complex array of different bureaucratic interests, classes, ethnicities, religions, and genders, but with non-humans and the non-living as well. Mountains, lichens, lakes, and salmon belonged to amalgams of influential actors that emerged during campaigns to industrialize the Kola Peninsula. Power in this sense is somewhat broader than the ability to enact one's will so as to achieve a desired result, since lakes and lichen possess no knowable intentions. An important distinction exists between agents, which may have willful intentions, and actors, which do not always but can still shape events unexpectedly.[9] Pegmatite rocks, unlike people, do not have desires, but, as I will show, they lured exploration geologists to the north. Non-human actors helped direct change even if they did not have human agency.

Seen as belonging to an interactive assemblage, Soviet power was both strikingly robust and rooted in inescapable materialities. The natural

6 Paul Robbins, *Lawn People: How Grasses, Weeds, and Chemicals Make Us Who We Are* (Philadelphia: Temple University Press, 2007) and Jane Bennett, *Vibrant Matter: A Political Ecology of Things* (Durham: Duke University Press, 2010).

7 Zsuzsa Gille, "From Nature as Proxy to Nature as Actor," *SR* 68, no. 1 (Spring 2009): 1–9. Two recent articles on Russian and Soviet history have brought in material actors, see Diana Mincyte, "Everyday Environmentalism: The Practice, Politics, and Nature of Subsidiary Farming in Stalin's Lithuania," *SR* 68, no. 1 (Spring 2009): 31–49 and Julia Fein, "Talking Rocks in the Irkutsk Museum: Networks of Science in Late Imperial Siberia," *The Russian Review* 72, no. 3 (July 2013): 409–426.

8 Among Latour's many works, one might best start with Bruno Latour, *Reassembling the Social: An Introduction to Actor-Network-Theory* (Oxford: Oxford University Press, 2005).

9 The language I use throughout this work attempts to reflect this difference. When I discuss elements of the natural environment "interfering with" or "inspiring" developmental programs, I imply a form of participation that involves action, but not agency.

world contributed to the regime's mobilization of resources for industrial and military projects, but also placed limits on the extension of the state authority. On the one hand, the ability of the Soviet Union to utilize northern nature for economic ends was profound and unprecedented. The country turned a frigid land at the end of the earth into a concentrated zone of industrial activity – a feat that required greater state power than existed almost anywhere before the twentieth century. Minerals and metals for mining, forests and peat for burning, and rivers for regulating allowed the Soviets to build up this region. In the view of one prominent Kola industrialist, Vasilii Kondrikov, "only under Soviet power, only under the leadership of the Communist Party, and only with socialist methods of labor, shock-work, and socialist competitions will it be possible to transform the desolate tundra of the north into an industrial and cultural territory."[10] Though at the time other countries certainly might have been able to industrialize the Arctic similarly, Kondrikov rightly foresaw that only the Soviet Union would actually undertake such an extensive endeavor.

On the other hand, the government did not eclipse nature's influence. Instead, the Soviet Union remained dependent on the material world and subject to its unpredicted intrusions. In one instance, Kola reindeer – with their migratory instincts and their tendency to evade rigid boundaries of domesticity and wildness – complicated Soviet programs for conservation and agriculture. Early Soviet designs to make nomads sedentary ended up accommodating seasonal reindeer migrations as an occupational necessity. The sustained willingness of wild and domestic animals to mix with each other also challenged both the restoration efforts of the Lapland Nature Reserve and the economic viability of socialist reindeer herding. In another case, the mineral nepheline, which could be used as a source for aluminum production, interfered with a campaign to reuse mining wastes. In the 1930s geochemist Aleksandr Fersman predicted that such schemes for the "complex utilization of natural resources" could entirely eliminate industrial pollution. Yet, in contrast to this hope, unused nepheline wastes accumulated and considerably degraded the surrounding environment over the proceeding decades.[11] The chasm between this conservationist

[10] V. I. Kondrikov, "Tri goda v Khibinakh," in A. E. Fersman, ed., *Khibinskie Apatity i nefeliny: Nefelinovoi spornik*, vol. 4 (Leningrad: Goskhimtekhizdat Leningradskoe otdelenie, 1932), 7.

[11] A. E. Fersman, *Kompleksnoe ispol′zovanie iskopaemogo syr′ia* (Leningrad: Izdatel′stvo Akademii Nauk SSSR, 1932) and Olga Rigina, "Environmental Impact Assessment of the Mining and Concentration Activities in the Kola Peninsula, Russia by Multidate Remote Sensing," *Environmental Monitoring and Assessment* 75, no. 1 (April 2002):

vision and the polluted outcome reflects limits on the manipulation of nature that existed in a period of the mass mobilization of resources and the abiding ability of inert matter to produce unintended consequences. It suggests as well that the Soviet Union fully controlled neither its natural environment, nor the people who lived in it.

Put another way, the Soviet Union never actually "conquered" the north, as regime propagandists and later observers often claimed. Boisterous assertions about the ascendance of people over nature abounded in Soviet rhetoric about industrialization, exploration, and technological development. In a routine utterance, a geologist concluded an article about his surveying work on the Kola Peninsula by referring to "the conquest of the north."[12] While historians have scrutinized the problems that emerged from such seemingly aggressive efforts, they have also tended to take "conquest" as the defining feature of the Soviet relationship to both the natural environment and the north.[13] By demonstrating how state representatives were forced to share power with the material world even as they accomplished radical industrial change in a particularly inhospitable region, I instead unearth a more complicated, nuanced, and accurate way to characterize Soviet interaction with northern nature.

A Dualistic Conception of Nature

Throughout the twentieth century, the human actors in the Kola north tended to understand the natural environment in two partially entangled, yet still discernable, ways. One idea was largely antagonistic. It envisioned the natural world as a wartime battlefield: a set of obstacles to be overcome in a bellicose manner. But the other view of the environment

11–31. Also see Andy Bruno, "How a Rock Remade the Soviet North: Nepheline in the Khibiny Mountains," in Nicholas Breyfogle, ed., *Eurasian Environments: Nature and Ecology in Eurasian History* (forthcoming at University of Pittsburgh Press).

12 G. Pronchenko, "V bor'be za ovladenie nedrami Khibinskikh gor," in G. Geber, M. Maizel', and V. Sedlis, eds., *Bol'sheviki pobedili tundry* (Leningrad: Izdatel'stvo pisatelei v Leningrade, 1932), 50.

13 Most recently and most relevantly, see Paul R. Josephson, *The Conquest of the Russian Arctic* (Cambridge, MA: Harvard University Press, 2014). Other works that stress the antagonism toward nature are Arja Rosenholm and Sari Autio-Sarasmo, eds., *Understanding Russian Nature: Representations, Values and Concepts* (Aleksanteri Papers 4/2005); John McCannon, "To Storm the Arctic: Soviet Polar Expeditions and Public Visions of Nature in the USSR, 1932–1939," *Ecumene* 2, no. 1 (January 1995): 15–31; Bernd Stevens Richter, "Nature Mastered by Man: Ideology and Water in the Soviet Union," *Environment and History* 3, no. 1 (1997): 69–96; and Alla Bolotova, "Colonization of Nature in the Soviet Union: State Ideology, Public Discourse, and the Experience of Geologists," *Historical Social Research* 29, no. 3 (2004): 104–123.

had the potential to be much more accommodating. It emphasized an amicable disposition toward nature: the notion that economic activity could bring mutual improvement for humanity and all that was outside of it. Those voicing these two conceptions – one hostile, one holistic – drew on a variety of imperial, militaristic, modernist, and socialist worldviews at different historical moments. The help and hindrance offered by the material world during specific projects also influenced which ideas people expressed. As the Soviet experiment unfolded and then unraveled, the balance between these two views of nature shifted. Sometimes industrialists tightly interwove them and at other times they kept them apart. Furthermore, each belief had some distinctive effects on how the Soviets treated the Kola environment. Aggressive notions helped give rise to much of the short-term destruction in the first half of the century, while integrationist ones often inspired the actions that came to place long-term pressures on the natural world.

The dualistic conception of nature predated the USSR. In the tsarist era some government officials and regional boosters began to espouse the notion that economic exploitation would enliven the Russian north. To people like biologist Sergei Averintsev, Kola nature was a "treasure chest" waiting to be discovered by committed colonists.[14] Indeed, this assimilationist view of the natural world aligned neatly with the empire-building project of the Russian state. In the early Soviet period developers maintained a similar integrationist idea that expanded economic activity benefited all. For instance, Gennadii Chirkin – a bureaucrat from the former Resettlement Administration of the Russian Empire who now served the new Soviet government – declared in 1922 that the Murmansk railroad should become "an industrial-transportation and pioneer-colonization enterprise with the goal of using its natural resources for the economic revival of Russia."[15] Yet when this railroad had been built during World War I, an alternative, more militaristic, way of describing industrial construction had dominated. Urgent labor with a recalcitrant environment fostered a view of nature as an object of conquest before the Bolsheviks even took charge in autumn 1917. Such belligerence during the erection of the railroad helped lead to a specific set of destructive and profligate practices, such as wastefully eliminating wide swaths of forest and

[14] S. Averintsev, "Neskol'ko slov o postanovke nauchno-promyslovykh issledovanii u beregov Murmana," *IAOIRS* 1, no. 2 (June 1, 1909): 37.

[15] G. F. Chirkin, *Puti razvitiai Murmansa* (Petrograd: Pravlenie Murmanskoi zheleznoi dorogi, 1922), 8.

dynamiting potentially useful landscape features for the sake of saving time.[16]

With Joseph Stalin's industrialization push in the 1930s, both assimilation and conquest acquired more extreme forms. The impulse for assimilating nature became a longing to establish socialist harmony with the natural environment, while the conquering drive of World War I and the Russian Civil War extended into the pursuit of militaristic dominance outside of a wartime context. I contend that "Stalinist" ecological relations emerged from the simultaneous pursuit of these contrasting environmental ideas.[17] Sergei Kirov, the Leningrad region party boss in the early 1930s, pithily captured this combination of hostility and hope with his frequently memorialized words about Kola nature: "This northern, severe, barren, useless wilderness turned out in reality to be one of the richest places on earth."[18] In the new nickel town of Monchegorsk, planners made a point of preserving a forested area in the city while exposing prison laborers from the Gulag to the polar tundra's calamities.[19] With the reindeer of the Kola north, authorities enacted programs aimed at both the strict preservation of wild animals and the aggressive expansion of herding activities through collectivization. The environmental consequences of the Stalinist mix of harmony and dominance in the Kola north included the rapid despoilment of proximate flora, fauna, and waterways. Such pollution fell especially hard on the area's new human inhabitants, but wrought much less ecosystem damage than what came later.

Authorities moderated some of the maximalist expressions of these two impulses after Stalin passed from the scene in the early 1950s. Both Nikita Khrushchev and Leonid Brezhnev infamously advanced their own

[16] M. Bubnovskii, "Po novomu puti (Iz dnevnika narodnogo uchitelia)," *IAOIRS* 9, no. 1 (January 1917): 7; V. A. Khabarov, *Magistral´* (Murmansk: Murmanskoe knizhnoe izdatel´stvo, 1986), 22–23; and A. A. Kiselev, *Kol´skoi atomnoi – 30: Stranitsy istorii* (Murmansk: Izdatel´stvo "Reklamnaia poligrafiia," 2003), 10.

[17] William Husband and Mark Bassin have also observed the presence of less antagonistic portrayals of nature in Stalinist culture. See William Husband, "'Correcting Nature's Mistakes': Transforming the Environment and Soviet Children's Literature, 1928–1941," *EH* 11, no. 2 (April 2006): 300–318 and Mark Bassin, "The Greening of Utopia: Nature, Social Vision, and Landscape Art in Stalinist Russia," in James Cracraft and Daniel Rowland, eds., *Architectures of Russian Identity: 1500 to Present* (Ithaca: Cornell University Press, 2003), 150–171.

[18] "Na stroike nikelevogo kombinata," *PP* (July 16, 1938), 3. This quotation also appears on the wall of the Murmansk Regional Studies Museum.

[19] V. Ia. Pozniakov, *Severonikel´ (Stranitsy istorii kombinata "Severonikel´")* (Moscow: GUP Izdatel´skii dom "Ruda i metally," 1999), 23 and A. A. Kiselev, "GULAG na Murmane: Istoriia tiurem, lagerei, kolonii," *SM* (October 22, 1992): 3.

gargantuan pet projects that seemed in line with Promethean desires, such as the Virgin Lands campaign and a scheme to reverse Siberian rivers. But the unrelenting growth of economic production most defined Soviet policy toward the natural world. Though dreams of harmony with nature became somewhat less idealistic than during the preceding period, the related yearning to assimilate nature ramped up to an even more all-encompassing drive to extract all economic value from the environment. The erection of a slew of new hydroelectric dams and the dramatic rise in the quantity of phosphates mined and enriched in the Khibiny Mountains in the 1950s and 1960s reflected this vision. So too did the consolidation of reindeer-herding enterprises into large state farms that tended more populous herds. Mid-century industrial expansion proceeded with enough caution to avoid some of the environmental and economic recklessness that had occurred in the Stalin era. Yet the total negative impact on the environment grew proportionally with increased production.

Environmental pressures and politics clashed most overtly in the final decades of the Soviet experiment. As environmentalism gained traction as an international movement in the 1970s and 1980s, the rhetoric of conquest became much more muted in the Soviet press. Instead, assurances that socialism, unlike capitalism, enabled the optimal balance between economic activity and nature protection frequently appeared. As an environmental monitor in Murmansk wrote in a local newspaper, "nature protection is valued as one of the most important state tasks of our socialist system. It is not profit at all cost as in capitalist countries."[20] Many commentators used such purportedly harmonious conceptions of nature to evade acknowledgment of the increasingly severe degradation of natural systems. Indeed, despite wider public discussion of ecological issues in the USSR than during previous periods, this era was also the most environmentally damaging. Sulfur emissions from the Kola Peninsula's nickel plants denuded huge areas of taiga forests, while the supposedly "clean" nuclear power industry stored massive amounts of radioactive waste in unsafe containment facilities.[21]

After the fall of the Soviet Union and the end of communist rule, a dualistic conception of nature continued to affect the treatment of

[20] F. Terziev, "Zabota o prirode – eto zabota o nashem zdorov′e: pis′mo pervoe," *PP* (June 20, 1973): 2.

[21] Robert G. Darst, *Smokestack Diplomacy: Cooperation and Conflict in East-West Environmental Politics* (Cambridge, MA: The MIT Press, 2001), 91–197; V. Berlin, "Kol′skaia AES i okruzhaiushchaia sreda," *KK* (August 20, 1976): 3; and V. Fedotov and B. Aleksandrov, "Bezvrednoe sosedstvo," *PP* (July 5, 1973): 4.

the environment. While economic collapse, technological upgrades, and restoration efforts ameliorated some pollution problems in the Kola north, industry leaders and state authorities persisted in parroting the Soviet rhetoric of harmony in order to deflect environmental concerns. For example, consulting scientists in the Khibiny Mountains still framed the quasi-conservationist Soviet idea of the "complex utilization of mineral resources" as "a foundation for advancing environmental safety in the region" in the early 2000s.[22] Meanwhile, the recent exploration of undersea resources has given new currency to discussions of Arctic subjugation. Thus, both unattainable views about the natural world, which appeared in the tsarist period and matured in the Soviet era, remain influential in Russia today.

A Modern Arctic and the Communist Anthropocene

As seen in the longevity of this bipolar disposition toward polar nature, the Soviet Union existed on a continuum in environmental matters with the other regimes that ruled the Eurasian landmass. It also closely resembled many other countries in the world. When compared either synchronically or diachronically, the Soviet relationship to the natural world more greatly reflects the common experience of modernizing states than the allegedly aberrant behavior of communist regimes. This book brings in a comparative focus in two overarching ways. First, it provides thorough discussions of the preceding tsarist era and proceeding post-communist period to reveal deep chronological continuities. By examining this long sweep of history, I attend to changes and legacies that do not easily fit within a standard periodization framework of twentieth-century political history based exclusively on regimes and leaders. Second, I look around to other countries at numerous points in the analysis to note convergences and divergences with the Soviet north. This approach is perhaps less directly comparative than that taken by some other scholars who have stressed the similarities between socialist and capitalist countries by writing about multiple locations.[23] But viewing the history of the Kola

22 A. I. Nikolaev, ed., *Kompleksnost' ispol'zovaniia mineral'no-syr'evyx resursov: osnova povysheniia ekologicheskoi besopasnosti regiona* (Apatity: KNTs AN, 2005).

23 Kate Brown, *Plutopia: Nuclear Families, Atomic Cities, and the Great Soviet and American Plutonium Disasters* (Oxford: Oxford University Press, 2013); Paul R. Josephson, *Industrialized Nature: Brute Force Technology and the Transformation of the Natural World* (Washington, DC: Island Press, 2002); and James Scott, *Seeing Like a State:*

region from this angle nevertheless exposes the abundant and disparate transnational influences at work in a particular place.

Many of the environmental practices embraced by Soviet leaders came from elsewhere in the world. State planners pursued patterns of northern development invented in the tsarist period and then closely followed global economic trends originating in capitalist countries. They emulated several strategies of twentieth-century growth economies from establishing self-sufficiency in nickel and fertilizers in the 1930s to constructing nuclear reactors to supply abundant electricity in the 1970s and 1980s. While the USSR shared many of the techniques for turning nature into a set of economic resources, it often declared them communist innovations. For instance, routine advancements in enrichment technology or geological surveying methods, which were comparable to ones made elsewhere in the world, would sometimes be described as specific achievements of Soviet socialism.[24] Such window dressing, however, should not conceal the more fundamental similarities.

A basic premise about the appropriate objective of modern states united the Soviet Union with other countries as well. Around the globe, governments of the last century usually privileged unrelenting economic expansion over limiting the pressures placed on natural systems. If anything, the Soviet Union followed this modern growth imperative more eagerly than most, due, at least initially, to an acute sense that it needed to rapidly overcome the country's supposed backwardness. Historians of the Soviet environment seem to concur on this point. In two recent syntheses, separate scholars have noted that an "exaggeration of modernity" characterized the country and that "the Soviet Union acted as a hyperbolically exaggerated version of a capitalist society."[25] This study of northwest Russia also echoes many of the conclusions of the "modernity" school of Soviet historiography.[26]

How Certain Schemes to Improve Human Condition Have Failed (New Haven: Yale University Press, 1998).

[24] Numerous examples of this appear in L. A. Potemkin, *U severnoi granitsy: Pechenga sovetskaia* (Murmansk: Murmanskoe knizhnoe izdatel'stvo, 1965) and L. A. Potemkin, *Okhrana nedr i okruzhaiushchei prirody* (Moscow: Nedra, 1977).

[25] Paul Josephson, et al., *An Environmental History of Russia* (Cambridge: Cambridge University Press, 2013), 2 and Stephen Brain, "The Environmental History of the Soviet Union," in J. R. McNeill and Erin Stewart Maudlin, eds., *A Companion to Global Environmental History* (Malden, MA: Wiley-Blackwell, 2012), 225.

[26] David Hoffmann and Yanni Kotsonis, eds., *Russian Modernity: Politics, Knowledge, Practices* (New York: St. Martin's Press, 2000).

The Soviet remaking of the Kola Peninsula also sheds particular light on the international history of the Arctic. It does so at a time when many are looking toward the future economic development of the region. As historian Andrew Stuhl points out, the current focus on the rise of a "New North" in the face of global warming, geopolitical competition, and offshore oil exploration tends to treat the Arctic as "a remote and unchanging place" that has hitherto been "outside of modernity."[27] Writers split into those who see the prospects of the circumpolar north in overly sanguine terms and those who embrace apocalyptic visions of environmental destruction and military conflict, but they unite in juxtaposing the future with a tranquil past.[28] In contrast, Stuhl shows how science and state power considerably changed the Western Arctic in the nineteenth and twentieth centuries. The transformation of the Kola Peninsula into the most industrialized section of the Arctic illustrates this corrective perhaps even more forcefully. Soviet newspapers described campaigns of the 1930s in language even more overblown than the current rhetoric about the rise of a "New North." A May 1938 article in *Polar Pravda* exclaimed, "By the will of the Bolsheviks under the leadership of great Stalin, the land of fearless birds is now transformed into an industrial outpost of socialism, into an indestructible fortress of the USSR in a northern periphery."[29] Whatever the hyperbole of this propaganda, the

[27] Andrew Stuhl, "Empires on Ice: Science, Nature, and the Making of the Arctic" (PhD diss., University of Wisconsin-Madison, 2013), 4. Also see Andrew Stuhl, "The Politics of the 'New North': Putting History and Geography at Stake in Arctic Futures," *The Polar Journal* 3, no. 1 (2013): 94–119.

[28] For sometimes thoughtful, but often highly speculative, prognosticating on the Arctic, see Charles Emmerson, *The Future History of the Arctic* (New York: PublicAffairs 2010). Environmental historians of the Arctic have usually been more circumspect. See John McCannon, *Red Arctic: Polar Exploration and the Myth of the North in the Soviet Union 1932–1939* (Oxford: Oxford University Press, 1998); Michael Bravo and Sverker Sörlin, eds., *Narrating the Arctic: A Cultural History of Nordic Scientific Practices* (Canton, MA: Scientific History Publications, 2002); David G. Anderson and Mark Nuttall, eds., *Cultivating Arctic Landscapes: Knowing and Managing Animals in the Circumpolar North* (New York: Berghahn Books, 2004); Liza Piper and John Sandlos, "A Broken Frontier: Ecological Imperialism in the Canadian North," *EH* 12, no. 4 (October 2007): 759–795; Stephen Bocking, "Science and Spaces in the Northern Environment," *EH* 12, no. 4 (October 2007): 867–894; Liza Piper, *The Industrial Transformation of Subarctic Canada* (Vancouver: University of British Columbia Press, 2009); John McCannon, *A History of the Arctic: Nature, Exploration, and Exploitation* (London: Reaktion Books, 2012); and Dolly Jørgensen and Sverker Sörlin, eds., *Northscapes: History, Technology, and the Making of Northern Environments* (Vancouver: University of British Columbia Press, 2013).

[29] "Pechati Zapoliarnia," *PP* (May 5, 1938): 3.

multifarious changes to the region speak of a tumultuous history in the Kola north, not a frozen stillness.

The sweeping scope of changes in the Soviet Arctic, moreover, overlaps with global environmental trajectories of the twentieth century. Narratives of rising environmental pressures have varied since the birth of modern environmentalism in the 1960s from fears of a population bomb to hopes for sustainable development. Evidence that carbon emissions from burning fossil fuels are now overwhelming the earth's climate system have led to recent theorizing about the Anthropocene: a new epoch in which humans have become a geophysical force. Proponents claim that human activities are no longer just reshaping the biological character of the earth's ecosystem but also the planet's geology. In typical accounts, the Anthropocene began with the advent of the industrial era in the late eighteenth century, but the pace of mounting environmental pressures accelerated to exponential rates after the 1950s.[30] The story of Kola industrialization clearly aligns with the planetary trends described by the concept of the Anthropocene, suggesting that global processes underpin this episode of exaggerated development by a communist country. The implications of the Anthropocene for human agency are also relevant here. Especially with global warming, humanity stumbled into an unforeseen, and potentially catastrophic, threat by disrupting existing climatic processes. Thus, the Anthropocene implies not just extensive human influence but also nature's abiding ability to bring about unanticipated and unpleasant consequences.

A New Vision of the Soviet Environment

Through its stress on the involvement of nature in this history, its attention to more multifaceted understandings of the natural world, and its comparisons to the environmental experience of other parts of the planet, this book offers a novel perspective on the Soviet environment. Advancing these arguments allows me to challenge some established interpretations in the existing literature and add fresh insights to scholarly discussions. It also helps me demonstrate the pertinence of the environment for Soviet history as a whole.

[30] Will Steffen, Paul J. Crutzen, and John R. McNeill, "The Anthropocene: Are Humans Now Overwhelming the Great Forces of Nature?" *Ambio* 36, no. 8 (December 2007): 614–621 and Dipesh Chakrabarty, "The Climate of History: Four Theses," *Critical Inquiry* 35, no. 2 (Winter 2009): 197–222.

One well-trodden genre of environmental writing on the Soviet Union has exposed the severe pollution problems that the country faced in its final decades. In the twilight of the Cold War, a number of Western social scientists declared the USSR a grievous culprit of ecocide, sometimes disingenuously implying that liberal capitalist countries had avoided comparable environmental problems.[31] More tempered appraisals generally came to the same consensus that an acute environmental situation existed in Russia as a legacy of communist-era development.[32]

To a greater extent than any other environmental historian, Paul Josephson has taken up this tragic theme. He has examined the spread of "brute force technologies" in a host of Soviet industries (ranging from hydroelectric dams to fisheries) and the creation of "industrial deserts" where concentrated economic activities caused extreme environmental destruction.[33] He blames the "Marxist industrial imperative" for accelerating environmental degradation in the "fragile" Arctic in particular.[34] An in-depth look at how the Severonikel′ and Pechenganikel′ nickel smelters came to despoil and entirely denude large portions of the Kola

[31] Boris Komarov [Ze′ev Vol′fson], *The Destruction of Nature in the Soviet Union* (White Plains: M. E. Sharpe, 1980); Joan DeBardeleben, *The Environment and Marxism-Leninism: The Soviet and East German Experience* (Boulder: Westview Press, 1985); Murray Feshbach and Alfred Friendly, *Ecocide in the USSR: Health and Nature Under Siege* (New York: Basic Books, 1992); D. J. Peterson, *Troubled Lands: The Legacy of Soviet Environmental Destruction* (Boulder: Westview Press, 1993); and Murray Feshbach, *Ecological Disaster: Cleaning Up the Hidden Legacy of the Soviet Regime* (New York: The Twentieth Century Fund Press, 1995).

[32] Marshall I. Goldman, *The Spoils of Progress: Environmental Pollution in the Soviet Union* (Cambridge, MA: The MIT Press, 1972); Charles E. Ziegler, *Environmental Policy in the USSR* (Amherst: University of Massachusetts Press, 1987); Philip R. Pryde, *Environmental Management in the Soviet Union* (Cambridge: Cambridge University Press, 1991); Ann-Mari Sätre Åhlander, *Environmental Problems in the Shortage Economy: The Legacy of Soviet Environmental Policy* (Brookfield: Edward Elgar Publishing Company, 1994); Natalia Mirovitskaya and Marvin S. Soroos, "Socialism and the Tragedy of the Commons: Reflections on Environmental Practice in the Soviet Union," *The Journal of Environmental Development* 4, no. 1 (Winter 1995): 77–110; and Jonathan D. Oldfield, *Russian Nature: Exploring the Environmental Consequences of Societal Change* (Burlington: Ashgate, 2005).

[33] Josephson, *Industrialized Nature* and Paul R. Josephson, *Would Trotsky Wear a Bluetooth: Technological Utopianism Under Socialism* (Baltimore: The Johns Hopkins University Press, 2010), 193–231. Donald Filtzer's research on Soviet cities after World War II shows the seriousness of pollution and sanitation issues in rivers in the 1940s. Donald Filtzer, *The Hazards of Urban Life in Late Stalinist Russia: Health, Hygiene, and Living Standards, 1943–1953* (Cambridge: Cambridge University Press, 2010), 105–126.

[34] Josephson, *The Conquest of the Russian Arctic*, 6, 11. Also see Paul R. Josephson, "Technology and the Conquest of the Soviet Arctic," *The Russian Review* 70, no. 3 (July 2011): 419–439.

landscape reveals an alternative cause for this extreme environmental damage. Global economic pressures of the 1970s and 1980s, along with the substitution of local ores for imported ones, nudged these metal works from the status of normally destructive polluters to particularly awful emitters. This explanation suggests that communism performed environmentally worse than capitalism in a specific historical context, but not that it was innately more ruinous.

This work also engages with historians who have explored conservation politics and policies in the USSR. The founding studies of Douglas Weiner demonstrate how early Bolshevik leaders initially welcomed a comparatively radical approach to nature protection that would cordon off selected territories from all economic activities in perpetuity. Despite setbacks, this system of nature reserves (*zapovedniki*) endured through even some of the most environmentally ominous moments in Soviet history.[35] The daring efforts of German Kreps and Oleg Semenov-Tian-Shanskii to preserve wild reindeer and land unblemished by pollution at the Lapland Nature Reserve provide vivid examples of Weiner's larger story on the Kola Peninsula. But the overall role of these conservation scientists in this book corresponds more closely with their ultimately narrow influence on Kola nature during the Soviet era. They managed to protect certain parcels of land from economic interference, but only while much larger areas came under the sway of industry.

Stephen Brain and Brian Bonhomme have more recently addressed the fate of the Russian forest from the revolutionary era through the end of Stalinism. Bonhomme's work highlights the conflict that existed between many peasants and foresters in the conservation of woodlands, while Brain offers an ambitious re-interpretation of Stalin's forest policies as possessing an environmentalist bent.[36] The disappearance of Kola forests

[35] Douglas Weiner, *Models of Nature: Ecology, Conservation, and Cultural Revolution in Soviet Russia* (Bloomington: Indiana University Press, 1988) and Douglas Weiner, *A Little Corner of Freedom: Russian Nature Protection from Stalin to Gorbachev* (Berkeley: University of California Press, 1999). On Soviet and post-Soviet conservation and environmentalism, also see Philip Pryde, *Conservation in the Soviet Union* (Cambridge: Cambridge University Press, 1972); Oleg Yanitsky, *Russian Environmentalism: Leading Figures, Facts, Opinions* (Moscow: Mezhdunarodnyje Otnoshenija Publishing House, 1993); Feliks Shtilmark, *History of the Russian Zapovedniks, 1895–1995*, trans. G. H. Harper (Edinburgh: Russian Nature Press, 2003); and Laura A. Henry, *Red to Green: Environmental Activism in Post-Soviet Russia* (Ithaca: Cornell University Press, 2010).

[36] Stephen Brain, *Song of the Forest: Russian Forestry and Stalinist Environmentalism, 1905–1953* (Pittsburgh: University of Pittsburgh Press, 2011) and Brian Bonhomme, *Forests, Peasants, and Revolutionaries: Forest Conservation and Organization in Soviet Russia, 1917–1929* (Boulder: East European Monographs, 2005).

during World War I and the revolutionary period and at the height of Stalinist industrialization followed the national trends that these authors describe. Yet the types of interactions that the mostly migrant population of the region had with their natural surroundings varied considerably from the situation of peasants in the forest heartland. Pre-existing land-use patterns on the Kola Peninsula mattered less for how these transplants experienced industrial development. Furthermore, though this study supports Brain's conclusions that a more holistic disposition toward the natural world existed in the throes of Stalinism than is often assumed, it does not take "Stalinist environmentalism" as a helpful category for making sense of these less antagonistic ideas and policies. For Brain, the fact that ideas about preserving ecological integrity made their way into decisions about how to treat the Soviet forest requires the presence of a unique top-down form of environmentalism. In contrast, I think it is best to avoid retrospectively using the term "environmentalism" when discussing an earlier historical period. I also show that it was precisely by evoking the notion of promoting harmony with nature that Stalinists often failed to acknowledge genuine contradictions between the imperatives of industry and the needs of nature protection.

From the initial focus on environmental problems and conservation, scholars are now taking increasingly diverse and inclusive approaches.[37] I join those who are investigating topics such as the environmental sciences, disasters, national identities, animals, agriculture, climate, and water under the rubric of environmental history. Some show how scientific concepts related to the environment – everything from permafrost, physical geography, and Arctic warming – developed distinctly Russian

[37] This brief overview of an ever-richer field invariably overlooks some work, and does not focus on contributions to the pre-Soviet era. Additional articles appear in a special issue of *The Soviet and Post-Soviet Review* 40, no. 2 (2013) on late Soviet environmentalism, edited by Laurent Coumel and Marc Elie, and in one of *The Slavonic and East European Review* 93, no. 1 (January 2015) on conceptualizing and utilizing the environment, edited by Jonathan Oldfield, Julia Lajus, and Denis J. B. Shaw. The reader also might refer to my earlier, and at the time fairly comprehensive, review of the field of Russian environmental history. Andy Bruno, "Russian Environmental History: Directions and Potentials," *Kritika* 8, no. 3 (Summer 2007): 635–650. Two more recent review essays are Brian Bonhomme, "Writing the Environmental History of the World's Largest State: Four Decades of Scholarship on Russia and the USSR," *Global Environment*, no. 12 (2013): 12–37 and Randall Dills, "Forest and Grassland: Recent Trends in Russian Environmental History," *Global Environment*, no. 12 (2013): 38–61. For a volume that introduces the field to a Russian audience, see Daniil Aleksandrov, Franz-Josef Brüggemeier, and Julia Lajus, eds., *Chelovek i priroda: ekologicheskaia istoriia* (Saint Petersburg: Aleteiia, 2008).

attributes and, conversely, how international exchange influenced Soviet sciences to a greater extent than has often been acknowledged.[38] Others turn to assorted disasters – famines, avalanches, mudslides, and radiation exposure – to better understand the Soviet experience with natural hazards in a comparative perspective.[39] Historically minded social scientists demonstrate how links between nation and nature shaped various groups' oppositional politics in the late Soviet era.[40] Contributors to thematic collaborations explore how relations with animals have mirrored Russia's own sense of otherness and how cold conditions have been a constitutive part of Russian culture.[41] Those examining agriculture deal with a range of topics from the symbolic significance of socialist farming to the proportional impact of climate variations on crop yields.[42] Finally, a number of historians research Soviet irrigation policies in various parts

[38] Julia Lajus, "Controversial Perceptions of Arctic Warming in the 1930s in the Context of Soviet-Western Contacts in Environmental Science" (paper presented at the National Convention of the Association for Slavic, East European, and Eurasian Studies in Washington, DC, November 2011); Denis J. B. Shaw and Jonathan D. Oldfield, "Totalitarianism and Geography: L. S. Berg and the Defence of an Academic Discipline in the Age of Stalin," *Political Geography* 27, no. 1 (January 2008): 96–112; and Pey-Yi Chu, "Mapping Permafrost Country: Creating an Environmental Object in the Soviet Union, 1920s-1940s," *EH* 20, no. 3 (July 2015): 396–421.

[39] Sarah I. Cameron, "The Hungry Steppe: Soviet Kazakhstan and the Kazakh Famine, 1921–1934" (PhD diss., Yale University, 2010); Andy Bruno, "Tumbling Snow: Vulnerability to Avalanches in the Soviet North," *EH* 18, no. 4 (October 2013): 683–709; Marc Elie, "Coping with the "Black Dragon": Mudflow Hazards and the Controversy over the Medeo Dam in Kazakhstan, 1958–66," *Kritika* 14, no. 2 (Spring 2013): 313–342; and Brown, *Plutopia*. Douglas Northrop is also working on a history of earthquakes in Eurasia.

[40] Jane Dawson, *Eco-nationalism: Anti-Nuclear Activism and National Identity in Russia, Lithuania, and Ukraine* (Durham: Duke University Press, 1996); Katrina Z. S. Schwartz, *Nature and National Identity after Communism: Globalizing the Ethnoscape* (Pittsburgh: University of Pittsburgh Press, 2006); and Katherine Metzo, "The Formation of Tunka National Park: Revitalization and Autonomy in Late Socialism," *SR* 68, no. 1 (Spring 2009): 50–69.

[41] Jane Costlow and Amy Nelson, eds., *Other Animals: Beyond the Human in Russian Culture and History* (Pittsburgh: University of Pittsburgh Press, 2010). Julia Herzberg is editing a forthcoming volume on the cold climate in Russian history based on a workshop that occurred in Moscow in February 2012.

[42] Nikolai M. Dronin and Edward G. Bellinger, *Climate Dependence and Food Problems in Russia 1900–1990* (Budapest: Central European University Press, 2005); Nikolai M. Dronin and Andrei P. Kirilenko, "Weathering the Soviet Countryside: The Impact of Climate and Agricultural Policies on Russian Grain Yields, 1958–2010," *The Soviet and Post-Soviet Review* 40, no. 1 (2013): 115–143; Mincyte, "Everyday Environmentalism," *SR* 68, no. 1 (Spring 2009): 31–49; and Jenny Leigh Smith, *Works in Progress: Plans and Realities on Soviet Farms, 1930–1963* (New Haven: Yale University Press, 2014). On the environment and agriculture before the Soviet era, see David Moon, *The Plough that*

of Central Asia, while other scholars of water write about famed lakes, rivers, and hydroelectric dams.[43]

This study incorporates aspects of these new and wide-ranging contributions into the history of a particular place. It touches on the conceptual development of the discipline of Soviet geochemistry, which owed much to fieldwork in the Arctic. Northerners faced threats from tumbling snow, gusty winds, treacherous thaws, and environmental contamination, which all feature in this story as well. The pages ahead explore debates about various ethnic groups' use of natural resources and the sometimes-evasive actions of Arctic fauna. I also discuss attempts to bring agriculture to the north, the problems and potentials created by the Arctic cold, and the reengineering of the Kola Peninsula's hydrology. Moreover, this book interweaves the everyday experiences of more marginal groups – prisoners of war, forcibly relocated peasant families, Gulag inmates, recruited migrant laborers, and reindeer herders – into its narrative of sweeping environmental change. As such, it responds to the still pressing need for environmental history to pay more attention to human livelihoods.[44]

In addition to interacting with the expanding scholarship on the Soviet environment, this book engages with a host of interpretive questions

Broke the Steppes: Agriculture and Environment on Russia's Grasslands, 1700–1914 (Oxford: Oxford University Press, 2013).

43 Maya K. Peterson, "Technologies of Rule: Water, Power, and the Modernization of Central Asia, 1867–1941" (PhD diss., Harvard University, 2011); Klaus Gestwa, *Die Stalinschen Grossbauten des Kommunismus: Sowjetische Technik- und Umweltgeschichte, 1948–1967* (Munich: Oldenbourg, 2010); Dorothy Zeisler-Vralsted, "The Cultural and Hydrological Development of the Mississippi and Volga Rivers," in Christof Mauch and Thomas Zeller, eds., *Rivers in History: Perspectives on Waterways in Europe and North America* (Pittsburgh: University of Pittsburgh Press, 2008); Julia Obertreis, "Soviet Irrigation Policies in Central Asia under Fire: The Ecological Debate in the Turkmen and Uzbek Republics, 1970–1991" (paper presented at Eurasian Environments: Nature and Ecology in Eurasian History, Columbus, Ohio, September 16–17, 2011); Christian Teichmann, "Canals, Cotton, and the Limits of De-Colonization in Soviet Uzbekistan, 1924–1941," *Central Asian Survey* 26, no. 4 (December 2007): 499–519; and Nicholas B. Breyfogle, "At the Watershed: 1958 and the Beginnings of Lake Baikal Environmentalism," *The Slavonic and East European Review* 93, no. 1 (January 2015): 147–180.

44 For calls to integrate social and environmental approaches to history, see Stephen Mosley, "Common Ground: Integrating Social and Environmental History," *Journal of Social History* 39, no. 3 (Spring 2006): 915–935 and Alan Taylor, "Unnatural Inequalities: Social and Environmental Histories," *EH* 1, no. 4 (October 1996): 6–19. Soviet environmental historians have only scratched the surface in this regard. For an earlier attempt I made, see Andy Bruno, "Industrial Life in a Limiting Landscape: An Environmental Interpretation of Stalinist Social Conditions in the Far North," *International Review of Social History* 55, S18 (December 2010): 153–174. Also see Brown, *Plutopia*.

about the history of the country more broadly. By doing so, it reveals the perhaps unexpected significance of the environment throughout the entire course of Soviet history. To start I show the connection that historians have noted between eras of War Communism and Stalinism applies to the economic treatment of nature.[45] I also make the case for interpreting Stalinism as an all-encompassing ecosystem instead of just a human-centered civilization.[46] While discussing the use of reindeer in ethnic relations on the Kola Peninsula, I synthesize institutionalist and knowledge-centered interpretations of Soviet nationality policy and draw on works of anthropologists of the Russian north.[47] The later chapters also address questions of dynamism and economic stagnation during the Khrushchev and Brezhnev years, showing how environmental problems and awareness shaped late communist authoritarianism.[48] As this history forays into the

45 Sheila Fitzpatrick offered an influential version of this thesis, while Peter Holquist and Donald Raleigh have more recently advanced alternative takes on it. See Sheila Fitzpatrick, "The Legacy of the Civil War," in Diane P. Koenker, William G. Rosenberg, and Ronald Grigor Suny, eds., *Party, State, and Society in the Russian Civil War: Explorations in Social History* (Bloomington: Indiana University Press, 1989), 385–398; Peter Holquist, *Making War, Forging Revolution: Russia's Continuum of Crisis, 1914–1921* (Cambridge, MA: Harvard University Press, 2002); and Donald Raleigh, *Experiencing Russia's Civil War: Politics, Society, and Revolutionary Culture in Saratov, 1917–1922* (Princeton: Princeton University Press, 2002).

46 Kotkin, *Magnetic Mountain.*

47 On Soviet nationalities policy, see Terry Martin, *The Affirmative Action Empire: Nations and Nationalism in the Soviet Union, 1923–1939* (Ithaca: Cornell University Press, 2001); Francine Hirsch, *Empire of Nations: Ethnographic Knowledge and the Making of the Soviet Union* (Ithaca: Cornell University Press, 2005); Yuri Slezkine, "The USSR as a Communal Apartment, or How a Socialist State Promoted Ethnic Particularism," *SR* 53, no. 2 (Summer 1994): 414–452; Yuri Slezkine, *Arctic Mirrors: Russia and the Small Peoples of the North* (Ithaca: Cornell University Press, 1994); and Ronald Grigor Suny and Terry Martin, eds., *A State of Nations: Empire and Nation-Making in the Age of Lenin and Stalin* (Oxford: Oxford University Press, 2001). For ethnographic work on the Russian north, see Bruce Grant, *In the Soviet House of Culture: A Century of Perestroikas* (Princeton: Princeton University Press, 1995); David G. Anderson, *Identity and Ecology in Arctic Siberia: The Number One Reindeer Brigade* (Oxford: Oxford University Press, 2002); Piers Vitebsky, *Reindeer People: Living with Animals and Spirits in Siberia* (London: HarperCollins Publishers, 2005); Joachim Otto Habeck, *What it Means to be a Herdsman: The Practice and Image of Reindeer Husbandry among the Komi of Northern Russia* (Münster: LIT Verlag, 2005); Yulian Konstantinov and Vladislava Vladimirova, "The Performative Machine: Transfer of Ownership in a Northwest Russian Reindeer Herding Community (Kola Peninsula)," *Nomadic Peoples* 10, no. 2 (2006): 166–186; and Niobe Thompson, *Settlers on the Edge: Identity and Modernization on Russia's Arctic Frontier* (Vancouver: University of British Columbia Press, 2008).

48 On the social and cultural dynamism of the Khrushchev and Brezhnev periods, see Polly Jones, ed., *The Dilemmas of De-Stalinization: Negotiating Social and Cultural Change*

post-Soviet period, I consider the proportional influence of the Soviet legacy and neoliberal reforms for the governance and treatment of the environment since the fall of communism.[49] Overall, these interventions should inspire scholars of the USSR to think anew about the relevance of the natural world in debates about social, political, cultural, and economic history.

History in an Ethnographic Vein

The Nature of Soviet Power is primarily a work of history, not ethnography. Despite numerous interdisciplinary flirtations and the many discussions I had with people on the Kola Peninsula during the time I spent there, the information I rely on comes mostly from the written record in archives, libraries, museums, and websites. Yet, in another sense, this study is deeply ethnographic. Instead of being primarily a regional history or a case study of broad phenomena in a particular place, I address general problems of Soviet environmental history through a fine-grained analysis of the local. In this way I follow a certain analytical logic not always present in historical scholarship. I eschew treating the specific history of the Kola Peninsula as directly representative of the entire Soviet Union, while interrogating placed-based nuances in order to come to a richer understanding of issues present elsewhere in the country. I write in an ethnographic vein precisely by using a thorough look at the peripheral to inform and complicate the picture of the general and offer insights that are often unattainable when only taking a broad view. For instance, by examining the actions of Soviet reformers in some of the remotest parts

in the Khrushchev Era (London: Routledge, 2006); Miriam Dobson, *Khrushchev's Cold Summer: Gulag Returnees, Crime, and the Fate of Reform after Stalin* (Ithaca: Cornell University Press, 2009); Christopher J. Ward, *Brezhnev's Folly: The Building of BAM and Late Soviet Socialism* (Pittsburgh: University of Pittsburgh Press, 2009); Alexei Yurchak, *Everything Was Forever, Until It Was No More: The Last Soviet Generation* (Princeton: Princeton University Press, 2006); Anne E. Gorsuch and Diane P. Koenker, eds., *The Socialist Sixties: Crossing Borders in the Second World* (Bloomington: Indiana University Press, 2013); and Denis Kozlov and Eleonory Gilburd, eds., *The Thaw: Soviet Society and Culture during the 1950s and 1960s* (Toronto: University of Toronto Press, 2013).

49 Beyond the numerous debates among social scientists about the post-Soviet transition, the following works by historians offer divergent interpretations of the Soviet collapse and post-communist reforms: Stephen F. Cohen, *Failed Crusade: America and the Tragedy of Post-Communist Russia*, 2nd edn. (New York: W. W. Norton and Co., 2001) and Stephen Kotkin, *Armageddon Averted: The Soviet Collapse, 1970–2000*, 2nd edn. (Oxford: Oxford University Press, 2008).

of the Kola tundra, I am able to demonstrate how the intimate knowledge of reindeer ecologies that they gained from local experience shaped ethnic politics in ways distinct from Moscow's central dictates.

The chapters ahead proceed along several narrative trajectories. Most basically, I survey a range of economic activities on the Kola Peninsula in separate chapters on railroads, phosphates, reindeer, nickel, and energy.[50] For each industry I use documentation from the Kola enterprises to reveal deep and discrete types of interaction with the natural environment. These range from profligate deforestation during the construction of the Murmansk railroad to the clandestine tampering of earmarks on reindeer, from toxic phosphine entering the water supply to re-engineered rivers and reservoirs, and from microbes and mosquitoes attacking forced laborers to well-provisioned northerners living with radiation risks. There is a looser chronological arc to the chapters as well. They begin concentrating on the late imperial and early Soviet periods and end focusing more on the second half of the twentieth century. This shift in emphasis partially charts the rising prominence of the different industries, but also aims to impart a better sense of the dramatic scope of change on the Kola Peninsula and the region's close connections to global trends at various moments. Finally, the book follows an analytical path that moves from the initial visions of northern development to the disparate Soviet strategies for achieving these goals, and then on to the results of an industrialized Arctic. Here the varied nature of Soviet power comes to the fore. As the material world variably assists and stymies state economic projects, the mobilizing capacity and persistent limitations of the Soviet Union become obvious.

The opening body chapter of the book examines the construction and operation of the Murmansk railroad. Built by the tsarist government during World War I, the Murmansk railroad brutally relied on forced

[50] I do not cover the large fishing industry that has operated out of the port of Murmansk. My decision to focus on other economic activities comes from the fact that commercial fishing has involved less interaction with the environment of the Kola Peninsula than with the ocean. For good research on the environmental history of the Kola fishing industry, see Julia A. Lajus, "Razvitie rybokhoziaistvennykh issledovanii barentseva moria: vzaimootnosheniia nauki i promysla, 1898–1934 gg." (PhD diss., Rossiiskaia akademiia nauk: Institut istorii estestvoznaniia i tekhniki, 2004); Alexei Yurchenko and Jens Petter Nielsen, eds., *In the North My Nest is Made: Studies in the History of the Murman Colonization, 1860–1940* (Saint Petersburg: European University at Saint Petersburg Press, 2006); and *"More – nashe pole": Kolichestvennye dannye o rybnykh promyslakh Belogo i Barentseva morei XVII – nachala XX vv.* (Saint Petersburg: European University at Saint Petersburg Press, 2010).

labor and reckless construction techniques – a pattern that would later be adopted during Soviet industrial projects in the 1930s. During the 1920s, the management of the railroad turned it into a device for regional colonization, enacting pre-Soviet schemes for Arctic development. Distinct environmental ideologies of assimilating and conquering nature accompanied these varying technocratic and militaristic approaches to industrialization. This look at railroads connects initial Soviet ideas and practices of northern development to the world situation in the early twentieth century and to the tsarist legacy.

The next chapter shifts from transportation infrastructure to the first major industrial project on the Kola Peninsula. During the first five-year plan (1928–1932), the state created an enterprise to excavate and process a phosphorus-rich mineral called apatite in the Khibiny Mountains. Opting for large-scale urban development instead of restricted mining activities, the Stalinist Soviet Union inaugurated a specific set of ecological relations characterized by the combination of a strong longing for harmony with nature and peculiar forms of peacetime environmental destruction. On the one hand, this endeavor marked a departure for the Soviet experience in the far north, as the country took the lead in Arctic industrialization. On the other hand, the perceived imperative to follow the industrialized West played a more influential role on this environmental evolution of Soviet socialism than the overt project of non-capitalism.

Then I turn to the mobilization of reindeer for the sake of ethnic and agricultural reform. The USSR upheld this single animal species over more complex and variegated tundra livelihoods as a means of permeating some of the most desolate territories of the country. Field workers collected ethnographic and biological information about the diverse economic practices of the Sami, Komi, and Nenets. This knowledge facilitated the local implementation of Soviet programs to integrate national minorities dwelling in the Kola tundra through the promotion of large-scale reindeer herding. Both the attempts to develop a socialist version of reindeer pastoralism and the campaigns to preserve wild reindeer arose from desires to alternately manipulate and cooperate with natural conditions. They together helped make the region more legible and governable to the state. At the same time, these efforts also depended on the knowledge of individuals familiar with the animals.

From the mid-1930s onward, a massive nickel and copper smelting industry burgeoned on the Kola Peninsula. The following chapter uses the rise of this heavy industry to investigate the history of pollution and waste in the region. A dualistic view of the environment remained at work as the regime tried out different economic strategies of autarky, militarization, and extensive growth in the nickel sector. In contrast to much of the literature on environmental problems in the Soviet Union, I show that shifts in the global economy and the depletion of local ores conspired to turn the Kola nickel industry from a typical heavy polluter to an egregious one in the 1970s. This interpretation implies that neither the inherent functioning of communist command economies nor the presence of political authoritarianism adequately account for the country's inglorious environmental record. I also demonstrate how the nickel industry has remained empowered over the treatment of the environment in the capitalist economy of post-Soviet Russia.

The final body chapter returns to another facilitator of economic development that, like railroads, enabled the other extractive industries: the energy sector. Kola industrialists sought to solve a regional dearth by harvesting a variety of sources of energy; they burned wood and peat, diverted rivers for hydroelectric dams, imported coal and oil, and split atoms at a nuclear power plant. Many felt confident that expanded energy use would allow humans to ascend over the natural environment, while also providing mutual improvement to both. Instead, as the mushrooming use of these different energy supplies dramatically altered the physical features of the region, new and intricate links to nature were simultaneously forged. Soviet rule transformed Kola lands but did not escape the confines of the material world. This dynamic of drastically changing but not overcoming nature provides an apt analogy for the contours of Soviet power.

2

Assimilation and Conquest

The dust of many years of combat was just beginning to settle, when Gennadii Chirkin published a sanguine pamphlet, *The Colonization of the North and the Means of Communication,* in 1920. A former official from the Resettlement Administration of the tsarist government, Chirkin now found himself ready to assist Russia's new communist leaders. "The productive forces and resources of the northern region of our motherland are extremely diverse," he proclaimed, but currently the territory is "uninhabited and deserted, making it, in an economic sense, 'geographic space.'" What was needed to revive this mere "space" was "a planned and consistent system of state measures aimed at developing the economic and industrial life of the region on the basis of the rational, intensive, and all-around use of natural resources and economic possibilities." In particular, "railroads should be colonization hubs."[1] Over the following decade Chirkin would work to make the recently built Murmansk railroad a multifaceted tool for settling and developing the Kola Peninsula. Throughout the 1920s, the administration of the railroad would be responsible for not only transporting goods and passengers, but also catching fish, harvesting timber, and drawing in new residents.

Chirkin's vision combined varied strands of thinking. It united imperial desires to populate the country more evenly with inspiration for northern development from Arctic territories abroad. At the most basic level, Chirkin and his colleagues maintained a notion that northern nature was inherently valuable because it presented opportunities to improve life in the region. This widely shared and enthusiastic view emerged in

[1] G. F. Chirkin, *Kolonizatsiia Severa i putei soobshcheniia* (Petrograd, 1920), 3, 7.

nineteenth- and early twentieth-century discussions about bringing a railroad connection to the Murman coast. Initially, the warm waters of the bays and inlets along Russia's western border with the Barents Sea sparked interest in establishing a port there that could remain open year-round along with a railroad connection.

But this understanding of the natural world as a treasure waiting to be uncovered lost currency during the period when the Murmansk railroad was actually built. Laborers, the majority of whom were prisoners of war (POWs), laid the track in a hasty and tempestuous fashion during the first several years of World War I as Russia teetered toward revolution in 1917. Officials in charge of the railroad militarized construction, which meant quickly mobilizing resources with a short-term outlook, accepting shoddy work for the sake of rapid completion, and exposing workers to deprivations and hazards related to the environment. In this context of wartime urgency, individuals involved in building the railroad described nature more as another enemy to be defeated than an ally to aid development. And indeed the frozen and swampy land of the north resisted this warlike approach, as newly laid roadbeds often sunk and flooded.

These two models of engagement with the environment – as a foe to vanquish or a potential friend of development – correspond to competing conceptions of nature, which were at the heart of the Soviet experiment on the Kola Peninsula. Should industrialists aim to assimilate the natural world into the national economy, or to conquer it? While related and often overlapping, these concepts also differed significantly.

Assimilation implied capture and integration, compelling detached landscapes to serve new purposes. It meant better understanding nature for the sake of using it more fully and promised economic benefits to new inhabitants of previously neglected territories. The most common term for assimilation in Russian is *osvoenie*, which also translates as mastery. The "word embodies a duality of knowledge and control," according to film scholar Emma Widdis. "*Osvoenie* articulated a relationship of exploitation . . . and was thus part of a colonizing process."[2] The deepening of this knowledge from abstract disposition to concrete thoughts about how to extract economic value from new territories depended on conceptual and physical interaction with specific environments. Kola nature presented a fixed array of possibilities for exploitation that made it possible for industrialists to assimilate it.

[2] Emma Widdis, *Visions of a New Land: Soviet Film from the Revolution to the Second World War* (New Haven: Yale University Press, 2003), 7.

Conquest, in contrast, involved subjecting a natural terrain to purposefully aggressive manipulation. To conquer nature was to destroy any obstacles in the way of making it serve human-dictated purposes. As a metaphor for industrialization, conquest often privileged speed, sacrificing thoroughness of change for the sake of rapid victory. Knowledge mattered less than will, in that the efforts to overcome impediments relied on volition more than careful consideration of existing opportunities. Approached as a wartime combatant, the environment frequently obliged in displaying obstinacy against such advances and in turn helped instigate more antagonistic understandings of it. This militaristic approach to building railroads reappeared in the Stalin years (1928–1953), forming a backbone of putatively "socialist" industrialization.

Therefore, in the Russian north the "conquest of nature" was more defined and specific, as well as less constant, than the definition scholars have used in other historical contexts. Distinguishing between conquest and assimilation allows for a clearer explanation for the variation in interactions with the natural world. In his magisterial study of German hydrological history, David Blackbourn instead adopts an all-encompassing and omnipresent meaning of the term. "I have called this book *The Conquest of Nature* because that is how contemporaries described what they were doing. The tone shifted over the years, from the sunny Enlightenment optimism of the eighteenth century to the earnest nineteenth century belief in science and progress, to the technocratic certainties that marked so much of the twentieth century.... What did not change is the basic idea that nature was an adversary to be manacled, tamed, subjugated, conquered, and so on through a dozen variations."[3] Unlike German waterways, the environmental ideologies behind railroad construction on the Kola Peninsula involved more than a shift in tone. Optimistic, scientific, and technocratic views stand on a different side of the ledger than impulses to manacle and subjugate the natural world.

[3] David Blackbourn, *The Conquest of Nature: Water, Landscape, and the Making of Modern Germany* (New York: W. W. Norton, 2006), 5. Paul Josephson similarly uses concept of conquest to capture the environmental dimensions of all economic, military, exploratory, scientific, and political activities in the Russian Arctic, while taking the Bolshevik revolution as a "sharp break" in the history of these endeavors. In contrast to this claim, I argue that the case of the Murmansk railroad shows how war, and not just revolution, gave birth to conquest and how tsarist legacies affected later Soviet actions. See Paul R. Josephson, *The Conquest of the Russian Arctic* (Cambridge, MA: Harvard University Press, 2014), 1–20.

Impulses toward assimilation and conquest ebbed in and out of late imperial and early Soviet history. I argue that the Soviet approach to the Kola environment owed a considerable amount to these divergent legacies of the tsarist era. Pre-war hopes for enlivening the north were enacted by Soviet officials in the 1920s, while the brutalities of wartime construction were repeated by the Stalinist regime. On the one hand, ideas of opening the north and integrating its resources appeared alongside early plans to establish a railroad line to the Murman coast at the end of the nineteenth century. Soviet railroad administrators largely implemented the technocratic plans of tsarist officials after the end of the Russian Civil War. On the other hand, ferocious and inhumane construction characterized the erection of the Murmansk railroad by the tsarist government during World War I and the frantic management of it during the Russian Civil War. After the consolidation of Joseph Stalin's rule at the end of the 1920s, the Soviet state emulated these wartime practices. Thus, the similarities between the Soviet and tsarist treatment of the natural environment shifted. In contrast to Widdis, who claims that in the Soviet period *osvoenie* "assumed a still more defined form, consistently linked to the more aggressive *zavoevanie* (conquest [through battle]) in descriptions of the transformation of territory," the relationship between assimilation and conquest was not evolutionary but instead characterized by fits and starts.[4] The history of Kola railroads, therefore, reveals varied forms of tsarist influence on the industrialization of the Soviet Arctic.

Colonization before the Railroad

Imperialism defined the pre-Soviet world. It was the age of the "scramble for Africa," foreign incursions into China, and German expansionism within Europe. In the nineteenth- and early twentieth century the Russian Empire participated in such endeavors in at least two distinct ways. The country incorporated new regions on the western and southern borderlands into the empire through violence and integration – a set of strategies that mirrored the overseas activities of many Western countries.[5] The tsarist government also promoted what it saw as "self-colonization": the

4 Widdis, *Visions of a New Land*, 7.

5 Imperial encounters have become a dominant theme in the history of the tsarist era. For works that highlight this expansionist imperialism, see Jane Burbank, Mark von Hagen, and Anatolyi Remnev, eds., *Russian Empire: Space, People, Power, 1700–1930* (Bloomington: Indiana University Press, 2007); Andreas Kappeler, *The Russian Empire: A Multi-Ethnic History*, trans. Alfred Clayton (Essex: Pearson Education, 2001); and

settlement of sparsely populated regions, which nominally had been part of Russia for a long time.[6] Contemporaneously, the United States practiced a similar type of imperialism in its western territories, as did Canada in its northern possessions.[7] In these contexts the term colonization often carried a specific connotation of economic development of the region itself, which distinguished it from imperial models based predominantly on resource extraction to serve the metropole. This "self-colonization" also possessed an ecological logic that would grow into one of the most influential and enduring conceptions of nature in the Soviet Union. As advocates for development debated how to colonize the Kola Peninsula in the second half of the nineteenth century, they started to view the natural world as a potential asset.

Until this time, the Kola Peninsula was a land in-between sovereignty. Russian authority over the region existed more in name than practice. A book published by the Russian government in 1916 to celebrate the completion of the Murmansk railroad even concluded that the region had been "a sad sight. The Murman coast, politically part of the Russian state, was in actuality at the disposal of Norway."[8] Beginning in the Middle Ages, political entities from Russia and Scandinavia took tribute from the Sami and other residents of the region. In the early seventeenth century most Sami on the Kola Peninsula stopped paying taxes to Denmark and those residing in Norwegian Finnmark ceased handing over wealth to Russia. However, intervening territorial conflicts stretching from seventeenth- and eighteenth-century confrontations with Denmark and Sweden to British activities in the region during the Napoleonic and

Jane Burbank and David L. Ransel, eds., *Imperial Russia: New Histories for the Empire* (Bloomington: Indiana University Press, 1998).

6 Efforts at purported "self-colonization" appear in Donald W. Treadgold, *The Great Siberian Migration: Government and Peasant in Resettlement from Emancipation to the First World War* (Westport: Greenwood Press, [1957] 1976); Willard Sunderland, *Taming the Wild Field: Colonization and Empire on the Russian Steppe* (Ithaca: Cornell University Press, 2004); Nicholas B. Breyfogle, *Heretics and Colonizers: Forging Russia's Empire in the South Caucasus* (Ithaca: Cornell University Press, 2005); and Nicholas B. Breyfogle, Abby Schrader, and Willard Sunderland, eds., *Peopling the Russian Periphery: Borderland Colonization in Eurasian History* (London: Routledge, 2007).

7 Mark Bassin, "Turner, Solov'ev, and the 'Frontier Hypothesis': The Nationalist Signification of Open Spaces," *Journal of Modern History* 65, no. 3 (September 1993): 473–511; Patricia Limerick, *The Legacy of Conquest: The Unbroken Past of the American West* (New York: W. W. Norton, 1986); and Liza Piper and John Sandlos, "A Broken Frontier: Ecological Imperialism in the Canadian North," *EH* 12, no. 4 (October 2007): 759–795.

8 *Murmanskaia zheleznaia doroga: Kratkii ocherk postroiki zheleznoi dorogi na Murman s opisaniem eia raiona* (Petrograd, 1916), 101.

Crimean wars further limited Russian control over the territory.[9] Indeed, dual taxation in the contested area between Neiden and Pechenga continued until an agreement in 1826 demarked the border between Russia and Norway (then part of Sweden).[10] In the pre-industrial era Russia's rule over far-flung areas like Siberia depended on paternalistic tribute-taking irrespective of religion and ethnicity, what historian Andrei Znamenski calls the country's "ethic of empire."[11] Without exclusive taxation – the most basic element of imperial rule for the tsarist state – the Kola Peninsula only partially belonged to the Russian Empire.

Very few people lived in this northern region up until this time as well. The population of the Kola Peninsula only reached approximately 5,200 permanent residents in 1858.[12] Slavic settlers began arriving from Novgorod in the thirteenth century and continued to trickle in after Muscovy consolidated its rule. They established garrison towns such as Kola and Kandalaksha and Orthodox monasteries. The schismatic upheavals of the seventeenth and eighteenth centuries also attracted several small groups of religious dissents.[13] In the interior of the peninsula over 1,000 Sami lived in migratory communities that engaged in hunting and freshwater fishing. The population increased during the summer when Slavic Pomors from the White Sea region migrated to the Murman coast to catch fish in the oceanic waters of the Barents Sea.[14]

Official efforts to populate the Kola north took off after Russia's defeat in the Crimean War in 1856. This campaign fit easily with the reformist agenda of the 1860s. Among other things, Tsar Alexander II's Great Reforms liberated Russia's serfs and created new elected institutions of

[9] I. F. Ushakov, *Izbrannye proizvedeniia: Tom 1: Kol'skaia zemlia* (Murmansk: Murmanskoe knizhnoe izdatel'stvo, 1997), 87–260.

[10] Jens Petter Nielsen, "The Murman Coast and Russian Northern Policies ca. 1855–1917," in Alexei Yurchenko and Jens Petter Nielsen, eds., *In the North My Nest is Made: Studies in the History of the Murman Colonization, 1860–1940* (Saint Petersburg: European University at Saint Petersburg Press, 2006), 12.

[11] Andrei A. Znamenski, "The 'Ethic of Empire' on the Siberian Borderland: The Peculiar Case of the 'Rock People,' 1791–1878," in Breyfogle, Schrader, and Sunderland, eds., *Peopling the Russian Periphery*, 106–127.

[12] "Vvodnyi ocherk," in A. A. Kiselev, ed., *Kol'skii entsiklopediia*, vol. 1 (Saint Petersburg/Apatity: IS/ KNTs RAN, 2008), 69–70.

[13] Ushakov, *Izbrannye proizvedeniia: Tom 1*, 29–260. Also see, Iu. P. Bardileva, "Religioznaia zhizn' Kol'skogo v nachale XX veka: osobennosti religioznye verovanii i religioznoi deiatel'nosti Severiane," in P. V. Fedorov, Iu. P. Bardileva, and E. I. Mikhailov, eds., *Zhivushchie na Severe: Vyvoz ekstremal'noi srede* (Murmansk: MGPU, 2005), 67–75.

[14] Julia Lajus, "Colonization of the Russian North: A Frozen Frontier," in Christina Folke Ax, et al., eds., *Cultivating the Colonies: Colonial States and their Environmental Legacies* (Athens, OH: Ohio University Press, 2011), 164–190.

local self-governance called *zemstva*. Emancipation mattered less for the Kola Peninsula, since serfdom had never taken root in the Russian north. Instead, the majority of rural residents already fell under the category of state peasants. The region also did not acquire *zemstva* after the Great Reforms. State administrators, nevertheless, initiated ambitious new programs to colonize this faraway periphery. The policies aimed to use the Arctic environment to buoy up the territory through improving existing industries and establishing new ones.

Anticipating the grandiose desires of later railroad developers, Leo Mekhelin, the Russian General Consul in Christiania (Oslo), argued that the Kola Peninsula should emulate northern Norway, which had dramatically expanded fisheries, transportation services, and communications during the 1840s and 1850s. With similar "climate, population, and livelihood," Mekhelin reasoned, Russian Lapland could undertake comparable growth.[15] The aquatic species in the Barents Sea provided an opportunity to develop a harsh land. To take advantage of this prospect, Mekhelin urged establishing a permanent and central fishing settlement on the Murman coast. This commercial center would improve the trading conditions of the fishers and eliminate the costly seasonal trek of the Pomors to the ocean. He also believed that allowing Norwegians to settle in the area could benefit Russian colonization by serving as a start-up population and demonstrating more advanced fishing techniques to the allegedly backward Pomors. This last proposal was controversial, but eventually found official support. Laws from 1860 and 1868 offered an array of benefits to settlers who were both Russian citizens and foreigners: exemption from taxes and military service, loans and subsidies, special trading privileges, and rights to hunt and fish on state lands.[16] These

[15] Quoted in Ruslan Davydov, "From Correspondence to Settlement: the Colonization of Murman 1860–1876," in Yurchenko and Nielsen, eds., *In the North My Nest is Made*, 29. On the use of international models in the colonization of the Kola north, see Julia Lajus, "In Search of Instructive Models: The Russian State at a Crossroads to Conquering the North," in Dolly Jørgensen and Sverker Sörlin, eds., *Northscapes: History, Technology, and the Making of Northern Environments* (Vancouver: University of British Columbia Press, 2013), 110–133.

[16] Nielsen, "The Murman Coast and Russian Northern Policies," Davydov, "From Correspondence to Settlement," and Tatiana Schrader, "Legislative Aspects of the Norwegian Colonization of Murman (1860–1915)," in Yurchenko and Nielsen, eds., *In the North My Nest is Made*, 12–24, 29–38, 47, 61–85. On Murman colonization, also see G. P. Popov and R. A. Davydov, *Murman: Ocherki istorii kraia XIX-nachala XX v.* (Ekaterinburg: Istitut ekologicheskikh problem Severa Ural′skoe otdelenie Akademii Nauk, 1999).

enticements attracted some Norwegian, Finnish, and Russian families to the Murman coast.

When they arrived, the ethnically diverse settlers interacted with the natural environment in divergent ways. Finns and Norwegians moved primarily to the area to the west of the Kola Bay. The land here had a much greater capacity to support livestock and vegetable gardening than the rocky shores east of the bay, allowing these settlers to supplement oceanic fishing with agriculture. Pomor and Karelian settlers chiefly migrated to the eastern part of the Murman coast and engaged more exclusively in cod fishing. Desperation drew many of them there after a famine struck northern Russia in 1868.[17] The varied occupations of these different groups meant that many Pomors continued to travel to the Murman coast only in the summer instead of permanently colonizing the region.[18] Occasionally, conflicts would arise among the different populations over access to natural resources. For instance, in the summer of 1870 one Norwegian settler complained to the Arkhangel'sk governor that the Pomors were taking wood for fuel and using hayfields without permission or payment.[19]

Such disputes played into the hands of nationalist critics of the tsarist government's colonization program. These conservative intellectuals and entrepreneurs bemoaned the increasing presence of foreigners on the Murman coast and romanticized the traditional livelihoods of the Pomors. Embodying what economic historian Thomas Owen has called "Slavophile capitalism," pan-Slavist philosopher Nikolai Danilevskii outlined an alternative vision of northern development.[20] Drawing on his own studies of fisheries in the Russian northwest, Danilevskii rejected Mekhelin's comparison of the Murman coast to Finnmark and many

[17] Yurchenko, "Economic Adaptation by Colonists on the Russian Barents Sea Coast," in Yurchenko and Nielsen, eds., *In the North My Nest is Made*, 94–110.

[18] For instance, in 1895 Arkhangel'sk governor Aleksandr Platonovich Engel'gardt reported that Western Murman had 1,063 permanent residents and Eastern Murman only 154. By contrast, 2,794 fishermen came in the summer that year. A. P. Engel'gardt, *Russkii sever": putevyia zapiski* (Saint Petersburg: Izdanie A. S. Suvorina, 1897), 95–96. For more on Engel'gardt's career, see Richard G. Robbins, *The Tsar's Viceroys: Russian Provincial Governors in the Last Years of the Empire* (Ithaca: Cornell University Press, 1987), 67–71 and David Moon, *The Plough that Broke the Steppes: Agriculture and Environment on Russia's Grasslands, 1700–1914* (Oxford: Oxford University Press, 2013).

[19] Davydov, "From Correspondence to Settlement," in Yurchenko and Nielsen, eds., *In the North My Nest is Made*, 40–42.

[20] Thomas C. Owen, *Russian Corporate Capitalism from Peter the Great to Perestroika* (Oxford: Oxford University Press, 1995), 126–138.

of his proposals. In his opinion the government should cease offering incentives to foreign colonists and concentrate on protectionist policies to shield the Pomors from competition. Danilevskii also advocated private entrepreneurial endeavors such as a steamship service to connect the Murman coast to Arkhangel′sk and northern Europe.[21] Moscow businessman Fedor Chizhov pursued this idea, creating the Murmansk Scheduled Steamship Company in the 1870s. Taken by the "cleverness and resourcefulness" of the Pomors whose ancestors had "conquered the land as far as the Arctic Ocean," Chizhov hoped to improve their lot. He explained that he organized the company, "not because I expect to make a profit – I do not expect that at all – but because I am convinced that region can be brought to life."[22] This view of development differed from Mekhelin's schemes in seeking to promote avowedly Russian ways of interacting with the environment. But these nationalist critics, as well as later opponents of foreign emulation, ultimately shared with government officials a conception of nature as a set of resources that could open up the north.

Campaigning for a Line

Disappointment with the tepid results of Murman colonization gave way to more ambitious plans to build a railroad line to the Kola Bay in the 1890s. Only a few thousand people had moved to the Murman coast by this time and the population of the Kola Peninsula remained under 10,000. Feeling heightened urgency to solidify and strengthen state dominance over the country's peripheries, the Ministry of Finance under Sergei Witte, Arkhangel′sk governor Aleksandr Engel′gardt, and the Ministry of Transportation lobbied to create a new naval and commercial port on the Murman coast with a railroad line to serve it. They viewed railroads as an optimal means of settling, economically developing, and asserting military control over sparsely populated territories – as tools of "self-colonization." Railroads had become an imperial technology in

[21] N. Ia. Danilevskii, "O merakh k obezpecheniiu narodnogo prodovol′stviia na krainem severe Rossii," in N. Ia. Danilevskii, ed., *Sbornik politicheskikh i ekonomicheskikh statei* (Saint Petersburg: Izdanie N. Strakhova, 1890), 588–601. Also see Nielsen, "The Murman Coast and Russian Northern Policies" and Davydov, "From Correspondence to Settlement," in Yurchenko and Nielsen, eds., *In the North My Nest is Made*, 35–37, 48–49, and 18–20.

[22] Quoted in Thomas C. Owen, *Dilemmas of Russian Capitalism: Fedor Chizhov and Corporate Enterprise in the Railroad Age* (Cambridge, MA: Harvard University Press, 2005), 138, 142, 134–148.

other continental states a bit earlier in the nineteenth century, but were now taking off in Russia.[23] Foremost among these projects was the construction of the Trans-Siberian railroad from 1891 to 1916. Marking a new era of expanded state involvement in population resettlements and managing the economy, this route brought millions of migrants to Siberia over the final decades of tsarist rule.[24]

Witte led the charge on a parallel project to establish a railroad to the Murman coast. The Minister of Finance ascended the ranks in the tsarist bureaucracy from a background in the Russian railroad industry and embraced the theories of German economist Frederick List about the active role states should play in industrialization.[25] He believed that state-sponsored railroad construction could surmount Russia's supposed economic and cultural backwardness: "The railroad is like a leaven, which creates a cultural fermentation among the population. Even if it passed through an absolutely savage people along the way, in a short time it would civilize them up to a necessary level." Witte added, "in Russia the influence of railroads should be even greater than in western European states" because the country had previously "lagged behind its western neighbors in cultural attitudes."[26] This conviction that industrial development elevated culture had a widespread environmental corollary – the belief that untouched nature represented a wasted opportunity for improvement.

However, the Ministry of Finance's advocacy for a railroad to the Kola Peninsula encountered opposition from other branches of the tsarist administration. Regional officials from the Olonets province (which

23 On railroads as an imperial tool in Canada and the United States, see Donald W. Roman, "Railway Imperialism in Canada, 1847–1865," in Clarence B. Davis, Kenneth E. Wilburn Jr., and Ronald E. Robinson, eds., *Railway Imperialism* (Westport: Greenwood Press, 1991), 7–24; Robert G. Angevine, *The Railroad and the State: War, Politics, and Technology in Nineteenth-Century America* (Stanford: Stanford University Press, 2004); and Richard White, *Railroaded: The Transcontinentals and the Making of Modern America* (New York: W. W. Norton, 2011).

24 Treadgold, *The Great Siberian Migration*, 32–34, 107–149 and Steven G. Marks, *Road to Power: The Trans-Siberian Railroad and the Colonization of Asian Russia, 1850–1917* (Ithaca: Cornell University Press, 1991).

25 On Witte's background, see Francis W. Wcislo, *Tales of Imperial Russia: The Life and Times of Sergei Witte, 1849–1915* (Oxford: Oxford University Press, 2011); Sidney Harcave, *Count Sergei Witte and the Twilight of Imperial Russia* (London: M. E. Sharpe, 2004); and Theodore Von Laue, *Sergei Witte and the Industrialization of Russia* (New York: Atheneum, 1969).

26 S. Iu. Vitte, *Konspekt lektsii o narodnom i gosudarstvennom khoziaistve*, 2nd edn. (St. Petersburg: Brokgauz" Efron", 1912), 344–345.

included most of Karelia) and Arkhangel'sk province (which included the Kola Peninsula) first floated the prospect of building a railroad there in the 1870s and 1880s. The project rose to the top of the agenda during the final years of Tsar Alexander III's reign as the Russian government considered where it should locate a new naval port. It wanted to bolster the country's security by developing a harbor that would be resistant to blockades, sufficiently close and connected to the Russian heartland, and stay unfrozen in the winter (unlike the ports in Saint Petersburg and Arkhangel'sk).[27] Against Witte's preference for the Murman coast, the War Ministry and Naval Ministry favored the Latvian city of Libau (Liepāja) for the new port. Despite higher blockade risks, Libau already possessed a railroad connection, a considerable population, and an ice-free harbor. A naval port on the Murman coast would require building a railroad up there, which the War Ministry considered costly and "premature." These opponents insisted that a population with economic interests should precede state support for a new railroad – the reverse of Witte's perspective.[28]

Behind the modernizing enthusiasm of Witte and his ilk lay a technocratic orientation toward the world. Such government officials, regional boosters, scholars, and businesspeople believed that scientific expertise and new technologies could be employed as drivers of economic growth. They often also thought that the state apparatus could and should help guide and regulate the process. These representatives of educated society in late imperial Russia shared this technocratic disposition with modernizers throughout the world. As political theorist Timothy Mitchell notes during the twentieth century, "the politics of national development and economic growth was a politics of techno-science, which claimed to bring the expertise of modern engineering, technology, and social science to improve the defects of nature, to transform peasant agriculture, to repair the ills of society, and to fix the economy."[29] The common conviction that technical expertise undergirded development also tied imperial era planners to their Soviet descendants. In his classic study of the technical intelligentsia in the Soviet Union, Kendall Bailes shows how engineers who came of age under the old regime often felt similar technocratic impulses as communist revolutionaries. Seeing a unified

[27] V. A. Khabarov, *Magistral'* (Murmansk: Murmanskoe knizhnoe izdatel'stvo, 1986), 12.

[28] *Murmanskaia zheleznaia doroga*, 15–16.

[29] Timothy Mitchell, *Rule of Experts: Egypt, Techno-Politics, Modernity* (Berkeley: University of California Press, 2002), 15.

cause on this matter at least, they embraced the new opportunities to use their expertise to solve social and political problems under the Bolsheviks.[30]

Adherents of this technocratic outlook understood the natural world as possessing inherent value that was waiting to be unleashed. The trick was for people to find ways to maximally utilize nature, thereby turning it into resources and bringing about mutual improvement to environment and society. Historian Ekaterina Pravilova describes how changes to Russia's system of property after the Great Reforms meant that the "natural world took on new value... New schemes for distributing natural resources that emerged in the late nineteenth to early twentieth century were based not on the grounds of social origin but on the grounds of knowledge, the ability to use resources effectively, and the exigencies of social justice presented as public good."[31] In places like the north, many experts shifted their attention to the prospects that nature offered for growth rather than the limitations it posed to livelihoods. While they planned the project, advocates of a railroad to the Kola Peninsula embraced a robust version of this assimilationist conception of nature.

As assorted expeditions inspected the Murman coast in the mid-1890s, the lands and waters of the Kola Peninsula presented their potential assets to the travelers. The Kola environment itself helped move impressions of the territory from desolate, harsh, and inhospitable to rich, valuable, and enticing. Above all, many of the inlets and bays of the Western Murman coast did not freeze in the winter, despite their polar locations. Thus, the territory could host a port that would remain open through the winter, unlike some of Russia's main waterfronts further south. One representative of the Ministry of Finance who traveled there with Witte in 1894 enthused "the importance of Murman lies in its splendid natural harbors that sit on the open ocean and do not freeze all winter" and echoed Mekhelin's earlier comparison to Finnmark.[32] Of the multiple parcels of the Murman coast the team surveyed, Witte left most impressed with the "remarkable" Ekaterina harbor in the northwest section of the Kola Bay, which he thought had good defensive capacities.[33]

30 Kendall E. Bailes, *Technology and Society under Lenin and Stalin: Origins of the Soviet Technical Intelligentsia, 1917–1941* (Princeton: Princeton University Press, 1978), 95–121.

31 Ekaterina Pravilova, *A Public Empire: Property and the Quest for the Common Good in Imperial Russia* (Princeton: Princeton University Press, 2014), 128.

32 Quoted in *Murmanskaia zheleznaia doroga*, 15–16.

33 S. Iu. Vitte, *Vospominaniia*, vol. 1 (Moscow/Tallinn: Skif Aleks, 1994), 389.

After his own expedition a year later, Arkhangel′sk governor Engel′gardt insisted that the natural treasures of the Kola Peninsula could enable regional development. Espousing a full vision of assimilating northern nature, he declared that fish, forests, and mineral ore could "not only develop and strengthen the welfare of the local population, but also benefit the entire state."[34] He also justified the desirability of a railroad line to the Murman coast as a needed investment to integrate this entire complex of the area's natural environment into the economy. Engel′gardt specifically refuted claims that the natural conditions of the region were too harsh for development: "While studying the issue of Murman, its climatic conditions, and the colonization of the Murman coast, we have quite often read and heard that one cannot live on Murman, that colonization of it is impossible, that its harsh climate prevents a healthy existence, etc. The above data testify to precisely the opposite." He concluded, "the time is already not far off when Murman will finally receive its proper commercial and political significance, which nature itself has specified."[35]

Despite the eagerness of these government officials, their plans to build the railroad in the 1890s faltered. At their final meeting, Witte gave Tsar Alexander III a report urging the construction of a naval and commercial port in the Ekaterina harbor and the establishment of a railroad line to connect it to the center. The notes Alexander III took before his sudden and unexpected death suggested his support for the project. According to Witte, Tsar Nicholas II – Alexander III's successor – initially intended to carry out his father's wishes, but then changed his mind and pursued the Libau port instead. A frustrated Witte eventually persuaded Nicholas II to create an exclusively commercial port and town on the Murman coast, but without any immediate plans to bring a railroad line up there.[36] In 1899 the port city of Aleksandrovsk in the Ekaterina harbor officially opened with a grand ceremony. Newspapers at the time predicted it would become a "natural center of economic life on the Murman coast."[37]

Without a railroad, Aleksandrovsk alone could serve as a conduit for neither settlement nor economic development. Most of the approximately 300 people who initially resided in the town came from nearby Kola. By the start of World War I, its population had barely doubled. The

[34] Engel′gardt, *Russkii sever″*, 1. [35] Engel′gardt, *Russkii sever″*, 130, 133.

[36] Sergei I. Witte, *The Memoirs of Count Witte*, trans. and ed. P. Sidney Harcave (Armonk: M. E. Sharpe, 1990), 210–212 and Khabarov, *Magistral′*, 12–16.

[37] Quoted in A. Zhilinskii, "Neskol′ko slov o zheleznoi dorogi na Murmane," *IAOIRS* 6, no. 14 (July 15, 1914): 421.

natural conditions of the Ekaterina harbor also proved less accommodating than its boosters had hoped. Strong winds and the port's distance from fishing grounds inhibited it from becoming a center for commercial fishing. The lands surrounding the harbor were almost exclusively steep rocky tundra without meadows or forests that could serve settlers' livelihoods in other ways. Most remarkably, the water in the Ekaterina harbor, unlike at other parts of the Murman coast, did occasionally freeze in the winter.[38] Arkhangel′sk journalist Aleksei Zhilinskii gave an unambiguously damning assessment of the port town: "it is hard to imagine so big a mistake and so big a disappointment as occurred with the opening of Aleksandrovsk."[39]

But neither this disappointment nor the tumult that gripped Russia deterred dreamers who sought to enhance the north with a railroad. While the maelstrom of the first decade of the twentieth century – the Russo-Japanese War, the 1905 Revolution, the establishment of a limited constitutional monarchy, and the dramatic land reforms of Prime Minister Petr Stolypin – delayed the railroad project, a new generation of technocrats grew more vocal and optimistic about the potential of the Kola Peninsula. Scientists undertook numerous explorations to the region in these years for the expressed purpose of gaining knowledge that would serve the economic interests of the state.[40] Activists in the imperial Resettlement Administration also energetically encouraged a thorough expansion of Russia's railroad network within government circles and through their journal *Problems of Colonization*. Several of the leaders of this body, including Genadii Chirkin and Vladimir Voshchinin, later became involved in Soviet efforts to develop the Murmansk region. In the years before World War I, Chirkin specifically wrote that "self-colonization" required the establishment of railroad lines to locations of desired resettlement and not just to existing economic centers.[41]

[38] Ushakov, *Izbrannye proizvedeniia: Tom 1*, 398–399; Zhilinskii, "Neskol′ko slov o zheleznoi dorogi na Murmane," *IAOIRS* 6, no. 14 (July 15, 1914): 421–422 and A. Zhilinskii, "K voprosu o porte na Murmane," *IAOIRS* 7, no. 5 (May 15, 1915): 135.

[39] Zhilinskii, "Neskol′ko slov o zheleznoi dorogi na Murmane," *IAOIRS* 6, no. 14 (July 15, 1914): 422.

[40] Julia A. Lajus, "Razvitie rybokhoziaistvennykh issledovanii barentseva moria: vzaimootnosheniia nauki i promysla, 1898–1934 gg." (PhD diss., Rossiiskaia akademiia nauk: Institut istorii estestvoznaniia i tekhniki, 2004), 33–147; Julia Lajus, "Whose Fish? Controversies between the State and Local Actors about the Knowledge and Practices of Resource Use in the Russian North," (Unpublished paper); and Ushakov, *Izbrannye proizvedeniia: Tom 1*, 410–414.

[41] *Voprosy kolonizatsii*, no. 10 (1912): 303–304.

According to historian Peter Holquist, these members of the Resettlement Administration "championed technocratic knowledge, advocated forms of scientized state intervention, and emphasized 'productive' labor over 'speculation.'"[42]

Meanwhile, a section of educated society in Arkhangel′sk began espousing a heightened sense of the value of northern nature, referring to it frequently as a diverse and inexhaustible treasure chest.[43] Nature's deficiencies resulted, many of them asserted, from an insufficient number of humans to use it economically. As the editors of the journal of the newly formed Arkhangel′sk Society for the Study of the Russian North put it: "The enlivening of the north can only stand on solid ground after a period of exploiting its resources." They continued, "the colonization system should be focused directly on the exploitation of natural resources of the north" and not on "one-sided goals."[44] Specifically addressing the Kola Peninsula, another article highlighted the need for colonization to enable the total use of nature: "the size of the current population of Murman does not correspond to its natural resources . . . a continual and significant influx of new forces and working hands is urgently required."[45] Many of these local advocates agreed with individuals in the Resettlement Administration that the construction of the delayed railroad line could solve these labor shortages. "The rich forests along the railroad would be

42 Peter Holquist, "'In Accord with State Interests and the People's Wishes': The Technocratic Ideology of Imperial Russia's Resettlement Administration," *SR* 69, no. 1 (Spring 2010): 157. Each of the traits that Holquist mentions here continues into the Soviet period. On the question of "speculation," I hasten to add that I depart from interpretations that take a distrust of markets and private property as one of the defining elements of technocracy. See, among other works, Walter McDougall, *The Heavens and the Earth: A Political History of the Space Age* (Baltimore: The Johns Hopkins University Press, [1985] 1997), which argues that the Soviet Union invented technocratic rule. Modern economic development often relied on such technocratic impulses, regardless of whether a country overtly embraced capitalism. Also, as I will argue in the next chapter, Soviet non-capitalism mattered little for environmental relations.

43 For example, "Ot redaktsii," *IAOIRS* 1, no. 1 (May 15, 1909): 3–6; "Chto nuzhno dlia kolonizatsii Murmana? (Murman i ego nuzhdy)," and S. Averintsev, "Neskol′ko slov o postanovke nauchno-promyslovykh issledovanii u beregov Murmana," *IAOIRS* 1, no. 2 (June 1, 1909): 5–18, 25–38; and Zhilinskii, "Neskol′ko slov o zheleznoi dorogi na Murmane," *IAOIRS* 6, no. 14 (July 15, 1914): 417–423. For an interesting discussion of competing identities of the European Russian north based on Arkhangel′sk and the Kola Peninsula, see Pavel V. Fedorov, "The European Far North of Russia and Its Territorial Constructions in the Sixteenth-Twenty-First Centuries," *Acta Borealia: A Nordic Journal of Circumpolar Studies* 28, no. 2 (2011): 167–182.

44 "Ot redaktsii," *IAOIRS* 1, no. 2 (June 1, 1909): 5–6.

45 "Chto nuzhno dlia kolonizatsii Murmana?," *IAOIRS* 1, no. 2 (June 1, 1909): 8.

objects of industrial extraction," wrote another journalist, "Life on the Murman and other coasts then would be turned toward vigorous labor and trading; mineral resources would not be left without exploitation."[46]

Even individuals who remained anxious about the negative influence of foreigners in the Kola north and were less inclined toward large-scale state solutions now embraced the railroad project. Maintaining a similar stance to Danilevskii decades earlier, these Russian nationalists felt a widespread ambivalence about economic modernity and hostility to indiscriminately relying on science from abroad. In this sense they were hardly technocrats. They blamed the activities of foreign trawling ships for depressing the economy of the Pomors and rejected calls to adopt new fishing technologies. In addition, they bemoaned the supposedly tragic influence of foreign settlers and saw their environmental practices as ill-suited for the Russian north.[47] One writer declared, "foreign industrialists succeeded in paying attention to the natural resources of Murman before us and exploit them for themselves as much as they can, recently reaching the point of almost open rapaciousness."[48] Yet, like the more ardent proponents of development, these critics praised northern nature as rich and supported strengthening the region's connections to Russia through a railroad line.[49] This consensus assured broad support among regional advocates during the wartime construction of the Murmansk railway.

Building the Murmansk Railroad

Total war gave birth to violence toward nature and society. As environmental historian Edmund Russell insists, "the control of nature formed one root of total war, and total war helped expand the control of nature."[50] The First World War (1914–1918) turned Russia's means of

46 A. G., "O zheleznoi doroge na Murmane," *IAOIRS* 2, no. 9 (May 1, 1910): 20.

47 A. Iaren′gin, "Zlo ot inostrannykh traulerov," *IAOIRS* 2, no. 12 (June 15, 1910): 18–19; A. S. Adrianov, "Inostrantsy na Murmane," *IAOIRS* 2, no. 14 (July 15, 1910): 25–27; and "Izvestiia Arkhangel′skogo obshchestva izucheniia Russkogo Severa," *IAOIRS* 9, no. 7–8 (July–August 1917): 333–339.

48 "Kolonizatsiia," *IAOIRS* 2, no. 10 (May 15, 1910): 38.

49 Sviashch. Arkh. Grandilevskii, "K istorii russkogo severa (Russko-norvezhskie otnoshcheniia)," *IAOIRS* 2, no. 11 (June 1, 1910): 21–42 and A. Rinek, "K voprosu o Murmanskoi zheleznoi doroge," *IAOIRS* 6, no. 11 (June 1, 1914): 321–324.

50 Edmund Russell, *War and Nature: Fighting Humans and Insects with Chemicals from World War I to Silent Spring* (Cambridge: Cambridge University Press, 2001), 2. On war and nature, also see Richard P. Tucker and Edmund Russell, eds., *Natural Enemy,*

mobilizing northern resources away from the enthusiastic proposals of the previous decades and toward militaristic strategies of industrial construction. Impossible time schedules, chaotic planning, major constraints in acquiring adequate supplies and finances, the use of prison labor, and shortsighted methods of nature use that undermined land health and subsequent economic growth characterized the building of the Murmansk railroad. This profligate approach to construction led to the loss of many workers' lives and foreshadowed later railroad projects of the Stalin era. Such militarism also contributed to a view of nature as above all an obstacle to be conquered, instead of an imperial treasure to be released.[51] In the midst of building the Murmansk railroad, the environment became an enemy – in part because the exigencies of war inhibited cautious planning and in part due to northern nature's recalcitrance to human manipulation.

Military concerns had been high on the agenda since Witte's abortive effort to establish a railroad to the Murman coast in the 1890s. They remained important as government officials and private entrepreneurs renewed preliminary planning for a railroad connection shortly before the outbreak of World War I.[52] In 1912 the regional government of the Olonets province cooperated with central state agencies to form a private company to build a connection from Saint Petersburg to Petrozavodsk. The Olonets railroad sought investments from Russian and foreign sources and began construction on the line by the summer of 1914.[53] At the time, members of the government and the educated public floated various ideas for a further expansion to the north, including several options for a railroad to Murman and the possibility of by-passing the Kola Peninsula and running the line through the Grand Duchy of Finland.[54]

Natural Ally: Toward an Environmental History of War (Corvallis: Oregon State University Press, 2004).

51 Historian Pavel Fedorov argues in a similar vein. He highlights the emergent militarism in regional development of the Kola Peninsula and a deep history of attraction and repulsion of the center toward the north. P. V. Fedorov, "Rossiiskaia okraina: prirodno-kul'turnyi landshaft i problema genezisa zapoliarnogo goroda" and P. V. Fedorov, "Rossiiskoe gosudarstvo i kol'skii sever: pritiazhenie i ottalkivanie," in P. V. Fedorov, Iu. P. Bardileva, and E. I. Mikhailov, eds., *Zhivushchie na Severe: Vyvoz ekstremal'noi srede* (Murmansk: MGPU, 2005), 87–90, 102–108.

52 *Murmanskaia zheleznaia doroga*, 18–19.

53 M. A. Press, "Istoriia sooruzheniia Murmanskoi zheleznoi dorogi," in *Proizvoditel'nye sily raiona Murmanskoi zheleznoi dorogi: Sbornik* (Petrozavodsk: Pravlenie Murmanskoi zheleznoi dorogi, 1923), 15–18; Khabarov, *Magistral'*, 14–15; and Ushakov, *Izbrannye proizvedeniia: Tom 1*, 549–551.

54 Prof A. Kh. Rinek, "Murmanskaia zheleznaia doroga," *IAOIRS* 5, no. 18 (September 15, 1913): 817–820; "Zheleznodorozhnye puti," *IAOIRS* 6, no. 4 (February 15, 1914):

Strategic calculations changed dramatically with the outbreak of war in August 1914. During the first few months of the conflict, the navies of the Central Powers effectively closed Russia's Baltic and Black Sea ports, thereby cutting off the most accessible hubs for trade with the Allies. These developments left Russia with the distant Pacific port of Vladivostok and the one in Arkhangel'sk, which closed for five months in winter.[55] The urgent need for greater access to foreign supplies inspired the government to move rapidly toward building the railroad line to the Murman coast. Accepting that Aleksandrovsk had been an inappropriate location for a major port, officials initially designated the town of Kola as the terminus of the railroad. They then revised the plans again, pushing the end of the railroad about eleven kilometers north to the Semenov bight – the future site of Murmansk – where the bay water remained unfrozen in winter.

The plan was for a single line track over a thousand kilometers long that would start at Petrozavodsk, traverse north along Lake Onega, and continue up to Soroka on the southern shore of the White Sea. The railroad would then cut through an extremely marshy area in northern Karelia and proceed to Kandalaksha in the southeast corner of the Kola Peninsula. Finally, it would follow a valley adjacent to Lake Imandra and eventually reach the Kola Bay. Pomors had historically passed through this last leg of the route when trekking to summer fishing grounds, as had Sami coachmen carrying mail, goods, and travelers. Building activities would revolve around these three separate segments of the railroad – Petrozavodsk to Soroka, Soroka to Kandalaksha, and Kandalaksha to Kola.[56] Russian officials struck a deal with Ambassador George Buchanan to bring British financiers and construction companies into the project. Imports of equipment, including rails, locomotives, and wagons, from Russia's wartime allies proved essential for the swift completion of the road.[57]

By accelerating the creation of the Murmansk railroad, the war in some ways proved a boon for technocratic advocates of northern development.

125–127; "Zheleznodorozhnye puti," *IAOIRS* 6, no. 5 (March 1, 1914): 155–156; "Zheleznodorozhnye puti," *IAOIRS* 6, no. 8 (April 15, 1914): 254–255; Rinek, "K voprosu o Murmanskoi zheleznoi doroge," *IAOIRS* 6, no. 11 (June 1, 1914): 321–324; Zhilinskii, "Neskol'ko slov o zheleznoi dorogi na Murmane," *IAOIRS* 6, no. 14 (July 15, 1914): 417–423; and "Zheleznodorozhnye puti," *IAOIRS* 6, no. 19 (November 15, 1914): 652–654.

55 Ushakov, *Izbrannye proizvedeniia: Tom 1*, 549–551.

56 *Murmanskaia zheleznaia doroga*, 20–22 and Khabarov, *Magistral'*, 15–17.

57 Reinhard Nachtigal, *Die Murmanbahn 1915 bis 1919: Kriegsnotwendigkeit und Wirtschaftinteressen* (Remshalden: BAG-Verlag, 2007), 39–48, 62–70.

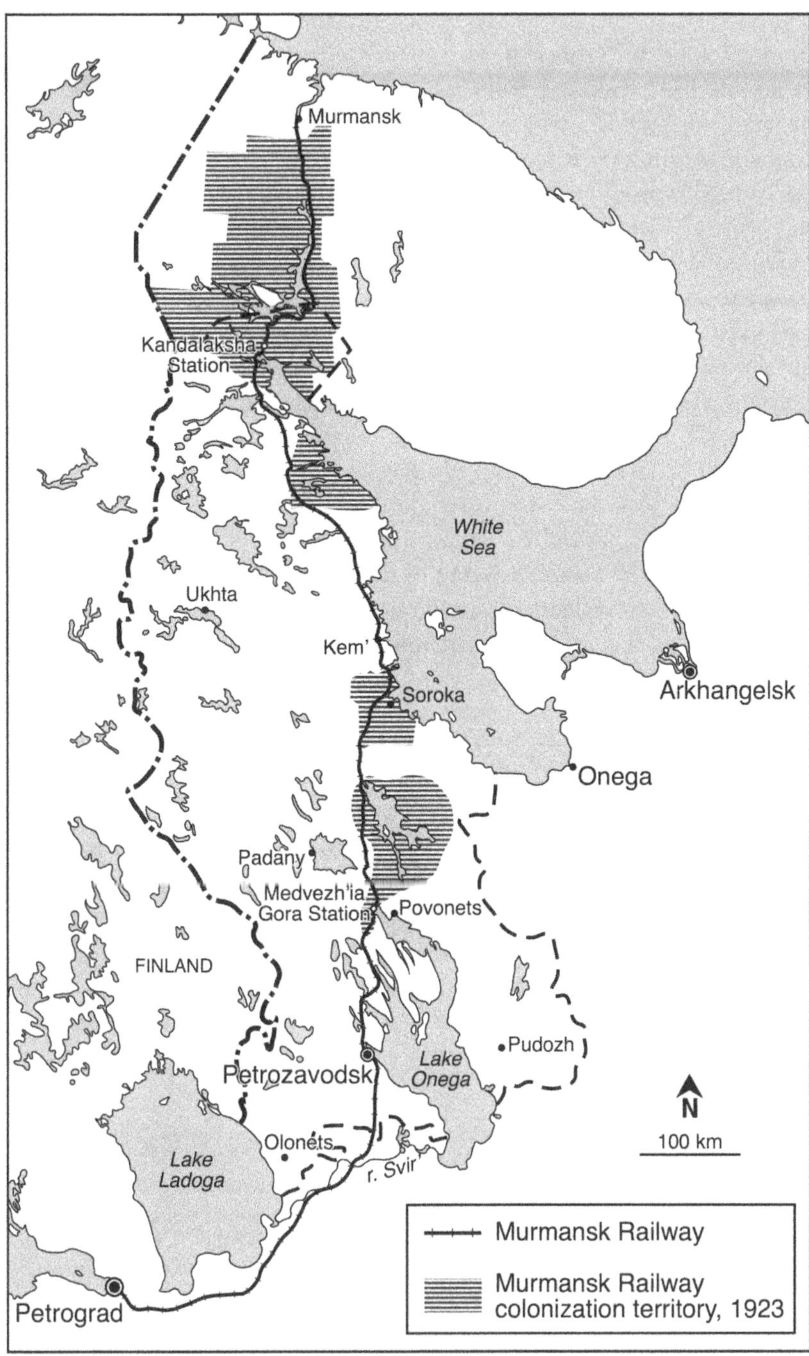

MAP 2. The Murmansk Railroad.
Source: Nick Baron, *Soviet Karelia: Politics, Planning and Terror in Stalin's Russia, 1920–1939* (London: Routledge, 2007), 73.

In a lecture for the Arkhangel′sk Society for the Study of the Russian North, Zhilinskii reportedly acknowledged the "dreadful upheaval of economic life" resulting from the conflict, but also insisted: "the war brought up a whole array of complex tasks for the economic life of the country, which have forced serious attention to the possible widening of the country's productive forces and strengthening of Russia's position on the world market. This last circumstance above all calls for the intensive pursuit of an exit to the open sea in our north through the erection of the Murmansk railroad."[58] At the Resettlement Administration, Chirkin and his colleagues turned their attention to regulating the country's food supply during the war, all the while concocting long-term plans to populate northern Russia.[59] The tsarist government declared, "the introduction of a railroad here opens up the brightest possibilities," such as "the development of productive forces." "In terms of the colonization of the vast Murman region – the current population of which does not correspond to its enormous natural resources – the railroad is destined to have a prominent role."[60] The bolstering of these desires for the future integration of the north while the war still raged fits with the growth of modern state practices that historians attribute to Russia's "continuum of war and revolution" during 1914–1921.[61]

All the same, assistance to the war effort took precedence during the construction of the Murmansk railroad. In these circumstances the ruthless exploitation of the natural world for military ends sidelined the optimistic pursuit of making sparse territories flourish. Instead of systematically unleashing nature's value, builders entered a battle with the Kola and Karelian environments. Initiating this conflict with the northern environment, they indeed encountered a formidable foe.

From the beginning of construction in the spring of 1915, several stable features of the environment resisted the railroad line. The long,

58 This summary of the report appeared in the journal without direct quotations. "Arkhangel′skogo obshchestva izucheniia Russkogo Severa,"*IAOIRS* 8, no. 9 (September 15, 1916): 369–370.

59 Holquist, "'In Accord with State Interests and the People's Wishes'," SR 69, no. 1 (Spring 2010): 164–171.

60 *Murmanskaia zheleznaia doroga*, 117. Discussions of the development potential of the Murmansk railroad after the war also appeared in A. F. Zaitsev and N. R. Rodionov, "Murmanskaia zheleznaia doroga i zadazhi ekonomicheskoi politiki na Severe," *Voina i ekonomicheskaia zhizn′*, no. 3 (1916): 1–45 and A. F. Zaitsev, "Murmanskaia zheleznaia doroga i zadazhi ekonomicheskoi politiki na Severe," *Russkaia mysl′* 37, no. 8 (1916): 1–16.

61 Peter Holquist, *Making War, Forging Revolution: Russia's Continuum of Crisis, 1914–1921* (Cambridge, MA: Harvard University Press, 2002).

dark, and snowy winter severely restricted the times of the year that work could be done. The abundant marshes and the rocky ground also sat along the path of the track. A total of 250 *verst* of the line (a *versta* is roughly equivalent to a kilometer) traversed through marsh, including a continuous fifty-two *verst* section from Soroka to the town of Kem. This waterlogged landscape required numerous bridges and curves in the track and the dredging of many swamps.[62] The inability to grow most crops forced a greater dependence on imported food than in agriculturally fertile regions.[63] Finally, the natural surroundings near the railroad provided insufficient construction materials. Forests in the north became sparser and only usable for fuel and not for sleepers or buildings. There was also a general lack of sandy land along parts of the line that could be used as ballast for the embankments.[64]

Unpredicted natural impediments also arose in response to destructive efforts to transform the landscape. Though management often classified these difficulties as technical, the anthropogenic control implied by this term was largely illusionary.[65] Massive effort went into erecting the roadbeds, which required approximately 15,000 cubic meters of land per *versta* and ended up using a total of ten million cubic meters of excavated earth. Builders stuffed rocks and logs into soggy bogs, blew up over a million cubic meters of earth with dynamite, and drilled into frozen rock that sometimes splintered in the process. Yet these roadbeds still frequently sank under the newly placed track. Near Soroka and the Kandalaksha Bay on the White Sea the tide sometimes flooded the high embankments of the track until engineers invented a means of letting the water drain out.[66] The freezing of the White Sea in the winter, which closed the Arkhangel′sk port, and the inaccessibility of the northern areas of the line made it harder for supplies shipped from abroad to reach the worksites.[67] Cattle and reindeer, which had been brought in to assist in

[62] Press, "Istoriia sooruzheniia Murmanskoi zheleznoi dorogi," in *Proizvoditel′nye sily raiona Murmanskoi zheleznoi dorogi*, 20; Nachtigal, *Die Murmanbahn 1915 bis 1919*, 198; and Bentley Historical Library, *Russia Route Zone A: Murman Railway and Kola Peninsula, Copy No. 706* (Washington, DC: Government Printing Office, 1918), 25.

[63] *Murmanskaia zheleznaia doroga*, 46–65.

[64] *Murmanskaia zheleznaia doroga*, 31; Nachtigal, *Die Murmanbahn 1915 bis 1919*, 39; and Khabarov, *Magistral′*, 18.

[65] *Murmanskaia zheleznaia doroga*, 43.

[66] Khabarov, *Magistral′*, 22; Bentley Historical Library, *Russia Route Zone A*, 25; and Norman Stone, *The Eastern Front, 1914–1917* (New York: Charles Scribner's Sons, 1975), 158.

[67] *Murmanskaia zheleznaia doroga*, 59 and Nachtigal, *Die Murmanbahn 1915 bis 1919*, 41, 60.

transportation and provided food for the laborers, also suffered from the cold and malnourishment and occasionally died in large numbers.[68]

Deforestation resulting from the felling of trees in large areas to lay the track, acquiring wood for fuel, and fires caused by industrial activity also exacerbated the lack of energy resources in the region. The administration of the railroad desperately tried to ration wood and arrange for fire prevention services, but these measures achieved little in terms of increasing the pace of construction, limiting forest destruction, or preventing human suffering.[69] No dried wood suitable for locomotive fuel remained in the region of the railroad by 1918 and the trains relied entirely on imported coal from England.[70] In a July 4, 1916 report, British Major-General Alfred Knox correctly predicted that these "natural difficulties of construction" combined with the wartime priority of rapidly completing the Murmansk railway would result in the line operating at less than half of its intended capacity.[71]

Contentious interactions with the natural environment contributed as well to the miserable experience of the thousands of individuals who built the Murmansk railroad. Memoirists used dramatic hyperbole to convey this point. British Major-General Charles Maynard later recalled wondering, "how many million trees must have been felled to clear the way for the line, and how many men must have been employed on the work, if it was really completed within sixteen months." He supposed, "that half Russia must have slaved at the job, and that each man, woman, and child must have felled at least one tree per minute."[72]

In reality, the leadership of the railroad failed to recruit a workforce to produce sufficient workers, since few people lived in the region and the demands of the Russian army severely diminished the potential labor pool.[73] Data are elusive, but according to its Chief Engineer, Vladimir

68 P. Surozhskii, "Kak stroilas′ Murmanskaia zheleznaia doroga," *Letopis′: Ezhemesiachnyi literaturnyi, nauchnyi politicheskii zhurnal* 11, no. 7–8 (July–August 1917): 240 and GAMO, f. I-72, op. 1, d. 3, l. 158.

69 GAMO, f. I-72, op. 1, d. 1a, ll. 24–26; GAMO, f. I-72, op. 1, d. 1b, ll. 64–66; GAMO, f. I-72, op. 1, d. 3, l. 37; GAMO, f. I-72, op. 1, d. 33, l. 12; and A. A. Kiselev, *Kol′skoi atomnoi – 30: Stranitsy istorii* (Murmansk: Izdatel′stvo "Reklamnaia poligrafiia," 2003), 10.

70 Bentley Historical Library, *Russia Route Zone A*, 26.

71 Nachtigal, *Die Murmanbahn 1915 bis 1919*, 197–198. On Knox's experiences in the Russian north during World War I, see Alfred Knox, *With the Russian Army*, 2 vols. (London: Hutchinson and Company, 1921).

72 Major-General C. Maynard, *The Murmansk Venture* (New York: Arno Press and the New York Times [1928] 1971), 42.

73 Khabarov, *Magistral′*, 18–20 and *Peter Gatrell, Russia's First World War: A Social and Economic History* (Harlow: Pearson Longman, 2005), 113–117.

FIGURE 3. Felling Trees for the Murmansk Railroad.
Source: Murmanskaia zheleznaia doroga: Kratkii ocherk postroiki zheleznoi dorogi na Murman s opisaniem eia raiona (Petrograd, 1916), 41.

Goriachkovskii, the administration of the Murmansk railroad employed approximately 32,000 Russian citizens, which included ethnic Russians, Pomors, Sami, Finns, Buryats, and Caucasians, and 8,000 Chinese workers in January 1917.[74] Many hired workers refused to renew their initial six-and-a-half month contracts.[75]

One of the railroad administration's contractors, the Pauling Company of Britain, also recruited several hundred Canadian railroaders to lay part of the track on the Kola Peninsula. The Canadians protested the poor conditions that greeted them, further souring the relationship between the Pauling Company and the Murmansk railroad administration and contributing to the withdrawal of foreign firms from the construction altogether in February 1916.[76] These workers' assertiveness exemplifies much more widespread grumbling about work conditions in

[74] Nachtigal, *Die Murmanbahn 1915 bis 1919*, 101 and D. L., "Ot Arkhangel'ska do Kandalaksha i obratno," *IAOIRS* 8, no. 12 (December 15, 1916): 484. These Russian citizens included at least 5,500 Finns and a considerable number of other non-Russian ethnicities. *Murmanskaia zheleznaia doroga*, 61. Upon arrival workers exchanged their passports for tokens. A total of 102,344 tokens were issued. Khabarov, *Magistral'*, 20.

[75] Nachtigal, *Die Murmanbahn 1915 bis 1919*, 198.

[76] Nachtigal, *Die Murmanbahn 1915 bis 1919*, 42–53.

FIGURE 4. Building a Bridge on Murmansk Railroad.
Source: Murmanskaia zheleznaia doroga: Kratkii ocherk postroiki zheleznoi dorogi na Murman s opisaniem eia raiona (Petrograd, 1916), 88–89.

the north and attempts to resist the railroad management. As the Russian government even acknowledged about the hired laborer: "the conditions he encounters and will be surrounded by for half a year are not attractive. An unpopulated region with a mass of marsh, dense untouched forests, and no ploughed fields or meadows loom around him, arousing melancholy."[77]

Most of the laborers, however, were prisoners of war in Russian detention. German historian Reinhard Nachtigal declares the abysmal situation for POWs on the Murmansk railroad to have been "one of the worst horrors of captivity in Russia during World War I."[78] Peter Gatrell and Alon Rachamimov agree.[79] According to the (likely inflated) estimates of Red Cross nurse Elsa Brändström, who lived with POWs in Russia during the war, 25,000 of 70,000 POWs sent to work on the Murmansk railroad died as a result. "Of the remaining 45,000 there were, in the autumn of

[77] *Murmanskaia zheleznaia doroga*, 64.

[78] Reinhard Nachtigal, "Murman Railway," in Jonathan Verne, ed., *Encyclopedia of Prisoners of War and Internment* (Santa Barbara: ABC-CLIO, 2000), 195. See Nachtigal's earlier book on the Murmansk railroad as well, Reinhard Nachtigal, *Die Murmanbahn: Die Verkehrsanbindung eines kriegswichtigen Hafens und das Arbeitspotential der Kriegsgefanfenen (1915 bis 1918)* (Grunbach: Verlag Bernhard Albert Greiner, 2001).

[79] Alon Rachamimov, *POWs and the Great War: Captivity on the Eastern Front* (New York: Berg, 2002), 107–115 and Gatrell, *Russia's First World War*, 183–186.

1916," wrote Brändström, "32,000 sick of scurvy, tuberculosis, rheumatism, and diarrhea."[80]

This terrible outcome for the people subjected to the work conditions on the Murmansk railroad, like the technical difficulties of the project, needs to be understood in relation to the natural setting. The weather conditions, the lack of food and shelter, and diseases worsened the experience of the laborers. Dark and frozen winters and constantly light summers with ravenous mosquitoes led to several tragedies and increased workers' exhaustion. The scarcity of foods that could grow in the region contributed to nutritional deficiencies. Crowded and unhygienic sanitary conditions allowed for viral and bacterial pathogens to thrive epidemically.

The labor force's vulnerability to these natural elements stemmed from deliberate decisions to build the railroad in this militaristic way.[81] Political ecologist Piers Blaikie and several of his colleagues have outlined a set of social and political factors that tend to generate vulnerabilities to biological hazards. They highlight lived environmental conditions (diet, shelter, sanitation, and the water supply), migration (especially forced displacements), and the limited capacities of degraded natural systems.[82] All of these features played a role in the construction of the Murmansk railroad as an imperial state pursued a recklessly urgent project while facing restricted means of obtaining necessary materials and supplies.

By late 1915 the situation had become so dire that Arkhangel′sk governor, Sergei Bibikov, wrote to the Minister of Transportation, Aleksei Trepov, to urge an evacuation of the line through Finland.[83] After an inspection in the summer of 1916, Bibikov filed an impassioned report surveying the harsh conditions and deprivations faced by POWs. "The majority of the barracks," he wrote, "do not account for the hygienic requirements of the severe northern climate." Lacking walls, adequate floors, windows, and sufficient kitchens, they were "completely unfit for the winter." Located in dense marshes, the barracks became filled

80 Elsa Brändstrom, *Among Prisoners of War in Russia and Siberia*, trans. C. Mabel Rickmers (London: Hutchinson and Co., 1929), 139.

81 On the social production of vulnerability, see Michael J. Watts and Hans G. Bohle, "The Space of Vulnerability: The Causal Structure of Hunger and Famine," *Progress in Human Geography* 17, no. 1 (March 1993): 43–67; Piers Blaikie, et al., *At Risk: Natural Hazards, People's Vulnerability, and Disasters* (London: Routledge, 1994); and Greg Bankoff, Georg Frerks, and Dorothea Hilhorst, eds., *Mapping Vulnerability: Disasters, Development, and People* (London: Earthscan, 2004).

82 Blaikie, et al., *At Risk*, 106–108.

83 Nachtigal, *Die Murmanbahn 1915 bis 1919*, 50, 84–86.

with filthy water, waste, and insects. Without adequate drinking water, bathing facilities, and medical help, diseases among the workers proliferated. Insufficient clothing exacerbated the problems caused by cold and unsanitary conditions, and pitiful food provisions, mostly consisting of rye flour, led to scurvy outbreaks, as Bibikov noted.[84]

A subsidiary project of the Murmansk railroad on the Kola Peninsula further illustrates how natural obstacles stymied construction and negatively affected human well-being. In March 1916, the Naval Ministry contracted the Murmansk railroad administration to build a military port at Iokanga on the eastern end of the Murman coast.[85] A lack of adequate supplies and food greeted the workers sent to erect the facility. The on-site engineer responsible for the Iokanga port wrote desperate telegrams in the summer of 1916. He reported that the workers slept in wet clothes in the cold, had no accessible wood for fuel, were falling ill from parasites, and lacked sufficient food.[86] The engineer purchased reindeer hides and venison to attempt to ameliorate the situation.[87] In the middle of October, the Iokanga laborers protested these conditions with a work stoppage. Repeatedly referring to the unaccommodating "climatic conditions" of "frosts, fogs, and short days," officials acquiesced to the workers' demand to be relocated to a more hospitable environment during the long winter.[88]

With diseases like typhus and scurvy haunting the population of POWs and hired workers in 1915 and 1916, tsarist officials and railroad administrators responded with a mixture of concern and cruelty. Though a low priority, they tried to arrange shipments of foodstuffs believed to prevent and cure scurvy and for evacuations of the ill.[89] The head of the Russian Sanitation and Evacuation Section, Prince Aleksandr Oldenburg, spoke out against the apparently illegal conditions and insisted that the administration of the railroad was responsible for the "sanitary well-being" of the prisoners and workers.[90] Also, at least according to government propaganda, the railroad administration sought to accommodate laborers' ethnic and religious differences. One publication discussed how railroad

84 Surozhskii, "Kak stroilas′ Murmanskaia zheleznaia doroga," *Letopis′* 11, no. 7–8 (July–August 1917): 242–243.
85 GAMO, f. I-72, op. 1, d. 2, ll. 12–14, 16–17.
86 GAMO, f. I-72, op. 1, d. 3, ll. 15–19, 29, 37, 112, 137–138.
87 GAMO, f. I-72, op. 1, d. 3, ll. 119, 158.
88 GAMO, f. I-72, op. 1, d. 4, ll. 62, 99 and GAMO, f. I-72, op. 1, d. 3, ll. 153, 166.
89 Nachtigal, *Die Murmanbahn 1915 bis 1919*, 83, 87–89.
90 GAMO, f. I-72, op. 1, d. 33, l. 65 and Nachtigal, *Die Murmanbahn 1915 bis 1919*, 87.

personnel transferred Muslim workers to a more southern part of the line during their summer Ramadan fast. The problem was that the polar day lasted for weeks in the areas north of the Arctic Circle on Kola Peninsula, depriving observers of the opportunity to eat at night. The railroad managers boasted that the relocation to Karelia allowed Muslim laborers the chance to break fast during the brief window when the sun fell below the horizon.[91]

But POWs' suffering frequently elicited more callous reactions. Since the beginning of construction, the railroad administration set prices for wood, kerosene, and food and prioritized supplying hired laborers, especially Russian ones, over POWs. The outbreaks of diseases forced a revision in these policies, but it maintained heavy-handed restrictions on trade and acceptable provisions.[92] Furthermore, the administration of the Murmansk railroad initially responded to the spread of diseases in March 1916 by attempting to reinforce labor discipline and restrictions on leaving the construction site to seek medical help.[93] In these circumstances many workers fled; some preferred to take their chances with the eastern front than to remain in the northern environment.[94]

The grievous conditions of the POWs on the Murmansk railroad turned into a diplomatic dispute in the summer of 1916. By this point, the international press knew about the line and Russia eased up on wartime censorship about it.[95] A martial celebration officially established the new port city of Romanov-on-Murman at the terminus of the railroad in June 1916.[96] Upon learning more about the deprivations their prisoners faced in the Russian north, the Central Powers began threatening reprisals and engaging in limited acts of retaliation against Russian POWs. With the Petrozavodsk-Soroka and Kandalaksha-Kola segments of the line already laid and only the difficult Soroka-Kandalaksha segment remaining, the

91 *Murmanskaia zheleznaia doroga*, 72.

92 GAMO, f. I-72, op. 1, d. 1, ll. 181–183, 191; GAMO, f. I-72, op. 1, d. 1a, ll. 24–26; and GAMO, f. I-72, op. 1, d. 33, ll. 97, 99. In general administrators prioritized providing for Russian workers. In the autumn of 1916, for instance, Russian workers earned four rubles a day and Chinese ones only received one ruble and eighty kopecks. D. L., "Ot Arkhangel'ska do Kandalaksha i obratno," *IAOIRS* 8, no. 11 (November 15, 1916): 459–460.

93 GAMO, f. I-72, op. 1, d. 33, l. 50.

94 Nachtigal, *Die Murmanbahn 1915 bis 1919*, 125–131.

95 Cyrus C. Adams, "Russia's Ice-Free Port," *The New York Times* (February 27, 1916), 16; "The Port of the Midnight Sun," *The Independent* (May 22, 1916), 274; "Gulf Stream Aids Czar," *The Washington Post* (November 19, 1916), 18; and Nachtigal, *Die Murmanbahn 1915 bis 1919*, 90.

96 Khabarov, *Magistral'*, 26–28.

tsarist government reacted to the reprisals by evacuating some sick POWs from the area while bringing in a large influx of new prisoners. It declared the Murmansk railroad complete in November.[97]

Throughout this brutal construction, the disruptions of the material world, the difficulties it posed for completing the railroad, and the challenges it created for the health of laborers compelled participants to view the northern environment in militaristic terms. Nature acted as another enemy in the belligerent context of wartime construction, bringing the idea of conquering nature to the fore. The press typically described the Murmansk railroad as "a struggle with harsh and primordial northern nature" and "an uninterrupted struggle with elemental obstacles."[98] Following this militaristic rhetoric, writers often elaborated the multiple ways that the environment inhibited the project. "This is a grandiose war with elemental forces and economic obstacles. The elemental obstacles were the local conditions. The conditions of the worksite included a harsh climate, the continuous polar night for a month-and-a-half, the short summer construction period, a negligible population, the absence of housing, the absence of transportation and a local means of transit, the distance and isolation of the road construction from the railroad network, and the lack of local medical help and hospitals because of the severe climate, etc."[99] Echoes of this theme of construction work as a war appeared in many places, including the standard letters of congratulations sent by Tsar Nicholas II to the administration of the Murmansk railroad after it finished the different segments of the line and the entire road. The tsar made a point to mention the administration's victory over "the technical difficulties and harsh local conditions."[100]

The conquest of nature rhetoric both vilified the natural world and celebrated heroic achievements over it. On the eve of the collapse of the monarchy in early 1917, one journalist referenced a litany of aggravating natural conditions on the Murmansk railroad. Instead of excoriating the deprivations of this lethal worksite, he addressed the railroaders as valiant and victorious troops. "It was hard for you to work in the winter freezes,

97 Nachtigal, *Die Murmanbahn 1915 bis 1919*, 71–75, 90–123; Khabarov, *Magistral′*, 17, 28; and *Murmanskaia zheleznaia doroga*, 7, 69–71.

98 Zaitsev, "Murmanskaia zheleznaia doroga i zadazhi ekonomicheskoi politiki na Severe," *Russkaia mysl′* 37, no. 8 (1916): 1 and *Murmanskaia zheleznaia doroga*, 23. Also see Surozhskii, "Kak stroilas′ Murmanskaia zheleznaia doroga," *Letopis′* 11, no. 7–8 (July–August 1917): 232–244.

99 *Murmanskaia zheleznaia doroga*, 31.

100 GAMO, f. I-72, op. 1, d. 13, ll. 136, 202 and *Murmanskaia zheleznaia doroga*, 6.

but no easier in the summer – not so much from the heat as from the troublesome midges and mosquitoes. When spring came many of you had neither clothes nor shoes, but you, ragged and half-barefooted, did not quit working. You slept in dirty, cold, gray barracks. During the day you suffered the cold or the heat and at night bedbugs and cursed midges." Against these varied vulgarities of the natural world, he triumphantly praised the railroaders, "you defeated the harsh north."[101]

These visions of the natural world were decidedly different from earlier enthusiasm for it as a source for human improvement. Initiating a wartime and warlike campaign to erect a railroad in the Arctic and encountering formidable resistance from the terrain itself, this more aggressive conception of nature gained widespread acceptance. And such views certainly continued after construction into the era of the Russian Civil War.

The War Zone

Months after the announced completion of the Murmansk railroad, the Russian monarchy ceased to exist. In October 1917 a socialist revolution followed the liberal one of the previous February. Civil War came the next year, turning the Kola Peninsula into part of the northern front of this conflict. The Provisional Government, the Bolsheviks, the White forces, and intervening British, American, and French armies all sought to exert authority over the north, which at times included arduous attempts to make the Murmansk railroad operational. Fighting inhibited the replacement of temporary structures with permanent ones and repeatedly involved the destruction of railroad infrastructure, leaving the line largely nonfunctional at the end of the war. Throughout the revolution and the Civil War, ideologically and internationally diverse combatants maintained militaristic approaches to the northern economy: the continued use of prisoner labor; hasty and chaotic responses to immediate difficulties; a pattern of shortsighted and destructive nature use; and an antagonistic view of the northern environment. These wartime practices united revolutionary Russian liberals and socialists, internal opponents of the Bolsheviks, and the ambivalent Allied Powers.

Upon overthrowing the monarchy, Russia's new revolutionary leaders publically disavowed the tsarist past, including the means that had been used to build the Murmansk railroad. A volatile system of governance

[101] M. Bubnovskii, "Po novomu puti (Iz dnevnika narodnogo uchitelia)," *IAOIRS* 9, no. 1 (January 1917): 7.

in which the self-appointed Provisional Government shared authority with the elected councils (Soviets) of workers, soldiers, and peasants had replaced tsarist rule. Amid the glow of revolutionary excitement, journalists penned exposés on the brutal construction of the railroad and the new minister overseeing the line evoked the democratic promise of the February Revolution to rally his staff.[102] Authorities also changed the name of Romanov-on-Murman to Murmansk in April 1917 to signal a decisive break with the disgraced Romanov dynasty.[103]

Despite this public departure, the Provisional Government by and large relied on similar bellicose oversight of the Murmansk railroad that had been used before the revolution. The railroad administration kept employing large numbers of POWs; some 12,000 remained on the line on the eve of the Bolshevik takeover.[104] It also relied on familiar tactics of regulating food prices, imposing sanitation rules, soliciting limited medical help, and trying to enforce discipline and surveillance over workers and prisoners.[105] Along the line, rampant deforestation persisted and under-fed and unsheltered livestock again perished.[106] Officials also grew increasingly alarmed about human wastes infecting the train wagons, stations, tracks, and storehouses of the Murmansk railroad, as this filth threatened the health of passengers and workers. An order from the head of the railroad in September 1917 called for mechanizing trash collection by installing more garbage bins and having workers burn or bury the contents of full receptacles. It insisted, however, that when "potentially infectious trash" contaminated the tracks, disinfection should occur "under the surveillance of medical personnel."[107]

At the construction site of the Iokanga base, the Provisional Government reacted only somewhat more attentively to the vagaries of the northern environment than had the tsarist regime. When scurvy again broke out

[102] Surozhskii, "Kak stroilas′ Murmanskaia zheleznaia doroga," *Letopis′* 11, no. 7–8 (July–August 1917): 232–244 and GAMO, f. I-72, op. 1, d. 1, l. 165.

[103] GAMO, f. I-72, op. 1, d. 1a, l. 232 and Khabarov, *Magistral′*, 32.

[104] Nachtigal, *Die Murmanbahn 1915 bis 1919*, 139–144; GAMO, f. R-488, op. 1, d. 13, ll. 5–6; and *Grazhdanskaia voina na Murmane glazami uchastnikov i ochevidtsev: sbornik vospominanii i dokumentov* (Murmansk: Murmanskoe knizhnoe izdatel′stvo, 2006), 24.

[105] GAMO, f. I-72, op. 1, d. 1, ll. 165, 181–183, 191; GAMO, f. I-72, op. 1, d. 16, l. 86; GAMO, f. I-72, op. 1, d. 17, ll. 174–177; GAMO, f. I-72, op. 1, d. 14, l. 152; GAMO, f. I-72, op. 1, d. 4, ll. 67–68; GAMO, f. I-72, op. 1, d. 33, ll. 128–131; and GAMO, f. R-488, op. 1, d. 13, ll. 5–6.

[106] GAMO, f. I-72, op. 1, d. 4, l. 180 and Kiselev, *Kol′skoi atomnoi – 30*, 10.

[107] GAMO, f. I-72, op. 1, d. 1a, l. 86 and GAMO, f. I-72, op. 1, d. 17, ll. 96, 98.

among the POWs there in September 1917, authorities decided to retreat from natural obstacles instead of going on the offensive.[108] They ordered most of the worksite to be abandoned for the winter months, explaining, "Among the conditions preventing work in the winter is first of all the difficult climate. Beginning with the autumn months a period of winds set in, which, according to common opinion, can be extremely sudden and forceful even during a comparatively low temperature. Doing any sort of work in the open air is physically impossible and labor productivity is reduced to a minimum."[109]

After the October revolution of 1917 transferred authority exclusively to the Bolshevik-controlled Soviets, the new government maintained militaristic management of the road. At this point the slogan "Soviet power," which had initially appealed to the idea of rule by a body representing multiple socialist parties, became primarily associated with Bolshevik governance. As the new rulers pursued their promise to get Russia out of World War I from November 1917 to March 1918, they set up a militia district along the Murmansk road and established new prices for an array of goods for its employees.[110] During these months, POWs and hired workers continued to face "extreme need," a lack of basic provisions, and the risk of "epidemics and excessive hunger."[111] Indeed, prisoners of war from the Central Powers remained on the Murmansk railroad through at least May 1918, after the Treaty of Brest-Litovsk traded peace with Germany for vast territories on Russia's western borderlands.[112]

Yet it was Russia's exit from World War I that turned the Murmansk railroad into a real war zone. Immediately after the signing of the Brest-Litovsk peace agreement in March, British marines landed in Murmansk with the initial approval of Bolshevik leaders. The Allied forces officially sought to protect large stores of munitions and the railroad line there from a potential Central Power invasion, but had tentative plans to confront the Bolsheviks if the conflict unraveled in particular ways. Disobeying orders from the Bolsheviks in the center to terminate cooperation in the spring of 1918, the Murmansk Regional Soviet supported the intervention of large forces of foreign troops the following summer. Eventually over 10,000 foreign troops came to the Murmansk front, which had grown in geopolitical significance relative to Arkhangel'sk

108 GAMO, f. I-72, op. 1, d. 4, l. 161.
109 GAMO, f. I-72, op. 1, d. 3, l. 394.
110 GAMO, f. R-488, op. 1, d. 15, ll. 8, 31–32.
111 GAMO, f. R-488, op. 1, d. 13, ll. 55, 58.
112 Nachtigal, *Die Murmanbahn 1915 bis 1919*, 123.

because of the railroad and the unfrozen port. Anti-Bolshevik forces took control of Arkhangel′sk in August 1918 and disbanded the Murmansk Soviet the next month, replacing the local soviet with a *zemstvo*. Increasingly ambivalent about being involved in the Russian Civil War after the November 1918 armistice ended World War I, the foreign interventionists remained in the area until the fall of 1919. These forces included American military units focused specifically on preserving the Murmansk railroad.[113]

International armies primarily approached the environment of northern Russia as something to overcome and subvert. Coordinating first with the short-lived socialist government in Arkhangel′sk under the renowned former revolutionary, Nikolai Chaikovskii, and then with the White leader in the north, General Evgenii Miller, the Allied Powers effectively ruled the Kola Peninsula during the first years of the Civil War.[114] With much of the Murmansk railroad under enemy control, the Red Army repeatedly bombed bridges on this strategic object, thereby compelling ongoing repair work by the foreign interventionists.[115] The Allies imposed their own food rationing system on Murmansk, not just for their troops but also as a means of gaining and maintaining the loyalty of the local population. Due to greater available provisions in these countries, they succeeded in obtaining enough to feed the population in spite of delays and conflicts between the British and American governments.[116] Delivery of food beyond Murmansk remained difficult because of natural factors. Frozen waters made Arkhangel′sk inaccessible and caused much alarm within the U.S. government, particularly about the women who had to deal with the harsh climate.[117] The military sought to use the

[113] Several works of political and military history review these developments. See Liudmila Novikova, *Provintsial′naia "kontrrevoliutsiia": Beloe dvizhenie i Grazhdanskaia voina na russkom Severe 1917–1920* (Moscow: Novoe literaturnoe obozrenie, 2011); Yanni Kotsonis, "Arkhangel′sk, 1918: Regionalism and Populism in the Russian Civil War," *Russian Review* 51, no. 4 (October 1992): 526–544; George F. Kennan, *The Decision to Intervene*, 2 vols. (Princeton: Princeton University Press, 1958); David S. Fogelsong, *America's Secret War against Bolshevism* (Chapel Hill: University of North Carolina Press, 1995); Ilya Somin, *Stilborn Crusade: The Tragic Failure of Western Intervention in the Russian Civil War 1918–1920* (New Brunswick: Transaction Publishers, 1996); and Robert L. Willett, *Russian Sideshow: America's Undeclared War* (Washington, DC: Brassey's, 2003).

[114] W. Bruce Lincoln, *Red Victory: A History of the Russian Civil War* (New York: Simon and Schuster, 1989), 270–286.

[115] Willett, *Russian Sideshow*, 131–138.

[116] NARA, Record Group 182, Box 1594.

[117] NARA, Record Group 120, Boxes 1–3, [Letter from W. Delano Osborne, February 21, 1919].

Murmansk railroad to bring supplies down to the White Sea coast, but the spring thaws flooded and destroyed much of the track and made it unreliable.[118]

Such impediments fostered deprecating discussion of the environment by the Allies. Thus, while diplomats inquired about possible contracts for northern timber and iron ore prospecting near Murmansk, international troops more frequently discussed the inhospitable features of the area.[119] One American soldier, who worked on repairing the Murmansk railroad and in general described the region as "bleak and dreary," joked in a letter home: "The only excitement to-day was a train leaving for Murmanska (sic). We call it the North Pole Limited or the Tri-weekly. It goes up one week and trys (sic) to get back the next."[120] At the same time the Allies also emphasized the defensive security that the harsh Kola environment could provide. A pamphlet of the American War Department given to soldiers noted that the "topographical conditions of the Murman region are such that in the north an enemy would have little chance of seizing the railroad."[121]

Solely in charge of the Murmansk region for several months in late 1919 and early 1920 after the departure of foreign armies, White forces struggled with Kola nature. They anxiously planned to procure forest materials from areas near Lake Imandra and bring in horses and forage for them.[122] Officials at the railroad feverishly sought to supply running water during the winter frosts and import food for the increasingly hungry population.[123] The road's staff also dealt with, but was largely outdone by, the heavy snowfalls and accumulating snowdrifts that prevented the road from effectively operating.[124] During this period, White forces again repaired destroyed bridges in the area just south of Kandalaksha.[125] They also kept political prisoners in such abysmal conditions at a prison at Iokanga that over a hundred inmates died from diseases exacerbated by the cold and isolation.[126]

118 NARA, Record Group 120, Boxes 1–3, [Situation in North Russia Theater, February 26, 1919], 9.

119 On inquires of the Allied Powers about Murmansk natural resources, see Novikova, *Provintsial'naia "kontrrevoliutsiia,"* 140–141.

120 Bentley Historical Library, Polar Bear Collection, Harry Duink Papers, 40–41.

121 Bentley Historical Library, *Russia Route Zone A*, 22.

122 GAMO, f. R-621, op. 1, d. 22, ll. 32, 73–76.

123 GAMO, f. R-621, op. 1, d. 22, ll. 32, 50, 75, 105.

124 GAMO, f. R-621, op. 1, d. 22, ll. 18, 67.

125 GAMO, f. R-621, op. 1, d. 22, l. 49.

126 A. A. Kiselev, "GULAG na Murmane: Istoriia tiurem, lagerei, kolonii," *SM* (October 7, 1992): 3 and Novikova, *Provintsial'naia "kontrrevoliutsiia,"* 201–202.

Just days before the Bolsheviks gained control of the Kola Peninsula in February and March 1920, a White engineer in charge of a northern section of line, Pavel Maslov, reported on the unaccommodating ecology along the Murmansk railroad. Heavy snows posed a major challenge for railroad operation, especially since only a small contingent of laborers – 60 percent of whom were women and adolescents – worked to clear the tracks. If blizzards continued several more weeks, "the struggle would be entirely beyond our strength, even with a snow plough." Maslov insisted that he needed more workers and proposed that "up to 100 prisoners of war" could be sent. He also wrote that "normal work in northern climate conditions is steadily being weakened by slow exhaustion" now that food rations have been cut. This situation was leading to "real starvation among the population and the railroad workers (more than 60% of their families live in horror)" and could easily result in another scurvy outbreak. "Without an increase in food rations, which are a question of life and death, any measures to improve transportation will not produce the desired results."[127]

Russia's new communist leaders had faced similar difficulties along the railway. They maintained possession of some of the southern sections of the line for periods of the Civil War. Desperate to supply other areas of the country with fuel but lacking skilled cadres of loggers and necessary equipment, the Office of Forest and Peat Procurement of the Murmansk railroad sought to exploit the "inexhaustible forest resources" along the line.[128] In autumn 1918 the officials labeled maximum procurement of forest materials as "rational" and requested "all possible assistance in gathering wood for the railroad, which has extremely important state significance at the present time."[129] Workers on the Red-controlled sections of the railroad also suffered from lacking food and basic provisions.[130]

After the defeat of the Whites in the north, the dearth of fuel and food deteriorated further as the new country descended into a major famine in 1921. Bolshevik railroad officials lamented the lack of available fuels on the Kola Peninsula in particular and deemed it "necessary to take heroic measures to collect wood as soon as possible."[131] By the end of

127 GAMO, f. R-621, op. 1, d. 22, l. 32.

128 GAMO, f. R-483, op. 1, d. 2, ll. 2–3, 21–24, 29–32, 169–171; GAMO, f. R-483, op. 1, d. 3, ll. 31–38, 53–54, 61–62; and GAMO, f. R-483, op. 1, d. 36, ll. 3–5, 13–16.

129 GAMO, f. R-483, op. 1, d. 2, ll. 21, 42.

130 GAMO, f. R-483, op. 1, d. 2, ll. 4–6, 22ob, 25 and GAMO, f. R-483, op. 1, d. 3, ll. 6, 16–20.

131 GAMO, f. R-483, op. 1, d. 100, l. 26, 30, 32, 37, 88, 94, 138.

the summer of 1920 malnutrition took its toll in the region as well: over 10 percent of the city of Murmansk's 5,000 residents had fallen ill with scurvy. The medical inspector who reported these figures blamed not only insufficient food provisions, but also northern nature itself. The "difficult conditions of this wild and neglected region" required transferring out railroad workers and medical staff who had already spent over a year in the Arctic.[132] To this doctor, Kola nature still seemed like an opponent – one that now, with the end of the war, could be evaded rather than confronted.

A Tool of Development

The cessation of warfare led not to a retreat from the north, but to a reorientation back toward enlivening it. Advocates of treating the Kola environment as a resource to be exploited instead of a foe to be defeated, returned to the fore. They renewed technocratic plans for colonizing and developing the Murmansk region that had emerged in the decades before Russia plunged into its interregnum of war and revolution. This link involved the participation of some tsarist-era government officials who had endorsed building a railroad to the Murman coast as well as similar conceptions of the natural world.

This preconceived development agenda also fit with the New Economic Policy (NEP) of the 1920s. In March 1921 Bolshevik leaders announced a resumption of small-scale private trade to allow the country's economy to recover. Billed as a deliberate retreat in the face of ruin, NEP revoked many of the centralized controls over agriculture and industry of the War Communism period (1918–1921). It also witnessed more free-ranging and pluralistic attempts to define Soviet culture and society than would be permitted in the subsequent Stalinist era. Most pertinent here, NEP offered opportunities to experiment with inexpensive means of reviving the economy.

In theory, the existing infrastructure of the Murmansk railroad should have immediately provided fertile ground for efforts to enliven the region. In actuality, though, much of the road had been destroyed during the Civil War. The road's ruined condition raised the question of what to do with it.[133] Several agencies in the central government floated the idea that the railroad should be closed for the time being and only restored in the

132 GARF, f. A-482, op. 2, d. 295, ll. 1–2.

133 Krentyshev, "Dostroika Murmanskoi zhel. dorogi," *VMZhD*, no. 2 (January 9, 1923): 15–16.

future. The leaders of the new Karelian Labor Commune – Finnish communists hoping for an eventual reunification of the newly independent Finland after the anticipated proletarian revolution there – supported repairing the line. But they opposed any development schemes that challenged their regional autonomy or denationalized the population of Karelia.[134] The leadership of the railroad, unsurprisingly, promoted not just fixing the line but expanding its role in the new Soviet north. A leading editorial in the first issue of their paper, *Herald of the Murmansk Railroad*, on January 2, 1923 insisted "the path to the rejuvenation of the north lies on the tracks of the Murmansk railroad." The road would assist the "colonization of the region" and integrate it with the "general cultural and productive life of the republic."[135]

Ultimately, officials in charge of the Murmansk railroad, members of the new State Colonization Institute, and the central People's Commissariats of the Navy, the Military, and Transportation pushed through a plan to make the railroad into a self-sustaining tool of development. With support from Bolshevik leader Vladimir Lenin and the infamous founder of the Cheka (the Soviet secret police) Feliks Dzerzhinskii, the Council of Labor and Defense passed a resolution on May 25, 1923 turning the Murmansk railroad into an "industrial-colonization-transportation combine." The order allocated the 241,000 square kilometers of land to the administration of the Murmansk railroad, with most of this vast territory located on the Kola Peninsula (see Map 2).[136] Proponents of this resolution thought this land allocation would substitute for state subsidies and allow for the self-financing of regional development. Timber along the track would fuel the railroad, provide local building materials, and generate profits from exports. The fishing industry and the efforts to establish agriculture in the far north would feed the new settlers.

The entire idea of an "industrial-colonization-transportation combine" offered a new opportunity for the officials from the prerevolutionary Resettlement Administration to put their technocratic ideas into practice. Voshchinin, and his colleague Ivan Iamzin described their

[134] Nick Baron, *Soviet Karelia: Politics, Planning and Terror in Stalin's Russia, 1920–1939* (London: Routledge, 2007).

[135] "Nash Put′," *VMZhD*, no. 1 (January 2, 1923): 1.

[136] V. V. Sorokin, "K istorii razrabotki postanovleniia STO ob osvoenii Karel′sko-Murmanskogo kraia," *Istoriia SSSR*, no. 4 (July–August 1970): 114. In the first years of Bolshevik rule railroads in general played an important role in state economic strategy, see Anthony Heywood, *Modernising Lenin's Russia: Economic Reconstruction, Foreign Trade and the Railways* (Cambridge: Cambridge University Press, 1999).

colonization work generally as fostering "a process of settlement and the use of productive forces of under-populated and economically under-developed territories by a significant mass of people emigrating from more densely populated regions."[137] In the Kola north, Chirkin specifically saw a "pioneering role of the Murmansk railroad," which, "as an organ of the state economy, should become a complex industrial-transport enterprise, waking this detached, uninhabited, and desolate region up to an economic life by all diverse means."[138] This was a call for a sweeping and encompassing extraction of value from the natural world – one that in theory should approach, but stop short of, predatory plundering. Calling the project the "Canada-ization" of the Soviet Arctic, Chirkin repeatedly evoked the role of the transcontinental railroads in North America. He insisted that "the railroad system created the American nation" and thought that the Murmansk railroad could similarly help the Soviet Union absorb the Kola Peninsula.[139] He focused mostly on Canada instead of the United States because of its more comparable northern climate.

At this time, discussion pivoted back toward an emphasis on the natural attractiveness of the Kola north. Reminiscent of Witte's and Engel′gardt's praise, Chirkin argued that "a whole treasure chest of untouched nature" would draw in new residents who could unleash "productive forces" and "enliven" the region.[140] The daring colonists, argued another writer, would become "a base for the further economic assimilation and development of the region."[141] Forests, fish, rivers, reindeer, minerals, and the ocean would serve them well as they transformed the northern landscape. As the head of the Murmansk railroad, Aron Arnol′dov, claimed, "The resources of the region are numerous. We have here mass deposits of iron ore, multiple deposits of mica, and a field of spar, quartz, barite, and various construction materials. Forests extend over the entire region along with fisheries on the Murman coast and in the White Sea, the vast reindeer pastures, and white coal [*rivers with*

137 I. L. Iamzin and V. P. Voshchinin, *Uchenie o kolonizatsii i pereseleniiakh* (Moscow: Gosudarstvennoe isdatel′stvo, 1926), 4.

138 G. F. Chirkin, "'Kanadizatsiia' Murmanskoi zheleznoi dorogi," in *Proizvoditel′nye sily raiona Murmanskoi zheleznoi dorogi*, 231 and G. Chirkin, "'Kanadizatsiia' Murmanskoi zheleznoi dorogi," *VMZhD*, no. 1 (January 2, 1923): 3.

139 G. F. Chirkin, "Sovetskaia Kanada (Karelo-Murmanskii krai)," *Priroda i liudi: ezhemesiachnoe prilozhenie k zhurnalu "Vestnik znaniia,"* no. 3 (1929): 3.

140 Chirkin, "'Kanadizatsiia' Murmanskoi zheleznoi dorogi," in *Proizvoditel′nye sily raiona Murmanskoi zheleznoi dorogi*, 225.

141 N. Raevskii, "Tri goda kolonizatsionnoi rabyty," *KMK* 5, no. 3 (March 1927): 7–9.

hydroelectric potential]."[142] The publicizing of ongoing scientific research contributed to this more alluring view of the environment as well. Geochemist Aleksandr Fersman popularized the expeditions he led on the Kola Peninsula, which had begun to reveal the presence of industrially significant mineral deposits, and specifically challenged common views of the far north as a polar desert that lacked value.[143]

Through the end of the 1920s, the Murmansk railroad led the charge to integrate the Kola environment into the Soviet economy. Railroad administrators created an array of subsidiary enterprises – Zhelles, Zhelryba, Zhelstroi, and Zhelsilikat – that were responsible for timber collection and processing, fishing, construction, and brick-making respectively.[144] Income from deforestation and investments from private and regional groups allowed for the quick restoration of the railroad line to working condition.[145] Timber harvesting under Zhelles grew from gathering 720,000 cubic meters of forest materials in 1924 to 1,460,000 cubic meters for the 1928–1929 accounting year.[146] Most of the higher quality forest material came from Karelia and Kola wood served almost exclusively as railroad fuel. The railroad administration also took over the Murmansk port in 1924 and expanded commercial trawl fishing out of it.[147] Zhelryba brought in 16,483 tons of fish from 1923 to 1929.[148] Finally, with a large amount of territory on the Kola Peninsula under its control the Murmansk railroad looked for new ways to use marshy and tundra lands.[149] In part this endeavor involved examining the potential to expand productive forces by creating a network of hydroelectric power stations, modernizing reindeer herding, and surveying mineral deposits.[150] It also entailed work by the colonization department of the

[142] A. Arnol′dov, *Vtorye Dardanelly: Murmanskii vykhod v Evropu* (Petrograd: "Petropechat′," 1922), 5–6.

[143] A. E. Fersman, *Tri goda za poliarnym krugom: Ocherki nauchnykh ekspeditsii v tsentral′nuiu Laplandiiu 1920–1922 godov* (Moscow: Molodaia gvardiia, 1924) and A. E. Fersman, *Novyi promyshlennyi tsentr SSSR za poliarnym krugom (Khibinskii apatit)* (Leningrad: Izdatel′stvo Akademii Nauk SSSR, 1931). On polar deserts, see A. E. Fersman, "Sovremennye pustyni," *Priroda*, no. 5–6 (1926): 15–26 and ARAN, f. 544, op. 1, d. 365, ll. 1–6.

[144] Each of these subsidiary names combines the term for railroad in Russian, *zheleznaia doroga*, which literally translates as "iron road," with the economic sphere it covered. Thus, Zhelles meant "iron-forest," Zhelryba meant "iron-fish," and so on. Clearly, these monikers associated these economic activities with industrial development as well. Khabarov, *Magistral′*, 41–62.

[145] Baron, *Soviet Karelia*, 77–78.

[146] ARAN, f. 544, op. 1, d. 115, l. 3.

[147] Khabarov, *Magistral′*, 55–56.

[148] ARAN, f. 544, op. 1, d. 115, l. 3.

[149] Baron, *Soviet Karelia*, 72–78.

[150] See the essays in *Proizvoditel′nye sily raiona Murmanskoi zheleznoi dorogi*.

railroad on land reclamation, afforestation, and preparing parcels into potential homesteads.[151]

If the Murmansk railroad achieved some success in harvesting the region's resources, it had a much more spotty record with settling the territory. Officials offered land and employment opportunities to migrants, but had a hard time convincing people to come and stay. In the first few years, only several hundred settlers moved to homesteads near railroad stations on the Kola Peninsula and many of them left after a short period of time. Greater numbers of the migrants moved to Karelia. But even here the new labor force was insufficient for the timber operations of the railroad, which continued to employ thousands of seasonal workers throughout the decade and began again relying on prisoners by the late 1920s.[152] Embarrassed by the lack of progress of the colonization department, Arnol′dov defensively wrote in 1925: "Such resettlement does not have a dominant significance but an auxiliary one; it is a means, not a goal, and it is only one of the elements of the colonization process." The main objective was "the organization of an entire range of enterprises for the industrial use of the natural resources of the colonized region."[153] This rationale reaffirmed that the personnel of the Murmansk railroad remained interested above all in the industrial transformation of the Kola landscape.

Officials made more headway in settling the region by the end of the decade. Chirkin boasted that the population of the city of Murmansk grew from 14,500 in 1923 to 23,000 in 1929.[154] But these results did not halt the transition in Soviet development models in the north from primarily assimilationist back to emphasizing conquest. Throughout 1930, the Murmansk railroad relinquished its role in regional settlement and by September it lost its status as an "industrial-colonization-transportation" combine.[155] The word colonization itself, disputed but accepted in the

151 *Murmanskaia zheleznaia doroga kak promyshlenno-kolonizatsionno-transportnyi kombinat* (Leningrad: Pravlenie Murmanskoi zheleznoi dorogi, 1926), 16–17 and GAMO, f. R-397, op. 1, d. 34, ll. 25–28.

152 *Murmanskaia zheleznaia doroga kak promyshlenno-kolonizatsionno-transportnyi kombinat*, 9; Raevskii, "Tri goda kolonizatsionnoi rabyty," *KMK* 5, no. 3 (March 1927): 7–9; and *Naselenie goroda Murmanska k nachalu 1925 goda* (Murmansk, 1925).

153 A. Arnol′dov, *Zheleznodorozhnaia kolonizatsiia v Karel′sko-Murmanskom krae: Po materialam razrabotannym kolonizatsionnym otdelom pravleniia dorogi* (Leningrad: Pravlenie Murmanskoi zheleznoi dorogi, 1925), 12–14.

154 Baron, *Soviet Karelia*, 77.

155 Khabarov, *Magistral′*, 68 and Sorokin, "K istorii razrabotki postanovleniia STO ob osvoenii Karel′sko-Murmanskogo kraia," *Istoriia SSSR*, no. 4 (July–August 1970): 115.

1920s, became increasingly marginalized in Soviet discourse with the onset of the first five-year plan (1928–1932).[156] As Politburo member Mikhail Tomskii admonished rising Kola industrialist Vasilii Kondrikov in December 1929, "the term 'colonization' (*kolonizatsiia*) needs to be thrown out."[157] What would replace it was a more warlike, but no less imperial, mode of regional development.

Militaristic Construction in the Stalin Era

The industrialization push of the early years of Joseph Stalin's undisputed dictatorship over the Soviet Union was a watershed in Russian history. With much attendant brutality, the country shifted from being predominantly agrarian to overwhelmingly industrial in short order. Historians have debated many aspects of the Soviet transition to the Stalin era, including the influence that the wartime origins had on the later communist regime. Numerous scholars have argued that war was a formative experience for the Bolsheviks that prefigured many features of Stalinist rule such as a militarized political culture, the centralization of authority, surveillance and secret policing, and the use of terror.[158] The economic treatment of northern nature during Stalinism also bears likeness to the martial practices of World War I and the Russian Civil War. In terms of both the forms of interaction with the landscape and some of the dominant environmental ideologies, Stalinism reintroduced historical trends of militarism into a peacetime setting. The environmental dimensions of railroad projects from 1928 to 1953 more closely resemble the tsarist building of the Murmansk railroad than the efforts to treat the line as a fountainhead of regional development in the NEP era.

156 Francine Hirsch, *Empire of Nations: Ethnographic Knowledge and the Making of the Soviet* (Ithaca: Cornell University Press, 2005), 87–98.

157 GAMO, f. 773, op. 1, d. 1, l. 103.

158 For some perspectives on this connection, see Robert C. Tucker, "Stalinism as Revolution from Above" in Robert C. Tucker, ed., *Stalinism: Essays in Historical Interpretation* (New York: Norton, 1977), 77–108; Sheila Fitzpatrick, "The Legacy of the Civil War," in Diane P. Koenker, William G. Rosenberg, and Ronald Grigor Suny, eds., *Party, State, and Society in the Russian Civil War: Explorations in Social History* (Bloomington: Indiana University Press, 1989), 385–398; Donald Raleigh, *Experiencing Russia's Civil War: Politics, Society, and Revolutionary Culture in Saratov, 1917–1922* (Princeton: Princeton University Press, 2002); Holquist, *Making War, Forging Revolution*; and Peter Holquist, "'Information is the Alpha and Omega of Our Work': Bolshevik Surveillance in its Pan-European Context," *The Journal of Modern History* 69, no. 3 (September, 1997): 415–450.

On the Kola Peninsula, Stalinist railroad construction possessed striking and multifaceted similarities with wartime efforts.[159] Determined to accomplish industrial transformation as rapidly as possible, state planners often moved forward with inadequate supplies, provisions, and labor. In part to overcome these shortcomings, they ordered the reckless, rapacious, and destructive use of local natural resources, which made little economic sense outside of exigencies of war. Continuing a tradition of using prisoner labor that extended back to the Trans-Siberian railroad of the early twentieth century and became entrenched during World War I, almost every new railroad on the Kola Peninsula in the Stalin era depended on some form of coerced labor: Gulag prisoners, forced peasant migrants, and POWs. Again the managers of these railroad construction projects exposed under-provisioned and barely sheltered forced laborers to environmental risks in the north. Contentious and militaristic interactions with the Kola environment also prompted another spike in aggressive rhetoric about nature. Descriptions of industrial activity as a military campaign involving "struggle," "conquest," and "victory" pervaded popular sources in the 1930s.[160]

Soviet planners first decided to expand the railroad network in the region with the establishment of an enterprise to mine and enrich phosphates – the Apatit trust based in the new city of Khibinogorsk in the Khibiny Mountains. Along with the decision to begin the project in September 1929, they ordered the construction of a railroad branch connecting the mainline of the Murmansk railroad to the new worksite. At the outset, they scheduled the branch for completion by August 1930 and specified that the labor could come from inmates of the Solovki prison camp.[161] By the end of 1930 about 2,000 prisoners worked on the railroad as the harsh winter approached and the project, like most of the construction in the Khibiny Mountains in these years, fell

159 On railroads elsewhere in the country during the Stalin era, see E. A. Rees, *Stalinism and Soviet Rail Transport, 1928–1941* (New York: St. Martin's Press, 1995) and Matthew J. Payne, *Stalin's Railroad: Turksib and the Building of Socialism* (Pittsburgh: University of Pittsburgh Press, 2001).

160 For example, *KhR* (October 18, 1932), 1; Fersman, *Novyi promyshlennyi tsentr SSSR za poliarnym krugom*, 5–7, 47–48; B. Vishnevskii, *Kamen′ plodorodiia* (Moscow/Leningrad: Partiinoe izdatel′stvo, 1932), 53–54; M. M. Kossov and B. I. Kagan, "Severnyi gorno-khimicheskii trest Apatit vo 2-m piatiletii," *KMK*, no. 3–4 (1932): 14; and G. Geber, M. Maizel′, and V. Sedlis, eds., *Bol′sheviki pobedili tundru* (Leningrad: Izdatel′stvo pisatelei v Leningrade, 1932).

161 "Chast′ ofitsial′naia," in A. E. Fersman, ed., *Khibinskie Apatity: Sbornik*, vol. 1 (Leningrad: Izdanie Gostresta "Apatit," 1930), 285.

behind schedule.[162] Similar diseases broke out among the workers as during the construction of the Murmansk railroad – typhus, tuberculosis, and scurvy – because of the unhygienic environment and natural deprivations.[163] Throughout the early 1930s, the Murmansk railroad itself also remained tangentially dependent on a different group of forced laborers for various upgrades. Forced peasant migrants, who had been subject to de-kulakization ("special settlers" in Soviet terminology) and faced conditions comparable to the Solovki prisoners, built the Niva-2 Hydroelectric Station that enabled the partial electrification of the railroad.[164] Along with Khibinogorsk, the Murmansk railroad was renamed the Kirovsk railroad in 1935 in honor of assassinated party boss Sergei Kirov.

Another extension line connected the Murmansk railroad to an emerging center for nickel mining and smelting, Monchegorsk, in the second half of the decade. In August 1935, the newly established Severonikel′ combine contracted with the fourteenth department of the White Sea-Baltic Combine, a Gulag organ, to build a line from the new nickel works to the Olen′ia railroad station north of Lake Imandra.[165] Economic planners initially hoped to have it operational by November 1935, but work dragged on into the summer of 1936.[166] The several thousand prisoners who labored on the railroad during 1935–1936 faced grievously insufficient supplies of equipment, food, and housing. The administration of the fourteenth department of the White Sea-Baltic Combine primarily provided military tents as housing, which required prisoners to sit and lie directly on the snow. One prisoner bitterly described these accommodations: "it was as filthy as a barnyard in them and often there was no hot water."[167] Food rations for them were unreliably shipped to the

162 GAMO, f. 773, op. 1, d. 1, ll. 318–319.

163 A. A. Kiselev, "GULAG na Murmane: Istoriia tiurem, lagerei, kolonii," *SM* (October 10, 1992): 3.

164 *Tekhnicheskie usloviia na dostroiku i rekonstruktsiiu Murmanskoi zheleznoi dorogi* (Leningrad: Izdatel′stvo Nauchno-tekhnicheskogo soveta Murmanskoi zheleznoi dorogi, 1934), 3–5; Khabarov, *Magistral′*, 78–81; and V. Ia. Shashkov, *Spetspereselentsy v istorii Murmanskoi oblasti* (Murmansk: "Maksimum," 2004), 147–151.

165 A. A. Eremeeva, "Stroitel′stvo kombinata 'Severonikel′' (period do nachala velikoi otechestvennoi voiny) v g. Monchegorske Murmanskoi oblasti," in V. P. Petrov and I. A. Razumova, eds., *Etnokul′turnye protsessy na Kol′skom Severe* (Apatity: Kol′skii nauchnyi tsentr Rossiisskoi Akademii nauk, 2004), 90–92; GAMO, f. 773, op. 1, d. 53, ll. 15–16, 60–61, 70, 229, 255–256, 264–265, 309–311; and GAMO, f. 773, op. 1, d. 55, ll. 132–133, 694, 711. On the operation of the White Sea-Baltic Combine in these years, see Baron, *Soviet Karelia*, 137–227.

166 GAMO, f. 773, op. 1, d. 53, ll. 15–16.

167 Quoted in A. A. Kiselev, "GULAG na Murmane," *SM* (October 22, 1992): 3.

camps from Kola. The cold, filth, and lack of nutrition took its toll as apparently almost a tenth of the prisoners working on the railroad line perished.[168]

Environmental interaction during the laying of the Monche-Olen′ia line mirrored that of wartime construction as well. Workers quickly chopped down any trees nearby to clear space for the track, supply firewood, and use as sleepers. They also gathered sand nearby to erect embankments for the roadbed.[169] This nature use hastily transformed the environment, but failed to adequately construct the road. The lack of material used for the roadbed and insufficient number of sleepers resulted in such sloppy construction that the spring thaws quickly destroyed the railroad.[170] Irate over this matter, Kondrikov, now the head of Severonikel′, described how nature retaliated in this instance: "The situation with the railroad branch is very distressing. Snow came off and clearly revealed the disgraceful work of the fourteenth department on the line. In essence there is no branch since along almost the entire length it proceeds at ground level and through swamps."[171] Time and again prisoners forced to engage in conquering the north disturbed the natural surroundings without rendering them more economically useful. With this railroad line still unusable after the prison camp leaders declared it completed, employees of Severonikel′ worked to repair it throughout the summer of 1936.[172]

The militarization of the regional economy in the years approaching World War II and its rebuilding afterward continued this pattern. With the outbreak of the Winter War between Finland and the Soviet Union in late 1939 the application of Gulag labor for assorted railroad repair and construction projects increased. It remained the norm in the 1940s and early 1950s.[173] A group of Gulag prisoners worked on the road from Ena to the future mining city of Kovdor in 1940. At the campsite they quickly chopped down all the trees in the area.[174] Additionally, prisoners of war during and after World War II helped with a variety of projects, including construction work on railroads and the redevelopment

168 Kiselev, "GULAG na Murmane," *SM* (October 22, 1992): 3.

169 Eremeeva, "Stroitel′stvo kombinata 'Severonikel′,'" in Petrov and Razumova, eds., *Etnokul′turnye protsessy na Kol′skom Severe*, 91.

170 GAMO, f. 773, op. 1, d. 63, ll. 250–252 and GAMO, f. 773, op. 1, d. 62, l. 387.

171 GAMO, f. 773, op. 1, d. 62, l. 160.

172 GAMO, f. 773, op. 1, d. 63, ll. 110, 248–252; GAMO, f. 773, op. 1, d. 62, ll. 160, 385–389; and GAMO, f. 773, op. 1, d. 64, ll. 191–194, 236–237.

173 M. B. Smirov, ed., *Sistema ispravitel′no-trudovykh lagerei v SSSR, 1923–1960* (Moscow: Zven′ia, 1998), 165–166, 169–170, 296, 397–398, 410–411, 430–433.

174 A. A. Kiselev, "GULAG na Murmane," *SM* (October 13, 1992): 3.

of the Pechenga region.[175] Efforts to lay down a railroad line to link the nickel deposits of the Pechenga territory to the mainline of the Murmansk railroad commenced in the early 1950s. But, yet again, the rocky and swampy landscape and seasonal fluctuations in weather undid previous work and caused significant delays. In this case the lines connecting the Pechenga region to Kola, as well as the railroad from Kovdor to Pinozero, only opened years after Stalin's death in 1953.[176]

The end of the Stalinist era nevertheless brought reprieve from the imperious and impetuous industrial techniques used during World War I and revamped in the 1930s. Regional economic leaders followed the enthusiastic, but cautious, assimilationist approach to development much more closely in the decades after Stalin. They undertook some additional projects to attach new mining sites, including Revda near Lovozero, to the mainline railroad (which officially became part of the October railroad after 1959). A railroad line connecting Kirovsk to Apatity, as well as an automobile highway extending from Murmansk to Leningrad, opened in the 1980s. By serving to integrate the natural resources of the region instead of waging battle with them, these construction projects entailed markedly different environmental relations than those of the first half of the century.

175 V. Rautio and O. A. Andreev, *Sotsial'naia restrukturizatsiia gornodobyvaiushchei promyshlennosti Pechengskogo raiona Murmanskoi oblasti* (Murmansk: Murmanskii gumanitarnyi institut / Barents tsentr issledovanii, 2004), 12–15; Eremeeva, "Stroitel'stvo kombinata 'Severonikel',"' in Petrov and Razumova, eds., *Etnokul'turnye protsessy na Kol'skom Severe*, 97; and V. A. Matsak, ed., *Pechenga: Opyt kraevedcheskoi entsiklopedii* (Murmansk: Prosvetitel'skii tsentr "Dobrokhot," 2005), 400.

176 Leonid Potemkin, *U severnoi granitsy: Pechenga sovetskaia* (Murmansk: Murmanskoe knizhnoe izdatel'stvo, 1965), 215–225.

3

Stalinism as an Ecosystem

As a doyen of Soviet science, geochemist Aleksandr Fersman often effused about the country's industrial expansion. He took particular pride in his own efforts in the far north. To him the exploitation of valuable phosphate deposits in the Khibiny Mountains on the Kola Peninsula represented a profound example of what socialism made possible. Near the end of the first five-year plan (1928–1932) in 1932, Fersman bragged about the achievements of the new town of Khibinogorsk (later Kirovsk) and the Apatit trust. "Over the past year I have had the occasion to familiarize myself with the sites of four of the giants of our industry: Magnitogorsk, Kuznetskstroi, Angarstroi, and the Khibiny. Before me passed images of the grandiose successes of socialist construction and socialist planning, but not one of the giants of metallurgy and energy can compare to the Khibiny in terms of the complexity of the problem and the grandiose difficulties of conducting work on an unprecedented scale in a polar realm."[1] Through a massive mobilization of resources and labor, the Soviet Union even managed bring ruler Joseph Stalin's dictum of "socialism in one country" to this Arctic periphery. For Fersman, nothing embodied the newfound capabilities of Soviet power more fully than this industrial reconfiguration of the Kola environment.

At the end of the 1920s, Soviet authorities decided to radically accelerate industrial development throughout the country. Desires to catch up economically with the capitalist West, to bolster state security in the aftermath of a war scare in 1927, and to reinvigorate the revolutionary

[1] A. E. Fersman, "Predislovie," in G. N. Solov'ianov, *Kol'skii promyshlennyi uzel* (Moscow: Gosudarstvennoe ekonomicheskoe izdatel'stvo, 1932), 3.

promises of the Bolsheviks in a Stalinist guise helped impel this general campaign. State planners chose to mine the Khibiny Mountains in particular in order to obtain a new domestic source for chemical fertilizers. They also sought to demonstrate that the Soviet Union could create industrial towns from scratch even in forbidding locations. With the development of the Khibiny during the first five-year plan, the Kola Peninsula embarked on the path toward becoming the most built-up and populated parcel of the global Arctic. Thousands came to the previously unpopulated mountain range in the early 1930s to help extract and process the phosphorus-rich mineral apatite. The industry there then served as a cornerstone for the dramatic rise of a regional mining sector over the following decades.

The spurt of industrial growth in the Soviet Arctic in the 1930s vitally depended on pre-existing ideas and the physical composition of the region. Apatite deposits that Fersman had recently discovered there and the area's close proximity to the Murmansk railroad gave the Khibiny advantages as a site for a new mining town. This geology and geography played into long-standing aspirations to enliven the north based on the opportunities that nature afforded. Conversely, the many less inviting features of the Khibiny environment challenged impetuous Soviet plans. State agents again showed a willingness to treat the natural world as a military foe.

Yet the building of an avowedly "socialist" settlement in the polar north was not simply a replay of railroad development. It also involved an attempt to forge a distinctive relationship with nature. Indeed, I argue here that the industrialization of the Khibiny Mountains involved efforts to refashion the ecosystem as Stalinist.

Borrowed from ecology, the term ecosystem captures the web of interaction that exists among people, plants, animals, climate, geological processes, geographic features, and inanimate matter. All beings and forces in a natural system act on, influence, and modify each other within an ecosystem. The elements of nature are thus potent actors in the story without necessarily possessing the capacity to pursue intentions. By focusing on the totality of the natural system, I look at issues beyond pollution, environmental management, and conservation, such as human health and habitat, population dynamics, seasonal variation in climate, the properties of mined material, and local flora and fauna. In fact, almost every facet of the industrial and urban development in the Khibiny entailed new ways of interacting with the environment. The ideas behind making the Arctic socialist, the treatment of individuals compelled to work there, and the endeavors to harness the tundra for economic ends relied on a revised ecology.

But what type of ecosystem did Soviet authorities seek to create in the Kola north? It was one that sought to combine outright ascendance over nature with an unprecedented level of socialist harmony. Industrialists mixed holism and dominance in both their rhetoric and their efforts to bring Stalinism to the Khibiny. The tension between these conflicting agendas helps account for the environmental contours of industrialization in the early 1930s, including some of its disastrous results. Hope for harmony with the natural surroundings inspired the decision to build a large city in the Khibiny Mountains and shaped the plans for the settlement. It featured in discussions about how polar nature would be improved through human activities and in schemes to limit industrial pollution affecting residents. Beyond assimilating northern nature for economic ends, the state's efforts to establish harmony aimed at crafting an improved and more livable environment. Dominance over nature, in contrast, meant severing dependence on the non-human world. In part, Soviet planners attempted to achieve this separation by renewing the vulgarities of warlike conquest. This hard-nosed stance toward the natural world directly undermined the confident hopes for a new type of industrial civilization that would be in accord with the Arctic environment. Instead, the choice to pursue militaristic dominance in a peacetime setting led to familiar troubles. Forced peasant migrants fell ill in a habitat not ready to accommodate them, waterways suffered from unplanned toxic dumping, and disorder struck the numerous ad hoc endeavors to mobilize local resources.

When Maksim Gor'kii visited the Khibiny Mountains in June 1929, he lamented the "meaningless work of the elemental forces of nature." No other mountain range provided "such a picture of premature chaos than this peculiarly beautiful and severe region. Here you get the impression that 'nature' wanted to do something, but only sowed this enormous space of the earth with rocks."[2] Such verbiage from Gor'kii should sound familiar to environmental historians of the Soviet Union, who have often noted the famed writer's open enmity toward nature.[3] But Gor'kii also

[2] Maksim Gor'kii, "Na kraiu zemli," in B. I. Nikol'skii and Iu. A. Pompeev, eds., *Pul's Khibin* (Leningrad: Sovetskii pisatel', 1984), 21.

[3] Arja Rosenholm and Sari Autio-Sarasmo, "Introduction," in Arja Rosenholm and Sari Autio-Sarasmo, eds., *Understanding Russian Nature: Representations, Values and Concepts* (Aleksanteri Papers 4/2005), 9–18; Alla Bolotova, "Colonization of Nature in the Soviet Union: State Ideology, Public Discourse, and the Experience of Geologists,"

insisted that the "reasonable activity of people" would prove mutually beneficial, serving human interests and helping polar nature achieve its potential.[4] This somewhat schizophrenic amalgam of subjugation and holism reflects the Stalinist approach to nature more generally. Its existence also points to two important corrections in scholars' understanding of Soviet environmental history.

First, the frequently noted antagonism toward the natural world in the Stalinist period was only part of the story. A number of historians suggest that a Promethean antipathy for nature defined the Soviet approach to the environment and even constituted a root cause of later environmental destruction.[5] But a more holistic disposition proved equally influential on what Soviet planners tried to accomplish in the Khibiny.[6] I do not mean to insinuate that Stalinist industrialization was more environmentally friendly than usually assumed, but to better capture the varied and contradictory elements of the system's economic relationship to the natural world. Second, the allegedly non-capitalist features of Soviet socialism were less pertinent for environmental interactions than one might presume from the scholarship emphasizing "Stalinism as a civilization."[7] The combined proclivity to overtake and harmonize delineated the ecosystems of Stalinism more than attenuated property

Historical Social Research 29, no. 3 (2004): 104–123; and Douglas Weiner, *Models of Nature: Ecology, Conservation, and Cultural Revolution in Soviet Russia* (Bloomington: Indiana University Press, 1988), 168–171.

4 Gor'kii, "Na kraiu zemli," in Nikol'skii and Pompeev, eds., *Pul's Khibin*, 21.

5 Stalinist antipathy toward nature is a major thread in the literature on Soviet environmental history. See, for example, Weiner, *Models of Nature*; Douglas Weiner, *A Little Corner of Freedom: Russian Nature Protection from Stalin to Gorbachev* (Berkeley: University of California Press, 1999); Paul R. Josephson, *Industrialized Nature: Brute Force Technology and the Transformation of the Natural World* (Washington, DC: Island Press, 2002); and Paul R. Josephson, *Would Trotsky Wear a Bluetooth: Technological Utopianism under Socialism* (Baltimore: The Johns Hopkins University Press, 2010). Alla Bolotova shows how residents dwelling in the Khibiny region in particular came to negotiate between loving nature and the dominant discourse of conquest in later eras. I'd add that this discourse of conquest was less uniform even among its initial proponents. Alla Bolotova, "Loving and Conquering Nature: Shifting Perceptions of the Environment in the Industrialised Russian North," *Europe-Asia Studies* 64, no. 4 (June 2012): 654.

6 This point largely concurs with Stephen Brain's reconceptualization of Stalinist forest policy, though not the author's categorization of these less harmful features as a type of environmentalism. See Stephen Brain, *Song of the Forest: Russian Forestry and Stalinist Environmentalism, 1905–1953* (Pittsburgh: University of Pittsburgh Press, 2011).

7 Stephen Kotkin, *Magnetic Mountain: Stalinism as a Civilization* (Berkeley: University of California Press, 1995).

rights and distorted markets. In many ways the environmental outcomes of the Soviet state's sweeping transformation of the Khibiny resembled the results of large-scale industrial projects elsewhere in the world. But the dualistic vision of Stalinist nature better accounts for the distinctions than attempts to avoid treating the natural world as a set of capitalist commodities.[8]

Searching for Minerals

Buried under a rugged, but confined, set of mountains in the Russian northwest was the "stone of fertility." It had been there for millions of years, but no one recognized its value. Geologists surveying the Khibiny Mountains in the 1920s discovered sizeable deposits of apatite and promoted the mineral's potential as a fertilizer. Their scientific work drew on international trends in the earth sciences and growing understandings of how to apply chemicals to soils to improve agricultural productivity. In less than a decade, these researchers helped change the Khibiny from a poorly known mountain range with no permanent residents to the subject of a grandiose scheme to create industrial socialism. Their insights into the range's geological properties relied on direct encounters with the Khibiny during fieldwork and not simply on armchair analysis from afar. Experience in the mountains set the stage for the region's environmental transformation.

Long before any attempts to remake the region through human interference, natural processes made the Khibiny Mountains and its environment. Volcanic magma from the depths of the earth began slowly to intrude into existing rock on the Fennoscandian shield over three hundred million years ago. When it cooled, this magma crystallized into a large mass of nepheline-syenite rock. Further geological activity formed a crescent within the igneous intrusion that came to contain veins of apatite embedded in the nepheline ore. Over the past sixty-five and a half million years, movements of tectonic plates pushed up this subterranean mass. It turned into a mountain range reaching over a kilometer above

[8] A recent forum in the journal *Kritika* broadly reconsiders the claim that anti-capitalism defined the Stalinist economy, not just its ecology. See, in particular, Andrew Sloin and Oscar Sanchez-Sibony, "Economy and Power in the Soviet Union, 1917–39," *Kritika* 15, no. 1 (Winter 2014): 7–22; Oscar Sanchez-Sibony, "Depression Stalinism: The Great Break Reconsidered," *Kritika* 15, no. 1 (Winter 2014): 23–50; and Marcie K. Cowley, "The Right of Inheritance and the Stalin Revolution," *Kritika* 15, no. 1 (Winter 2014): 103–124.

sea level and filling about 1,327 square kilometers in area.[9] Henceforth, the Khibiny Mountains stood in sharp juxtaposition to the surrounding territory. In the center of the south side of the range sat a valley with two small lakes, Lake Large Vud″iavr and Lake Little Vud″iavr. The White River drained out of Large Vud″iavr into Lake Imandra on the western edge of the Khibiny. Towering over the valley of the Vud″iavr lakes were several of the mountains containing apatite: Rasvumchorr, Kukisvumchorr, and Iuksporr. The pre-industrial ecosystem of the region varied between marshy taiga forests with a predominance of pines in the lowlands and alpine tundra at the higher altitudes where little grew besides some mosses and lichens. Some large fauna such as wolves, wolverines, arctic fox, and reindeer resided on the land and diverse aquatic species lived in the rivers and lakes of the range.[10]

Knowledge about the mountains trickled in during the late imperial period. Sami living nearby had long understood certain possibilities and perils of the Khibiny. They tended to avoid the steep and dangerous terrain in the winter, but periodically entered the range in the summer for hunting or grazing reindeer herds.[11] Beginning in the late nineteenth century, occasional foreign researchers traveled to the Khibiny and applied a scientific lens to understanding its mineral composition. Rock samples collected by French explorer Charles Rabot in the mid-1880s first revealed traces of apatite in the mountains. Several years later, Swedish geologist Wilhelm Ramsay proposed a rough date for the origin of the Khibiny and described the crystallization process of the nepheline-syenite rock. All the same, these initial encounters left "the mineral resources of

9 On the geological formation of the Khibiny Mountains, see Victor Yakovenchuk, et al., *Khibiny* (Apatity: Laplandia Minerals, 2005), 3–31; F. M. Onokhin, *Osobennosti struktury Khibinskogo massiva* (Leningrad: Izdatel′stvo "Nauka," 1975); F. Wall and A. N. Zaitsev, *Phoscorites and Carbonites from Mantle to Mine: The Key Example of the Kola Alkaline Province* (London: Mineralogical Society of Great Britain and Ireland, 2004); and Francis Wall, "Kola Peninsula: Minerals and Mines," *Geology Today* 19, no. 6 (November-December 2003): 206–211.

10 L. F. Forsh and G. V. Nazarov, eds., *Ozera razlichnykh landshaftov Kol′skogo poluostrova: Gidrologiia ozer i kharakteristika ikh vodosborov*, vol. 1 (Leningrad: Izdatel′stvo "Nauka," 1974); L. F. Forsh and V. G. Drabkova, eds., *Bol′shie ozera Kol′skogo poluostrova* (Leningrad: Izdatel′stvo "Nauka," 1976); B. L. Mishkin, *Flora khibinskikh gor, ee analiz i istoriia* (Moscow: Izdatel′stvo Akademii Nauk SSSR, 1953); and G. D. Rikhter, *Sever evropeiskoi chasti SSSR: Fiziko-geograficheskaia kharakteristika* (Moscow: Gosudarstvennoe izdatel′stvo geograficheskoi literatury, 1946).

11 A. E. Fersman, *Nash Apatit* (Moscow: Izdatel′stvo "Nauka," 1968), 24–25 and Iu. L. Ziuzin, *Khibinskaia laviniada* (Vologda: Poligraf-Kniga, 2009), 5–6.

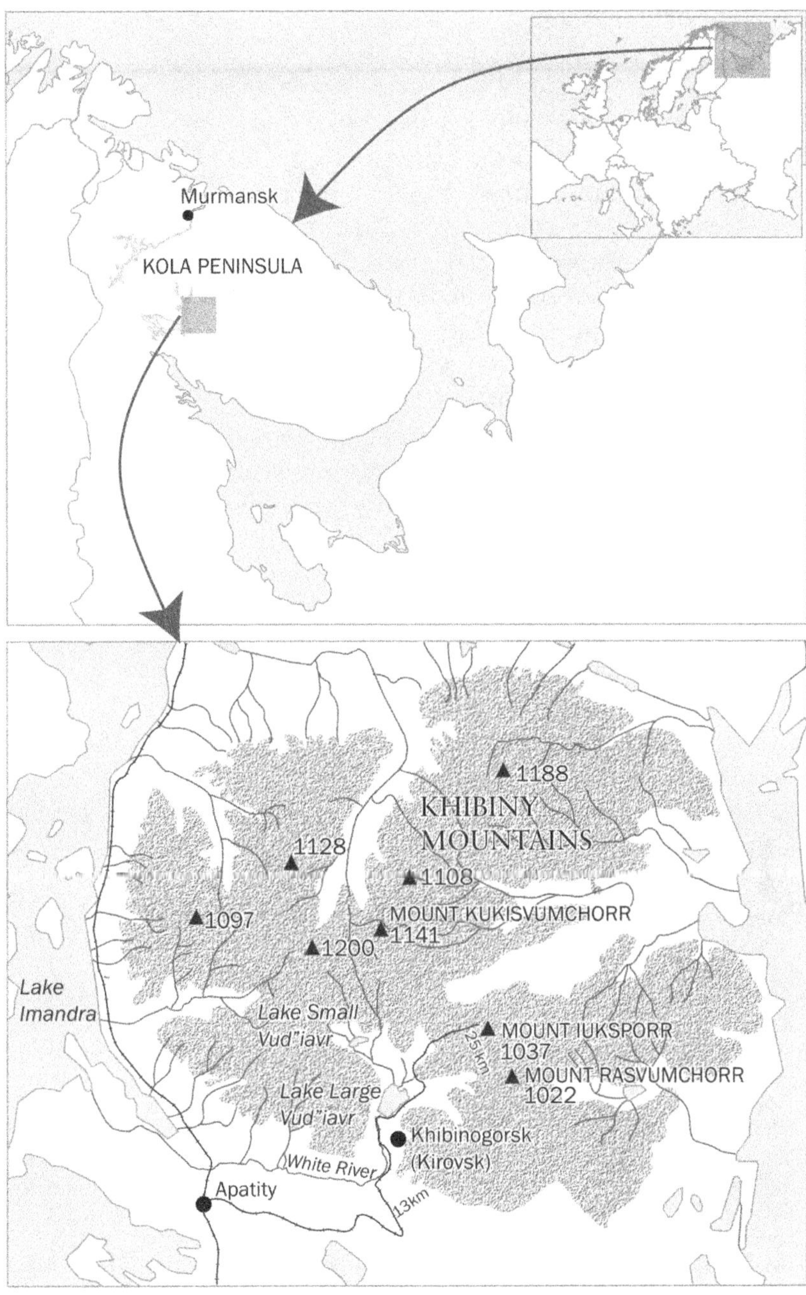

MAP 3. The Khibiny Mountains.
Source: Andy Bruno, "Industrial Life in a Limiting Landscape: An Environmental Interpretation of Stalinist Social Conditions in the Far North," *International Review of Social History* 55, S18 (December 2010): 160. Map produced by www.cartographicstudio.eu.

the region still little known" at the end of the century before geological research staggered for a couple of decades.[12]

Meanwhile, scientists and entrepreneurs abroad devised ways to produce artificial fertilizers from phosphorus-rich rock, thereby increasing the economic potential for the material inside the Khibiny Mountains. Attempts to enrich the nutrient content of soil had long revolved around crop rotation, the use of legumes, and the spreading of manure. In the middle of the nineteenth century guano from Latin America became a heavily traded commercial fertilizer. European soil chemists in the same period figured out how to use sulfuric acid to concentrate phosphate from ores. Apatite (a form of calcium phosphate with an extra ion of fluorine, hydroxyl, or chlorine) was an ideal source material for enriching superphosphate fertilizers, which companies from North America to Morocco sold on the international market. Worldwide, superphosphate dominated the chemical fertilizer industry until nitrogen-fixating technologies proliferated after World War II.[13]

Despite this basic information about the range's geology and the uses of apatite ore, even advocates for enlivening the Kola Peninsula remained unaware of the minerals in the Khibiny by the revolutionary spring of 1917. An overview of mineral resources in the north at the time failed to mention the presence of apatite in the mountains.[14] While travelers frequently hoped to find economic value in the range, they also expressed diverse views about the sparse and desolate Khibiny landscape. Writer Mikhail Prishvin, for instance, saw inherent value in northern wilderness. His moniker for the north, "the region of fearless birds," sought to inspire awe at the uniqueness of environments putatively beyond human influence.[15] As an adolescent who had already absorbed Prishvin's books

[12] Yakovenchuk, et al., *Khibiny*, 3–6 and A. P. Engel′gardt, *Russkii sever″: putevyia zapiski* (Saint Petersburg: Izdanie A. S. Suvorina, 1897), 60.

[13] Vaclav Smil, *Enriching the Earth: Fritz Haber, Carl Bosch, and the Transformation of World Food Production* (Cambridge, MA: MIT Press, 2001); J. R. McNeill, *Something New Under the Sun: An Environmental History of the Twentieth-Century World* (New York: W. W. Norton and Company, 2000), 22–26; B. M. Gimmel′farb, *Chto takoe fosfority, gde i kak ikh iskat′* (Moscow: Gosudarstvennoe nauchno-tekhnicheskoe izdatel′stvo literatury po geologii i okhrane nedr, 1962); and Richard A. Wines, *Fertilizer in America: From Waste Recycling to Resource Exploitation* (Philadelphia: Temple University Press, 1985).

[14] M. N. Artleben, "Gornopromyshlennye ressursy Severa," *IAOIRS* 9, no. 3–4 (March–April 1917): 155–160.

[15] M. M. Prishvin, *V Kraiu nepuganykh ptits/Osudareva doroga* (Petrozavodsk: Izdatel′stvo "Kareliia," [1907] 1970) and M. M. Prishvin, *Za volshebnym kolobkom: povesti* (Moscow: Moskovskii rabochii, [1908] 1984). Prishvin's descriptions of the natural

when he visited the Khibiny in 1914, Gavriil Rikhter, a future geographer of the Kola Peninsula, remembered being impressed by the "astonishing beauty and simultaneous originality of untouched nature."[16]

Such reverence for an unchanged environment contrasted sharply with Soviet commentators' later descriptions of the Khibiny as it existed in the late imperial era. Evoking an idea that unused nature lacked meaning, the local press in the 1930s recast the phrase, "the region of fearless birds," as a derisive reference to the pre-industrial north and labeled the territory "a blank spot on the map."[17] Others insisted on the "backwardness" of such undeveloped territories, blaming the tsarist regime for isolating these areas from European modernity. Several Khibiny industrialists evoked orientalist stereotypes as well when they declared in 1933, "The Kola Peninsula (the Murmansk district) in old times was one of the most neglected and backward borderlands... wild conservatism, sluggishness, and the Asiatic tempos of the Tsarist government kept this huge region untouched and unstudied."[18] Many living in the final years of the monarchy shared this critical attitude.

Scientists who believed that the Khibiny had been understudied before the revolution leapt at the opportunity to research it immediately after the Bolsheviks retook the Kola Peninsula from White forces. In May 1920 the Petrograd Soviet Executive Committee formed a commission

surroundings resonate with historian Christopher Ely's argument about artists in the late imperial era who embraced the "meagerness" of Russian nature as a national landscape aesthetic. Christopher Ely, *This Meager Nature: Landscape and National Identity in Imperial Russia* (DeKalb: Northern Illinois University Press, 2002).

16 G. D. Rikhter, "Chest′ otkrytiia: vosponimaniia pervoprokhodtsev," *MR* (April 7, 1977): 2.

17 *KhR* (October 8 1932): 1; *PP* (November 20, 1936): 2; *PP* (May, 5 1938): 3; *KR* (February 28, 1939): 2; *Bogatstva Murmanskogo kraia – na sluzhbu sotsializmu: Itogi i perspektivy khoziaistvennogo razvitiia Kol′skogo poluostrova* (Leningrad: Gosudarstvennoe sotsial′no-ekonomicheskoe izdatel′stvo, 1934), 7; I. Brusilovskii and N. Markova, "Magnetity Kol′skogo poluostrova," *KMK*, no. 1–2 (1933): 55; and S. Barsuk, "Kul′turnaia revoliutsiia pobezhdaet za poliarnym krugom," in G. Geber, M. Maizel′, and V. Sedlis, eds., *Bol′sheviki pobedili tundry* (Leningrad: Izdatel′stvo pisatelei v Leningrade, 1932), 69. Writers also made a similar point by giving an arbitrary estimate of the number of people per square kilometer in the tsarist era. B. Vishnevskii, *Kamen′ plodorodiia* (Moscow/Leningrad: Partiinoe izdatel′stvo, 1932), 4–8 and V. I. Osinovskii, "Rol′ khibinskikh apatitov v kolonizatsii Kol′skogo poluostrova," in A. E. Fersman, ed., *Khibinskie Apatity: Sbornik*, vol. 1 (Leningrad: Izdanie Gostresta "Apatit," 1930), 204.

18 B. I. Kagan and M. M. Kossov, *Khibinskie Apatity* (Leningrad: Izdatel′stvo Lenoblizspolkoma i Lensoveta, 1933), 91. The head of the Apatit trust, Vasilii Kondrikov, repeated these lines without attribution a year later in V. I. Kondrikov, "Itogi i perspektivy Kol′skogo promyshlennogo kompleksa," *KMK*, no. 1–2 (1934): 49.

of the Academy of Sciences to inspect the postwar condition of the Murmansk railroad. During a brief trip with the commission, Aleksandr Fersman became excited at the mineral composition of the Khibiny Mountains. Soon after returning, he arranged a full geological expedition of the massif. Despite his early ambivalence toward the Bolsheviks, Fersman, like his renowned academic advisor and collaborator Vladimir Vernadskii, had long desired to use expertise to provide assistance to the state.[19] Obliging both his sense of patriotic duty and scientific curiosity, Fersman commenced an intensive study of the range's mineral resources that would lay the groundwork for the industrialization.

A team comprised of professors and students, including some of the young women whom Fersman taught in Petrograd, joined these geological expeditions in the early 1920s. During three trips in 1920, 1921, and 1922, they traversed some 1,450 kilometers in the Khibiny Mountains, spent a total of 106 days up there, and collected about three metric tons of samples. The field workers tended to experience the mountains as a threatening and unfamiliar landscape that required them to exercise caution. Only able to transport limited provisions for short summer sojourns, the group relied on local railroad workers and Sami families for sustenance and guidance. When entering the high mountains, the scientists ventured out in pairs and regrouped after several days. Environmental conditions indeed created both difficulties and possibilities for their fieldwork. The polar day allowed them to stay out into the night but also inhibited their ability to sleep. Warm periods allowed them to leave the base for a few days without tents, but the harsh winds and rain during cold spells impeded research. Ravenous summer mosquitoes annoyed the geologists at lower altitudes and the flat plateaus of the Khibiny caused them to lose track of their location in the highlands.[20]

Some prospectors wrote about the challenges they encountered. By dwelling on the hardships and unpleasant experiences of the Khibiny environment, the geologists offered stories that would fit into their

[19] On Fersman, see A. I. Perel'man, *Aleksandr Evgen'evich Fersman, 1883–1945*, 2nd edn. (Moscow: Izdatel'stvo "Nauka," 1983); D. I. Shcherbakov, *A. E. Fersman i ego puteshestviia* (Moscow: Gosudarstvennoe izdatel'stvo geograficheskoi literatury, 1953); M. I. Novgorodova, ed., *Neizvestnyi Fersman: 120-letiiu so dnia rozhdeniia A. E. Fersmana posviashchaetsia* (Moscow: EKOST, 2003); and Kendall E. Bailes, *Science and Russian Culture in an Age of Revolutions: V. I. Vernadsky and His Scientific School, 1863–1945* (Bloomington: Indiana University Press, 1990).

[20] A. E. Fersman, *Tri goda za poliarnym krugom: Ocherki nauchnykh ekspeditsii v tsentral'nuiu laplandiiu 1920–1922 godov* (Moscow: Molodaia gvardiia, 1924) and Fersman, *Nash Apatit*, 58–122.

subsequent portrayals as heroic pioneers of the north. Mineralogist Aleksandr Labuntsov described how his team overcame "Khibiny weather" by huddling in a cold tent during a frigid summer downpour.[21] While in the field, another researcher penned the following lines in a poem about the Khibiny: "The landscape is dejected. Severe nature / Only provided the north with dull tones: / Scorched forest, a boulder, sad marshes, / Melancholic rain and a dim moon."[22] At the time the deprivations of this "severe" nature seemed to induce depression in the author, but later these traits would provide evidence of the meaninglessness of the area before industrial development.

The time spent in the range in the early 1920s allowed the geologists to confirm that Mount Kukisvumchorr and Mount Iuksporr possessed large sections of green apatite ore. Though the quantity of the material remained a mystery, Fersman quickly realized its potential utility as a source for phosphoric acid. Research then turned from a general assessment of the mineral composition of the mountains to determining the size of the apatite deposits. Over the next several years, surveyors discovered another deposit on Mount Rasvumchorr and raised the estimate of known apatite reserves in the Khibiny to eighteen million tons.[23] Labuntsov was now convinced that "Khibiny apatite" could serve "as a new factor in the colonization and revival of the Murmansk Region."[24]

Lingering uncertainties about the industrial significance of the deposits ended after a conclusive expedition in 1928. Researchers now knew that the mountains possessed at least ninety million tons of apatite ore. Simultaneously, the Scientific Institute for Fertilizer and the Institute of Mechanical Processing of Mineral Resources showed that they could enrich the ore to above a 36 percent concentration of phosphorus pentoxide, the active substance in superphosphate fertilizers.[25] With

21 A. Labuntsov, "Kak byl otkryt khibinskii apatit," *KMK*, no. 11–12 (1929): 17–19.

22 Printed in "Letopis′ sobytii goroda Khibinogorska," *ZhA*, no. 1 (October 2001): 20.

23 "Letopis′ sobytii goroda Khibinogorska," *ZhA*, no. 1 (October 2001): 17; B. Kupletskii, "Khibinskie i Lovozerskie tundry," *KMK* 5, no. 3 (March 1927): 11–13; I. Eikhfel′d, "V Khibinakh za apatitami (Iz dnevnika uchastnika ekspeditsii)," *KMK* 5, no. 2 (February 1927): 8–13; A. Labuntsov, "Kak byl otkryt khibinskii apatit," *KMK*, no. 11–12 (1929): 17–19; A. V. Barabanov, et al., *Gigant v Khibinakh: Istoriia otkrytogo aktsionernogo obshchestva "Apatit" (1929–1999)* (Moscow: Izdatel′skii dom "Ruda i metally," 1999), 16; and Yakovenchuk, et al., *Khibiny*, 3–8.

24 A. Labuntsov, "Poleznye iskopaemye Khibinskikh tundr i Kol′skogo poluostrova," *KMK*, no. 5–6 (1927): 9.

25 A. E. Fersman, "Ot nauchnoi problemy k real′nomu delu," in Geber, Maizel′, and Sedlis, eds., *Bol′sheviki pobedili tundry*, 28; "Letopis′ sobytii goroda Khibinogorska," *ZhA*, no. 1 (October 2001): 20; and Barabanov, et al., *Gigant v Khibinakh*, 16.

these developments, science had prepared the mountains for the Stalinist onslaught.

Going Big

Far from the Khibiny a groundswell was brewing. A complicated array of political, economic, military, and social pressures convinced the Soviet leadership in Moscow to abandon the New Economic Policy of the 1920s. As Stalin undertook the final steps to consolidate his status as an undisputed dictator, he launched a revolutionary "Great Break" to hastily bring socialism to the USSR. This chaotic and often violent program involved the collectivization of agriculture, rapid industrialization, the mobilization and uprooting of urban and rural populations, and the creation of a command economy structure with at least a pretense of central planning. It inspired a cultural outpouring during which writers and artists sought to frame these reforms as a decisive departure from past oppression and the restrictions that the natural world had imposed. One commentator on the Khibiny celebrated the Great Break for bringing about "the giant growth of culture in what up until now was an uninhabited region" and allowing for "the creation of a new man who in the struggle with nature transforms himself into an active builder of a classless socialist society."[26] Large and new industrial settlements like the one in the Khibiny became microcosms of how Stalinism changed ecological relations.

Economic calculations about the benefits of investing in agriculture, reducing phosphate imports from Morocco, and exporting chemical fertilizers did not alone inspire decisions to go big in the far north.[27] Planners mulled over proposals for small-scale mining operations in the Khibiny before dramatically ramping up the project. Limited extraction of apatite would have left the scope of Soviet industrialization of the Arctic more comparable to what occurred in North America. Historian Liza Piper shows how some mining operations began appearing in subarctic Canada at the time, while Andrew Stuhl describes the more restrained endeavors to study and exploit the U.S. and Canadian Arctic. More ambitiously, the Soviet state overtly pushed forward to forge its own socialist "New North" in the 1930s.[28] It did so in the context of countrywide

[26] M. Maizel′, "Bor′ba za apatit v svet sovremennoi khudozhestvennoi literatury," in Geber, Maizel′, and Sedlis, eds., *Bol′sheviki pobedili tundry*, 222.

[27] RGAE, f. 3106, op. 1/2, d. 367, ll. 62–81 and Solov′ianov, *Kol′skii promyshlennyi uzel.*

[28] Liza Piper, *The Industrial Transformation of Subarctic Canada* (Vancouver: University of British Columbia Press, 2009) and Andrew Stuhl, "Empires on Ice: Science, Nature,

hyper-development, as fervor for ratcheting up the first five-year plan spread and the specific material and geographical features of the Khibiny Mountains seduced industrialists into enlarging the endeavor. A number of planners also felt that only a major project could overcome natural constraints to make the Arctic Soviet.

Early on, as they continued to learn about the copious apatite deposits in the Khibiny Mountains, Soviet decision makers wanted to know more about the range's unwelcoming natural features. Investigators studied the limited ability to grow food locally, the dramatic seasonal fluctuations, the bothersome tundra insects, and the meteorological conditions of the area. Plant biologist Iogan Eikhfel′d organized the Khibiny Experimental Agricultural Point in the 1920s, which quickly refuted enduring ideas that agriculture was impossible in the north. Station workers annually planted many varieties of edible crops, applied different types of organic and chemical fertilizers, and gradually expanded arable territory by draining marshes and felling forested areas. Despite a low ratio of success, the station managed to grow potatoes, cereals, grains, grasses, cabbage, peas, lettuce, and other crops.[29] Regional leaders likewise wondered about the effects on the human population of the several weeks around the winter solstice when the sun did not rise above the horizon and the month-and-half in the summer without darkness at night. But only by the mid-1930s, well after the establishment of the new city, did a health inspector in the region reject theories that the polar night caused depression and the polar day led to insomnia. He claimed that polar seasonality did not harm human health and dismissed reports of adverse conditions as part of the process of adaptation.[30]

The Academy of Sciences and industrial personnel additionally sponsored research on Khibiny mosquitoes in 1930. Vladimir Fridolin, the head of the study, declared the insects to be "one of the biggest

and the Making of the Arctic" (PhD diss., University of Wisconsin-Madison, 2013). Stuhl also argues that the recent prophecies of a "New North" need to be placed in a deeper historical context. His claim seems doubly the case for the Soviet north.

29 S. A. Diuzhilov, "Nauchnoe reshenie problemy poliarnogo zemledeliia," in P. V. Fedorov, Iu. P. Bardileva, and E. I. Mikhailov, eds., *Zhivushchie na Severe: Vyvoz ekstremal′noi srede* (Murmansk: MGPU, 2005), 82–86; Iu. Iordanskii, "Sel′sko-khoziaistvennye opytnye raboty za Poliarnym Krugom," *KMK*, no. 21 (1926): 1–4; ARAN, f. 544, op. 1, d. 161, l. 10; I. Eikhfel′d, "Pobeda poliarnogo zemledeliia," in Geber, Maizel′, and Sedlis, eds., *Bol′sheviki pobedili tundru*, 151–157; and Osinovskii, "Rol′ khibinskikh apatitov v kolonizatsii Kol′skogo poluostrova," in Fersman, ed., *Khibinskie Apatity*, vol. 1, 204–211.

30 GAMO, f. R-163, op. 1, d. 141, ll. 9–26.

obstacles for the colonization of the region" and claimed that they had been known to kill horses and small children through excessive blood loss.[31] Mosquitoes in the area were indeed ravenous creatures whose brief life span in the Arctic required them to forage and mate quickly and aggressively when the opportunity arose. Fridolin's study assessed the entirety of the mosquito habitat in the Khibiny, the relationship of the insects with predators and prey, and the potential presence of the protozoans that cause malaria in them. The ecologically-minded researcher argued against a standard belief at the time that the draining of marshes was the primary tactic in the "struggle with mosquitoes." He showed that drainage of certain peat bogs and marshes could alter the hydrology of the area and cause new moist zones to emerge. Drainage of black poplar marshes, in particular, could actually increase the mosquito population by destroying the larvae of dragonflies, one of the few local predators. The main finding of this research, however, was that Khibiny mosquitoes did not carry malaria. In this case the cold ameliorated a threat.[32]

The challenges of alpine climate and topography also demanded further information. Though atmospheric and oceanic currents kept temperatures comparatively mild for its latitude, the Khibiny winters were still harsher than the rest of the Kola Peninsula. It was colder, windier, and snowier in the mountains, especially as elevation increased. Compared to the rest of the peninsula, the period of constant snow cover lasted on average forty days more – totaling 220 days a year – and the range received double to triple the amount of precipitation with frequent blizzards.[33] These snowy conditions, combined with the steep inclines of the mountains, made the region prone to avalanches and slush flows. Augmenting more anecdotal evidence and periodic observations, a meteorological station in the mountains started systematically recording wind, temperature, and precipitation with the onset of industrial activities.[34]

[31] V. Iu. Fridolin, "Izuchenie nasekomykh Khibinskikh gor v sviazi s voprosom o kolonizatsii kraia," in A. E. Fersman, ed., *Khibinskie Apatity*, vol. 2 (Leningrad: ONTI VSNKh SSSR Lenzkimsektor, 1932), 446.

[32] ARAN, f. 544, op. 1, d. 161, ll. 19–26, and Fridolin, "Izuchenie nasekomykh Khibinskikh gor v sviazi s voprosom o kolonizatsii kraia," in Fersman, ed., *Khibinskie Apatity*, vol. 2, 446–451.

[33] "Vvodnyi ocherk," in A. A. Kiselev, ed., *Kol'skii entsiklopediia*, vol. 1 (Saint Petersburg/Apatity: IS/ KNTs RAN, 2008), 39–41.

[34] B. M. Belen'kii, "Iz istorii issledovaniia snega i lavin v khibinakh," in E. Ia. Zamotkin and N. M. Egorova, eds., *Priroda i khoziaistvo Severa*, vol. 2, part 2 (Apatity: Akademiia Nauk SSSR Geograficheskoe Obshchestvo SSSR Severnyi filial, 1971), 305–310.

Concern about these various hazards of the Khibiny at first seemed to elicit some caution from industrial planners in the late 1920s. An early draft of the chemical industry's first five-year plan in December 1928 recommended mining in the Khibiny Mountains, but declared it more expedient to build enrichment facilities in Leningrad and not "directly at the Khibiny deposits of apatite."[35] Planners also proposed using the White River for hydroelectric energy and connecting the deposits to the mainline of the railroad. Presumably they believed that labor would be supplied by a combination of invigorated colonization efforts of the Murmansk Railroad and continued seasonal hires.[36] Even as the newly formed Apatite-Nepheline Commission became more ambitious over the next year, the location of the Khibiny and the lack of population there militated against building a large new settlement. With increased mining targets, one geologist on the commission proposed creating a 5,000-person mining town near Mount Kukisvumchorr that would enable working on the deposit throughout the polar night and long snowy winter. Apatite ore would still be enriched in Leningrad under this proposal.[37] This model of development would have treated the Khibiny more as an extraction periphery to bolster the overall Soviet economy than a natural stage for acting out socialism. However, at the same September 1929 meeting, as Fersman later recalled, "the majority of participants resolutely pronounced that the issue cannot be limited to organizing extraction and should include the building of an enrichment factory on site. Consequently, they underscored the necessity of erecting large-scale urban settlements."[38]

The expansion of industrial projects was a nationwide phenomenon during the Great Break and regional authorities were especially prone to advocate overly lofty goals on absurdly unrealistic timetables.[39] Nevertheless, enthusiasm for the apparent physical advantages of the Khibiny

35 RGAE, f. 3106, op. 1/2, d. 367, ll. 62–79.

36 "Chast′ ofitsial′naia," in Fersman, ed., *Khibinskie Apatity*, vol. 1, 281–283.

37 GAMO, f. 773, op. 1, d. 1, ll. 8–9. 38 *KDF*, 33.

39 On regional lobbying for increased resources and attention from central authorities, see James R. Harris, *The Great Urals: Regionalism and the Evolution of the Soviet System* (Ithaca: Cornell University Press, 1999) and Nick Baron, *Soviet Karelia: Politics, Planning and Terror in Stalin's Russia, 1920–1939* (London: Routledge, 2007). On the chaotic growth of output quotas throughout the USSR during the first five-year plan, see the following histories of Stalinist industrialization: Donald Filtzer, *Soviet Workers and Stalinist Industrialization: The Formation of Modern Soviet Production Relations, 1928–1941* (London: Pluto Press, 1986); Hiroaki Kuromiya, *Stalin's Industrial Revolution: Politics and Workers, 1928–1932* (Cambridge: Cambridge University Press, 1988); Kotkin, *Magnetic Mountain*; and David Shearer, *Industry, State, and Society in Stalin's Russia, 1926–1934* (Ithaca: Cornell University Press, 1996).

also played a role here. Despite being located in sparsely populated tundra, this polar region enjoyed proximity to a functioning railroad line that connected it to Leningrad and the Murmansk port. After 1927, the Kola Peninsula also belonged to the Leningrad region, placing the Khibiny under one of the most powerful regional administrations in the country.[40] Perhaps even more pertinent, the value of the apatite in the mountains seemed to be increasing by the day. By the fall of 1929 geologists believed at least half a billion tons of apatite rock existed in the range that could be enriched to increasingly high concentrations. According to the Apatite-Nepheline Commission, "we can say with certainty that by quantity and quality Khibiny apatite is the best in the world."[41] Excited commentators began calling the mineral "the stone of fertility," animating this inorganic substance with potent vitality.[42] As writer Aleksei Tolstoi later opined, "If these mountains were pure gold, they would not be so precious."[43]

To capture this treasure, the Supreme Council of the National Economy (VSNKh) officially created the Apatit trust to manage industrial activities in the Khibiny Mountains and appointed Vasilii Kondrikov to head the new enterprise on November 13, 1929.[44] Typical of his generation, Kondrikov was an under-educated and under-prepared Communist Party member who was promoted to a position of authority during the Stalinist revolution.[45] Upon learning of his job as the manager of an apatite mining enterprise, Kondrikov asked, "What is apatite?"[46]

During his first few months at the helm of Apatit, Kondrikov advocated enlarging the project to an unprecedented scope for the Arctic. In a December 1929 meeting, he confronted Mikhail Tomskii on the

40 D. A. Fokin, "Obrazy prostranstva: Kol'skii sever v administrativno-territorial'noi politike Sovetskogo gosudarstva (20–30-e gg. XX v.)," in P. V. Fedorov, et al., eds., *Zhivushchie na Severe: Obrazy i real'nosti* (Murmansk: MGPU, 2006), 101–103.

41 GAMO, f. 773, op. 1, d. 1, ll. 6–8.

42 References to the "stone of fertility" appear in Vishnevskii, *Kamen' plodorodiia*; A. E. Fersman, *Vospominaniia o kamne* (Moscow: Izdatel'stvo Akademii nauk SSSR, [1940] 1960), 9–20; and *PP* (April 27, 1946): 2–3. This description of apatite resonates with the symbolic veneration of metal in Soviet culture. See Rolf Hellebust, *Flesh to Metal: Soviet Literature and the Alchemy of Revolution* (Ithaca: Cornell University Press, 2003).

43 Aleksei Tolstoi, "Novyi materik," in Nikol'skii and Pompeev, eds., *Pul's Khibin*, 68.

44 GAMO, f. 773, op. 1, d. 1, l. 18; *KDF*, 38–39; and "Chast' ofitsial'naia," in Fersman, ed., *Khibinskie Apatity*, vol. 1, 286–291.

45 On such promoted individuals (*vydvizhentsy*), see Shelia Fitzpatrick, *Education and Social Mobility in the Soviet Union, 1921–1934* (Cambridge: Cambridge University Press, 1979) and Sheila Fitzpatrick, *The Cultural Front: Power and Culture in Revolutionary Russia* (Ithaca: Cornell University Press, 1992).

46 "Boi za nikel': Vospominaniia I. L. Kondrikovoi-Tartakovskoi," *MR* (September 13, 1986): 3–4.

issue, who at the time led the organization overseeing Apatit (the All-Union Association of the Chemical Industry). As an opponent of Stalin's plans for agriculture and industry, the once-powerful Tomskii had already fallen into disrepute.[47] In addition to outlining proposals for an enrichment factory in the Khibiny and a hydroelectric station on the Niva River, Kondrikov ramped up the mining program to three and a half million tons by the end of the first five-year plan. To accomplish this task the Khibiny would need a large work force, which could be supplied, Kondrikov asserted, by hiring laborers and temporarily using prisoners for tasks like building a railroad extension into the range.[48] In contrast to Tomskii's gradualism, Kondrikov espoused Stalinist views about industrializing nature. He favored the wholesale and aggressive transformation of the northern environment for the sake of achieving a more harmonious world. "We made a revolution, we will remove snow and difficulties – we are masters of life," argued Kondrikov. "I am a maximalist: either nothing or a very large management. You cannot create a small business in the Khibiny, even if you want. We came there not to waste our time on trifles. The Kola Peninsula should be a son of industry."[49]

Envisioning Town and Enterprise

A big project begot big plans. Over the next couple of years as thousands of people came to the Khibiny, architects, planning commissions, and enterprise personnel devised and debated proposals for how this new site of Soviet industry should look. To a considerable degree their visions revolved around re-organizing the mountain ecosystem. Participants in these discussions sought ways to force industrial infrastructure into the range while accentuating the aesthetics of the landscape. Paying homage to the serene alpine tundra as an alluring feature of the region, authorities named the new town Khibinogorsk (Khibiny Mountain City).[50] As they drew on a shared repertoire of the ideal features for socialist cities and narratives of heroically conquering the north, planners wavered between attempts to accommodate the natural surroundings and reckless decisions that, in spite of stated intentions, would make life in this terrain more difficult.

47 I. O. Gorelov, *Tsugtsvang Mikhaila Tomskogo* (Moscow: ROSSPEN, 2000).
48 GAMO, f. 773, op. 1, d. 1, l. 103.
49 "Letopis′ sobytii goroda Khibinogorska," *ZhA*, no. 1 (October 2001): 32.
50 *KDF*, 33–34.

During the Great Break, architects offered schemes for establishing socialist cities throughout the country. The ideological contours of their visions and the troubles they faced in converting their plans into reality have garnered considerable attention from scholars of Stalinism. Some projects like the steel town of Magnitogorsk – and less famously the apatite works in the Khibiny – imposed an industrial settlement on an unpopulated territory. In the case of Magnitogorsk, historian Stephen Kotkin argues that the city "ended up faithfully reflecting the circumstances of its conception and construction as the urban form for a new world founded on heavy industry," despite the ad hoc implementation of early plans.[51] Elsewhere, Stalinist urban designers confronted pre-existing cities with complicated histories. For Tashkent, Paul Stronski argues that "the regime's ideological stress on industrial development, its uncompromising faith in Marxist theories of development, its desire for total control over the population, and its bureaucratic inefficiency complicated efforts to build an ideal capital city" in Central Asia.[52] In contrast to this stress on ideological shortcomings, Heather DeHaan proposes that the "agency of the material" undermined Soviet "visionary planning" in Nizhnyi Novgorod.[53] Each of these cities seem to have followed a familiar path of incompletely and often haphazardly reworking the physical surroundings for the sake of fulfilling socialist promises.

This story played out in the Khibiny as well. Many espoused bullish ideas of how this Arctic landscape would be improved. Oscar Munts, an architect from Leningrad who drafted plans for a socialist city in the Khibiny, wrote soaringly about his environmental aims. "It is necessary," he insisted, "that man, simultaneously with a victory over nature and the disturbance of its majestic tranquility, is able to accord his labor with its eternal beauty." To achieve such harmony with nature, "a wild, almost uninhabited, region will need to be transformed into a populated one and will need to supply its population with all of the requirements for a normal and cultured existence in the unique conditions of the far north." Munts specifically sketched out how housing for workers, a transportation network, illumination, heating, telephone service, a water supply, a sewer system, and various municipal services could be built. He also envisioned three parks in the city that would preserve the sections of forest remaining

51 Kotkin, *Magnetic Mountain*, 107.

52 Paul Stronski, *Tashkent: Forging a Soviet City, 1930–1966* (Pittsburgh: University of Pittsburgh Press, 2010), 8.

53 Heather D. DeHaan, *Stalinist City Planning: Professionals, Performance, and Power* (Toronto: University of Toronto Press, 2013), 40–63.

on the site and serve the sanitary purpose of protecting the settlement from noise and dust generated by the enrichment factory.[54] Others described how the creation of schools, research institutions, pioneer camps, red corners, cinemas, theaters, conservatories, clubs, libraries, parks, and health facilities would change the Khibiny from being "held in the pincers of ignorance, a lack of culture, and darkness" to a "blossoming industrial and cultural region."[55] In their view a habitat that included these cultural and industrial installations was inherently more suitable for communists to thrive.

Many of the suggestions for Khibinogorsk were boilerplate features of Soviet urban design that had only slightly been altered to the conditions of the north. In one example of overlooking the local landscape, Munts's plan for a major central road failed to adequately account for the topography of the city's location.[56] Yet planners did acknowledge a need to adjust their program for greenery to the polar climate. Admitting the current difficulties of cultivating plants in a polar region, Munts proposed that acclimatization could still be used in the future to create green belts throughout the city that would connect the proposed parks.[57] The task of introducing new flora to the Khibiny fell on the shoulders of botanist Nikolai Avrorin, who headed the new Polar-Alpine Botanical Garden. Researchers there studied characteristics that made the region's environment unique – its polarity and high altitude – and began testing different species of plants, trees, and bushes to see if, and under what conditions, they could grow there. Their results served as a basis for adding green spaces to polar cities over the following decades.[58] Avrorin saw this

54 O. R. Munts, "Gorod Khibinogorsk i ego planirovka," in Fersman, ed., *Khibinskie Apatity*, vol. 2, 192–207, 193, 207.

55 Barsuk, "Kul'turnaia revoliutsiia pobezhdaet za poliarnym krugom," in Geber, Maizel', and Sedlis, eds., *Bol'sheviki pobedili tundru*, 54. In 1935, Kondrikov celebrated the supposed fulfillment of this vision, writing that not long ago "it was considered impossible to create a normal life in the mountains of the Kola Peninsula. Today, this territory has already been assimilated by man, and industry and culture with him." GAMO, f. 773, op. 1, d. 55, l. 23.

56 Bolotova, "Loving and Conquering Nature," *Europe-Asia Studies* 64, no. 4 (June 2012): 654.

57 Munts, "Gorod Khibinogorsk i ego planirovka," in Fersman, ed., *Khibinskie Apatity*, vol. 2, 192–207.

58 N. A. Avrorin, *Poliarno-al'piiskii botanicheskii sad v khibinakh (proekt)* (Leningrad: Izdatel'stvo Akademii Nauk SSSR, 1931); *KDF*, 81–83; N. A. Avrorin, *Chem ozeleniat' goroda i poselki Murmanskoi oblasti i severnykh raionov Karelo-Finskoi SSR* (Kirovsk: Izdanie Ispolnitel'nogo Komiteta Murmanskogo oblastnogo Soveta deputatov trudiashchikhsia, 1941); and GAMO, f. 773, op. 1, d. 52, l. 506.

work of the botanical garden as part of "a wide front of the struggle for succulent meadows, unprecedented berry gardens, splendid parks, and a healthy and comfortable life for the laborers of the socialist north!"[59]

Geologists and engineers shared this botanist's zeal for making the new town not only a site of industry but also a center of science. They succeeded in organizing the Khibiny Mountain Station of the Soviet Academy of Sciences. Over the ensuing decades, this institute grew into the Kola Base of the Academy of Sciences, then the Kola Branch of the Academy of Sciences, and finally the Kola Science Center in 1988.[60] Many researchers at the station strongly believed in directing expert knowledge about the natural world toward practical state concerns and saw their work in the early 1930s as part of socialist construction in the Khibiny.[61]

Still others believed that the Khibiny should become a tourist destination. The Society of Proletarian Tourism and Excursions set up a base on Mount Kukisvumchorr and began organizing summer trips for hikers.[62] In the winter the region began hosting downhill skiing competitions at events like the annual Holiday of the North.[63] To promote the Khibiny, tourism writers frequently cited the benefits of spending time in polar nature. One declared, "I would not exchange the nature of the north for even a section of the Caucasus... It would be much nicer to relax here on

59 N. A. Avrorin, "Poliarnyi botanicheskii sad v zapoliarnoi tundre," in Geber, Maizel', and Sedlis, eds., *Bol'sheviki pobedili tundru*, 170.

60 E. I. Makarova, "Kol'skii nauchnyi tsentr Rossiisskoi Akademii nauk v istorii Kol'skogo severa," *Ushakovskie chteniia: Materialy pervoi nauchno-prakticheskoi mezhregional'noi kraevedcheskoi konferentsii pamiati professors I. F. Ushakova* (Murmansk: MGPU 2004), 159–164; E. I. Makarova, "Ot tietty – k Kol'skoi base AN SSSR: Istoriia organizatsii geologicheskogo otdela po arkhivnym dokumentam," *Mineralogiia vo vsem prostranstve seto slova* (Apatity: Kol'skii nauchnyi tsentr Rossiisskoi Akademii nauk, 2006), 27–30; V. T. Kalinnikov and A. N. Vinogradov, "Stanovlenie i razvitie Kol'skogo nauchnogo tsentra RAN kak istoricheskii opyt Rossiiskogo puti promyshlennoi tsivilizatsiia severnykh territorii v XX veke," in V. T. Kalinnikov, ed., *Prirodopol'zovanie v Evro-Arkticheskom regione: Opyt XX veka i perspektivy* (Apatity: KNTs RAN, 2004), 3–14; and S. A. Duizhilov, "Sud'by nauki na Kol'skom Severe (Po materialam Kol'skoi bazy AN SSSR)," in V. P. Petrov and I. A. Razumova, eds., *Etnokul'turnye protsessy na Kol'skom Severe* (Apatity: Kol'skii nauchnyi tsentr Rossiisskoi Akademii nauk, 2004), 101–116.

61 A. E. Fersman and B. M. Kupletskii, eds., *Khibinskaia gornaia stantsiia* (Leningrad: Izdatel'stvo Akademii Nauk SSSR, 1934).

62 Barsuk, "Kul'turnaia revoliutsiia pobezhdaet za poliarnym krugom," in Geber, Maizel', and Sedlis, eds., *Bol'sheviki pobedili tundru*, 68. The Academy of Sciences also released a guidebook for hikers. A. E. Fersman, ed., *Putevoditel' po khibinskim tundram* (Leningrad: Izdatel'stvo Akademii Nauk, 1932).

63 M. Dubnitskii and A. Khrapovitskii, *Prazdnik Severa* (Murmansk: Murmanskoe knizhnoe izdatel'stvo, 1984).

the shore of a river or, having climbed up one of the high mountains, to rest with real pleasure after the descent. This tempers and strengthens the organism...From the north you always arrive vigorous and strong."[64] To provide visitors with this vitality involved more than directing them uphill; to many it required subduing the craggy landscape.

Soviet propagandists often evoked the catchphrase, "the Bolsheviks defeated the tundra," when describing the campaign to develop the region.[65] This pervasive rhetoric of conquest implied that Stalinist industrialization would bring newfound dominance over the natural world. The significance of this idea was multidimensional. As I showed in the case of railroad construction, aggressive language about nature spiked during the rash treatment of physical environs and often was partially a response to encountering recalcitrance from the material features of the landscape. But in the Stalinist era such allusions to dominance not only referred to a militaristic assault, but also to a strategy for attaining a holistic relationship with the environment. Through subjugation, Soviet citizens would make peace with their harsh surroundings. As Fersman explained this vision, "the path to economic, industrial, and cultural assimilation of distinct territories lies above all on the scientific mastery of them and the conquest of all sides of nature, life, and man – not in separation but in the complete envelopment of all the complex economic and social diversity of their mutual relationship."[66]

Once officials moved toward relying on forced laborers in the Khibiny, they also extended this dualistic view of nature to visions of rehabilitating class enemies among the peasantry. The country was in the midst of an outright attack on rural society that targeted wealthier peasants known as kulaks. De-kulakization wound up supplying Apatit with the bulk of its workforce. Thousands of repressed peasants were sent to the Khibiny, where they helped build the city, mine the mountains, and operate the enrichment plant.[67] The enterprise also contracted out imprisoned

64 Barsuk, "Kul′turnaia revoliutsiia pobezhdaet za poliarnym krugom," in Geber, Maizel′, and Sedlis, eds., *Bol′sheviki pobedili tundru*, 68. On campaigns to create a new form of purposeful proletarian relaxation in this era, see Diane P. Koenker, "The Proletarian Tourist in the 1930s: Between Mass Excursion and Mass Escape," in Anne E. Gorsuch and Diane P. Koenker, eds., *Turizm: The Russian and East European Tourist under Capitalism and Socialism* (Ithaca: Cornell University Press, 2006), 119–140.

65 Geber, Maizel′, and Sedlis, eds., *Bol′sheviki pobedili tundru*.

66 A. E. Fersman, *Novyi promyshlennyi tsentr SSSR za poliarnym krugom (Khibinskii apatit)* (Leningrad: Izdatel′stvo Akademii Nauk SSSR, 1931), 7.

67 Lynne Viola, *The Unknown Gulag: The Lost World of Stalin's Special Settlements* (Oxford: Oxford University Press, 2007); Oxana Klimkova, "Special Settlements in

technical specialists from Gulag camps, since "the severe climate" had prevented it from acquiring these experts "through the usual means of hiring and mobilization."[68] When mentioned publically, compulsory migrants were often depicted as engaged in a process of reforging.[69] Hard work in the severe northern environment allegedly played a therapeutic role of turning social pariahs into proper Soviet people. A book celebrating the building of the White Sea-Baltic Canal by prisoners in Karelia around the same time opened with the words, "Man, in changing nature, changes himself."[70] This phrase implied that industrial mastery of the natural world could reincorporate class enemies.

As they made specific decisions about the future of the city, enterprise leaders and planning commissions grappled with a host of environmental considerations. A group met in January 1930 to review options for where to locate a settlement for approximately 20,000 workers with room to expand. Among other issues, they discussed access to the worksite, climatic and topographical conditions, and the organization of a sewer system and water supply. Four possibilities stood out: on Mount Kukisvumchorr; in a section of a valley along the Iuksporiok River; near the Apatity station of the Murmansk railroad; and on the south side of the Lake Large Vud″iavr. The option near the main mining site on Mount Kukisvumchorr had particularly poor climatic conditions such as strong winds and snowdrifts and lacked the possibility of arranging a sewage system "without pollution of Vud″iavr which is the single source of a water supply." The valley of the Iuksporiok River would have similar problems with sewage, but would offer protection from winds. Though the area around the railroad had a better climate than the locations within the mountain range, its distance from the mines prevented it from garnering much support.[71]

Soviet Russia in the 1930s-50s," *Kritika* 8, no. 1 (Winter 2007): 105–135; V. Ia. Shashkov, *Spetspereselentsy v istorii Murmanskoi oblasti* (Murmansk: "Maksimum," 2004); and Andy Bruno, "Industrial Life in a Limiting Landscape: An Environmental Interpretation of Stalinist Social Conditions in the Far North," *International Review of Social History* 55, S18 (December 2010): 153–174.

[68] *KDF*, 91–93. These once imprisoned experts included Petr Vladimirov, who had been involved in the Shakhty trial and later ascended to the post of main engineer at Apatit. See Sergei Tararaksin, *Sudeb sgorevshikh ochertan'e* (Murmansk: "Sever," 2006), 91–103.

[69] On political work among declassed peasants on the Kola Peninsula, see V. Ia. Shashkov, *Spetspereselentsy na Murmane: Rol' spetspereselentsev v razvitii proizvoditel'nykh sil na Kol'skom poluostrove (1930–1936 gg.)* (Murmansk: MGPU, 1993), 105–126.

[70] M. Gor'kii, L. Averbakh, and S. Firin, eds., *Belomorsko-Baltiiskii Kanal imeni Stalina: Istoriia stroitel'stva* (Moscow: Istoriia Fabrik i Zavodov, 1934).

[71] GAMO, f. 773, op. 1, d. 1, ll. 107ob.

In the end the group endorsed the south side of the Large Vud″iavr as most ideal for the city. Despite strong winds and heavy snow cover, this spot possessed fir trees, sandy soil, sunlight, and a comparatively level surface in a dry area.[72] This proposal immediately came under fire from the Academy of Sciences and the Colonization Department of the Murmansk Railroad. Encouraging an urban design with "good sanitary conditions based on the self-purifying properties of water, soil, and air," the consultants noted that the chosen location would create tremendous difficulties with street design due to the steep inclines, winds, and preserved green sections.[73] Others foresaw problems in building a sewer system in the city if it was placed there.[74] Apatit responded to these criticisms by slightly adjusting its plans, but still moved forward with this site.[75]

The placement of Apatit's enrichment factory featured prominently in the decisions about the Khibinogorsk's layout. To determine its location within the city, a commission at the enterprise evaluated the ease of delivering ore from the mines, safety during explosions at the mines, avalanche hazards, the options for a loading route, the possibility of arranging the equipment in a cascade, the quality of the ground, the presence of an adequate water supply, and the ability to divert tailings (the solid residue of processed mineral ore). It considered three potential sites for the enrichment factory: on the southern incline of Mount Iuksporr; in the Iuksporr valley on the northeast shore of Large Vud″iavr; and on the southern shore of Large Vud″iavr. Of all of the factors mentioned, the possibility of disposing tailings without polluting Large Vud″iavr predominated in their decision to recommend the third location at the mouth of the White River on lower ground than the lake. Planners hoped to maintain the lake as a supply of water for both the city and the enterprise and wanted to avoid immediate expenditures on water purification. In this model the White River would serve as a sewer for industrial wastes. Trust employees drew up estimates of the maximum amount of tailings that could be dumped in the river.[76]

Neither ignorance nor disregard for nature inspired this environmentally destructive decision about what to do with industrial waste. Instead, enterprise leaders felt unjustifiably confident in the possibility of balancing industrial and environmental needs down the road. They saw pollution

72 GAMO, f. 773, op. 1, d. 1, ll. 107–108. 73 GAMO, f. 773, op. 1, d. 1, ll. 149–152.

74 GAMO, f. 773, op. 1, d. 1, l. 154. 75 *KDF*, 33–34.

76 G. F. Smirnov, "Obogashchenie apatito-nefelinovoi porody Khibinskogo mestorozhdeniia," in Fersman, ed., *Khibinskie Apatity*, vol. 1, 122–139 and GAMO, f. 773, op. 1, d. 51, ll. 209–210.

FIGURE 5. Construction of the Original Enrichment Factory at Apatit with the Khibiny Mountains in the Background.
Source: V. Iu. Brandt and G. F. Smirnov, "Proekt obogatitel′noi fabriki dlia khibinskikh apatitov i proverka ego ispytaniiami i konsul′tatsiei v Amerike" in A. E. Fersman, ed., *Khibinskie Apatity*, vol. 2 (Leningrad: ONTI VSNKh SSSR Lenzkimsektor, 1932), 179.

of the White River as only a temporary problem. Nikolai Vorontsov, the head of the enrichment factory, insisted that soon the wastes from apatite enrichment would be recycled to produce a variety of subsidiary products, thereby reducing the amount of tailings being dumped into the river.[77] At the time scientists consulting Apatit were developing a model of industrial organization called the "complex utilization of natural resources," which promised to minimize wastes through reuse. Always enthusiastic, Fersman declared complex utilization as "the idea of the protection of our natural resources from their predatory squandering, the idea of using raw material to the end, the idea of the possible preservation of our natural supplies for the future," where "not one gram of extracted mining mass is lost, where there is not one gram of waste, where nothing is emitted into the air and washed away by water."[78]

Laboring in the Mountains

Stalinism is less known today for lofty idealism than abject brutality. Struggling to enact their plans to industrialize the Khibiny, the leaders of the Apatit trust embraced strategies that hardly seemed to reflect the promises of socialism. They consulted foreign representatives of capitalist countries to solve basic questions about processing and tried to orient production toward international exports. Unable to recruit enough workers to the Arctic tundra, they increasingly depended on the coerced labor of forced migrants who suffered greatly in this harsh environment. But this underwhelming and duplicitous experience did not signal a conscious abandonment of hopeful visions for a bright future in the Soviet north. Instead it represented an unsurprising outcome of an economic strategy based on blending holism and heavy-handed control in relations with the Khibiny environment. Gainsaying both of these aspects of the Soviet agenda, the natural features of the mountain range continued to demonstrate their potency.

As they planned the city, project leaders faced significant setbacks in getting the enterprise up and running. At the apogee of the first five-year plan, a dearth of necessary supplies, funds, and labor struck firms

77 GAMO, f. 773, op. 1, d. 2, ll. 238–244.

78 A. E. Fersman, *Kompleksnoe ispol'zovanie iskopaemogo syr'ia* (Leningrad: Izdatel'stvo Akademii Nauk SSSR, 1932), 19; Olli Salmi and Aino Toppinen, "Embedding Science in Politics: 'Complex Utilization' and Industrial Ecology as Models of Natural Resource Use," *Journal of Industrial Ecology* 11, no. 3 (2007): 93–111; GAMO, f. 773, op. 1, d. 9, ll. 8–10; and GAMO, f. 773, op. 1, d. 5, l. 174.

throughout the USSR. The state's wide-ranging and impatient push for breakneck industrialization caused a temporary paralysis in production at the exact moment it was supposed to be rapidly expanding.[79] Apatit predictably staggered in this period. In February 1930, the All-Union Association of the Chemical Industry slashed Apatit's budget for the year in half. While agencies further up the chain of command reversed this cut in May, it still led to delays in construction.[80]

Questions about the appropriate enrichment process prompted these erratic funding decisions. Would the factory be based on selective crushing or flotation? Chemists consulting Apatit realized that they could not attain high enough concentrations of phosphorus pentoxide from the ore to produce superphosphate through selective crushing (a method in which only specific, apatite-rich segments of the mined material would be used to make superphosphate). Enrichment required flotation (a method that involved pulverizing large blocks of the removed ore and then separating the contents in liquid solutions).[81] Though still seen as a valuable treasure, the rock from the Khibiny was not making it easy for Stalinist industrialists.

Input and interference from abroad also shaped the controversy about Apatit's enrichment process. Around the time that foreign purchasers received a contaminated shipment of unprocessed ore and started canceling their orders, Krügel, a German specialist on phosphates, questioned whether it was even possible to enrich Khibiny apatite into usable superphosphate.[82] At a conference in Interlaken, Switzerland in July 1930, Krügel opined, "It is very doubtful that those big hopes that the USSR has for apatite were at any point justified. The climate of the place where the deposits are found is unfavorable and people can hardly live there. In my view there remains very little of the proud hopes of the Soviets."[83] To resolve the issue Apatit sent two engineers to Salt Lake City, Utah to consult with the General Engineering Company, which relied on flotation enrichment to process copper ore. The visit

79 Kuromiya, *Stalin's Industrial Revolution*, 137–172.

80 GAMO, f. 773, op. 1, d. 1, ll. 109–144.

81 GAMO, f. 773, op. 1, d. 5, ll. 58–70; Barabanov, et al., *Gigant v Khibinakh*, 45; and *KDF*, 39–40.

82 GAMO, f. 773, op. 1, d. 6, ll. 25–26; "Letopis′ sobytii goroda Khibinogorska," *ZhA*, no. 1 (October 2001): 57; GAMO, f. 773, op. 1, d. 7, ll. 154–176, 184–187; and V. I. Kondrikov, "Sostoianie i perspektivy stroitel′stva v raione Khibinskikh razrabotok," *KMK*, no. 5–6 (1931): 8.

83 Quoted in P. A. Nevskii, "Apatity – na vneshnii rynok," in Fersman, ed., *Khibinskie Apatity*, vol. 2, 121.

revealed crucial adjustments that needed to be made to the size of filters and allowed Apatit's representatives to purchase required equipment.[84] Espousing a cosmopolitan ethos that until recently many scholars of Stalinist culture have overlooked, the Soviet engineers insisted that the trip to America helped them avoid "a whole array of major defects in the work of the factory."[85] A redesigned apatite-nepheline enrichment factory opened its doors in September 1931 and completed a large expansion in 1934.[86] Recalling Krügel's suspicions, the Kola press acrimoniously denounced him as a "bourgeois specialist" and proclaimed "Overcoming the 'unfavorable climate,' we successfully capture the natural resources wasting away in the earth above the polar circle. We build a large mining and chemical industry in the far north."[87]

Mining the Khibiny began haphazardly as well. Small teams of geologists and engineers began hacking out chunks of the mountains even before Apatit opened shop at the end of 1929. When workers started setting up basic mining infrastructure on the southwest incline of Mount Kukisvumchorr the next year, they encountered unexpected troubles that, according to Kondrikov, almost put a halt to "the entire Khibinogorsk affair." The enterprise planned to start with surface mining on Kukisvumchorr and later transition to underground operations. But the slides that engineers installed to move the material out of the mountain did not have steep enough inclines for the highly frictional apatite-nepheline ore to descend. The angles they used were standard for removing coal and iron. Ruing the rock's chicanery, Kondrikov wrote, "without a sufficiently precise scheme all the work of the trust in the summer of 1930 was its own form of a 'university' for learning the particular properties of apatite ore, primarily in terms of how to lower it from the pit faces onto the loading

84 GAMO, f. 773, op. 1, d. 7, ll. 108–109 and V. Iu. Brandt and G. F. Smirnov, "Proekt obogatitel'noi fabriki dlia khibinskikh apatitov i proverka ego ispytaniiami i konsul'tatsiei v Amerike" and V. Iu. Brandt, "Ocherk obogatitel'nykh fabrik SASSh," in Fersman, ed., *Khibinskie Apatity*, vol. 2, 153–181.

85 *KDF*, 43. On the importance of the international audience to the Soviet Union in the 1930s, see Katerina Clark, *Moscow, the Fourth Rome: Stalinism, Cosmopolitanism, and the Evolution of Soviet Culture, 1931–1941* (Cambridge, MA: Harvard University Press, 2011) and Michael David-Fox, *Showcasing the Great Experiment: Cultural Diplomacy and Western Visitors to the Soviet Union, 1921–1941* (Oxford: Oxford University Press, 2012). Of course, the engineers' justification for the trip also seemed designed to protect themselves against the accusations of disloyalty that were often made against technical experts in this period. Loren R. Graham, *The Ghost of the Executed Engineer: Technology and the Fall of the Soviet Union* (Cambridge, MA: Harvard University Press, 1993).

86 Barabanov, et al., *Gigant v Khibinakh*, 44–59.

87 *KhR* (October 18, 1932), 1.

FIGURE 6. Apatit's Leaders Experiment with Slides (Vasilii Kondrikov on the Left and Aleksandr Fersman on the Right).
Source: A. I. Chistiakov, "Razvitie i organizatsiia gornykh rabot po dobyche apatita" in A. E. Fersman, ed., *Khibinskie Apatity*, vol. 2 (Leningrad: ONTI VSNKh SSSR Lenzkimsektor, 1932), 151.

platforms." To meet its production quota for 1930, Apatit forced workers to break the ore off the mountain with handheld sledgehammers and relied on reindeer to haul the material down the slopes.[88] The situation improved over the next couple of years as the company partially mechanized the mine, which included using drills powered by compressed air. It also began some underground mining on Kukisvumchorr and extracted about one million tons of ore by the end of 1932.[89]

Needless to say, the miners labored arduously in these polar mountains. Because of the frequent snowfalls and constant darkness in the winter, management increased from one mining shift the first year to a three-shift, twenty-four hour regime. With the snow melt each spring, abrasive and sharply cleaved rocks from the mine rained down from above, imperiling the miners' safety. Indeed, at least twenty-seven workers died on the job between 1930 and 1934.[90] To spin this grim reality into narratives of Soviet triumph, authors often dwelt on the dangerous environment where the work took place. As poet Lev Oshanin described the labor at the Kukisvumchorr mine: "The all-out wind blows along the ledges, / Thundering on the grounds, sliding on the slopes. / One might freeze under a wolf-skin coat, / But must never simply stand before the wind. / It is morose, the face of the mine, and won't allow for a full swing, / It would be glad to bury you under itself, / But with strokes of a black and red-hot sledgehammer / The guys hack up the face of the mine all shift long."[91] In this lyrical fragment the threatening wind and frost produced the conditions for miners to become heroes of Stalinist industrialization.

Of course, Oshanin referred not to all of the laborers in the Khibiny, but to the pool of individuals that the Apatit trust had managed to recruit. The company wanted "qualified cadres" who would feel "love for the region" and lay down "healthy roots."[92] But as rapid industrialization led

[88] Kondrikov, "Sostoianie i perspektivy stroitel′stva v raione Khibinskikh razrabotok," *KMK*, no. 5–6 (1931): 10; Barabanov, et al., *Gigant v Khibinakh*, 44–45; and P. V. Vladimirov and N. S. Morev, *Apatitovyi rudnik im. S. M. Kirova* (Leningrad: Seriia izdatel′stva po khibinskoi apatitovoi probleme, 1936), 24–34, 84.

[89] *KDF*, 119 and S. I. Tiul′panova, ed., *Istoriia industrializatsii SSSR. Industrializatsiia Severo-zapadnogo raiona v gody vtoroi i tret′ei piatiletok (1933–1941 g.g.): Dokumenty i materialy* (Leningrad: Isdatel′stvo LGU, 1969), 176.

[90] Vladimirov and Morev, *Apatitovyi rudnik im. S. M. Kirova*, 42, 114–120.

[91] Lev Oshanin, "Povest′ ob udarnikakh gory Kukusvum (Otryvok iz poema)," in Geber, Maizel′, and Sedlis, eds., *Bol′sheviki pobedili tundru*, 185–188. A reprint of a part of the poem appears in Lev Oshanin, "Rabochaia noch′," *ZhA*, no. 1 (October 2001): 60–61.

[92] GAMO, f. 773, op. 1, d. 51, l. 204.

to a sharp labor shortage nationwide, Apatit found itself in a particularly unenviable position for hiring a voluntary workforce. The harsh climate, faraway location, and lack of sufficient housing and services made the project much less attractive to free workers. One report declared that "remoteness and natural wildness of the Khibiny" made it "impossible" for the enterprise to meet its need by "hiring a free labor supply."[93] Some skilled workers, including a mobilized squad of Communist Party affiliates from Leningrad, came to the Khibiny, but many new voluntary migrants left soon after encountering the conditions there.[94] So while Apatit estimated that it would have 9,500 recruited workers by the end of 1931, less than half that number was on its rolls in late October.[95] This overall shortage meant that the entire industrial project depended on another group of laborers – declassed peasants exiled to the north.

Soviet authorities decided to send de-kulakized migrants – known as "special settlers" in government parlance – to live and work in the Khibiny without much forethought. The mass collectivization and de-kulakization campaign of the winter of 1929–1930 stripped huge numbers of comparatively well-off peasants of their property, excluded them from the new collective farms, and slated them for exile. With only a general idea of using these de-kulakized peasants to exploit natural resources in distant peripheries, the Unified State Political Organization (OGPU, the secret police) began resettling them into "special settlement" camps that winter.[96] Close to 1,000 arrived in the Khibiny region in mid-March.[97] Soon afterward, OGPU head Genrikh Iagoda outlined the idea of turning these camps into more or less permanent, self-sustaining "colonization settlements." Relocated peasants would work in timber, agriculture, and mining and help "colonize the north in the shortest possible time."[98] As with the building of the Murmansk railroad, forced labor again allowed state officials to populate the Kola Peninsula to a much greater extent than offering incentives to colonists had. In the early 1930s a total of approximately 45,000 special settlers came to the Kola Peninsula,

93 RGASPI, f. 17, op. 120, d. 26, l. 151.
94 GAMO, f. 773, op. 1, d. 1, l. 315; GAMO, f. 773, op. 1, d. 5, ll. 22ob, 185–189, 247; GAMO, f. 773, op. 1, d. 8, l. 34; and GAMO, f. 773, op. 1, d. 15, l. 225.
95 GAMO, f. 773, op. 1, d. 5, l. 22ob and *KDF*, 41, 95.
96 Viola, *The Unknown Gulag*, 14–88.
97 Shashkov, *Spetspereselentsy na Murmane*, 51.
98 Oleg V. Khlevniuk, *The History of the Gulag: From Collectivization to the Great Terror* (New Haven: Yale University Press, 2004), 23–24.

which alone more than doubled its 1926 population of 32,200. All but a few thousand of these peasant expellees directly served the apatite industry.[99]

Legally, special settlers occupied an intermediate status between citizens and labor camp prisoners, being deprived of mobility and civil rights but contractually entitled to wages and (frequently unfulfilled) amenities. Within the settlements they were not kept under guard surveillance, but had to periodically check in with secret police authorities. In the summer of 1931 the Apatit trust signed a contract with the OGPU, which stipulated that the enterprise would supply up to 15,000 special settlers with equivalent levels of food, material provisions, and wages (except for the 15 percent that would be paid to the camp administration) as offered to other workers. It additionally bore responsibility for providing housing, sanitation infrastructure, medical facilities, and schools. To make use of their labor, the trust also needed to train these agriculturalists for construction work, mining, factory operation, and other jobs. The OGPU offered funds for heating, illumination, and certain communal services. On the more punitive side, the contract prohibited special settlers from going on vacation, demanded that they live in separate areas or buildings, limited their ability to serve in administrative positions without the approval of the OGPU commandant's office, and put the OGPU commandant in charge of disciplinary issues.[100]

Not only did this mandatory relocation bring members of agricultural communities to a new industrial site, it also moved people from more central regions of Russia into the Arctic. Small numbers of special settlers made their way to the Khibiny from all over the USSR, but the vast majority of them came from elsewhere in the Leningrad region or from areas around the Ural Mountains. Approximately 69 percent of the population of the Khibiny were special settlers as of late October 1931 and 52 percent and 26 percent of adults, respectively, were from these two regions. Most arrived as family units: 49 percent were women and 32 percent were under sixteen years old.[101] Yet their cows, horses, pigs, and other livestock did not join them, since the state had confiscated these animals. Even for migrants accustomed to the long and dark snowy

99 Shashkov, *Spetspereselentsy na Murmane*, 32; Shashkov, *Spetspereselentsy v istorii Murmanskoi oblasti*, 108–113; and "Vvodnyi ocherk," in Kiselev, ed., *Kol'skii entsiklopediia*, vol. 1, 70.

100 Viola, *The Unknown Gulag*, 92–96 and GAMO, f. 773, op. 1, d. 6, ll. 230–232.

101 *KDF*, 94–96.

winters of the Leningrad region and the less steep, but still mountainous, landscapes of the Urals, the Khibiny must have seemed particularly severe. This rocky polar tundra was a far cry from rural villages in more temperate territories. One expellee from a village in the southern Urals later described entering the range, "We looked all around and mountains were everywhere." He also noted how in the winter the family's clothing froze to the canvas tents where they slept.[102]

Upon arrival the special settlers disproportionately moved into encampments outlying Khibinogorsk. Many of the settlement camps were either high up in the mountains near the mines or in a valley along the recently placed railroad servicing the Khibiny. All of them were away from the spot along the southern side of Lake Large Vud″iavr that had been chosen as the location for a socialist city, where the administration of Apatit, recruited laborers, and technical experts often lived.[103] The Khibiny also contrasted with the isolated colonies serving the forestry sector, which were a more common destination for special settlers in the north. Here the large-scale project of setting up a new industrial town required greater integration among forced and voluntary migrants and over time more and more special settlers relocated into the city itself.[104]

After being dropped off by a train and processed by police officials, a range of ad hoc housing structures greeted the new migrants. At first almost all of the special settlers moved into tents, mud huts, and makeshift barn-like structures built with thin boards and wood beams called *shalmany*.[105] One former kulak recalled thousands grieving "over the whistling of the raging northern wind, over the wailing blizzards, and, yes, over the cries of our own young children trembling from the cold in canvas tents and in boarded, hard to heat, *shalmany*."[106] At the

[102] V. M. Lebednik, "Stranitsy detstva," *Spetspereselentsy v Khibinakh: Spetspereselentsy i zakliuchennye v istorii osvoeniia Khibin (Kniga vospominanii)* (Apatity: Khibinskoe obshchestvo "Memorial," 1997), 24–25. For a discussion of special settlers' reactions to the Khibiny environment, also see Alla Bolotova and Florian Stammler, "How the North Became Home: Attachment to Place among Industrial Migrants in the Murmansk Region of Russia" in Lee Huskey and Chris Southcott, eds., *Migration in the Circumpolar North: Issues and Contexts* (Edmonton: CCI Press, 2010), 193–220.

[103] *KDF*, 95.

[104] Close to 20,000 special settlers resided in Khibinogorsk by 1933. V. Ia. Shashkov, *Raskulachivanie v SSSR i sud′by spetspereselentsev, 1930–1954 gg.* (Murmansk: Murmanskii gosudarstvennyi pedagogicheskii institut, 1996), 167.

[105] In late 1930 close to 12,000 of 14,000 residents in the Khibinogorsk region lived in such houses. A. V. Barabanov and T. A. Kalinina, *"Apatit": vek iz veka* (Apatity: Laplandia Minerals, 2004), 38.

[106] L. E. Gudovskaia, "Chto sokhranila pamiat′," in *Spetspereselentsy v Khibinakh*, 37.

end of 1930 a regional inspector of housing and communal sanitation alarmingly reported that the "*shalmanov*, mud huts, and tents that act as surrogates of housing" are "unacceptable for the conditions of the polar winter." Despite this knowledge, the tents and *shalmany* remained for years, though the sharp mountain relief, the hard rocky ground, and the long winter prevented the mud huts from lasting long in this region.[107]

Such disregard for the unsuitability of this temporary housing in the perilous Khibiny worsened the suffering of its new inhabitants. It allowed these cold, crowded, and filthy dwellings to create a sanitary nightmare. Doctors in Khibinogorsk wanted to limit the tents to forty-five residents each after inspecting one of the special settlements in September 1931. "The contamination of the settlement with garbage, overcrowding, the absence of a basic stock of everyday items, and the dirtiness of the area undoubtedly is a favorable atmosphere for the development of disease."[108] Special settlers remembered these hardships of the Stalinist ecosystem vividly. "Only at night could I find a place. If you arrived late, you would sleep on the edge in the cold. Typhus took people down. Twenty children died from our *shalman* alone. I crept among the sick in the cold and dirt."[109] Another commented, "It is hard to say how many people lived in this barrack. There was no thought about hygiene. Diseases began and every morning we brought out the dead."[110] As in other special settlements in the north, typhus, typhoid fever, tuberculosis, and measles spread among the new residents of the Khibiny.[111] So too did ailments related to malnutrition such as scurvy and rickets.[112] Since they were the lowest priority in terms of housing, food, and medical services, the special settlers fell ill more frequently. As a result, their mortality rates exceeded the voluntary migrants for the first several years.[113]

In spite of these torments, some forced migrants later took pride in having helped transform the Khibiny. "In daytime we worked the best we could. We laid the roads, built the city, mined apatite and processed it at the enrichment plant that we constructed, and struggled with snowdrifts.

[107] *KDF*, 60–61, 67 and Shashkov, *Spetspereselentsy v istorii Murmanskoi oblasti*, 271–278.

[108] GAMO, f. R-163, op. 1, d. 26, ll. 8–10.

[109] Tat'iana Shishkina, "Iablonskie," *KhR* (October 5, 2006): 6.

[110] Lebedik, "Stranitsy detstva," in *Spetspereselentsy v Khibinakh*, 24.

[111] Viola, *The Unknown Gulag*, 34–141; A.A. Kiselev, "GULAG na Murmane: Istoriia tiurem, lagerei, kolonii," *SM* (October 8, 1992): 3; and *KDF*, 152–153.

[112] Shashhkov, *Spetspereselentsy v istorii Murmanskoi oblasti*, 278–279 and GAMO, f. R-163, op. 1, d. 141, l. 13.

[113] Shashkov, *Spetspereselentsy v istorii Murmanskoi oblasti*, 143, 191.

This was all done in large part by the hands of the kulaks."[114] The leadership of Apatit, however, did quite not see it this way. Instead, they resented the low labor productivity of these unskilled peasant migrants, who usually brought along their entire families.[115] Irritated, Kondrikov reportedly remarked, "I do not care whether these peasants die like flies. But if they had worked as free laborers, I could have built three such towns instead of one."[116]

The Altered Ecosystem

For all of the setbacks, for all of the mistreatment of those conscripted to the region, for all of the ways that the physical environment countered grandiose visions, the Soviet Union managed to industrialize the Khibiny Mountains. During the second five-year plan (1933–1937), Apatit steadily mined increasing quantities of apatite-nepheline ore and enriched more and more apatite concentrate. Imports from Morocco ceased as Apatit supplied Soviet fertilizer factories with more than three-fourths of the material they used to make superphosphate by 1934.[117] Khibinogorsk expanded to a city of more than 30,000 residents by 1935, when local party cells pushed to rename the town Kirovsk after the murder of Leningrad party boss, Sergei Kirov.[118] This industrial growth altered environmental relations within the mountain range. The new population cut down forests and cultivated crops. They polluted air and water and installed sanitation infrastructure. And they succumbed to natural hazards and addressed health risks. Such outcomes lay bare some of the contradictions within the Stalinist agenda toward the natural world.

Much of the forest within the settled valley of the Khibiny soon disappeared. This ecological change involved not only abandoned agendas,

114 Gudovskaia, "Chto sokhranila pamiat′," in *Spetspereselentsy v Khibinakh*, 37.

115 *KDF*, 41. Reflecting these anxieties, the All-Union Association of the Chemical Industry ordered that male special settlers should not be used to complete tasks that women could do. GAMO, f. 773, op. 1, d. 1, ll. 246–247. On the experience of women in Khibinogorsk, see A. G. Samorukova, "Mir zhenshchiny v istorii Khibinogorska (K 75-letiiu goroda)," *Tretie Ushakovskie chteniia: Spornik nauchnykh statei* (Murmansk: MGPU 2006), 141–146.

116 Harvard Project on the Soviet Social System, Schedule B, Vol. 3, Case 49 [i.e. 31] (interviewer A.P.), Widener Library, Harvard University, 5, accessed May 24, 2012, http://nrs.harvard.edu/urn-3:FHCL:964366?n=5.

117 Barabanov, et al., *Gigant v Khibinakh*, 44–66; GAMO, f. 773, op. 1, d. 5, ll. 62–70; and Vladimirov and Morev, *Apatitovyi rudnik im. S. M. Kirova*, 10–12.

118 *KDF*, 99–101, 189.

but also the participation of trees, fires, and dust. As wood became a scarce, and rapidly depleted, resource, plans to preserve forested areas for parks fell by the wayside.[119] Frequent fires along the Murmansk railroad and within the city and the steady cutting and burning of forests near Lake Little Vud″iavr further exhausted the local wood supply.[120] Since most of the trees on the Kola Peninsula were too thin anyway, the town ended up importing wood for construction from the Arkhang′elsk region.[121] Once the apatite enrichment factory came online, a new threat confronted Khibiny flora. Dust from the factory spewed out so thickly that it blocked sunlight "like during a forest fire."[122] By 1935 a layer of this dust covered the foliage and buildings in the area and had begun to kill coniferous trees. V. E. Lebedeva, a sanitation inspector sent to the region, suggested installing new electric filters at the enrichment factory and greening the area to bulwark air quality. Ultimately, though, she saw the enrichment facility's location as presenting "definite insalubrities for the city."[123]

The dearth of local building materials extended beyond forests. As Apatit's leadership noted in 1931, "Unfortunately, large supplies of limestone on the Kola Peninsula have still not been found, there is comparatively little wood, the renewal period of which extends here up to 200 years, and until very recently there was a large deficit of clay."[124] In a desperate effort to compensate, the company relied heavily on a type of nepheline rock from the mountains called khibinite as a cheap substitute for concrete and bricks.[125]

[119] GAMO, f. 773, op. 1, d. 51. ll. 279–281 and GAMO, f. 773, op. 1, d. 52. l. 506.

[120] ARAN, f. 544, op. 1, d. 161, l. 40; Shashhkov, *Spetspereselentsy v istorii Murmanskoi oblasti*, 278; and Ivan Kataev, "Ledianaia Ellada," in Nikol′skii and Pompeev, eds., *Pul′s Khibin*, 42–66.

[121] Barabanov and Kalinina, "*Apatit,*" 38.

[122] ARAN, f. 544, op. 1, d. 161, l. 41.

[123] GAMO, f. 773, op. 1, d. 51, l. 92.

[124] Kondrikov, "Sostoianie i perspektivy stroitel′stva v raione Khibinskikh razrabotok," *KMK*, no. 5–6 (1931): 9. On Apatit's failures to meet housing construction quotas: RGASPI, f. 17, op. 120, d. 26, l. 85; GAMO, f. 773, op. 1, d. 5, l. 190; GAMO, f. 773, op. 1, d. 5, ll. 9–10; and GAMO, f. 773, op. 1, d. 44, ll. 191–193.

[125] GAMO, f. 773, op. 1, d. 51, ll. 84, 215 and GAMO, f. 773, op. 1, d. 59, ll. 258–262. Trust leaders proved largely unwilling or unable to use this material from the mountains for municipal purposes. They argued instead that the "harsh climate of the polar tundra" and "the mountain relief of the location with rocky ground," along with insufficient state funds to purchase supplemental materials, inhibited the construction of housing. *KDF*, 66 and Shashkov, *Spetspereselentsy v istorii Murmanskoi oblasti*, 277. According to Kirov, special settlers in the region still lived in less than two square meters of space per person in 1934. GAMO, f. 773, op. 1, d. 9, ll. 22–23, 191–193.

To feed and clothe the new population, state, party, enterprise, and police organs mostly shipped supplies into the region. Local agencies opened several stores and set up a network of cafeterias where people ate most of their meals.[126] Apatit also combined forces with agricultural researchers such as Eikhfel′d and Avrorin to establish a state farm, Industriia, designed to help supplement the food supply. Over its first few years, Industriia drained and reclaimed hundreds of hectares of marshland, thereby modifying the Khibiny landscape. On this territory, it cultivated potatoes, vegetables, and edible roots and planted grasses to provide forage for cattle, horses, pigs, sheep, and goats. Despite these successes, several of the animals kept by the state farm lacked adequate shelters and froze to death in the winter. And though it established milk, meat, and vegetable production in the Khibiny, Industriia did not grow much grain.[127] Polar conditions still imposed limits on agricultural development.

To supplement their diets residents also made use of other familiar features of this new environment. Many caught freshwater fish in the nearby lakes and rivers and collected mushrooms and berries in the summer. One special settler recalled how his family had lived in a region with many fish-filled ponds. In the Khibiny, his father "went into the mountains where there were already pools and caught fish.... In the White River there used to be a lot of fish, only they've gone away."[128] Indeed, pollution of Khibiny waters soon killed off many of the aquatic species in them.

Wastewater came from both municipal and industrial sources. The absence of an adequate sewage system helped despoil the Khibiny. Planners had tried to layout the city and enterprise so as to avoid polluting water sources, while still delaying investments on sewer infrastructure. But this scheme did not work. Referring to the lakes and streams of the Khibiny, a sanitation inspector wrote at the end of 1930, "the mountain character of the place with a sharp incline represents an almost insuperable obstacle to the protection of them from pollution." Already he considered "all of the available sources of a water supply to be contaminated to a greater or lesser degree" by human wastes. When migrants arrived

126 GAMO, f. 773, op. 1, d. 2, ll. 183–186; GAMO, f. 773, op. 1, d. 6, ll. 230–232; GAMO, f. 773, op. 1, d. 15, ll. 76–79; and *KDF*, 64–65, 68–74.

127 *KDF*, 54, 74–75, 94–95, 132–133; Osinovskii, "Rol′ khibinskikh apatitov v kolonizatsii Kol′skogo poluostrova," in Fersman, ed., *Khibinskie Apatity*, vol. 1, 204–211; and RGASPI, f. 17, op. 122, d. 104, l. 163.

128 L.D. Zverev, "Rasskaz o zhizni bogatoi," in *Spetspereselentsy v Khibinakh*, 16.

in the region, they immediately began drawing water from the closest sources to their settlements for drinking, cooking, cleaning, bathing, and extinguishing fires. The contaminated liquids from laundries, trash receptacles, cesspits, and bathhouses soon seeped into the water supply.[129]

In response to an outbreak of diseases connected to infected water in Khibinogorsk and its outlying settlements, the local government attempted to regulate migrants' use of water. In order to enhance the safety of the aqueous environment, it sought to modify the behavior of the human population of mostly forced settlers. The Khibinogorsk City Council created a fifty-meter territory around Lake Large Vud″iavr in the summer of 1931 that was to be on a "strict regime" of reduced human activity and construction for the sake of preserving this water source.[130] A follow-up decree prohibited dumping wastes on the ground; placing cafeterias, bathhouses, cesspits, lavatories, stables, and pigsties within fifty meters of any water body; doing laundry in living quarters; and taking water from a specific lake and river for any reason besides housing construction. The City Council printed one hundred copies of this order and presumably posted it around the area.[131]

While seeking this interventionist remedy, authorities kept postponing the installation of sewer canals, water pipes, and a purification station. At the end of 1930, Apatit still intended to begin construction on this infrastructure the next year, making the river Loparki the source of drinking water instead of Large Vud″iavr, which would only supply water to the enterprise.[132] As the firm lagged in its production quotas in 1931 and 1932, it repeatedly deferred making this basic municipal expenditure for the provision of safe water.[133] The city did, however, begin onsite chlorination of drinking water, but this stopgap measure did not prevent both the White River and Large Vud″iavr from becoming increasingly polluted even before wastes from enrichment became a major threat.[134] Alarmed, Kirov described the situation in 1934: "In Khibinogorsk and its settlements there is a complete lack of a sewer system and it does not have an independent system for the municipal water supply – the supply of the city is produced with unpurified water from Lake Large Vud″iavr through a pumping station of the industrial water supply. Further postponing the urgent construction of the sewer system might bring mass diseases of an

129 *KDF*, 62–63. 130 GAMO, f. R-163, op. 1, d. 26, ll. 15–16.

131 GAMO, f. R-163, op. 1, d. 26, l. 17. 132 *KDF*, 63.

133 GAMO, f. 773, op. 1, d. 5, ll. 62–70, 192–193; Barabanov, et al., *Gigant v Khibinakh*, 51; and GAMO, f. 773, op. 1, d. 51, ll. 92–94.

134 *KDF*, 152.

epidemic character to the population."[135] Construction of these services did finally begin the next year, but the sewer network only approached completion near the end of the decade.[136]

The dumping of the enrichment factory also disturbed the rivers and lakes in the area. Unfiltered wastewater from the enterprise included "resinous substances and kerosene" that "can spoil the water of the lake and kill the fish it has there."[137] This pollution deprived freshwater species such as salmon (*losos′*) of the oxygen that they needed to survive. Nepheline tailings from enrichment also turned the White River literally white and began making their way to Lake Imandra. Even ostensibly protected water bodies suffered from Apatit's wastes.[138] By the end of the decade Fridolin, who had earlier studied mosquito abatement in the Khibiny, reported that "factory wastewaters and the abundance of thin dust from crushed apatite has so changed the character of Large Vud″iavr – previously the absolutely pure and typical mountain lake on whose shore the city of Kirovsk is located – that the fish that once passed through already do not live there."[139]

Recall that Apatit's leadership had thought that the reprocessing of nepheline tailings would allow them to avoid this problem. All by-products of production could be turned into useful substances leaving minimal waste, under Fersman's rosy plan. The enterprise actively pursued this agenda by pressing for the construction of a new plant in nearby Kandalaksha to reprocess nepheline tailings into aluminum.[140] Aluminum usually came from bauxite, but Soviet geochemists determined that nepheline could also serve as a suitable source material.[141]

135 GAMO, f. 773, op. 1, d. 9, ll. 192–193.
136 *KDF*, 143–146.
137 GAMO, f. 773, op. 1, d. 51, l. 92ob.
138 S. A. Diuzhilov, "'Arkhipelag Svobody' na Murmane (vtoraia polovina 1920-kh – 1930-e g.g.)," in Fedorov, et al., eds., *Zhivushchie na Severe*, 100; ARAN, f. 544, op. 1, d. 161, ll. 40–42; and GAMO, f. 773, op. 1, d. 51, ll. 92–94.
139 ARAN, f. 544, op. 1, d. 161, ll. 40–41. Fridolin's ecological sympathies ran deep. Among other scientific ideas, he embraced Lev Berg's landscape theories of physical geography. On Berg's science, see Denis J. B. Shaw and Jonathan D. Oldfield, "Totalitarianism and Geography: L. S. Berg and the Defence of an Academic Discipline in the Age of Stalin," *Political Geography* 27, no. 1 (January 2008): 96–112. Fridolin also lost his job at the Kola Base of the Academy of Sciences during a purge in 1938. E. I. Makarova, "Istoriia Kol′skogo nauchnyi tsentr Rossiisskoi Akademii nauk v istorii Kol′skogo severa," *Tietta*, no. 7 (2009): 15–17.
140 GAMO, f. 773, op. 1, d. 9, ll. 7–11; and GAMO, f. 773, op. 1, d. 15, ll. 102–104.
141 A. E. Fersman and N. I. Vlodatsev, "Nefelin, ego mestorozhdeniia, zapasy, primenenie, i ekonomika," in A. E. Fersman, ed., *Khibinskie Apatity*, vol. 3 (Leningrad: Gosudarstvennoe nauchno-tekhnicheskoe izdatel′stvo Lenkhimsektor, 1931), 33–44.

Beseeching Stalin to support the project, one chemist from the trust evoked the desire for Fersman's pollution-free "complex utilization of the minerals of the Khibiny."[142] Though temporarily approved in 1932, a nepheline reprocessing facility subsequently faced funding cuts and revisions. The Soviet aluminum industry argued against the project, especially after the discovery of new rich bauxite deposits in the Urals in the mid-1930s. Consequently, construction staggered until just before World War II, at which point the war postponed the project further.[143] These delays meant that the substance itself – nepheline from the Khibiny Mountains – played a very different role than planners had hoped. Instead of serving as a valuable subsidiary resource, it functioned as a potent pollutant that "bit back" against Khibiny waterways.[144]

A major debate about industrial pollution within the city broke out in early 1935 as authorities considered an expansion that would have raised the population of Kirovsk and the mining settlements at Kukisvumchorr and Iuksporiok to 68,000.[145] Lebedeva reported that the experimental phosphorus factory near Iuksporiok (in a spot planners had rejected for the enrichment factory) discharged "extraordinarily dangerous water and air." But now this unit emitted directly into Lake Large Vud″iavr and belched out gases such as carbon monoxide that threatened human health.[146] Then, in March 1935, an engineer for Apatit noticed a stench from the water in the Iuksporr valley. After his tests showed the presence of poisonous phosphine in the water, he called for immediate action to reduce this hazard.[147]

Over the next few weeks, anxieties about poisonous drinking water and toxic dust circulated throughout the city. On April 8 local party and enterprise leaders met with researchers to discuss the concerns about pollution from the phosphorus factory. One expert presented some of

142 GAMO, f. 773, op. 1, d. 9, l. 8.

143 ARAN, f. 544, op. 1, d. 378, l. 90b; GAMO, f. 773, op. 1, d. 9, ll. 11, 283; Kossov and Kagan, "Severnyi gorno-khimicheskii trest 'Apatit' vo 2-m piatiletii," *KMK*, no. 3–4 (1932): 14–22; GAMO, f. 773, op. 1, d. 55, ll. 237–265; and GAMO, f. R-990, op. 1, d. 3, l. 19.

144 I tell the story of pollution in the Khibiny from nepheline's perspective in Andy Bruno, "How a Rock Remade the Soviet North: Nepheline in the Khibiny Mountains," in Nicholas Breyfogle, ed., *Eurasian Environments: Nature and Ecology in Eurasian History* (under consideration at University of Pittsburgh Press). On material wastes "biting back," see Zsuzsa Gille, *From the Cult of Waste to the Trash Heap of History: The Politics of Waste in Socialist and Postsocialist Hungary* (Bloomington: Indiana University Press, 2007).

145 GAMO, f. 773, op. 1, d. 51, ll. 88–90.

146 GAMO, f. 773, op. 1, d. 51, l. 92ob.

147 GAMO, f. 773, op. 1, d. 51, ll. 317–318.

the preliminary results of an ongoing government study, indicating that sewage water from the phosphorus factory had indeed reached Large Vud″iavr. Though the current levels seemed safe, the enterprise urgently needed to purify the industrial sewage from the phosphorus factory and add fluorine to the water, which could oxidize and stabilize phosphoric substances.[148] A sanitation inspector at the session also focused on dust from the enrichment and phosphorus factories. He claimed that these particles could cause tuberculosis and encouraged better ventilation of the work sites, concluding, "if we do not take sanitary measures, there will be poisoning."[149]

But the dominant voices at this meeting dismissed the seriousness of these issues. One obstreperous speaker, Isakov, complained that he was receiving calls day and night about phosphorus in the water and that "panic is already beginning to be felt" in the city. He blamed the local Society for Regional Studies for making an "unwarranted racket" about water quality and considered public discussion of this problem before the completion of testing to be "indecent" if not "politically disloyal." Isakov was also quick to rely on his own impressions to assuage concerns. "But in the meantime the drinking water from Vud″iavr in my opinion does not represent a danger in relation to poisoning. People not only have not been poisoned, but over the last two years our mortality rate has not increased."[150] The technical director of Apatit's enrichment factory employed a similar tactic to discount the consequences of air pollution, stating that he felt fine after four years there, including two years when no filters were being used.[151] Kondrikov agreed, noting that the dust-collecting filters that Apatit had installed were more effective than anticipated.

The enterprise manager also had the final word on the phosphine question, which he summarized as "perhaps something will happen" to the water supply. "Well, you know, perhaps the Kola Peninsula will collapse and we will not extract apatite then. Give figures. If we ourselves do not understand, then the issue needs to be put before an authoritative commission and not confessed to all gods, not confessed at all intersections. All analyses need to be checked thoroughly. Do not speak of an off-chance, because we will not give one kopeck for an off-chance."[152]

148 GAMO, f. 773, op. 1, d. 51, ll. 297–301.
149 GAMO, f. 773, op. 1, d. 51, ll. 276–278.
150 GAMO, f. 773, op. 1, d. 51, ll. 281–283.
151 GAMO, f. 773, op. 1, d. 51, l. 288.
152 GAMO, f. 773, op. 1, d. 51, ll. 305–310.

Kondrikov's cavalier use of uncertainty to avoid expenditures on environmental protection would make many contemporary business leaders proud. Though Apatit addressed pollution issues over the next few years by organizing more greening campaigns and reducing dust emissions from the enrichment facilities, it kept the phosphorus factory open.[153]

At the end of 1935 Kirovsk faced another challenge that prompted efforts to modify the alpine environment. Despite knowledge that snow avalanches occurred in the range, officials chose to erect apartment buildings right under Mount Iuksporr and to invest only meagerly in meteorological services. These decisions placed northern migrants at grave risk. On the night of December 5 a major avalanche from Mount Iuksporr destroyed two buildings, killing eighty-nine of the 249 individuals housed inside, including forty-six special settlers.[154] Several years later another avalanche took the lives of twenty-one miners. The bosses at the mine had failed to evacuate a workers' cafeteria near the mountains after wind speeds exceeded ten meters per second, as required by a protocol. Still in the crux of the Stalinist terror, attendees at a party meeting mentioned rumors circulating around that the Bolsheviks had intentionally killed people.[155]

Authorities reacted to the considerable loss of life with an invigorated "struggle with avalanches." The Apatit trust established a snow service, began to use controlled explosions to reduce the randomness of avalanches, instituted new safety requirements for mining work, and closed down its lovchorrite mine on Mount Iuksporr. The city allocated more money for stone buildings that could better withstand the tumbling snow and four-meter high walls to protect the settlements. Local scientific organizations established a permanent meteorological base on Iuksporr, held conferences to discuss the issue, researched the morphological dynamics of snow cover, and attempted to determine zones most prone to avalanches.[156] In the long run these adaptations and alterations made

153 GAMO, f. 773, op. 1, d. 52, l. 506; GAMO, f. 773, op. 1, d. 55, ll. 238, 241, 251, 256, 388ob, 442–443; and GAMO, f. 773, op. 1, d. 63, ll. 162–169.

154 *KDF*, 101–102 and S. N. Boldyrev, "Lavina s gory Iukspor," in G. I. Rakov, ed., *Khibinskie Klady: Vospominaniia veteranov osvoeniia Severa* (Leningrad: Lenizdat, 1972), 290–300.

155 GAMO, f. P-152, op. 1, d. IV, ll. 18–21.

156 ARAN, f. 544, op. 1, d. 334, ll. 1–6; ARAN, f. 544, op. 1, d. 335, ll. 1–22; ARAN, f. 544, op. 8, d. 388, ll. 1–2; GAMO, f. P-152, op. 1, d. IV, ll. 18–21; GAMO, f. 773, op. 1, d. 63, ll. 162–169; Barabanov and Kalinina, "*Apatit,*" 78; Belen'kii, "Iz istorii issledovaniia snega i lavin v khibinakh," in Zamotkin and Egorova, eds., *Priroda i khoziaistvo Severa*, vol. 2, part 2, 305–310; G. M. Rzhevskaia and B. N.

the Khibiny a safer place, though avalanches continued to occasionally wreak havoc, destroying equipment and injuring people.

On the whole the region became more livable for humans, vegetables, livestock, and bacterial pathogens and less livable for fish and forests during the 1930s. Pulverized particles and liquefied sludge from the mountains despoiled rivers and lakes as chemical substances and cascading snow threatened the population. But the frequently chaotic imposition of homes, farms, mines, and protective structures allowed the range to become a habitat for considerable numbers of *Homo sapiens* who lived with the whims of the polar north. Stalinism succeeded neither in surmounting the limits of the tundra nor in creating an ideal space for residents to find accord with nature, but it did manage to reorder the Khibiny environment into something unprecedented.

Linchpin for Development

These changes of the early 1930s not only altered the Khibiny. They also helped set the stage for a burst in industrial activity on the Kola Peninsula as a whole. If the Murmansk railroad further integrated the region nationally and internationally, phosphate production decisively showed that large-scale heavy industry was feasible in northwest Russia. From serving as an organizational hub for new ventures to rampantly expanding its output, Apatit provided a cornerstone for turning the Kola north into one of the most developed sections of the Arctic worldwide.

In the 1930s the population of the Kola Peninsula as a whole rose to almost 300,000, the fishing industry out of the Murmansk port grew sharply, the government established the Northern Fleet of the Soviet Navy on the Barents Sea, and the corridor along Lake Imandra became a center of mining, non-ferrous metallurgy, hydroelectricity, and chemical processing. Beyond modeling northern development for these subsequent endeavors, Apatit directly managed many of them in their early phases. It drew up plans for the future aluminum processing plant in Kandalaksha and coordinated the erection of hydroelectric power plants along the Niva and Tuloma rivers. Severonikel′ – the massive nickel mining and smelting combine on the west side of Lake Imandra – began as a side

Rzhevskii, "'Malye' rudniki tresta 'Apatit' kak popytka kompleksnogo osvoeniia mineral′nykh bogatst Khibin," in *Chetvertye Ushakovskie chteniia: Sbornik nauchnykh statei* (Murmansk: MGPU, 2007), 121; Andy Bruno, "Tumbling Snow: Vulnerability to Avalanches in the Soviet North," *EH* 18, no. 4 (October 2013): 683–709; and Iu. L. Ziuzin, *Khibinskaia laviniada* (Vologda: Poligraf-Kniga, 2009).

project of Apatit and the new firm Kol′stroi grew out of the trust's construction operations.[157] The ill-fated Vasilii Kondrikov personally spent time at the helm of most of these entities.

During the Stalinist state's violent conflagration of 1937–1938, extensive influence over a burgeoning industrial center became a deadly liability. The Great Terror turned the previously periodic purges of Communist Party members into a murderous witch-hunt to root out imagined conspiracies. Much of the leadership in industry, the military, and the government, along with groups of national minorities and former kulaks, became targeted as "counter-revolutionary" enemies.[158] Mirroring the inquisitional dynamics that occurred throughout the country, agents of the People's Commissariat of Internal Affairs (the NKVD, the successor organization of the OGPU) arrested and executed Kondrikov in 1937. He had faced denunciations for poor planning, immoral behavior, misusing his authority, and even for his enthusiasm for recycling nepheline wastes in aluminum production. Many other figures in the upper management of Apatit and on the Kirovsk City Council also lost their lives at the time.[159]

The company town endured another ordeal with World War II. Frequently bombed during the first couple of years of the conflict as the USSR almost fell to Germany, Kirovsk evacuated most of its population and much of its industrial infrastructure. Apatit turned to making chemical weapons for the Red Army.[160] Local authorities also conscripted the Khibiny lakes into the region's defensive strategy – not only ordering extra measures to preserve them during the war, but also using them as frozen landing pads in the winter.[161]

After the Soviet victory, as Apatit rebuilt its facilities and people moved back to Kirovsk, similar types of environmental problems from the 1930s

[157] A. A. Kiselev, *Rodnoe Zapoliar′e: Ocherki istorii Murmanskoi oblasti (1917–1972 gg.)* (Murmansk: Murmanskoe knizhnoe izdatel′stvo, 1974), 244–315 and Kossov and Kagan, "Severnyi gorno-khimicheskii trest 'Apatit' vo 2-m piatiletii," *KMK*, no. 3–4 (1932): 14–22.

[158] On the Stalinist terror, see J. Arch Getty, *The Road to Terror: Stalin and the Self-Destruction of the Bolsheviks* (New Haven: Yale University Press, 1999); Wendy Goldman, *Terror and Democracy in the Age of Stalin. The Social Dynamics of Repression* (Cambridge: Cambridge University Press, 2007); Paul Gregory, *Terror by Quota* (New Haven: Yale University Press, 2009); and David Shearer, *Policing Stalin's Socialism: Repression and Social Order in the Soviet Union, 1924–1953* (New Haven: Yale University Press, 2009).

[159] Tararaksin, *Sudeb sgorevshikh ochertan′e*, 81–90 and *KDF*, 104–105.

[160] Slightly over 10,000 people lived in the region after the evacuation. *KDF*, 203–208, 212–225.

[161] *KDF*, 199–200, 202.

struck again. Contaminated water and air posed direct threats to people's health. Nazi air attacks had destroyed much of the city's sewage infrastructure and rebuilding it took a backseat to restoring production to pre-war levels. By 1948 purification equipment had still not been reinstalled and "sewage without preliminary treatment drained into the waterways not used for drinking."[162] Wastewater from Apatit's enrichment factory still only underwent a process of clarification, using coagulants to lump substances together and then pouring the water through basic filters into the White River, rather than more comprehensive treatment. In 1957 the company finally opened its first tailing dump to divert some of the contaminated water.[163] Dust also continued to cause respiratory diseases and other ailments among miners and residents living near the enrichment factory. Even after the replacement of malfunctioning electro-filters and other measures reduced dust emissions from 58.5 tons a day in 1954 to 4.4 tons a day in 1961, people living near the enrichment facility fell ill at considerably higher rates. A journalist in *Polar Pravda* declared, "the air in Kirovsk is highly polluted" at this point.[164] Glossing over the objections raised in the early debates about the urban layout, the director of Apatit now claimed, "the necessary sanitary-defense zone for the Apatit combine had not been foreseen when working out the general plan for the city of Kirovsk in 1930."[165]

Acknowledging constraints embedded in the Stalinist model of developing the Khibiny, enterprise leaders turned to new strategies for expanding industrial activities in the region after the dictator's death. Apatit started opening additional mines, built new enrichment facilities outside of the cramped mountain valley, and supported the creation of a new

[162] GARF f. A-482, op. 47, d. 7670, l. 15. On the acute sewage problems in postwar Soviet cities, see Donald Filtzer, "Standard of Living versus Quality of Life: Struggling with the Urban Environment in Russia During the Early Years of Postwar Reconstruction," in Juliane Fürst, ed., *Late Stalinist Russia: Society Between Reconstruction and Reinvention* (London: Routledge, 2006), 81–102 and Donald Filtzer, *The Hazards of Urban Life in Late Stalinist Russia: Health, Hygiene, and Living Standards, 1943–1953* (Cambridge: Cambridge University Press, 2010).

[163] GARF f. A-482, op. 49, d. 7243, l. 130 and G. S. Goppen, "Sostoianie okruzhaiushchei prirodnoi sredy v Khibinskom rudnom raione Murmanskoi oblasti," in A. I. Nikolaev, ed., *Kompleksnost′ ispol′zovaniia mineral′no-syr′evyx resursov: osnova povysheniia ekologicheskoi besopasnosti regiona* (Apatity: KNTs AN, 2005), 108.

[164] "Vtoraia sessiia oblastnogo soveta deputatov trudiashchikhsia: Okhrana prirody – delo gosudarstvennogo znaheniia," *PP* (June 18, 1961): 2.

[165] GARF f. A-482, op. 50, d. 6178, ll. 47–52; GARF f. A-482, op. 47, d. 7670, ll. 24, 31; and GARF f. A-482, op. 49, d. 7243, l. 125.

town called Apatity.[166] Officially established in 1966 and located just southwest of the range along the mainline railroad, Apatity enjoyed a considerably milder climate than Kirovsk. It also became a much larger town, while managing to maintain forested areas within the city.[167] Instead of outright coercion, financial incentives now enticed increasing numbers of individuals to the north.[168] This revised urban and economic planning led to an astronomical growth in production. By the mid-1960s, Apatit was mining as much ore and enriching as much apatite concentrate annually as it had during all of the 1930s. It was on the path to more than doubling that output over the subsequent decade (see Table 1).

With industrial expansion, residents of the Khibiny region developed new ways of understanding their relationship to the natural world. As sociologist Alla Bolotova shows, people living in Kirovsk and Apatity did not simply imbibe Soviet discourses of subjugating the tundra. Instead, many came to view "nature" as a distinctive "taskscape" of recreation. Relying on the theories of Tim Ingold, Bolotova defines a taskscape as a space through which the "predominant type of activity in a territory with expressed goals and objectives strongly influences one's perception of the surrounding environment." For city residents in the Khibiny, "the area beyond the urban territory and the industrial zone" became "primarily a space for leisure." They often preferred recreation "connected with staying out of town: skiing during winter time, barbequing beginning in the spring, hiking in the hills and mountains, visiting summer houses (dacha), picking mushrooms and berries, hunting and fishing."[169] Increasingly in the 1960s and 1970s tourists joined in treating the mountains as a space for outdoor adventures. Kirovsk became one of the more prominent centers of downhill skiing in the USSR, attracting thousands of visitors every year.

The enterprise also tried to address some environmental problems with new abatement technologies or by simply moving industrial activities into

166 RGAE, f. 4372, op. 62, d. 565, ll. 1–7, 44, 171 and RGAE, f. 4372, op. 67, d. 1961, ll. 1–3, 18, 59–63,112–119.

167 Bolotova, "Loving and Conquering Nature," *Europe-Asia Studies* 64, no. 4 (June 2012): 654 and "Vvodnyi ocherk," in Kiselev, ed., *Kol'skii entsiklopediia*, vol. 1, 72.

168 A. L. Epshtein, *L'goty dlia rabotnikov Krainego Severa* (Moscow: "Iuridicheskaia literatura," 1968) and L. Ia. Gintsburg and N. M. Smirnova, *L'goty rabotaiushchim na Krainem Severe* (Moscow: "Iuridicheskaia literatura," 1975).

169 Bolotova, "Loving and Conquering Nature," *Europe-Asia Studies* 64, no. 4 (June 2012): 649, 662. On taskscapes, see Tim Ingold, *The Perception of the Environment: Essays in Livelihood, Dwelling, and Skill* (London: Routledge, 2000).

TABLE 1. *Reported Production Output from Apatit (in 1,000 Tons)*

Year	Ore Mined	Apatite Concentrate	Nepheline Concentrate
1930	250		
1931	416	18	
1932	385	157	
1933	687	213	
1934	1,117	400	
1935	1,600	768	
1936	2,001	1,049	
1937	2,121	1,157	4
1938	2,303	1,300	
1939	2,627	1,460	
1944	290	160	
1948	1,861	980	8
1949	2,342	1,198	32
1950	2,856	1,482	52
1951	3,463	1,674	92
1952	3,762	1,849	99
1953	3,850	1,826	151
1954	4,483	2,293	127
1955	5,315	2,632	173
1960	8,510	3,826	624
1961	9,349	4,156	815
1962	10,215	4,479	950
1963	11,310	4,634	1,045
1964	15,941	6,377	1,082
1965	19,078	7,576	1,090
1976	40,200	15,212	1,502
1977	41,600	15,818	1,581
1978	42,300	15,962	1,595
1979	43,060	16,003	1,600
1980	46,400	17,359	1,630
1986	54,591	19,300	1,500
1987	55,404	19,500	1,600
1988	56,200	20,400	1,640
1991	49,500	15,500	239

Note: Some of these figures were given as "more than" or "up to." They should only be used to capture the general trend and not as an entirely accurate reflection of output. PhosAgro, the company that now owns Apatit, claims that between 1929 and 2013 more than 1.86 billion tons of ore, 649 million tons of apatite concentrate, and 66.8 million tons of nepheline concentrate have been produced in the Khibiny. "OAO 'Apatit'," PhosAgro, accessed June 2, 2014, www.phosagro.ru/about/holding/item49.php#tab-activity-link.

Sources: A. V. Barabanov, et al., *Gigant v Khibinakh: Istoriia otkrytogo aktsionernogo obshchestva "Apatit" (1929–1999)* (Moscow: Izdatel′skii dom "Ruda i metally," 1999), 44–66, 74, 78–82, 102, 173, 192, 193, 201, 213; P. V. Vladimirov and N. S. Morev, *Apatitovyi rudnik im. S. M. Kirova* (Leningrad: Seriia izdatel′stva po khibinskoi apatitovoi probleme, 1936), 3–4; and *KDF*, 119.

new locations.[170] These decisions amounted to a tacit acceptance that the initial hopes for arranging optimal relations between people and nature in the Khibiny had not come to fruition. Apatit further upgraded its gas purifiers and tailing dumps in the 1960s, though these measures did not always prove effective.[171] It later introduced a system of using recycled water in enrichment, which entailed making an economic sacrifice for the environment. The new process extracted slightly less of the active ingredient in phosphate fertilizers, but it reduced freshwater intake and cut wastewater dumping.[172] In the late 1970s, Apatit admitted that the air and water emissions from the initial enrichment factory in Kirovsk were "incompatible with active legislation on nature protection" and decided to shut down this "morally and physically out-of-date" unit. According to the director, the mountain relief of the Khibiny made it practically impossible to update the facility.[173]

Nevertheless, environmental threats from the mounting scale of production at Apatit outpaced the effects of these closures, relocations, and technologies. As the years passed, there were more tailings to divert, more dust and gases to capture, deeper cuts into the mountains, and larger rock piles near the mines. All of this activity increased the size of the industrial landscape in the Khibiny region to well over fifty square kilometers in area.[174] The deployment of martial metaphors against polluters in the local party newspaper, which published an article declaring that "the dumping of industrial enterprises is a serious enemy" of Kola waterways, did little to improve the situation.[175] In the late 1970s the company divulged that "all remaining surface waters" besides Lake Imandra "are unsuitable for the water supply, since they are polluted with discharged wastewater."[176] On top of that even a section of Lake Imandra – the White Bay – had already accumulated a nepheline-rich layer sediment up

170 GARF f. A-482, op. 54, d. 5009, ll. 51–52 and GARF f. A-482, op. 54, d. 350, l. 57.

171 GARF f. A-482, op. 54, d. 350, ll. 46–48, 52, 54–55; RGAE, f. 4372, op. 62, d. 565, ll. 12–14; and GARF f. A-482, op. 54, d. 5009, ll. 48–50.

172 RGAE, f. 4372, op. 67, d. 1961, ll. 123, 163–166 and P. A. Markov, "Prirodokhrannaia deiatel′nost′ OAO 'Apatit'," in Nikolaev, ed., *Kompleksnost′ ispol′zovaniia mineral′no-syr′evyx resursov*, 17–21.

173 RGAE, f. 4372, op. 67, d. 1961, ll. 81–82, 175.

174 Olga Rigina, "Environmental Impact Assessment of the Mining and Concentration Activities in the Kola Peninsula, Russia by Multidate Remote Sensing," *Environmental Monitoring and Assessment* 75, no. 1 (April 2002): 18–19.

175 N. Aleinikov and A. Smirov, "Problemy and mneniia. 'Apatit' i Imandra. Chto nuzhno dlia dobrogo sosedstva," *PP* (September 4, 1973): 2.

176 RGAE, f. 4372, op. 67, d. 1961, l. 180.

to eight meters deep, which reduced the transparency of the water and harmed the fish and native zooplankton there. One cause of the pollution in Imandra was the failure of nepheline reprocessing to keep pace with the explosion in mining and apatite enrichment. Without reuse in the aluminum industry, this mining waste either spoiled waterways or ended up in the rapidly expanding and filling tailing dumps, which came to pose a toxic threat themselves.[177]

As a springboard of massive industrial growth throughout the Kola north, the Khibiny faced continual change to its natural surroundings in the second half of the twentieth century. The environmental effects of late socialist productionism ultimately overshadowed the optimistically aggressive intrusion of the Stalin era. In a sense environmental problems that more robustly challenged the integrity of the non-human world supplanted ones that more immediately threatened people's health. Similar shifts occurred in the nickel industry, while reindeer farms deep in the tundra witnessed their own dramatic expansion in the post-Stalin period. To put the changes of latter part of the twentieth century in another way, a Soviet ecosystem replaced a Stalinist one.

177 Rigina, "Environmental Impact Assessment of the Mining and Concentration Activities in the Kola Peninsula, Russia by Multidate Remote Sensing," *Environmental Monitoring and Assessment* 75, no. 1 (April 2002): 11–31. Ze′ev Vol′fson's *samizdat* exposé of Soviet environmental problems discussed the issue of nepheline tailings being dumped into Lake Imandra. Boris Komarov [Ze′ev Vol′fson], *The Destruction of Nature in the Soviet Union* (White Plains: M. E. Sharpe, 1980), 93.

4

Deep in the Tundra

In the height of Nikita Khrushchev's Thaw, Vladimir Charnoluskii at last returned to the Kola north. Like many others involved in remaking the region, this expert on Sami folklore and the Kola reindeer economy had endured years of state repression. But unlike many who were less fortunate, he survived a stint in the Gulag and lived long enough to return to his early academic passion in retirement. The Kola Peninsula he visited in 1961 was already vastly different than the one he first traveled to as a young ethnographer in the 1920s.[1] Towns and factories now filled a thoroughly Soviet landscape. Even wayfaring reindeer had undergone a revolution.

On the trip Charnoluskii journeyed to the Lapland Nature Reserve – a protected territory dedicated to preserving wild reindeer. Not long before the Kola Sami had mostly hunted reindeer instead of herding them. Indeed, this not-too-distant past was part of what attracted him to the Lapland Nature Reserve. "It was impossible to shake off the idea that it is precisely here that wild reindeer, its lifestyle, and the legends about it in Sami consciousness should be preserved in inviolability."[2] Yet only a few Sami lived on the reserve to convey such cultural knowledge to Charnoluskii. In fact, Sami herders at the Krasnoe Pulozero collective

[1] For background on Charnoluskii's biography, see O. V. Shabalina, "Iz istorii entografich-eskikh issledovanii V. V. Charnoluskogo: Risunki i pis'ma uchenogo iz fonda muzeia-arkhiva TsGP RAN," in V. P. Petrov and I. A. Razumova, eds., *Regional'noe soobshch-estvo v period sotsial'nykh transformatsii: Kol'skii Sever, nachalo XXI veka: Spornik statei* (Apatity: Kol'skii nauchnyi tsentr Rossiisskoi Akademii nauk, 2007), 146–170.

[2] V. V. Charnoluskii, *V kraiu letuchego kamnia* (Moscow: Izdatel'stvo "Mysl'," 1972), 107.

farm were the main group of suspected poachers being excluded at the time. What had caused the isolation of these "reindeer people" from the wild creatures that they had once preyed upon? Moreover, what had even turned them into practitioners of large-scale herding of domestic reindeer to begin with?

To answer these questions requires looking at the depth of Soviet changes in the far north. At the same time that heavy industrial enterprises like Apatit and cities like Kirovsk and Apatity increasingly infiltrated the Kola Peninsula, the populations of both wild and domestic reindeer boomed. At first glance, it might seem odd that building up the north included accentuating a pastoralist economic activity while protecting wildlife. After all, many scholars depict conservation and nomadism as anathema to Stalinist planners. At second glance, it is even weirder. For contrary to common assumptions, reindeer herding on the Kola Peninsula was neither a remnant of a pre-modern past nor a tradition destroyed by state interference. Instead, the USSR helped turn the territory into a center of "industrial" or "socialist" reindeer husbandry. Most indigenous peoples on this land had hitherto practiced a mixed economy of hunting, fishing, and small-scale husbandry instead of large-scale herding.[3] Deploying monoculture as a technology of rule, authorities used reindeer to reorganize the rural economy and reorder ethnic relations among non-Russian communities. I argue that this tactic of promoting reindeer helped extend Soviet power into the furthest reaches of the peninsula's taiga and tundra lands.

The Soviet elevation of reindeer depended on diverse forms of ecological knowledge. Overarching economic conceptions of the natural world as something variably to assimilate, dominate, conquer, and harmonize found expression in opposing ways of understanding animals and their habitats. In particular, some reformers embraced a more heavy-handed strand of Soviet thinking about the environment as they sought to make ethnic, economic, and ecological complexities "legible" by prioritizing reindeer. Yet others adopted a seemingly more accommodating perspective as they drew on more intimate sentience for comprehending the

[3] The impact of the Soviet modernization drive on indigenous peoples has been astutely discussed in, among other works, Yuri Slezkine, *Arctic Mirrors: Russia and the Small Peoples of the North* (Ithaca: Cornell University Press, 1994) and Bruce Grant, *In the Soviet House of Culture: A Century of Perestroikas* (Princeton: Princeton University Press, 1995). For a historical overview of northern peoples, see James Forsyth, *A History of the Peoples of Siberia: Russia's North Asian Colony 1581–1990* (Cambridge: Cambridge University Press, 1992).

animal's place in the Kola landscape. Collectively both forms of knowledge contributed to an environmental outcome in which reindeer herds grew in number and prominence.

As James Scott defines it, legibility is a tool for states to manipulate societies and nature. Legible knowledge functions through standardizing, simplifying, classifying, abstracting, and making "rational" thorny and irreducible phenomena, thereby enabling state management and control. Scott cites the careful cultivation of timber forests, the creation of large reservoirs for dams, and the use of monoculture in farming as environmental examples of modern governments around the world relying on legible knowledge.[4] Scientists, state agents, and rural residents offered similar pragmatic information to help reform the most distant outreaches of the Kola Peninsula. During the decades of Soviet rule, they used this knowledge to establish reindeer-herding collective farms, open a nature reserve to protect wild reindeer, promote techniques of certain ethnic groups over others, focus the livelihoods of minorities on venison production, and consolidate numerous collective farms into a few state farms. Though the uniform and rigid frameworks that they imposed distorted messy realities, such legibility provided space for reindeer in an industrial Arctic.

In contrast to legibility, sentient ecological knowledge involves understanding specific animals and environments through practical, communicative, and tactical interaction. David Anderson develops this concept in his ethnography of Evenki reindeer herders who "act and move on the tundra in such a way that they are conscious that animals and the tundra itself are reacting to them."[5] Expanding on Anderson's theory,

[4] James Scott, *Seeing Like a State: How Certain Schemes to Improve Human Condition Have Failed* (New Haven: Yale University Press, 1998). In a similar vein, Mark Nuttall notes how people throughout the Arctic have faced "common experiences" with "how various capitalist and socialist states claimed control over their lands and animals" through resource-use policies, wildlife management, and political and economic interventions to cultivate northern landscapes. Mark Nuttall, "Epilogue: Cultivating Arctic Landscapes," in David G. Anderson and Mark Nuttall, eds., *Cultivating Arctic Landscapes: Knowing and Managing Animals in the Circumpolar North* (New York: Berghahn Books, 2004), 200.

[5] David G. Anderson, *Identity and Ecology in Arctic Siberia: The Number One Reindeer Brigade* (Oxford: Oxford University Press, 2002), 116. In another work on the Evenki, Nikolai Ssorin-Chaikov highlights the complexities of their relationship with the state throughout history. Like Anderson, he shows how a lot more has occurred in on-the-ground interactions than the imposition of simplified abstractions from central authorities. Nikolai V. Ssorin-Chaikov, *The Social Life of the State in Subarctic Siberia* (Stanford: Stanford University Press, 2003).

Tim Ingold discusses sentient ecology as "knowledge not of a formal, authorized kind, transmissible in contexts outside those of its practical application. On the contrary, it is based in feeling, consisting of the skills, sensitivities and orientations that have developed through long experience of conducting one's life in a particular environment."[6] Such ecological intuition allowed people in close contact with reindeer to engage with the animals as living beings with which they held reciprocal relations. Referring to Komi and Nenets pastoralism, anthropologists Kirill Istomin and Mark Dwyer show that reindeer and herders undergo "mutual behavioral adaptations" as they learn to respond to changes in the other species.[7] Reindeer's capacity for sentience means that they did more than enable, confine, inspire, and shape economic activities in the region, as inanimate substances such as snow and apatite and climatic phenomena such as wind and cold temperatures did. The ungulates also reacted to schemes to manage them through deliberate behaviors of both compliance and evasion.

Not only pastoral communities and northern wildlife shared in this sentient ecology. State reformers and scientists also benefited from practical experiences, intimate interactions, and intangible understandings that informed their efforts to transform the Kola reindeer economy.[8] They grew aware of ethnic distinctions in herding techniques by spending time with Sami, Komi, Nenets, and Russians in the tundra. Encountering social and environmental challenges when organizing collective farms, party activists unleashed recently attained know-how to find solutions. Conservation scientists fused indigenous insights into their knowledge about wild reindeer and developed passionate commitments to this particular creature based on their own personal experiences. For instance, Oleg Semenov-Tian-Shanskii – the botanist who hosted Charnoluskii at the Lapland Nature Reserve in 1961 – felt deeply attached to the animals. When advocating tough hunting restrictions to limit the time of the year

[6] Tim Ingold, *The Perception of the Environment: Essays in Livelihood, Dwelling, and Skill* (London: Routledge, 2000), 25.

[7] Kirill Istomin and Mark Dwyer, "Dynamic Mutual Adaptation: Human-Animal Interaction in Reindeer Herding Pastoralism," *Human Ecology* 38, no. 5 (October 2010): 613–623. Also see Hugh Beach and Florian Stammler, "Human-Animal Relations in Pastoralism," *Nomadic Peoples* 10, no. 2 (2006): 6–30 and Anderson and Nuttall, eds., *Cultivating Arctic Landscapes.*

[8] My argument here therefore resonates with Fernando Coronil's rejoinder to Scott. "States embody both the abstract logic Scott associates with high modernism and also the practical knowledge he identifies with *metis.*" Fernando Coronil, "Smelling Like a Market," *American Historical Review* 106, no. 1 (February 2001): 127.

wild reindeer could be pursued, he went beyond abstractly stressing the reproductive cycle of the species and decried shooting calves during their third trimester of pregnancy as outright "barbarism."[9]

This story of how Kola reindeer became Soviet traverses the twists and turns in the animal's fate over the long haul. It starts well before the revolution when migrants from the Pechora River basin uprooted the reindeer economy on the Kola Peninsula and helped set off contentious discussions about nationality and agriculture in the pre-Soviet north. These debates changed dramatically in the 1920s and 1930s when proponents of promoting ethnic minorities, advocates for modernizing agriculture, and conservation ecologists clashed over the question of what to do with the region's reindeer population. The turbulent and sometimes violent resolution to this conflict involved embracing Komi herding practices while labeling them as Sami and, more importantly, Soviet. Soon afterwards, the successful rehabilitation of wild reindeer eventually came to loggerheads with the interests of collectivized herders. This tension played into the forced relocation of animals and herding communities into two consolidated centers of Kola reindeer husbandry in the 1960s and 1970s. Despite its relatively recent origin in the region and the drastic changes it experienced since that time, Kola reindeer herding increasingly became imagined as a traditional livelihood of the Sami in the late Soviet and post-Soviet periods. Though a potent source of political capital for Kola Sami today, this neo-traditionalism often glosses over the ways that the Soviet era more thoroughly entrenched a herding economy into the region in the first place. With the loss of Soviet state backing, Kola reindeer husbandry in many ways has been in decline since the 1990s.

Pastoralism Arrives

Reindeer have been some of the most prominent mammalian megafauna on the Kola Peninsula for millennia. Numbering in the millions in the circumpolar Arctic, reindeer (*Rangifer taranda*) (or caribou as they are known in North America) are medium-sized creatures with dense furs and seasonal antlers. They possess strong shovel-like hoofs that can dig deeply into the snow to reach the smallest quantities of vegetation, often lichens and mosses growing on the rocky Arctic landscape. Reindeer also instinctively form migrating herds, which offer them protection from predators and the capacity to traverse tremendous distances to take advantage of

[9] GARF, f. A-358, op. 4, d. 1521, ll. 83–89.

sparse pastures of northern flora. As glacial sheets retreated at the end of the last Ice Age, reindeer migrated from the heartland of Eurasia and North America into their northern edges. They might have begun arriving on the Kola Peninsula sometime around 9000 BCE as early human hunters, the Komsa, followed the animals there.[10]

The ancestors of a group that came to be called the Sami (Laplanders and Lapps in earlier terminology) likely first arrived in the region sometime after 2000 BCE, though some have argued that they descended from earlier inhabitants. These Sami spoke dialects of a Finno-Ugric language common to a number of other, more populous, groups of Sami in northern Scandinavia. For much of their history the economy of both the Sami and the Pomors – the Slavic-speakers who inhabited the Tersk coast as far back as the thirteenth century – focused predominantly on fishing. Both groups also hunted wild reindeer and kept limited numbers of domesticated draft animals as subsidiary activities. Due partially to their inland orientation, the Sami allocated reindeer a more significant place in their culture and spiritual beliefs than the Pomors. The imperatives of reindeer hunting also shaped the Sami system of territorial organization. Loosely defined *pogosty* (parishes) often included different seasonal settlements for kin groups and incorporated areas officially belonging to the Orthodox Church and imperial government.[11]

Reindeer domestication depended on intimate understandings of the animal and positive responses of reindeer to the protection offered by humans. Northern communities throughout Eurasia first invented methods for training individual wild reindeer for transportation, milk, and as hunting decoys. They do not seem to have relied on much selective breeding, as often occurred in the domestication of other animals. Instead, their training gradually led the reindeer to modify their behavior and become more willing to interact with humans. In the seventeenth and eighteenth centuries, some groups began manipulating the grazing, migration, and reproduction patterns of entire herds, thereby providing the basis for

[10] Piers Vitebsky, *Reindeer People: Living with Animals and Spirits in Siberia* (London: HarperCollins Publishers, 2005), 17–39; Igor Krupnik, *Arctic Adaptations: Native Whalers and Reindeer Herders of Northern Eurasia*, trans. and ed. Marcia Levenson (Hanover: University Press of New England, 1993), 86–127, 160–185; and John McCannon, *A History of the Arctic: Nature, Exploration, and Exploitation* (London: Reaktion Books, 2012), 40–48.

[11] I. F. Ushakov, *Izbrannye proizvedeniia: Tom 1: Kol'skaia zemlia* (Murmansk: Murmanskoe knizhnoe izdatel'stvo, 1997), 29–165 and I. F. Ushakov and S. N. Dashchinskii, *Lovozero* (Murmansk: Murmanskoe knizhnoe izdatel'stvo, 1988), 40.

pastoralism (reindeer herding). Those tending to reindeer adapted more nomadic lifestyles to accommodate the abiding herding instinct of the domesticated animals.[12]

In the late nineteenth century, the Kola Sami still relied more on fishing and hunting wild reindeer than on harvesting the products of domestic reindeer. This sustenance pattern put them in notable contrast to Sami populations in northern Norway, Sweden, and Finland, which already possessed a well-developed herding economy.[13] Ethnographer Nikolai Kharuzin reported that a dwindling stock of wild reindeer on the Kola Peninsula was causing a decline in the hunting economy at the time. "[F]inding wild reindeer now is extremely rare," he noted, adding that "not only the Lapps but also the Russian residents unanimously say that the Lapps are becoming poor in reindeer." In response to these resource limitations, the Kola Sami had already begun to increase the numbers of the domestic reindeer they kept after the 1860s.[14] But they still organized their herding as to allow time for fishing and to take advantage of other opportunities for sustenance. Most Kola Sami families kept only about fifteen to nineteen reindeer. They would release them for grazing in the summer and collect them again in the fall. Migration patterns varied considerably between the western and eastern sides of the peninsula, in part because of topographic differences.[15]

Wild reindeer held deep spiritual significance for the Kola Sami in this era. Though Sami communities nominally had converted to Orthodox

[12] Vitebsky, *Reindeer People*, 17–39; Krupnik, *Arctic Adaptations*, 160–184; Ingold, *The Perception of the Environment*, 61–76; and Robert Paine, "Animals as Capital: Comparisons among Northern Nomadic Herders and Hunters," *Anthropological Quarterly* 44, no. 3 (July 1971): 152–172.

[13] Tim Ingold, *Hunters, Pastoralists and Ranchers: Reindeer Economies and Their Transformations* (Cambridge: Cambridge University Press, 1980).

[14] Nikolai Kharuzin, *Russkie lopari (Ocherki proshlago i sovremennago byta)* (Moscow: Izvestiia imperatorskago obshchestva liubitelei estestvoznaniia, antropologii i etnografii, 1890), 105, 108–109, 101–120. Nathaniel Knight demonstrates how Kharuzin became one of the first Russian ethnographers to embrace evolutionist theory in his scholarship. However, this monograph on the Kola Sami fit more with an earlier framework of Russian ethnography: one that concentrated on gathering and systematizing information about peoples without the application of theory. See Nathaniel Knight, "Nikolai Kharuzin and the Quest for a Universal Human Science," *Kritika* 9, no. 1 (Winter 2008): 83–111.

[15] T. V. Luk′ianchenko, *Material′naia kul′tura saamov (loparei) Kol′skogo poluostrova v kontse XIX–XX v.* (Moscow: Izdatel′stvo "Nauka," 1971), 31–32 and Robert P. Wheelersburg and Natalia Gutsol, "Babinski and Ekostrovski: Saami Pogosty on the Western Kola Peninsula, Russia from 1880 to 1940," *Arctic Anthropology* 45, no. 1 (2008): 81.

Christianity centuries earlier and regularly attended church services in the late nineteenth century, they still held religious beliefs in shamans, sorcerers, rock formations, and animal spirits.[16] One of their rituals involved sacrificing wild reindeer under the direction of village sorcerers and displaying the animals' horns on the roofs of their dwellings.[17] Additionally, legends of a man-reindeer called Miandash who traversed between human and non-human worlds circulated among the Kola Sami. These stories drew on Miandash's ability to transform from a wild reindeer into a human and associated separate lands of the Sami and reindeer with the realms of the living and the dead.[18] Among other things, such reindeer-centric myths and rituals reflected Sami awareness of the active role of these creatures in their lives.

Across the Arkhangel′sk province in the Pechora River basin, a very different reindeer economy and ecology existed among the Komi. Nenets (or Samoedy) pastoralists in the region began to keep large numbers of reindeer comparatively early and taught herding to the Komi-Izhemtsy (hereafter Komi) migrants of the sixteenth century.[19] Having actively collected and traded furs with Russian merchants, these Komi embraced market-oriented economic practices in their reindeer herding. Well-off Komi maintained massive herds, hired other herders, profited from selling reindeer products to traders, and managed a total of close to twenty times the number of domestic reindeer as the Sami. Their reindeer also roamed around in a different way. Unlike the Kola ungulates, which lived on a confined and significantly forested peninsular environment, reindeer in the Pechora-Izhma River basin traversed hundreds of kilometers in the

[16] Edward Rae, *The White Sea Peninsula: A Journey in Russian Lapland and Karelia* (London: John Murray, 1881), 262–277; Kharuzin, *Russkie lopari*, 235–236; and Veli-Pekka Lehtola, *The Sámi People: Traditions in Transition* (Fairbanks: University of Alaska Press, 2004), 29.

[17] N. N. Volkov, *The Russian Sami: Historical-Ethnographic Essays*, eds. Lars-Nila Lasko and Chuner Taksami (Kautokeino: Nordic Sami Institute, 1996), 95–107 and Kharuzin, *Russkie lopari*, 182–190, 214–236.

[18] Enn Ernits, "Folktales of Meandash, the Mythic Sami Reindeer: Part 1," *Folklore: Electronic Journal of Folklore* 11 (October 1999): 31; Enn Ernits, "Folktales of Meandash, the Mythic Sami Reindeer: Part 2," *Folklore: Electronic Journal of Folklore* 13 (May 2000): 66–92; V. V. Charnoluskii, *Legenda o olene-cheloveke* (Moscow: Izdatel′stvo "Nauka," 1965); and V. I. Nemirovich-Danchenko, *Strana kholoda* (Saint Petersburg/Moscow: Izdanie knigoprodavtsa-tipografa M. O. Vol′fa, 1877), 208–209.

[19] I am usually translating references to the Izhemtsy in my primary sources as Komi here. The Izhemtsy are a small subgroup of Komi, which included those who migrated to the Kola Peninsula. I am doing so for the sake of readability. This practice differs from how I refer to the Sami and Nenets. For them I keep the words Lapp and Samoed when they appear in a primary source.

expansive tundra every year. Komi herders also played a more intensive protective role than the Kola Sami; they guarded the animals during every season, including while the reindeer grazed in the summer. Large-scale herding also led to mounting environmental pressures such as the crowding of lichen pastures and outbreaks of epizootics. Faced with these hurdles, several Komi started searching for new lands to occupy.[20]

In the 1880s a group of Komi from Izhma moved to the Kola Peninsula. Suffering from a decline in their herds at the time, they had learned of abundant lichen pastures and a lack of reindeer disease there. According to anthropologist Nikolai Konakov, Komi migrants tended to seek similar environments that could support the basis of their current economic complex. The Kola Peninsula only partially fitted this model because of its distance and detachment from other Komi lands and its different climate. These features dissuaded most pastoralists with smaller herds from making the trek. Yet two wealthier herders, Ivan Terent′ev and Polikarp Rochev, provided several thousand domestic reindeer for a group of sixty-five individuals, including several Nenets herders, to resettle. They set out from the Pechora-Izhma River basin in the autumn of 1883 and arrived the following spring. After a few itinerant years checking out different parts of the Kola Peninsula, the Komi and Nenets families settled in the small Sami settlement of Lovozero. A large anthrax outbreak in 1896 among reindeer on the Komi homelands compelled more families to join the migrant herders.[21]

The Komi brought their large-scale reindeer pastoralism with them to the Kola Peninsula. Their arrival alone dramatically increased the quantity of domestic reindeer there. Furthermore, the herding they did resulted in an over sevenfold growth in the domestic reindeer population in the region by World War I. Komi pastoralists continued to employ many of their conventional herding methods, some of which conflicted with Sami practice. In particular, the Sami preference to release reindeer in the

[20] Joachim Otto Habeck, *What it Means to Be a Herdsman: The Practice and Image of Reindeer Husbandry among the Komi of Northern Russia* (Münster: LIT Verlag, 2005), 63–68; N. P. Isaeva, "K izucheniiu protsessov adaptatsii izhemskikh komi na Kol′skom severe," in V. P. Petrov and I. A. Razumova, eds., *Severiane: Problemy sotsiokul′turnoi adaptatsii zhitelei Kol′skogo poluostrova* (Apatity: Kol′skii nauchnyi tsentr Rossiisskoi Akademii nauk, 2006), 42; and N. D. Konakov, "Ecological Adaptation of Komi Resettled Groups," *Arctic Anthropology* 30, no. 2 (1993): 97.

[21] Konakov, "Ecological Adaptation of Komi Resettled Groups," *Arctic Anthropology* 30, no. 2 (1993): 92–102 and Isaeva, "K izucheniiu protsessov adaptatsii izhemskikh komi na Kol′skom severe," in Petrov and Razumova, eds., *Severiane*, 42–47.

summer contrasted with the year-round surveillance of the Komi.[22] Antagonism between the groups grew especially tense as some Sami accused Komi of stealing free-grazing Sami reindeer and branding them with their own earmarks. Sami also opposed the Komi use of lichen pastures that they had intentionally set aside in reserve.[23]

Confronted with competition from the Komi and the disappearing population of wild reindeer available for hunting, some groups of Sami altered their own herding practices. They began to keep much larger numbers of animals, to construct fences during summer grazing, and to more vigilantly attempt to round up all their animals before the autumn rut.[24] These changes marked a shift among the Kola Sami to pastoralism. It should be noted that the state played hardly any role in this pre-Soviet transformation of the Kola reindeer economy, which instead relied on northern communities using their knowledge of shifting ecological conditions to adapt. But even with these changes, one researcher still claimed on the eve of the First World War that the "Lapps of the Kola Peninsula" were "not reindeer herders in the true sense of the word."[25]

Late Imperial Debates

Tsarist officials, scientists, journalists, and regional enthusiasts centered in other parts of the Arkhangel′sk province responded to the evolving reindeer economies of the Sami, Komi, Nenets, and Pomor with divergent proposals for reform. They filtered many of their ideas about the animal's future role in tundra and taiga ecosystems through the lens of nationality. Some more technocratic commentators in the final decades of the Russian empire fantasized about the potential to expand reindeer husbandry based on Komi methods. Other writers echoed Slavophile sentiments and pined

22 N. N. Gutsol, S. N. Vinogradova, and A. G. Samorukova, *Pereselenie gruppy kol′skikh saamov* (Apatity: Kol′skii nauchnyi tsentr Rossiisskoi Akademii nauk, 2007), 24–25; Konakov, "Ecological Adaptation of Komi Resettled Groups," *Arctic Anthropology* 30, no. 2 (1993): 98–99; I. Budovnits, *Olenevodcheskie kolkhozy kol′skogo poluostrova* (Moscow/Leningrad: Gosudarstvennoe izdatel′stvo sel′skokhoziaistvennoi i kolkhozno-kooperativnoi literatury, 1931), 10–11; and Isaeva, "K izucheniiu protsessov adaptatsii izhemskikh komi na Kol′skom severe," in Petrov and Razumova, eds., *Severiane*, 44.

23 V-r, "Iz oblasti olenevodstva," *IAOIRS* 1, no. 7 (August 15, 1909): 45–47 and Ushakov and Dashchinskii, *Lovozero*, 68–69.

24 Luk′ianchenko, *Material′naia kul′tura saamov (loparei) Kol′skogo poluostrova v kontse XIX–XX v.*, 29–34.

25 K. V. Regel′, "Puteshestvie po Kol′skomu poluostrovu letom 1913 goda," *IAOIRS* 6, no. 12 (June 15, 1914): 375.

for ways to make the harsh lands of the far north more suitable for ethnic Russians by replacing reindeer with livestock from the heartland.

In his 1897 economic survey of northwest Russia, Arkhangel′sk governor Aleksandr Engel′gardt evaluated the ethnic organization of the Kola reindeer economy. A passing summer encounter with the Kola environment affirmed his preconceived stereotypes that the Sami appeared "gnome-like" and were themselves on the path to extinction. He also criticized them as bad pastoralists who did not care about increasing their herds. In his view they squandered the plentiful natural resources available to them on state lands by letting their reindeer roam freely in the summer. The recent Komi migrants, in contrast to the Sami, "conduct the reindeer trade correctly and sensibly guard reindeer against attack from predatory beasts."[26]

A little over a decade later, another author, who wrote under the pseudonym V – r, evoked a slightly different ethnic hierarchy to describe reindeer husbandry in the region. After observing how different groups tended transportation animals, he inverted the established order and placed the Russian Pomors below the other ethnicities. V – r criticized the "excessive exploitation of the strength of the reindeer" by some Kola herders. "[T]his carelessness is very harmful and unprofitable, but worst of all it has penetrated not only the life of savages or semi-savages, but also of the Russian peasant who is almost fully deprived of cultural influence on the Kola Peninsula." In this rendering, the environmental and social context of the region undermined the Pomors' status as the allegedly superior group and spoke of the dire need for reform. V – r believed that "the more rational use of resources from the natural environment" could allow reindeer herding to become profitable.[27] By "more rational" he meant, like Engel′gardt, adopting commercially-oriented Komi methods of husbandry and land use.

In the years immediately preceding the outbreak of World War I, a divergent ecological vision of the national economy of the north arose among specialists elsewhere in the Arkhangel'sk province. The proprietor of the Pechora Experimental Agricultural Station, Andrei Zhuravskii, described reindeer herding as an inherently productive activity

[26] A. P. Engel′gardt, *Russkii sever″: putevyia zapiski* (Saint Petersburg: Izdanie A. S. Suvorina, 1897), 1, 64–68. On representations of the Komi among policy makers and others in late imperial Russia, see Indreek Jääk, "The Komi, Ethnic Stereotypes, and Nationalities Policy in Late Imperial Russia," *The Russian Review* 68, no. 2 (April 2009): 199–220.

[27] V-r, "Iz oblasti olenevodstva," *IAOIRS* 1, no. 7 (August 15, 1909): 41–42, 48.

that required minimal labor, thereby dissuading proper crop cultivation. Estimating that reindeer could give pastoralists an 800 percent return on invested capital after five years, he stressed that indigenous practitioners were on the whole well-off economically. Other commentators on the reindeer economy in the Arkhangel′sk province, including the Kola Peninsula, shared this assessment of tundra nature use. One wrote, "receiving everything from the tundra and nothing from humans, reindeer give them everything."[28] The ease of the herding economy, rather than a lack of culture, served to prevent northern realms from being worked for crops.

Indeed, Zhuravskii's real interest in reindeer came from his desire to expand traditional Russian agriculture into herders' tundra lands. Believing in the superiority of Russian "self-knowledge" over "Western European science" for developing the "primitive landscape" of the north, he apparently considered "the polar tundra" to be "an ordinary uncultivated plot of land that is superficially marshy and thus easily transformed into a meadow." The only problem was that migrating reindeer trampled tundra mosses preventing the regeneration of grasslands that supported less mobile livestock and fertile soils that would be capable of cultivating crops. Zhuravskii felt confident that, "wherever there is the donkey of a settler in two, three, or four years magnificent meadows appear in the places of former 'marshes' (tundra)."[29] The notion that Russians could and should bring their national agricultural habits to tundra ecosystems mirrored the late-imperial efforts to encourage the colonization of lands on the southern frontier and the afforestation of steppe grasslands. Many nationalists thought that Russifying inhospitable natural environments could give the variegated empire better coherence and uniformity.[30] It

[28] Quoted in V-r, "Iz oblasti bibliografii i kritiki: A. N. Makarevskii i V. D. Petrushevskii, Severnyi olen′. Domashnee zhivotnoe poliarnykh stran (SPb: Izdatel′stvo zhurn. Vystn. Obsh. Vserinarii, 1909)," *IAOIRS* 2, no. 4 (February 15, 1910): 28.

[29] A. V. Zhuravskii, *Evropeiskii Russkii Sever″: K voprosu o griadushchem i proshlom ego byta* (Arkhangel′sk: Gubernskaia Tipografiia, 1911), 32–33 and S. V. Kertselli, *Po bol′shezemel′skoi tundre s kochevnikami* (Arkhangel′sk: Gubernskaia Tipografiia, 1911), 70–77, 81–82. Zhuravskii was close, financially and intellectually, to conservative journalist Mikhail Men′shikov at the newspaper, *The New Times* (*Novoe Vremia*). Also around this time Zhuraveskii was involved in a major scandal with Lev Shternberg at the Museum of Anthropology and Ethnography in Saint Petersburg in which the former's anti-Semitism and conservatism came out even more strongly. See Sergei Kan, *Lev Shternberg: Anthropologist, Russian Socialist, Jewish Activist* (Lincoln: University of Nebraska Press, 2009), 172–177.

[30] Discussions of Russian colonization and landscape modification in the southern borderlands include Judith Pallot and Denis J. B. Shaw, *Landscape and Settlement in Romanov*

is not a surprise, then, that figures like Zhuravskii drafted reindeer into larger questions about the ethnic makeup of the north. As Jane Costlow and Amy Nelson argue, "Russian culture is marked by preoccupations with issues of identity, marginalization, and uniqueness that extend the basic concern with an 'animal other' to broader patterns of (human) self-definition."[31]

Promoters of Komi-style herding, V – r and Sergei Kertselli, who were likely the same person, attacked Zhuravskii's position. They accused him of exaggerating the ease of reindeer pastoralism and using pseudoscience in his study of tundra landscapes. V – r, for instance, remarked on Zhuravskii's ignorance of veterinary medicine and blamed him for spreading the inaccurate idea that reindeer herding was especially profitable.[32] For his part, Kertselli polemically mocked Zhuravskii's position and challenged his ideas about tundra landscapes and their mutability, specifically refuting the historical and contemporary examples that his foe had cited to show that meadows existed in the region. He also claimed that the tundra was less marshy than Zhuravskii thought, denied that reindeer trample moss, and demonstrated the heavy loads of manure required to make these lands agriculturally fertile. Generally emphasizing the comparative immutability of the tundra, Kertselli saw it as most suitable for Komi-style reindeer herding.[33]

Despite the distinctions in nationality politics and the models of economic development present in these two positions, both coalesced around the stance that the current reindeer economy of the Kola Sami needed to be changed. Few members of educated society believed that the Sami could avoid losing their cultural distinctiveness. As Arctic oceanographer Vladimir Vize wrote in January 1917, "the process of 'Russification' and the infection of Russian Lapps with new ideas is going very quickly and

Russia, 1613–1917 (Oxford: Oxford University Press, 1990); Thomas Barrett, *At the Edge of Empire: The Terek Cossacks and the North Caucasus Frontier, 1700–1860* (Boulder: Westview Press, 1999), 57–83; Nicholas Breyfogle, *Heretics and Colonizers: Forging Russia's Empire in the South Caucasus* (Ithaca: Cornell University Press, 2005), 87–127; David Moon, *The Plough that Broke the Steppes: Agriculture and Environment on Russia's Grasslands, 1700–1914* (Oxford: Oxford University Press, 2013); and Stephen Brain, *Song of the Forest: Russian Forestry and Stalinist Environmentalism, 1905–1953* (Pittsburgh: University of Pittsburgh Press, 2011), 143.

31 Jane Costlow and Amy Nelson, "Introduction: Integrating the Animal," in Jane Costlow and Amy Nelson, eds., *Other Animals: Beyond the Human in Russian Culture and History* (Pittsburgh: University of Pittsburgh Press, 2010), 3.

32 V-r, "Iz oblasti bibliografii i kritiki," *IAOIRS* 2, no. 4 (February 15, 1910): 28.

33 Kertselli, *Po bol'shezemel'skoi tundre s kochevnikami*, 70–77, 81–82, 106–107.

will hasten even further with the installation of the Murmansk railroad. That is why we should realize that it is not far from the moment when the legends of olden times will completely fade from the memory of the Russian Lapps."[34] A sense that the indigenous knowledge of this historically defined "other" was irretrievably slipping away inspired a number of journalists and researchers to collect Kola Sami folklore and write ethnographic accounts.[35] This information would soon influence early Soviet strategies to reform desolate areas of the region. But had Zhuravskii's Russian nationalism carried the day, reindeer herding might have been abandoned altogether in favor of experiments with traditionally Slavic forms of agriculture.

Promoting a Sami Animal

As it happened, many outside experts and reformers rallied to the side of Sami reindeer after the Bolsheviks seized power. They hoped to elevate the status of minority ethnicities and nationalities as part of the USSR's socialist experiment. Several observers now argued for the suitability of Sami land use patterns in the region, though others continued to stress the advantages of Komi husbandry. Along with a campaign to protect wild reindeer in the 1920s, the efforts of new organizations and visiting ethnographers to aid the Sami helped position reindeer as an important creature for developing the regional economy.

After prospering in the early twentieth century, Kola reindeer suffered dramatically as wars and revolutions engulfed Russia in 1914–1921. The total regional population of domestic reindeer fell from somewhere between 74,000 to 81,000 animals in 1914 to 23,000 in 1923, with the Sami in particular losing 70–75 percent of their herds (see Table 2).[36]

34 V. Vize, "Narodnyi epos russkikh loparei," *IAOIRS* 9, no. 1 (January 1917): 16.

35 Sviashchennik V. Meletiev, "Iz zhizni loparei," *IAOIRS* 2, no. 3 (February 1, 1910): 13–18; Sviashchennik V. Meletiev, "V vezhe (Iz zhizni loparei)," *IAOIRS* 2, no. 4 (February 15, 1910): 13–15; N. Pinegin "Iz skazov Laplandskogo Severa (Listki iz zapisnoi knizhki turista)," *IAOIRS* 2, no. 17 (September 1, 1910): 27–33; Regel′, "Puteshestvie po Kol′skomu poluostrovu letom 1913 goda," *IAOIRS* 6, no. 12 (June 15, 1914): 372–377; A. Zhilinskii, "Lopari i nashe zakonodatel′stvo," *IAOIRS* 6, no. 19 (November 15, 1914): 657–663; Kir Kozmin, "Laplaniia i laplandtsy," *IAOIRS* 7, no. 6 (June 15, 1915): 176–187; Vize, "Narodnyi epos russkikh loparei," *IAOIRS* 9, no. 1 (January 1917): 15–24; V. Vize, "Narodnyi epos russkikh loparei," *IAOIRS* 9, no. 2 (February 1917): 65–73; and Nik. Briskin, "Loparskie skazki," *IAOIRS* 9, no. 5 (May 1917): 213–223.

36 Slezkine, *Arctic Mirrors*, 132.

TABLE 2. *Reported Population of Domestic Reindeer in the Murmansk Region*

Year	Domestic Reindeer Population	Year	Domestic Reindeer Population	Year	Domestic Reindeer Population
1886	13,000	1929	56,500	1963	78,152
1887	18,000	1932	63,100	1968	79,117
1896	45,000	1934	54,000	1971	82,832
1905	59,000	1937	76,918	1981	63,000
1910	67,200	1940	70,300	1985	71,449
1914	81,000/ 74,000	1947	42,045	1991	73,356
1923	23,000	1950	53,883	1998	72,438
1927	48,300	1959	74,800	2002	57,000

Note: Konakov and Kiseleva report different figures for 1914.
Sources: O. A. Makarova, "Dikii severnyi olen′ Kol′skogo poluostrova v kontse XX – nachale XXI vekov," *Nauka i biznes na Murmane*, no. 4 (August 2003): 43; N. D. Konakov, "Ecological Adaptation of Komi Resettled Groups," *Arctic Anthropology* 30, no. 2 (1993): 98–99; I. Budovnits, *Olenevodcheskie kolkhozy kol'skogo poluostrova* (Moscow/Leningrad: Gosudarstvennoe izdatel′stvo sel′skokhoziaistvennoi i kolkhozno-kooperativnoi literatury, 1931), 10–11; E. V. Bunakov, "Ekonomicheskoe obosnovanie razvitiia olenevodstva Murmanskogo okruga," *Sovetskoe olenevodstvo* 4 (1934): 125; T. A. Kiseleva, "Vliianie sotsial′no-ekonomicheskikh faktorov na razvitie olenevodstva Kol′skogo poluostrova v 1900–1980 gody," in *Voprosy istorii Evropeiskogo Severa (Problemy ekonomiki i kul′tury XX v.)* (Petrozavodsk: Petrozavodskii gosudarstvennyi universitet, 1994), 72; and A. A. Kiselev and T. A. Kiseleva, *Sovetskie Saamy: Istoriia, ekonomikam kul'tura* (Murmansk: Murmanskoe knizhnoe izdatel′stvo, 1987), 119.

Botanist German Kreps also discovered a major decline in the wild reindeer population during this period (see Table 3). He cited multiple causes for the drop, including the disruption to traditional migration routes of herds by the new Murmansk railroad, the increased competition from domestic reindeer, and the general cycle of booms and busts that occurred as wild reindeer over-consumed the available lichen pastures.[37]

Fairly minor policy interventions accompanied the recovery of domestic reindeer in the 1920s. In order to help revamp the herding economy from wartime devastation, new state-backed credit cooperatives provided subsidized loans to over half of the individual herders.[38] The government

[37] German Kreps, "Dikii severnyi olen′ na Kol′skom poluostrove i proekt organizatsii laplandskogo zapovednika," *KMK* 6, no. 10–11 (October–November 1928): 37.

[38] V. I. Osinovskii, "Opyt kreditovaniia olenevodcheskikh khoziaistv," in D. A. Zolotarev, ed., *Kol′skii sbornik: Trudy antropologo-etnograficheskogo otriada kol′skoi ekspeditsii* (Leningrad: Izdatel′stvo Akademii Nauk, 1930), 103–117.

TABLE 3. *Reported Population of Wild Reindeer in the Western Part of the Murmansk Region*

Year	Wild Reindeer Population	Year	Wild Reindeer Population	Year	Wild Reindeer Population
1929	99	1959	563	1975	3,420
1931	150	1960	2,168	1981	100
1937	415	1963	3,974	1985	270
1940	935	1967	12,640	1990	600
1948	380	1968	2,280	1998	1,270
1957	1,964	1971	6,447	2001	200–300

Sources: O. A. Makarova, "Dikii severnyi olen′ Kol′skogo poluostrova v kontse XX – nachale XXI vekov," *Nauka i biznes na Murmane*, no. 4 (August 2003): 43; S. A. Diuzhilov, "'Arkhipelag Svobody' na Murmane (vtoraia polovina 1920-kh – 1930-e g.g.)," in P. V. Fedorov, et al., eds., *Zhivushchie na Severe: Obrazy i real′nosti* (Murmansk: MGPU, 2006), 95; GARF, f. A-358, op. 2, d. 111, l. 25; and GARF, f. A-358, op. 2, d. 231, l. 32.

also created the Murmansk Experimental Reindeer-Herding Point near Krasnoshchel′e to research pasture use, feeding techniques, breed differences, predator protection, and herding methods.[39] Whether due to state aid, or more likely due to regularities in reindeer demography, the domestic reindeer population doubled between 1923 and 1929 (see Table 2). At this point Kola herders began to export venison abroad and offered transportation services to northern developers.[40] Geological surveyors, construction workers, and miners also employed draft reindeer in the Khibiny Mountains to haul loads of ore and other materials from otherwise inaccessible places.[41]

Journalists and reformers started speaking more frequently about the potential for reindeer pastoralism to serve the Kola economy. Kertselli

39 "Predislovie," in *Murmanskaia olenevodcheskaia opytnaia stantsiia (Sbornik nauchnykh rabot)*, vol. 1 (Murmansk: Murmanskoe knizhnoe izdatel′stvo, 1967), 3–5; S. V. Kertselli, "Olenevodstvo RSFSR," in P. G. Smidovich, S. A. Buturlina, and N. I. Leonova, eds., *Sovetskii Sever: pervyi sbornik statei* (Moscow: Komitet sodeistviia narodnostiam severnykh okrain pri prezidiume VTsIK, 1929), 125; Budovnits, *Olenevodcheskie kolkhozy kol′skogo poluostrova*, 106–120; and GAMO, f. 169, op. 1, d. 7, l. 13.

40 *PP* (January 24, 1928), 3; *PP* (February 4, 1928), 4; and Ushakov and Dashchinskii, *Lovozero*, 100.

41 V. I. Osinovskii, "Rol′ khibinskikh apatitov v kolonizatsii Kol′skogo poluostrova," in A. E. Fersman, ed., *Khibinskie Apatity: Spornik*, vol. 1 (Leningrad: Izdanie Gostresta "Apatit," 1930), 206; "Letopis′ sobytii goroda Khibinogorska," *ZhA*, no. 1 (October 2001): 27, 38, and P. V. Vladimirov and N. S. Morev, *Apatitovyi rudnik im. S. M. Kirova* (Leningrad: Seriia izdatel′stva po khibinskoi apatitovoi probleme, 1936), 26.

continued to advocate the "industrial reindeer herding" of the Komi over that of the Sami, which "can be regarded as subsidiary reindeer herding of a hunting and fishing tribe." If all pastoralists tended large herds and maintained year-round surveillance like the Komi, then the Soviet Union could eventually support up to fifteen-to-twenty million domestic reindeer.[42] More popular writers extolled reindeer as the "gold of the tundra" and proclaimed, "no animal in nature is more industrially productive than reindeer."[43]

Meanwhile, Kreps campaigned to establish a nature reserve (*zapovednik*) to help restore the dwindling population of wild reindeer.[44] Along with Fedor Arkhipov, a Sami hunter who could distinguish between wild and domestic reindeer from a distance, Kreps conducted a population estimate in 1929 that showed only ninety-nine wild reindeer remained in the western territories of the Kola Peninsula.[45] Since current hunting prohibitions were impossible to enforce, the "only effective measure for the protection of wild reindeer" was to set aside a territory of approximately 200,000 hectares in which all forms of economic activity would be prohibited. The reserve would have the "goal not only of protecting a single animal, but also of preserving the entire geographical landscape in natural inviolability." To justify the utility of the reserve, Kreps cited its value for science, the future hunting economy, and the domestic reindeer industry.[46] Government agencies responded positively to this lobbying and officially created the Lapland *zapovednik* on January 17, 1930.[47]

Even more so than dreams about the animal's economic potential or the efforts to preserve it, the Soviet Union's policies toward national

42 S. V. Kertselli, "Olenevodstvo Murmanskogo kraia," in *Proizvoditel'nye sily raiona Murmanskoi zheleznoi dorogi: Sbornik* (Petrozavodsk: Pravlenie Murmanskoi zheleznoi dorogi, 1923), 93, 133.

43 Zinaida Rikhter, *Pervoe desiatiletie: zapiski zhurnalista* (Moscow: Sovetskii pisatel', 1957), 133 and A. Zorich, *Sovetskaia Kanada: Ocherki* (Moscow: Izdatel'stvo "Federatsiia," 1931), 201.

44 On the history of *zapovedniki* in this period, see Douglas Weiner, *Models of Nature: Ecology, Conservation, and Cultural Revolution in Soviet Russia* (Bloomington: Indiana University Press, 1988) and Feliks Shtilmark, *History of the Russian Zapovedniks, 1895–1995*, trans. G. H. Harper (Edinburgh: Russian Nature Press, 2003).

45 GARF, f. A-358, op. 4, d. 1521, ll. 17–18.

46 *PP* (March 24, 1928), 1; *PP* (April 24, 1928), 4; and Kreps, "Dikii severnyi olen' na Kol'skom poluostrove i proekt organizatsii laplandskogo zapovednika," *KMK* 6, no. 10–11 (October–November 1928): 37, 40.

47 GARF, f. A-358, op. 2, d. 231, l. 28 and O. Semenov-Tian-Shanskii, *Laplandskii gosudarstvennyi zapovednik (nauchno-populiarnyi ocherk)* (Murmansk: Murmanskoe knizhnoe izdatel'stvo, 1960), 6.

minorities brought increased attention to Kola reindeer. As a post-colonial and avowedly non-imperial empire, the USSR was bent on nation-building as a way to operationalize socialism. In the north it sought to make tundra-dwellers and their ecosystems legible by promoting selective ethnic groups and animals in specific territories. This attempt critically involved the acquisition of ecological and ethnographic information based on both practical experiences and universalizing theories.

Historical scholarship on nationality has shown the significance of the Soviet commitment to self-determination, in particular in terms of the reliance on territorial units aimed at making populations national in form but socialist in content. It has also elucidated policy makers' belief that encouraging ethnic identities was part of a temporary, but historically necessary, process to advance the country culturally and economically. Special opportunities for members of minority groups coexisted alongside the repression of overly assertive articulations of nationality. Some scholars treat these measures as a coherent policy devised and implemented by Soviet institutions, while others point to how knowledge production shaped the Bolsheviks' response to their imperial dominion.[48] Both state institutions and ethnographic knowledge played an interconnected and instrumental role in Kola reindeer country.

The Soviet state placed the Sami, as well as the Nenets and twenty-four other ethnic groups, into the category of the "small peoples of the north." This designation meant that they belonged at the bottom of an imagined evolutionary scale of national minorities. It also associated them more closely with hunter-gathering societies than nomadic pastoralists. Reformers designed aid programs to quickly overcome the supposedly extreme backwardness of these groups so that they could be incorporated fully into a modern socialist state. As Anatolii Skachko, head of the

[48] Terry Martin represents the former position and Francine Hirsh the latter one. In general, see Yuri Slezkine, "The USSR as a Communal Apartment, or How a Socialist State Promoted Ethnic Particularism," *SR* 53, no. 2 (Summer 1994): 414–452; Ronald Grigor Suny and Terry Martin, eds., *A State of Nations: Empire and Nation-Making in the Age of Lenin and Stalin* (Oxford: Oxford University Press, 2001); Terry Martin, *The Affirmative Action Empire: Nations and Nationalism in the Soviet Union, 1923–1939* (Ithaca: Cornell University Press, 2001); and Francine Hirsch, *Empire of Nations: Ethnographic Knowledge and the Making of the Soviet Union* (Ithaca: Cornell University Press, 2005). Older works tended to view early Soviet nationality policy as unwaveringly hostile to minority nations or as a cynical and insincere manipulation of nationalist movements. See Richard Pipes, *The Formation of the Soviet Union: Communism and Nationalism, 1917–1923* (Cambridge, MA: Harvard University Press, 1954) and Robert Conquest, *The Nation Killers: The Soviet Deportation of Nationalities* (London: Macmillan, 1970).

Committee of the North (officially, the Committee for Assistance to the Peoples of the Northern Borderlands), put it, "the small peoples of the north, in order to catch up with the advanced nations of the USSR, must, during the same ten years, cover the road of development that took the Russian people one thousand years to cover, for even one thousand years ago the cultural level of Kievan Rus′ was higher than that of the present-day small peoples of the north."[49]

Neither the Russian Pomors nor the Komi belonged to the small peoples of the north, nor were they seen as geographically indigenous to the Kola Peninsula. In contrast to the special attention they garnered in the imperial era, the Pomors received no ethnically-based aid and witnessed a total government embrace of the industrial fishing practices that had earlier threatened their livelihood.[50] The Komi, despite being a native group living in the north and engaging in reindeer pastoralism, had a status closer to other large nationalities. In the regional realignments of the 1920s and 1930s the Komi mainland first became an autonomous region and then an autonomous republic. With this separate territory and a higher status among Soviet nationalities, the Kola Komi attracted little institutional support and even less anthropological interest.[51]

Instead, reformers and ethnographers collaborated to elevate and assimilate the Kola Sami. Under the leadership of Vasilii Alymov, the Murmansk Branch of the Committee of the North focused on lifting the economic and cultural level of the "small peoples" in the region.[52] The Russian State Geographic Society sponsored the Lapp Expedition in 1927, which used on-site fieldwork to evaluate the physical anthropology,

49 Quoted in Slezkine, *Arctic Mirrors*, 220. Originally from Anatolii Skachko, "Ocherednye zadachi sovetskoi raboty sredi malykh narodov Severa," *SS*, no. 2 (1931): 20.

50 Julia A. Lajus, "Razvitie rybokhoziaistvennykh issledovanii barentseva moria: vzaimootnosheniia nauki i promysla, 1898–1934 gg." (PhD diss., Rossiiskaia akademiia nauk: Institut istorii estestvoznaniia i tekhniki, 2004) and Paul R. Josephson, *Industrialized Nature: Brute Force Technology and the Transformation of the Natural World* (Washington, DC: Island Press, 2002), 197–229.

51 Habeck, *What it Means to Be a Herdsman*, 75–86 and Hirsch, *Empire of Nations*, 62–98. Some funding for cultural bases apparently went to Komi pastoralists on the Kola Peninsula in the mid-1930s, but this support drew disapproval from the organizers overseeing it. See Paul R. Josephson, *The Conquest of the Russian Arctic* (Cambridge, MA: Harvard University Press, 2014), 230–232.

52 E. V. Fedorova, "Murmanskii komitet Severa," *NBM*, no. 4 (August 2003): 54–57; V. V. Sorokazherd′ev, "Alymov i Komitet Severa," *NBM* 16, no. 2 (April 2004): 12–16; GAMO, f. R-169, op. 1, d. 7, ll. 3–5; and A. A. Kiselev and T. A. Kiseleva, *Sovetskie Saamy: Istoriia, ekonomikam kul′tura* (Murmansk: Murmanskoe knizhnoe izdatel′stvo, 1987), 58–59, 84–107.

FIGURE 7. Kola Reindeer Herders.
Source: D. A. Zolotarev, *Loparskaia ekspeditsiia* (Leningrad: Izdanie Gosudarstvennogo Russkogo Geograficheskogo Obshchesvta, 1927), 11.

health, culture, and economic conditions of the Sami.[53] Vladimir Charnoluskii served as the primary ethnographer on this expedition. To better understand the material life and folklore of the Sami, he spent months living among them. He left this experience with special sympathy for Sami communities and a desire to make his research assist them.[54] Based on this ethnographic work and discussions with local populations, the Murmansk Committee of the North drew up plans for two Lapp native districts in the east and the west of the Kola Peninsula.[55]

53 F. G. Ivanov-Diatlov, *Nabliudeniia vracha na Kol'skom poluostrove* (Leningrad: Izdanie Gosudarstvennogo Russkogo Geograficheskogo Obshchesvta, 1928); D. A. Zolotarev, *Loparskaia ekspeditsiia* (Leningrad: Izdanie Gosudarstvennogo Russkogo Geograficheskogo Obshchesvta, 1927); D. A. Zolotarev, *Kol'skie lopari: Trudy loparskoi ekspeditsii russkogo geograficheskogo obshchestva po antropologii loparei i velikorusov kol'skogo poluostrova* (Leningrad: Izdatel'stvo Akademii Nauk, 1928); Zolotarev, ed., *Kol'skii sbornik*; and Marina Kuropjatnik, "Expeditions to Sámi Territories: A History of the Studies of the Kola Sámi in the 1920s–1930s," *Acta Borealia* 16, no. 1 (1999): 117–124.

54 V. V. Charnoluskii, "Zametki o past'be i organizatsii stada u loparei," in Zolotarev, ed., Kol'skii sbornik, 23–70 and V. V. Charnoluskii, *Materialy po bytu loparei: Opyt opredeleniia kochevogo sostoianiia loparei vostochnoi chasti Kol'skogo poluostrova* (Leningrad: Izdanie Gosudarstvennogo Russkogo Geograficheskogo Obshchesvta, 1930).

55 Sorokazherd'ev, "Alymov i Komitet Severa," *NBM* 16, no. 2 (April 2004): 14; Fedorova, "Murmanskii komitet Severa," *NBM*, no. 4 (August 2003): 61–62; and GAMO, f. R-169, op. 1, d. 7, ll. 3–5.

Reindeer stood at the center of the plans for ethnic reform. Both Alymov and Charnoluskii believed that the proper regulation of lichen pastures was a key element in serving Sami interests and increasing the profitability of their herding. The Murmansk Committee of the North engaged in a program of territorial formation (*zemleustroistvo*) to try to fix the Kola reindeer economy.[56] Territorial formation involved surveying landscapes to assess the presence and varieties of lichen, figuring out the optimal arrangement for seasonal grazing and migration paths, establishing the quantity of reindeer that could live on certain territories, and performing a number of other tasks to develop a basis for economic and administrative reform.[57] It also provided a means to prevent the Komi from using Sami pastures.[58]

For his part, Charnoluskii produced ethnographic scholarship that explicitly valorized the Sami treatment of reindeer and the land. He intentionally chose a research site on the eastern part of the Kola Peninsula that had been the least influenced by the reindeer herding of the Komi and Nenets.[59] While attentive to the significance of fishing and hunting in the Sami economy, Charnoluskii also stressed the primacy of reindeer: "Reindeer in the everyday life of a Lapp is everything: food, a means of transportation and a source of secondary earnings." He further posited that aspects of Sami grazing, which contrasted with those of the Komi, were appropriate for the Kola Peninsula. The Kola Sami felt "deep indignation" at the "the Komi methods of using lichen" because it unnecessarily trampled and destroyed pasturelands through overgrazing. According to Charnoluskii, the Sami desired a "totally conditional designation of the boundaries of several sections of land (in general land that no one owns) with natural markers, which are necessary for avoiding the mixing of herds." Outlining his vision of how to improve the Kola reindeer

[56] I follow David Anderson in translating *zemleustroistvo* as territorial formation. Anderson, *Identity and Ecology in Arctic Siberia*, 148–170.

[57] GAMO, f. R-169, op. 1, d. 6, ll. 10, 23, 41, 52, 60–64, 72–74 and GAMO, f. R-169, op. 1, d. 7, ll. 3–5.

[58] GAMO, f. R-169, op. 1, d. 6, ll. 6–10, 21.

[59] Charnoluskii, *Materialy po bytu loparei*, 77. At about this time the Polar census collected statistics on nomadism in the Kola tundra. It estimated that 286 Sami households (277 of which owned reindeer) were nomadic and eighty-five (seventy-two of which owned reindeer) were sedentary in 1926–1927. The census also recorded that of the households that had reindeer herding as a main occupation, forty-seven of them were "settled, native" and eighty-five were "nomadic." See *Pokhoziaistvennaia perepis' pripoliarnogo Severa SSSR 1926/1927 goda: Territorial'nye i gruppovye itogi pokhoziaistvennoi perepisi* (Moscow: Tsentral'noe statisticheskoe upravlenie SSSR, 1929), 13–26, 140–141 and Luk'ianchenko, *Material'naia kul'tura saamov (loparei) Kol'skogo poluostrova v kontse XIX–XX v.*, 20, 24.

economy, Charnoluskii insisted that the "prudent herd management" of the Komi and Nenets be combined with Sami means of "carefully treating the pastures of their region, which are disappearing before our eyes."[60]

Geobotanist Aleksandr Salazkin at the Murmansk Committee of the North also rejected the Komi pasture usage in favor of Sami practice. His detailed surveys of flora on Kola lands indicated that reindeer herders were only using a quarter of the abundant foraging resources available. But "despite the far from full use of foraging resources, one observes places with crowded pastures in the tundra." A big part of the problem was that the "Komi-Nenets system of grazing herds for the whole year certainly does not respond to the particularities of the local lichen pastures and quite harmfully affects their condition during summer pasturage." The ecology of the Kola Peninsula set it apart from the lands where Komi herding first developed. While the region possessed rich lichen pastures, most of them existed in forests instead of tundra areas. According to Salazkin, the predominance of forested lands made the Kola environment better suited for Sami pasture usage, including the free release of reindeer during the summer. Through this emphasis on the proper foraging techniques, Salazkin, like Charnoluskii, posited historic Sami practice as an appropriate foundation for the development of "socialist reindeer herding."[61]

Reindeer Collectivization

Wholesale agricultural reform then collided with the ethnic politics of the tundra. Starting at the end of the 1920s, the Soviet government pushed to collectivize reindeer pastoralism. As contested, confused, and cruel as collectivization was, these policies succeeded in making the reindeer economy more comprehensible and manageable to the state as an agricultural activity. In this way, it extended Soviet authority into the sparsest outposts of the Kola Peninsula and focused rural livelihoods more on a single mammal.

Above all, collectivization was a program designed to establish central control over food production. In most instances, it involved restructuring farms engaged in crop cultivation or livestock breeding, improving state capacity to acquire grain, and putting a socialist veneer over the peasantry. As seen in the case of the special settlers in the

[60] Charnoluskii, "Zametki o past′be i organizatsii stada u loparei," in Zolotarev, ed., *Kol′skii sbornik*, 23, 38–39, 69.

[61] A. S. Salazkin, "Estestvennye kormovye ugodiia Murmanskogo okruga," in *Sovetskoe olenevodstvo* (Leningrad: Institut izdatel′stva olenevodstva, 1934), 55.

Khibiny Mountains, a class war against wealthier rural inhabitants (de-kulakization) took place alongside collectivization and ended up providing expropriated land, property, and animals to the new collective and state farms. While in theory poor and middle class peasants would volunteer to create or join collective farms, in practice many were coerced into them by party activists.[62] Instead of bolstering the rural economy, collectivization disrupted grain production in the immediate term and created widespread discontent among the peasantry. Yet its institutional structure served as the foundation of Soviet agriculture.

To collectivize rural society on the Kola Peninsula, government officials and consulting specialists spun out plans to expand reindeer herding astronomically. By this thinking, reindeer should be used for meat, milk, and fur production to accumulate capital instead of simply for providing food and clothing to local communities. More meat required more animals and thus bigger herds. Some reformers fancifully boasted that the lichen supplies in the Murmansk region could feed up to 300,000 animals and even Alymov agreed that "the multiplicity of farms with few reindeer" held back the growth rate of the domestic reindeer population.[63] To achieve an intended tenfold improvement in the productivity of Kola herding, the initial collectivization plans anticipated getting 91 percent of households to join the fourteen new collective farms and a state farm by 1933.[64] Their earliest proposals mentioned that this state farm would include 50,000 reindeer, which was close to the entire population of this species on the peninsula at the time.[65]

The state also sought to gain greater control over the movement of herders and reindeer. One reindeer-herding researcher expressed a widespread Soviet desire to transform nomadic peoples into sedentary animal breeders whose occupation, as opposed to way of life, required some seasonal movement. "[W]e believe that a system of year-round stationary pasturage based on an increased herd size and the organization of steady corralling is more progressive and advantageous for the socialist reconstruction of the reindeer economy."[66] Though officials accepted

[62] Moshe Lewin, *Russian Peasants and Soviet Power: A Study of Collectivization* (New York: W. W. Norton, 1975) and Lynne Viola, *The Best Sons of the Fatherland: Workers in the Vanguard of Soviet Collectivization* (Oxford: Oxford University Press, 1989).

[63] E. V. Bunakov, "Ekonomicheskoe obosnovanie razvitiia olenevodstva Murmanskogo okruga," *SO* 4 (1934): 148; Zorich, *Sovetskaia Kanada*, 206; and Fedorova, "Murmanskii komitet Severa," *NBM*, no. 4 (August 2003): 56–57.

[64] GAMO, f. 169, op. 1, d. 11, l. 56. [65] GAMO, f. 169, op. 1, d. 11, l. 27.

[66] Bunakov, "Ekonomicheskoe obosnovanie razvitiia olenevodstva Murmanskogo okruga," *SO* 4 (1934): 159–160.

the need for reindeer to roam for pasturage, they also wanted to use collectivization to restrict mobility and resettle communities of native northerners, thereby making them easier to rule.

At the same time, some local experts did use their on-the-ground knowledge about the Kola environment to moderate the government's agenda. Insisting that "the observations of the Lapps about weather and other geographical phenomena in the tundra" and "about the life and habits of wild and domestic reindeer" could aid Soviet science, Charnoluskii detailed the complex and diverse "indigenous knowledge" (*znatkikh*) of herders in the eastern half of the Kola Peninsula.[67] Relying on some of the biological aspects of Charnoluskii's research, including his classification system of the different types of reindeer, one party activist suggested embracing a model of diversified herding. He claimed that "the exploitation of a herd would produce much better results if part of it was specially suited for the goal of cultivating venison, another part of it for hides, a third would be selected to produce milk, a fourth would be used for transit, etc."[68] Alymov additionally attempted to utilize these insights, arguing that "Every reindeer-herding settlement, every *pogost* requires its own particular approach when organizing collective farms." He proposed that in order to build up the domestic reindeer population, herding communities should reduce slaughter numbers, cease venison exports, and rely more on subsidiary activities like fishing and hunting during the first years of collectivization.[69] Partially in response to all of these concerns, the Murmansk Committee of the North drafted a scaled back plan for the state farm that would require importing fewer reindeer from other parts of the country and thus reduce the likelihood of disease among the animals.[70]

These researchers and reformers played a less commendable role in allowing ethnic distinctions in the Kola reindeer economy to influence class politics. Advocates at the Committee of the North initially sought to sidestep class distinctions within indigenous communities by associating them with the primitive communist stage of development. However, they ceded ground after this notion came under attack. Then part of their

[67] Charnoluskii, "Zametki o past'be i organizatsii stada u loparei," in Zolotarev, ed., *Kol'skii sbornik*, 23.

[68] Budovnits, *Olenevodcheskie kolkhozy kol'skogo poluostrova*, 111–117 and Charnoluskii, "Zametki o past'be i organizatsii stada u loparei," in Zolotarev, ed., *Kol'skii sbornik*, 53–57.

[69] GAMO, f. 169, op. 1, d. 11, ll. 70–78 and GAMO, f. 169, op. 1, d. 7, l. 13.

[70] GAMO, f. 169, op. 1, d. 11, l. 24–27, 44–48.

strategy in the Murmansk region was to help establish separate Sami, Nenets, and Komi collective farms.[71] Beginning in 1928 several Sami families joined small collective farms, including the work association Saam in the Voron′e *pogost* and one called Olenevod (later Krasnaia Tundra) in the Semiostrov *pogost*.[72] These on-paper collective farms essentially broke up when herders left their winter pastures in the spring and soon afterwards authorities abandoned the principle of ethnically-based collective farms in the area.[73] In an attempt to defend gradualist reforms, Skachko also proposed a scheme that denied measurable class stratification among hunters and fishers, but admitted to the existence of kulaks among reindeer herders.[74] Individuals who owned more reindeer could be ascribed the class status of kulak.[75] This meant the traits that had previously garnered successful herders' praise now put them in peril.

Those assisting the Kola Sami made it abundantly clear that these kulak herders were disproportionally Komi. The Murmansk Committee of the North supplied information about the class composition of minority groups that was vital for the implementation of de-kulakization on the Kola Peninsula. Though Alymov bemoaned the efforts to apply class categories to local ethnic groups, complaining that the middling group (*sredniaki*) was so porous that it rendered simple indices of economic stratification inaccurate, he ultimately complied. Crunching different data sets he had compiled, Alymov showed that a much higher quantity of Komi households owned larger reindeer herds and hired laborers (see Table 4). In his continual promotion of Sami herding methods, he relayed "the unanimous opinion" of "Lapps and their Russian neighbors" that the presence of "rich Komi" with 600–700 reindeer "systematically harms their reindeer herding."[76] These critiques of Komi herders became more

[71] The Murmansk Committee of the North's specific advocacy of ethnic collective farms appears in GAMO, f. 169, op. 1, d. 11, ll. 70–78.

[72] Luk′ianchenko, *Material′naia kul′tura saamov (loparei) Kol′skogo poluostrova v kontse XIX–XX v.*, 20 and Gutsol, Vinogradova, and Samorukova, *Pereselenie gruppy kol′skikh saamov*, 27.

[73] Kiselev and Kiseleva, *Sovetskie saamy*, 68.

[74] Slezkine, *Arctic Mirrors*, 192–193.

[75] On the process of attributing class identity in the Soviet Union, see Sheila Fitzpatrick, "Ascribing Class: The Construction of Social Identity in Soviet Russia," *Journal of Modern History* 65, no. 4 (December 1993): 745–770.

[76] Fedorova, "Murmanskii komitet Severa," *NBM*, no. 4 (August 2003): 58–59; GAMO, f. 169, op. 1, d. 6, ll. 7, 21, 23; V. Ia. Shashkov, *Spetspereselentsy v istorii Murmanskoi oblasti* (Murmansk: "Maksimum," 2004), 78–79; Konakov, "Ecological Adaptation of Komi Resettled Groups," *Arctic Anthropology* 30, no. 2 (1993): 100; and V. Alymov, "Znachenie olenia v tundrovykh khoziaistvakh Murmanskogo okruga," *KMK* 6, no. 9 (September 1928): 14–16.

TABLE 4. *Quantity of Reindeer Belonging to Kola Ethnic Groups in 1926, as Reported by Vasilii Aymov*

Quantity of Reindeer	Sami (%)	Nenets (%)	Komi (%)
Zero	4.3	0	2.8
Up to 20	30.6	3	10.2
21–50	34	28	25.2
51–100	17	28	25.2
101–200	8.9	31	17.8
201–300	2.3	10	6.5
301–500	2		10.3
More than 500	0.9		2

Source: E. V. Fedorova, "Murmanskii komitet Severa," *Nauka i biznes na Murmane*, no. 4 (August 2003): 59.

vocal as the forced collectivization campaign neared. Alymov reported that he "more and more frequently" received grievances from Sami about the "unauthorized occupation of Lapp pastures by large and predominantly Komi reindeer herders," and urged the Murmansk Executive Committee "to raise the issue of prohibiting the unauthorized occupation of reindeer pastures by large herds and the unauthorized migration of reindeer herders to already settled places."[77]

Among Kola pastoralists, the axe of class war therefore fell hardest on the Komi. The majority of herders oppressed as kulaks during collectivization in the 1930s belonged to this group.[78] In one instance at the Krasnaia Tundra collective farm in Ivanovka the conflict between Komi and Sami fell on the ancestors of the village's founder Ivan Artiev – a Komi herder who had migrated there in the nineteenth century.[79] Authorities targeted several of the Artievs as kulaks, arrested them, expropriated their animals,

77 GAMO, f. 169, op. 1, d. 6, ll. 7, 21, 23.

78 T. A. Kiseleva, "Iz istorii kollektivizatsii olenevodcheskikh khoziaistv Kol′skogo poluostrova," in *Voprosy istorii Evropeiskogo Severa* (Petrozavodsk: Petrozavodskii gosudarstvennyi universitet, 1979), 24. Reverberations of the sentiment that the majority of kulaks were Komi and that few were Sami appear in a statement by I. M. Isaichikov in Kiselev and Kiseleva, *Sovetskie saamy*, 73 and in Budovnits's explanation for the existence of a Sami kulak in the Pulozero region because of the lack of Komi in the area, Budovnits, *Olenevodcheskie kolkhozy kol′skogo poluostrova*, 37.

79 A. V. Simanovskaia, "Chal′mny-Varre: Likvidirovanniia derevnia kak mesto pamiati," in Petrov and Razumova, eds., *Severiane*, 70–73. Also see Isaeva, "K izucheniiu protsessov adaptatsii izhemskikh komi na Kol′skom severe," in Petrov and Razumova, eds., *Severiane*, 44–45.

and excluded them from the collective farm.[80] Around this time, Charnoluskii continued to complain of Komi dominance to the Committee of the North, protesting that, "labor was assigned improperly" at Krasnaia Tundra. "The Lapp group carried a large load and completed more difficult work than others."[81] Meanwhile, collectivizers attributed some of the setbacks they encountered to ethnic tensions. Trying to explain the minimal Sami presence in the Tundra collective farm in Lovozero, one reporter vividly evoked the existence of atavistic national antipathies: "Lapps, who sucked in hatred for the Komi nationality (the great power in the conditions of the Kola Peninsula) from their mother's milk, do not understand that among the Komi there are farm hands, the poor (*bedniaki*), and a middle class (*sredniaki*), as well as predatory money-lenders, thieves, and exploiter-kulaks."[82]

On top of fostering ethnic strife during collectivization, reformers clumsily applied central policies to the northern landscape. Up to 62.5 percent of the Kola reindeer economy was temporarily collectivized during the winter of 1930 before many of the new farms broke apart in the spring.[83] The hapless experience of the state's representative at Krasnaia Tundra is illustrative here. As the head of the collective farm, Ivan Pen′kov instituted a wage and investment system used in agricultural communes elsewhere in the country. In the distinct conditions of an Arctic reindeer economy, this policy simply antagonized the population and soon he faced threats that he chalked up to kulak resistance. Pen′kov also found few obliging organizations in the regional center of Murmansk when he tried to procure supplies for the herders' tents and faced an almost farcical series of pleas, negotiations, and bargains with provisioning agencies.[84] Furthermore, one specialist mocked the influential view that reindeer herding could thrive anywhere with sufficient food, snidely retorting, "in Africa there is also a foraging base, as giraffes know well, but reindeer aren't there and certainly won't be."[85] The warnings of the Committee of the North members about importing reindeer from other

[80] Budovnits, *Olenevodcheskie kolkhozy kol′skogo poluostrova*, 79–83.

[81] GAMO, f. 169, op. 1, d. 11, l. 172.

[82] Budovnits, *Olenevodcheskie kolkhozy kol′skogo poluostrova*, 101.

[83] Gutsol, Vinogradova, and Samorukova, *Pereselenie gruppy kol′skikh saamov*, 27.

[84] Budovnits, *Olenevodcheskie kolkhozy kol′skogo poluostrova*, 62–71 and Kiselev and Kiseleva, *Sovetskie saamy*, 70–71. Pen′kov was a participant in the 25,000er movement, which recruited urban communist workers to bring collectivization forcefully to the village. Viola, *The Best Sons of the Fatherland*.

[85] P. Semerikov, "Kak ne nado pisat′ programmy po olenevodcheskim kolkhozam," *SS* 4 (1933): 120.

parts of the country also proved prescient. After purchasing a large number of animals, the new state farm suffered an outbreak of hoof disease (*kopytka*) and many reindeer perished. Indeed, the difficulties that reindeer had in surviving collectivization undermined the economic rationale of the policy. Thus, while approximately 40 percent of households and 75 percent of reindeer on the Kola Peninsula belonged to collective or state farms in 1932, the domestic reindeer population after this point declined to below pre-collectivization levels (see Table 2).[86]

Interactions with reindeer and social bonds among herders shaped how these communities opposed collectivization and de-kulakization. Throughout the country, rural residents slaughtered and feasted on animals slated for state expropriation and sometimes let carcasses rot to prevent authorities from profiting from a policy they denounced as a second serfdom.[87] The 1932–1933 famine caused some to turn to this tactic out of desperation, but such episodes of killing animals constituted a form of resistance as historians Lynne Viola and Sheila Fitzpatrick have shown.[88] Soviet researchers blamed the supposed sabotage of kulak herders for helping lead to the loss of approximately 7,500 Kola reindeer during 1932.[89] In one instance, a Sami man in the Pulozero region, Kondrat Arkhipov, faced accusations of being a kulak and a sorcerer who stole and burned other herders' reindeer. The details of his apprehension and trial, however, point more to community cohesion and his paternal position in Sami society than his status as a class pariah. Arkhipov evaded prosecutors for months and villagers, who likely knew his approximate location the whole time, only helped find him when compelled to do so.[90] In another case, the state convicted six individuals from the Tundra

[86] Bunakov, "Ekonomicheskoe obosnovanie razvitiia olenevodstva Murmanskogo okruga," *SO* 4 (1934): 125, 132 and Kiselev and Kiseleva, *Sovetskie saamy*, 73–74.

[87] For instance, Fitzpatrick cites that peasants slaughtered an astounding 25 percent of cattle, 53 percent of pigs, 55 percent of sheep, and 40 percent of chickens in the Central Black Earth region during the winter of 1930. Sheila Fitzpatrick, *Stalin's Peasants: Resistance and Survival in the Russian Village After Collectivization* (Oxford: Oxford University Press, 1994), 66.

[88] Fitzpatrick, *Stalin's Peasants*, 62–69 and Viola, *Peasant Rebels under Stalin*, 69–79.

[89] Bunakov, "Ekonomicheskoe obosnovanie razvitiia olenevodstva Murmanskogo okruga," *SO* 4 (1934): 126–127 and Kiselev and Kiseleva, *Sovetskie saamy*, 73. As part of a national policy of correcting "excesses," the government transferred approximately 2,000 reindeer directly to non-collectivized herders, including to nine Sami who had been classified as kulaks. Local party cells at the Apatit trust approved these "corrections." GAMO, f. P-152, op. 1, d. 1, l. 32.

[90] Budovnits, *Olenevodcheskie kolkhozy kol'skogo poluostrova*, 37–41; Zolotarev, *Kol'skie lopari*, 184; Kiselev and Kiseleva, *Sovetskie saamy*, 94–95; and Z. E. Cherniakov, *Ocherki etnografii saamov* (Rovaniemi: University of Lapland, 1998).

collective farm for killing at least 144 reindeer of other herders. Though authorities wanted to frame such actions as kulak exploitation, all of the herders had been deemed lower class and, indeed, two of them had begun to forge Communist Party affiliations.

Moreover, both of these instances of resistance involved duplicitous interactions with the animals themselves. The Sami carved personalized earmarks to distinguish their reindeer, which would frequently herd with other pastoralists' animals. Arkhipov had supposedly refused to let others search his herd for reindeer with their earmarks, while the six Tundra herders had apparently tried to cut new earmarks into stolen reindeer in order to make them resemble their own animals.[91] Only individuals with intimate knowledge of Sami-reindeer relations could employ these tactics. Though such acts of opposition created setbacks and delays, they ultimately did not stop the state from intruding into the realm of reindeer.

Stalinist Challenges

Over the next couple of decades efforts to further reform the Kola reindeer economy, like much of the agricultural sector, subsided. Time, policy compromises, and the recovery of wild and domestic reindeer stocks helped stabilize remote terrains as nominally integrated into the Soviet system. Yet a series of disruptive crises related to terror, war, and a waning interest in conservation challenged the role of reindeer in the rural Kola economy. These ordeals had the potential to shift the region away from being a reindeer landscape. Only the renewed focus of the government on promoting large-scale herding in the post-Stalin era prevented such an outcome.

A collectivized reindeer economy gradually took root after the initial drive of the Great Break. Though Soviet-era sources claimed that almost all Kola reindeer herders belonged to collective farms by the end of the 1930s, it would be safer to assume that this only occurred with the post-World War II reconstruction.[92] Collectivization created something of an industrialized reindeer economy in which the number of animals and

[91] Budovnits, *Olenevodcheskie kolkhozy kol'skogo poluostrova*, 37–38, 91–100 and Zolotarev, *Kol'skie lopari*, 184.

[92] Luk'ianchenko, *Material'naia kul'tura saamov (loparei) Kol'skogo poluostrova v kontse XIX–XX v.*, 20–24 and Kiselev and Kiseleva, *Sovetskie saamy*, 80–83. I base the assertion about full collectivization occurring after the war on the vagueness of the Soviet-era sources and Alymov's claim, albeit made under considerable duress, from March 1938 that no more than 45 percent of households in the Lovozero district were collectivized. V. V. Sorokazherd'ev, "Po stranitsam sledstvennogo dela No. 46197," *NBM* 16, no. 2 (April 2004): 58.

amount of venison served as the ultimate criteria of success. It witnessed the rise of demarcated pastures, the reliance on techniques like territorial formation to maximize effective land use, the constriction of migration routes, and the replacement of the historic *pogost* system of regional organization.[93]

Authorities also instituted new forms of surveillance, including a notoriously inaccurate bi-annual count of the reindeer population that occurred once after the birthing period in the spring and again after the annual slaughter of reindeer in the early winter.[94] Within each collective farm, herders split into several brigades that tended to large herds composed of both commonly-held and private reindeer. The private animals were roughly equivalent to the private plots that peasants kept as their personal gardens in more temperate terrains.[95] In the collective farms the herders were now supposed to watch over the animals year-round, abandoning the Sami technique of free summer grazing for the Komi practice.[96]

Overall, this move toward even larger-scale herding meant that many Sami stopped knowing their reindeer individually, as they often had in earlier periods. It also split the newly collectivized herders off from the rest of their communities. Only the herders, who were men, and a few camp workers, often the wives of senior herders, traveled with the animals to the tundra; many residents, including herders' families, started staying in the villages year-round.[97]

Both domestic and wild reindeer stocks grew in the latter part of the 1930s. By 1937 the domestic reindeer population in the Murmansk

93 GAMO, f. 169, op. 1, d. 6, ll. 6, 9–10, 21–23, 29–50, 60–64, 72–74 and Kiselev and Kiseleva, *Sovetskie saamy*, 67–83.

94 Anderson, *Identity and Ecology in Arctic Siberia*, 32; Yulian Konstantinov, "Pre-Soviet Pasts and Reindeer-Herding Collectives: Ethnographies of Transition in Murmansk Region," *Acta Borealia: A Nordic Journal of Circumpolar Societies* 17, no. 2 (2000): 49–64; and Yulian Konstantinov, "From 'Traditional' to Collectivized Reindeer Herding on the Kola Peninsula: Continuity or Disruption?" *Acta Borealia: A Nordic Journal of Circumpolar Societies* 22, no. 2 (2005): 170–188.

95 Yulian Konstantinov, "Reinterpreting the Sovkhoz," *Sibirica* 6, no. 2 (Autumn 2007): 1–25.

96 Luk'ianchenko, *Material'naia kul'tura saamov (loparei) Kol'skogo poluostrova v kontse XIX–XX v.*, 32–33.

97 N. N. Gutsol, S. N. Vinogradova, and A. G. Samorukova, "Istoricheskie usloviia i sotsial'no-ekonomicheskie posledstviia pereselenii Kol'skikh saamov v sovetskii period (na primere trekh saamskikh pogostov)," in V. P. Petrov and I. A. Razumova, eds., *Chelovek v sotsiokul'turnom prostranstve: Evropeiskii Sever Rossii* (Apatity: Kol'skii nauchnyi tsentr Rossiisskoi Akademii nauk, 2005), 99–100, 111.

region had more than recovered from the disruptions of collectivization, reportedly reaching 76,918 animals (see Table 2). It is unclear whether productivist Soviet policies contributed to this increase. At the very least, the new dictate to frequently report the size of herds gave authorities a number to track. The Lapland Nature Reserve played a more obvious role in rehabilitating the wild reindeer population. It protected the creatures from predation and established a research program to study their ecology. Kreps informed Charnoluskii in 1931 that the wild reindeer population had already increased one-and-a-half times. This steady rise continued through the end of the decade when it reached over 900 wild reindeer (see Table 3). At this point wild reindeer's tendency to travel outside the territory of the Lapland Nature Reserve helped scientists lobby to expand its borders.[98] In agreeing to enlarge the *zapovednik* in early 1941, officials stated, "in connection with the increased numbers of wild reindeer and elk in the Lapland Nature Reserve, the insufficient foraging resources led these animals to be displaced into the regions of the Monche tundra beyond the border of the nature reserve, where they are deprived of effective protection from poaching."[99]

But a new bout of violent interference interrupted the burgeoning reindeer economy. In the years approaching the terror of 1937–1938, the ethnographers and reformers of the Kola Sami continued to try to develop a Sami literary culture and renewed their campaigns to create an autonomous Sami region in the western part of the Kola Peninsula.[100] A series of arrests connected to the mass operations against Finns in Karelia then halted these efforts.[101] Soviet mass operations scheduled specific populations – former kulaks, criminals, anti-Soviet elements, and specific nationalities believed to pose a potential military threat to the country – for arrests and exterminations by quota. They uprooted and undermined many of the class and ethnic distinctions that the state had previously encouraged.

[98] GARF, f. A-358, op. 2, d. 32, ll. 2–11, 18–28; GARF, f. A-358, op. 2, d. 19, l. 170; GARF, f. A-358, op. 4, d. 1521, l. 19; and GARF, f. A-358, op. 2, d. 231, ll. 28, 37. The other rationale for expanding the territory of the Lapland reserve was that its staff discovered that it only occupied 138,000 hectares instead of the officially sanctioned 200,000 hectares.

[99] GARF, f. A-358, op. 2, d. 32, l. 10.

[100] Kiselev and Kiseleva, *Sovetskie saamy*, 84–107; Sorokazherd′ev, "Po stranitsam sledstvennogo dela No. 46197," NBM 16, no. 2 (April 2004): 47–61; and Aleksei Kiselev, "Saamskii zagovor (Delo No. 46197)," *ZhA*, no. 3–4 (December 1999): 58–60.

[101] Nick Baron, *Soviet Karelia: Politics, Planning and Terror in Stalin's Russia, 1920–1939* (London: Routledge, 2007).

In 1938 state security agents accused Kola reindeer herders and Sami advocates of participating in a conspiracy with Finnish fascists and Karelian nationalists to unite the Kola Peninsula with Finland. Part of this plot included creating an independent Sami state that would help extend Greater Finland into the Urals. Alymov was to be the president and Salazkin the war minister. Eliding ethnic differences among Kola herding communities, the secret police implicated Komi in promoting "Sami nationalism." Several Komi herders, who earlier faced repression as kulaks, now lost their lives as Sami separatists. In fact, fewer than half of the approximately thirty individuals repressed for alleged involvement in a counter-revolutionary Sami nationalist plot were actually Sami; just as many were Komi or Nenets. At least eighteen were reindeer herders. On October 22, 1938 state agents executed fifteen individuals, including Alymov, Salazkin, and a group of Sami, Komi, and Russians.[102]

Part of the suspicious behavior in this case involved the treatment of reindeer and the land. The police accused individuals of destroying lichen pastures, leaving the reindeer without supervision, and slaughtering calves. Under duress during interrogations, Alymov affirmed: "These instructions of mine were carried out every summer, especially during the years 1935–1937. A large area of lichen was burned in the tundra, collective farm pastures were cut, and because of inadequate food a significant decline in the number of reindeer in herds occurred." Reindeer lichen "only grows back in thirty years after a fire." He also acknowledged that the plotters intentionally spread "hoof disease among the reindeer," which annually killed around 25,000 animals.[103] These coaxed confessions reveal more about the state's unease about its inability to fully manage the Kola environment than about acts of enemy sabotage. Fires naturally occur in such regions and the efforts to systematize and regulate the pastures of the collective farms before adequate fire prevention services existed likely impeded herders' ability to adapt. The spread of hoof disease was a predictable outcome of pursuing the relentless increase in herd numbers without adequate veterinary facilities.

102 Sorokazherd′ev, "Po stranitsam sledstvennogo dela No. 46197," NBM 16, no. 2 (April 2004): 46–64; Kiselev, "Saamskii zagovor (Delo No. 46197)," *ZhA*, no. 3–4 (December 1999): 58–60; and "Vozvrashchennye imena: Severo-zapad Rossii," Rossiiskaia natsional′naia biblioteka, accessed November 2, 2009, http://visz.nlr.ru/search/lists/murm/224_0.html.

103 Sorokazherd′ev, "Po stranitsam sledstvennogo dela No. 46197," *NBM* 16, no. 2 (April 2004): 55–64.

Questions about the optimal reindeer ecology also played into a campaign against Kreps at the Lapland Nature Reserve. In contrast to his initial claims about the benefit of preserving wild reindeer for the domestic reindeer economy, Kreps shifted to favoring isolation among wild and domestic herds. He now emphasized the future possibility of hunting wild reindeer as conservation's primary economic utility.[104] In September 1933 he evoked criticism from the head of the Apatit trust, Vasilii Kondrikov, who commented, "wild reindeer are a good thing, but I should say that comrade Kreps with his wild reindeer should still be more concerned with practical issues," including assisting collective agriculture.[105] Later the author of a 1937 newspaper exposé assailed the Lapland Nature Reserve's research program for not prioritizing the study of lichen restoration in an area where there had been a forest fire and accused Kreps of issuing "a call to exterminate wild reindeer." He based this attack on Kreps's observations that wild reindeer contribute "to domestic reindeer going wild," are not genetically unique from domestic reindeer, and "can disturb the work of rescuing domestic reindeer from gadflies and therefore are harmful in reindeer-herding regions."[106] Kreps lost his job amid such incriminations and left the wild reindeer reserve.[107]

The Second World War disturbed Kola reindeer much more than the terror. More than 1,000 herders served in the Red Army, forcing them to abandon their animals during the war. In addition, over 6,000 reindeer assisted the army on the Finnish front as an unsustainable means of transport and sustenance.[108] Desperate state-sanctioned hunting caused a sharp decline in the reindeer population, which almost completely disappeared from Karelia and fell from 70,300 domestic animals in 1940 to 42,900 in 1945 on the Kola Peninsula (see Table 2).[109] The wild reindeer population in the western part of the peninsula likewise fell from over 900 animals in 1940 to 380 in 1948 (see Table 3). This aggressive hunting apparently affected the psychology of the animals. Artamon Sergin, a Sami security guard at the Lapland reserve, described "the extremely

104 German Kreps, "Domashnii i dikii olen′ v Laplandii," *SS*, no. 3 (1934): 68–74.

105 V. I. Kondrikov, "Sostoianie i zadachi issledovatel′skikh rabot (Vstupitel′noe slovo)," in A. E. Fersman, ed., *Khibinskie Apatity: Itogi nauchno-issledovatel′skikh i poiskovykh rabot*, vol. 6 (Leningrad: NIS-NKTP Lenoblispolkom, 1933), 19.

106 D. Davydov, "Na beregu Chunozera," *KR* (February 9, 1937): 3.

107 GARF, f. A-358, op. 2, d. 32, l. 30 and V. E. Berlin, *Grazhdanin laplandii: Odisseia Germana Krepsa* (Moscow: "Mysl′," 1985), 110–121.

108 McCannon, *A History of the Arctic*, 230 and Kiselev and Kiseleva, *Sovetskie saamy*, 108–120.

109 GARF, f. A-358, op. 4, d. 1640, l. 25 and Kiselev and Kiseleva, *Sovetskie saamy*, 119.

alarmed behavior of wild reindeer" in his diary in February 1942. "Wild reindeer now began to move very quickly. If you frighten them away, they will go thirty kilometers and not eat but go straight. If one or two reindeer stay on the path, then they go in pursuit of them and scare away the herd."[110]

As the war wound down, central party and economic organizations sought to shore up the local food supply in the north by again expanding the Kola reindeer economy and further developing polar agriculture.[111] Still, pastoralists' actions likely contributed more to the postwar recovery of reindeer stocks than new policy interventions.

A final challenge to the status of reindeer on the Kola Peninsula came with the liquidation of nature reserves. The Soviet Union reduced the amount of territory under protection from 12,600,000 hectares to 1,384,000 hectares and eliminated eighty-eight of 128 *zapovedniki*, including the Lapland Nature Reserve, in 1951.[112] Environmental historians have viewed this decision from contrasting perspectives. On the one hand, Douglas Weiner depicts liquidation as related to the ascent of charlatan agronomist Trofim Lysenko and his Promethean views about the natural world to the apex of their influence.[113] Infamous for his attacks on genetics and other scientists, Lysenko was in the midst of distorting a potentially sensible tree-planting program into the absurdly unrealistic Stalin Plan for the Transformation of Nature.[114] On the other hand, Stephen Brain argues that the Ministry of Forest Management, which took over much of the territory of the closed *zapodvedniki*, actually had no interest in economically exploiting these lands. Instead, it wanted to expand its own program of forest conservation.[115]

Whether it was bureaucratic wrestling or the growing sway of an unsavory agronomist behind the liquidation of the *zapovedniki*, the leadership of the Lapland Nature Reserve responded steadfastly. Oleg Semenov-Tian-Shanskii and others at the reserve first did everything they could to

110 GARF, f. A-358, op. 4, d. 1521, ll. 20–21.

111 RGASPI, f. 17, op. 122, d. 104, ll. 162–168.

112 Douglas Weiner, *A Little Corner of Freedom: Russian Nature Protection from Stalin to Gorbachev* (Berkeley: University of California Press, 1999), 129.

113 Weiner, *A Little Corner of Freedom*, 63–103.

114 Stephen Brain, "The Great Stalin Plan for the Transformation of Nature," *EH* 15, no. 4 (October 2010): 670–700. Also on Lysenko, also see David Joravsky, *The Lysenko Affair* (Cambridge, MA: Harvard University Press, 1970) and Ethan Pollock, "From Partinost′ to Nauchnost′ and Not Quite Back Again: Revisiting the Lessons of the Lysenko Affair," *SR* 68, no. 1 (Spring 2009): 116–138.

115 Brain, *Song of the Forest*, 135–136.

try to prevent its closure. They then successfully pushed to reopen it with the initial round of *zapovedniki* restoration in 1957.[116]

The gap in protection also turned out to be less harmful for wild reindeer than conservation scientists had feared. Though timber collection began in the area and supposedly one third of the forests burned down (destroying a significant portion of lichen pastures) while the reserve was closed, the number of wild reindeer there actually grew substantially (see Table 3).[117] Any predation that occurred did not overshadow the boom cycle in the animal's population. The state hunting inspection also started using aerial photography to estimate reindeer populations during liquidation – a technique that reserve scientists quickly picked up after the Lapland *zapovednik* reopened.[118] This method of counting animals replaced an earlier practice of relying on the practical skills and knowledge of reindeer herders. Lost in the process was the ability to distinguish between wild reindeer and the domestic ones that had joined the group.[119] Soon, though, these groups of animals would be kept further apart.

Consolidation

Lovozero only became the center of "Sami reindeer herding" on the Kola Peninsula after the death of Stalin. Visitors today are greeted by standard five-story Soviet apartment buildings along with quasi-modernist structures such as a hotel shaped like a teepee and a stylized socialist-realist reindeer on the town's entrance sign. One cannot help but notice the jarring contrast between the place's identity as a pastoral village and the urban architecture adorning the streets. There are also plenty of reminders of Sami culture, such as the Museum of the History of Kola Sami and the National Cultural Center of the Sami, which celebrate Lovozero's status as a traditional homeland for Sami and their reindeer.[120] Yet such an impression reveals only part of the story.

116 Weiner, *A Little Corner of Freedom*, 88–93, 232, 258.

117 Semenov-Tian-Shanskii, *Laplandskii gosudarstvennyi zapovednik*, 60; Weiner, *A Little Corner of Freedom*, 224; and O. I. Semenov-Tyan-Shanskii, "Wild Reindeer of Kola Peninsula," in E. E. Syroechkovskii, ed., *Wild Reindeer of the Soviet Union (Proceedings of the First Interdepartmental Conference on the Preservation and Rational Utilization of Wild Reindeer Resources)* (New Delhi: Oxonian Press, [1975] 1984), 165.

118 GARF, f. A-358, op. 3, d. 1375, ll. 1–29; GARF, f. A-358, op. 3, d. 1011, ll. 1–3; and Semenov-Tian-Shanskii, *Laplandskii gosudarstvennyi zapovednik*, 62.

119 GARF, f. A-358, op. 4, d. 1521, l. 55 and Semenov-Tian-Shanskii, *Laplandskii gosudarstvennyi zapovednik*, 62–77.

120 Kiselev and Kiseleva, *Sovetskie saamy*, 157–184.

FIGURE 8. The National Cultural Center of the Sami in Lovozero.
Source: Author's photograph.

An old yet average-sized settlement of the Sami dating back to the sixteenth century, Lovozero first became a home of large-scale reindeer herding with the Komi migration in the late nineteenth century. At the time of collectivization, Komi households dominated the Tundra collective farm based there.[121] It was the influx of 435 Sami from resettled villages to Lovozero in the 1960s that more than doubled its Sami population.[122] As Natalia Gutsol, Svetlana Vinogradova, and Antonina Samorukova observe, "the contemporary role of Lovozero as an ethnic and reindeer-herding center on the Kola Peninsula came about as the result of historical, political, and socio-economic processes and events that occurred in the Murmansk region during the twentieth century."[123]

A specific "high-modernist" policy concentrated Sami and reindeer into an urbanized village: collective farm consolidation.[124] While

[121] Ushakov and Dashchinskii, *Lovozero*, 108 and Budovnits, *Olenevodcheskie kolkhozy kol'skogo poluostrova*, 45, 100.

[122] Gutsol, Vinogradova, and Samorukova, *Pereselenie gruppy kol'skikh saamov*, 48.

[123] Gutsol, Vinogradova, and Samorukova, *Pereselenie gruppy kol'skikh saamov*, 6.

[124] In labeling consolidation "high-modernist," I am again referring back to James Scott's theories of legible knowledge as a tactic of rule. Scott, *Seeing Like a State*. For a study

collectivization expanded surveillance and control over the tundra in part through prioritizing a specific animal, the consolidation of numerous collective farms into a few state farms further isolated ethnic minorities from historically important forms of nature use. It also confined them and their reindeer to more restricted territories, often to make way for energy, industrial, conservation, and military installations. Through this very process of eliminating space and access to other natural resources, amalgamation further accentuated the role of large-scale reindeer herding among native northerners of the Kola Peninsula. In a sense, the result was the Arctic equivalent of the global expansion of monoculture and domesticated fauna in the twentieth century.[125] Consolidation brought the Soviet campaign to manage territories by concentrating on a single species to its apex.

After decades of focusing on heavy industry while leaving the rural economy depressed, the Soviet government turned to a variety of programs to increase grain outputs and agricultural productivity in the 1950s. Most famously, Nikita Khrushchev eagerly sought to revive Soviet agriculture with the Virgin Lands program, which transformed millions of hectares of unplowed steppe grasslands into farming territories. He also expanded the cultivation of corn as a fodder crop.[126] In addition, Khrushchev continued the late Stalinist consolidation of collective farms: in 1950 the total number of collective farms in the USSR fell by half and between 1953 and 1958 they again dropped by over a quarter.[127] As this push to eliminate and combine small agricultural units extended into the 1960s, central agencies used 1959 census data to draw up a list of 580,000 "non-viable" villages scheduled for liquidation. The general idea was to leave only two concentrated agricultural towns in each region.[128]

that explores the varied ways that Scott's ideas relate to Soviet agricultural consolidation of the 1950s, see Auri C. Berg, "Reform in the Time of Stalin: Nikita Khrushchev and the Fate of the Russian Peasantry" (PhD diss., University of Toronto, 2012).

125 On the spread of monoculture and growth in the populations of domestic animals, see J. R. McNeill, *Something New Under the Sun: An Environmental History of the Twentieth-Century World* (New York: W. W. Norton, 2000), 212–226, 262–264.

126 Martin McCauley, *Khrushchev and the Development of Soviet Agriculture: The Virgin Lands Program 1953–1964* (New York: Holmes & Meier Publishers, 1976).

127 Ronald Grigor Suny, *The Soviet Experiment: Russia, the USSR, and the Successor States*, 2nd edn. (Oxford: Oxford University Press, 2011), 394; Gregory L. Freeze, "From Stalinism to Stagnation, 1953–1985," in Gregory L. Freeze, ed., *Russia: A History* (Oxford: Oxford University Press, 1997), 366; and Fitzpatrick, *Stalin's Peasants*, 174–203.

128 Neil J. Melvin, *Soviet Power and the Countryside: Policy Innovation and Institutional Decay* (New York: Palgrave Macmillan, 2003), 64.

These mergers led to a remarkable reduction in the number of reindeer herding enterprises on the Kola Peninsula from over a dozen before World War II to only two state farms by the end of the Soviet era.[129] Many factors shaped the implementation of this policy. For one thing, consolidation aimed at increasing the productivity and profitability of the herding economy by enlarging the scale of operations. Collective farms with economic difficulties were often the first to be eliminated and combined with more successful ones. Thus, Vpered in Chudz′iavr, which had mostly been in the red since its creation in 1939, closed its doors in 1959. Eighteen households from the primarily Sami community, which had already been forced out of Kildin Island in the 1930s, moved to Lovozero. Vpered's herders and reindeer joined the Tundra collective farm. Over time, though, economic considerations mattered less. In 1969 the Bol′shevik collective farm in Varzino, which had been fulfilling its production plans consistently in the 1950s and 1960s, also united with Tundra.[130]

The desire to make room for new industrial installations and the military also helped determine the pattern of resettlement. Hydroelectric power stations displaced several small reindeer-herding villages. In the early 1960s the profitable Dobrovolets collective farm (renamed from the cooperative Saam in 1937) moved from Voron′e to Lovozero, where it merged with Tundra. This occurred so that the village, including an old Sami cemetery, could be submerged under a reservoir for the Serebriansk Hydroelectric Station.[131] Likewise, residents of Chal′mny-Varre (Ivanovka) relocated to nearby Krasnoshchel′e in the 1960s after authorities slated the village for flooding to serve a planned electric station on the Ponoi River. The Krasnaia Tundra collective farm combined with one in the new village and eventually became the state farm Imeni V. I. Lenina (In the Name of Lenin).[132] Moreover, the expanding presence of

129 Luk′ianchenko, *Material′naia kul′tura saamov (loparei) Kol′skogo poluostrova v kontse XIX–XX v.*, 23 and Yulian Konstantinov, *Reindeer-herders: Field-notes from the Kola Peninsula (1994–95)* (Uppsala: Uppsala University Press, 2005), 25–27.

130 Gutsol, Vinogradova, and Samorukova, *Pereselenie gruppy kol′skikh saamov*, 27–33, 37–43.

131 Gutsol, Vinogradova, and Samorukova, *Pereselenie gruppy kol′skikh saamov*, 33–37, 52 and Gutsol, Vinogradova, and Samorukova, "Istoricheskie usloviia i sotsial′no-ekonomicheskie posledstviia pereselenii Kol′skikh saamov v sovetskii period," in Petrov and Razumova, ed., *Chelovek v sotsiokul′turnom prostranstve*, 104–108.

132 Simanovskaia, "Chal′mny-Varre," in Petrov and Razumova, eds., *Severiane*, 70–82 and I. I. Gokhman, T. V. Luk′ianchenko, and V. I. Khartanovich, "O pogrebal′nom obriade i kraniologii loparei," in *Polevye issledovaniia instituta etnografii* (Moscow: "Nauka," 1978), 51–67, accessed October 8, 2009, http://qwercus.narod.ru/chalmny-varre_1976.htm.

the Soviet military on the Kola Peninsula during the Cold War generally encouraged more rigid boundaries with civilian terrains. Officials designated areas where reindeer had roamed as excluded zones for the Soviet navy and facilities serving the country's nuclear arsenal.[133]

Local conservationists also supported relocating reindeer herders away from the wild animals that they wanted to protect. Over the years a conflict surfaced between reindeer pastoralists at the Krasnoe Pulozero collective farm and the scientific staff at the nearby Lapland Nature Reserve. The herders seem to have resented their exclusion from the land and resources on the protected territory, while scientists saw them and their animals as a threat to wild reindeer. In 1949 Semenov-Tian-Shanskii accused the members of Krasnoe Pulozero of illegally hunting approximately fifty wild reindeer the previous year.[134] During another incident in 1960, Pulozero pastoralists claimed that 400 of their domestic reindeer escaped to the reserve. They purposefully came to investigate while Semenov-Tian-Shanskii was away. Entering the *zapovednik* with a security guard from the reserve, this group of herders shot fourteen reindeer. Instead of checking the animals' earmarks to verify that they belonged to the herders, the security guard covered up the matter. Outraged when he learned of this episode, Semenov-Tian-Shanskii declared the "reindeer herders of the Pulozero collective farm" to be "the main poachers on the territory of the nature reserve."[135] Having lost a large portion of their reindeer in the late 1950s, the Pulozero pastoralists did not relent in the face of this opposition. In 1961 the Pulozero village council sought "to take all measures to retrieve the reindeer that had broken away and to fire in the regions of the Lapland Nature Reserve."[136]

The behavior of the reindeer played a role in this conflict. Wild and domestic herds in the western part of the Kola Peninsula indeed competed for foraging resources. In the postwar years wild reindeer's search for lichen ended up leading them to pastures outside of the Lapland Nature Reserve, where collective farm reindeer also grazed. For their part,

[133] Geir Hønneland and Anne-Kristin Jørgensen, *Integration vs. Autonomy: Civil-Military Relations on the Kola Peninsula* (Aldershot: Ashgate, 1999) and Konstantinov, "Pre-Soviet Pasts and Reindeer-Herding Collectives," *Acta Borealia* 17, no. 2 (2000): 51.

[134] GARF, f. A-358, op. 2, d. 788, l. 7 and Valerii Berlin, "Khraniteli prirodnogo naslediia," *ZhA*, no. 1 (2004): 7.

[135] GARF, f. A-358, op. 5, d. 101, ll. 2–3 and GARF, f. A-358, op. 4, d. 1521, ll. 72–73. Between 1960 and 1962 *zapovednik* workers had discovered eight reindeer with earmarks indicating that they belonged to Krasnoe Pulozero. GARF, f. A-358, op. 4, d. 1521, ll. 57–58.

[136] GARF, f. A-358, op. 4, d. 1521, l. 81 and GAMO, f. R-955, op. 1, d. 2, ll. 23–24, 75–76.

domestic herds had also begun using *zapovednik* pastures.[137] Furthermore, the mixing of wild and domestic reindeer created problems for all of the people involved in protecting, harvesting, and hunting them. Wild animals that joined domestic herds brought out less complacent behaviors in the other reindeer, making it more difficult for pastoralists to manage their herds. Domestic animals that escaped into wild herds challenged the integrity of conservationists' campaign to strictly preserve a distinct type of fauna and threatened to spread diseases to the protected reindeer. Such lichen competition and the perils of mixing made it hard for a large-scale reindeer economy to coexist alongside a vibrant wild reindeer population.[138] Ultimately, wild reindeer gained the upper hoof in this standoff. Authorities closed the Krasnoe Pulozero collective farm and transferred its reindeer to the Murmansk Experimental Reindeer-Herding Station.[139]

While decision-making remained top-down in the Soviet 1960s, herding communities did offer input on consolidation and tried to get the most out of it. For instance, before their resettlement the members of the collective farm Bol′shevik voted convincingly, but not unanimously, in favor of it. They cited the lack of supplies and electricity in the village, the distance from amenities, and the fact that young people were already abandoning Varzino in support of their decision. When the members of Tundra took up the issue, they expressed concern about limited pastureland for reindeer herds. Tundra member V. A. Podoliak declared, "the most complicated question concerns pastures for reindeer. We have so few winter pastures and will need to accommodate another herd of three thousand animals."[140] Tundra ultimately agreed to accept Bol′shevik on the condition that they receive pastureland back from the Imeni V. I. Lenina collective farm and that current members of Tundra would be allowed to move into any new building before the migrants. During the earlier resettlement of Dobrovolets, collective farm members had secured

[137] In the early 1950s the Murmansk Experimental Reindeer-Herding Station built fences and awnings to allow Krasnoe Pulozero reindeer the chance to graze without supervision in the summer. These structures do not seem to have effectively stopped the animals from mixing with wild herds. A. Poliakov, "V kolkhoze 'Krasnoe Pulozero,'" *PP* (September 17, 1953): 2 and G. V. Ivanova, P. A. Mashistova, and A. V. Gavrilova, "Izgorodi na olen′ikh pastbishchakh murmanskoi olenevodcheskoi opytnoi stantsii," in *Murmanskaia olenevodcheskaia opytnaia stantsiia (Sbornik nauchnykh rabot)*, vol. 2 (Murmansk: Murmanskoe knizhnoe izdatel′stvo, 1972), 97–103.

[138] GARF, f. A-358, op. 4, d. 1521, ll. 2–98.

[139] *Murmanskaia olenevodcheskaia opytnaia stantsiia*, vol. 1, 3; Luk′ianchenko, *Material′naia kul′tura saamov (loparei) Kol′skogo poluostrova v kontse XIX–XX v.*, 23; and GAMO, f. R-955, op. 1, d. 2, ll. 21–24, 75–76.

[140] Gutsol, Vinogradova, and Samorukova, *Pereselenie gruppy kol′skikh saamov*, 42.

moving expenses and two new apartment buildings in Lovozero from the new hydroelectric plant. But this time housing planners botched this construction project and many former members of Bol′shevik remained without the promised residences for years.[141]

In the end, amalgamation remade the tundra. As the pinnacle of the Soviet industrialization of reindeer herding, it left the Kola Peninsula with only Tundra in Lovozero and Imeni V. I. Lenina in Krasnoshchel′e in the 1970s. Both of these large and concentrated state farms included an array of Sami, Komi, Nenets, and Russian members among their ranks. They also reduced the space devoted to reindeer herding, while maintaining the quantity of animals kept. Dobrovolets, Vpered, and Bol′shevik alone lost 120,000 hectares as they combined with Tundra.[142] Meanwhile, the population of domestic reindeer on the Kola Peninsula reached a twentieth-century peak of 82,832 animals in 1971 (see Table 2). The environmental interactions of rural inhabitants also changed in the process. Throughout the 1930s to the 1950s, fishing and hunting remained key to, if not the dominant components of, herding communities' economies. For the inhabitants of Varzino in particular, salmon (*semga*) fishing at numerous points on the rivers of the Semiostrov region was more significant than reindeer herding.[143] Consolidation separated many small Kola communities from these fishing grounds and hunting territories, while one edible organism grew in prominence – reindeer.

Soviet Stability and Globalized Changes

"You won't drive us back to the stone age!" exclaimed one Kola reindeer herder after the collapse of the Soviet Union.[144] Opposed to the deliberate efforts to save the traditions of indigenous communities, this outraged tundra dweller implied a widely-shared preference for late Soviet pastoralism. The state farms of the 1970s and 1980s afforded the Kola

[141] Gutsol, Vinogradova, and Samorukova, *Pereselenie gruppy kol′skikh saamov*, 33–37, 41–43, 51–54 and Gutsol, Vinogradova, and Samorukova, "Istoricheskie usloviia i sotsial′no-ekonomicheskie posledstviia pereselenii Kol′skikh saamov v sovetskii period," in Petrov and Razumova, ed., *Chelovek v sotsiokul′turnom prostranstve*, 104–108.

[142] Gutsol, Vinogradova, and Samorukova, *Pereselenie gruppy kol′skikh saamov*, 60.

[143] Gutsol, Vinogradova, and Samorukova, "Istoricheskie usloviia i sotsial′no-ekonomicheskie posledstviia pereselenii Kol′skikh saamov v sovetskii period," in Petrov and Razumova, ed., *Chelovek v sotsiokul′turnom prostranstve*, 97–114.

[144] Quoted with a slightly different translation in Vladislava Vladimirova, *Just Labor: Labor Ethic in a Post-Soviet Reindeer Herding Community* (Uppsala: Uppsala University Press, 2006), 405. Vladimirova included the original Russian as "*V kamennom veke nas ne zagonish*."

reindeer economy with a comparatively durable set of herding practices. Reindeer served their intended purpose of incorporating distant outreaches into the Soviet state and many pastoralists enjoyed the security and social benefits of late socialism. Perestroika and the Soviet collapse then ushered in a reorientation toward international markets and activist groups. These events brought yet another round of disruptive reforms. While reindeer have retained a central role in providing remote territories with legibility to the outside world, the changes of the post-Soviet decades now leave the future of Kola herding in doubt.

Unlike the collective farms where members bore the brunt of the risks of agricultural production (and in theory could reap the rewards), the state farms turned reindeer herders into government employees with guaranteed salaries. The state also took greater responsibility for keeping Tundra and Imeni V. I. Lenina financially afloat by providing loans and investments. Indeed, though the state farms failed to earn profits for the government, herders still earned higher wages than the national average. Paid only once a year, management deducted purchases from their salaries and awarded bonuses based on meeting production quotas. Each of the state farms' brigades included about a dozen herders who tended to several thousand animals and maintained bases out in the tundra for herding activities. Increasingly, the herders relied on modern equipment such as snowmobiles, radios, helicopters, and all-terrain vehicles, though sleds drawn by draft reindeer, lassos, and dogs remained important as well. The division of pasturelands among the different brigades largely succeeded in supplying all of the reindeer with adequate grazing grounds. Most of the venison culled each year went to the Murmansk Meat Combine, which made sausage out of it. Tundra and Imeni V. I. Lenina also sold furs and antlers for souvenirs, clothing, and exported elixirs.[145]

Herders acquired new ways of relating to reindeer in the state farms. Slowly but surely after World War II, the various herding enterprises switched back from constant surveillance over the animals to free release in the summer. This resurgent Sami practice became standard after consolidation.[146] With each brigade responsible for even larger numbers of animals than in the collective farms, the amount of interaction

[145] Hugh Beach, "Reindeer Herding on the Kola Peninsula – Report of a Visit with Saami Herders of Sovkhoz Tundra," in Roger Kvist, ed., *Readings in Saami History, Culture and Language III* (Umeå: University of Umeå, 1992), 113–141. On collectivized herders in this period in another location of the Soviet Union, see Caroline Humphrey, *Marx Went Away but Karl Stayed Behind* (Ann Arbor: University of Michigan Press, 1998).

[146] Luk′ianchenko, *Material′naia kul′tura saamov (loparei) Kol′skogo poluostrova v kontse XIX–XX v.*, 19–34.

with the reindeer declined further. Calving operations continued to occur in the spring, during which time herders led the mothers toward the best grazing spots, helped protect the calves, and marked the ears of newborns. After frozen conditions returned in the autumn, they rounded up the reindeer into corrals. Here they counted them and slaughtered a portion of older animals. For much of the year, the herders spent time in the urban villages of Lovozero and Krasnoshchel′e, or fishing and hunting (often illegally) away from the herds. The state farm system also altered pastoralists' relations with their personal reindeer. On the one hand, these animals became a greater concern since they could provide more profit to individuals than the state farm reindeer. On the other hand, herders encountered them even less frequently. Only really at slaughter time did herders check the distinguishing earmarks on the animals. Most of the reindeer would belong to the state farm, but any personal animals killed would be credited to the owner.[147]

As Kola herders enjoyed the relative and often incongruous comforts of late socialism, they witnessed a burgeoning interest in reindeer and Sami ethnicity as regional symbols. Some of this veneration extended back to the 1930s, when the annual Holiday of the North first started featuring reindeer races. By the 1960s and 1970s these competitions were some of the most popular spectator events at the sports festival. The athletes and animals routinely adorned the historic attire of native groups and several of the reindeer races specifically required the use of Sami sleds.[148] Writers and artists in this period also more frequently celebrated Sami folklore, which often involved reindeer themes and evoked phrases such as "We are reindeer people."[149] A postwar industrial town even acquired the name of Olenegorsk (Reindeer Mountain City).[150]

In the middle of the 1980s individuals promoting indigenous livelihoods of the Kola Sami started looking abroad and becoming more political. At first, some of them increased interaction with Sami communities

[147] Konstantinov, "Pre-Soviet Pasts and Reindeer-Herding Collectives," *Acta Borealia* 17, no. 2 (2000): 49–64; Beach, "Reindeer Herding on the Kola Peninsula," in Kvist, ed., *Readings in Saami History, Culture and Language III*, 113–141; and Yulian Konstantinov, "Soviet and Post-Soviet Reindeer-Herding Collectives: Transitional Slogans in Murmansk Region," in Erich Kastern, ed., *People and the Land: Pathways to Reform in Post-Soviet Siberia* (Berlin: Dietrich Reimer Verlag, 2002), 171–188.

[148] M. Dubnitskii and A. Khrapovitskii, *Prazdnik Severa* (Murmansk: Murmanskoe knizhnoe izdatel′stvo, 1984).

[149] Charnoluskii, *V kraiu letuchego kamnia*, 16–21; Charnoluskii, *Legenda o olenecheloveke*; and Kiselev and Kiseleva, *Sovetskie saamy*, 172.

[150] A. A. Kiselev, *Rodnoe zapoliar′e: ocherki istorii murmanskoi oblasti (1917–1972 gg.)* (Murmansk: Murmanskoe knizhnoe izdatel′stvo, 1974), 412–413.

in Scandinavia by participating in foreign-funded programs to reforge ethnic ties. Nordic Sami already possessed a strong and growing political movement at this time. With the newfound acceptance of oppositional politics during perestroika, ethnic activists on the Kola Peninsula formed a social movement focused on protecting Sami culture. In 1989 they created the Association of Kola Sami, which soon joined the Sami Council – an international umbrella organization that advocates on behalf of the group. Many of the people who became involved in Sami politics came from the better-educated and more urban part of the population. Most were women and few were herders.[151]

Efforts to preserve wild reindeer similarly turned in an international direction. Pollution from the nearby Severonikel′ smelter destroyed vegetation on parts of the Lapland Nature Reserve in the 1970s and 1980s, just as the wild reindeer population crashed (see Table 3). In response, the Soviet government nearly doubled the total territory of the reserve in 1983, adding more potential reindeer pastureland.[152] The United Nations Educational, Scientific and Cultural Organization (UNESCO) also designated the Lapland *zapovednik* as a biosphere reserve in February 1985.[153] As state funding for nature protection dropped precipitously in the 1990s, the UN and the newly multinational corporation Noril′sk Nikel′ gained considerable influence over wild reindeer conservation. Through its funding of new infrastructure for tourists and the promotional materials it provided, Noril′sk Nikel′ accentuated the symbol of reindeer in the place over its own history of pollution.[154] One children's book that the company put out in the 2000s featured a girl and boy searching for Grandfather Frost's missing reindeer on the Lapland reserve and calling the nickel industry "the main Guardian of Nature."[155]

Even more so than it did with conservation, the collapse of the USSR at the end of 1991 set Kola pastoralism off on another turbulent course.

151 Indra Overland and Mikkel Berg-Nordlie, *Bridging Divides: Ethno-Political Leadership among the Russian Sámi* (New York: Berghahn Books, 2012); Vladimirova, *Just Labor*, 66–74, 317–358; and Kiselev and Kiseleva, *Sovetskie saamy*, 185–194.

152 V. E. Berlin, "O. I. Semyonov-Tyan-Shansky – naturalist, researcher, citizen," in *Laplandsky Zapovednik: Year-book of the Laplandsky State Nature Biosphere Zapovednik*, no. 7 (2005–2006), 8.

153 From the website of the Lapland Nature Reserve, accessed September 25, 2009, www.lapland.ru/.

154 S. Shestakov, "Benefits Beyond Boundaries," in *Laplandsky Zapovednik: Year-book of the Laplandsky State Nature Biosphere Zapovednik*, no. 5 (2003), 3–4.

155 Gennadii Leibenzon, *Tainy Laplandskogo zapovednika: istoriia odnogo prikliucheniia* (Monchegorsk/Moscow: Kol′skaia GMK, 2006).

President Boris Yelstin's new government responded to Russia's acute economic strife with shock-therapy policies designed to swiftly switch the country from socialism to capitalism – an eerie reversal of Stalin's campaign to build socialism in one country during the first five-year plan. This neoliberal approach to transitioning Russia into a market democracy included hasty privatization, the deregulation of price controls, the withdrawal of state subsidies, and increased openness to foreign trade. Predictably, these measures impoverished and disempowered huge portions of the population just as the country was trying to erect a more democratic form of governance. The fate of agricultural property in these reforms involved legal and practical complexities over the distribution of rights and moral anxieties in society regarding the reorganization of ownership.[156] One outcome from these tensions was that in certain sectors, like Kola reindeer herding, post-Soviet reforms allowed important elements of the state farm system to remain in place.

In 1992 the Russian government initially privatized the Kola state farms Tundra and Imeni V. I. Lenina as Limited Liability Partnerships, allocating the majority of shares in the enterprises to employees and managers. Imeni V. I. Lenina later reverted to its original moniker, Olenevod. Members of both entities voted to reconstitute themselves as cooperatives, officially Agricultural Production Cooperatives, in 1998. This latter status eased loan requirements and their tax burden. Legally focused on a common activity instead of accruing profit, these cooperatives demanded that everyone in them work, paid out salaries instead of just dividends, and offloaded some debt obligations to members.[157] Since the cooperatives

156 Ethnographic research has effectively probed the on-the-ground contradictions in many realms of the post-socialist world that complicate understandings of how capitalist property regimes function. See Katherine Verdery, *The Vanishing Hectare: Property and Value in Postsocialist Transylvania* (Ithaca: Cornell University Press, 2003); Ruth Mandel and Caroline Humphrey, eds., *Markets and Moralities: Ethnographies of Postsocialism* (Oxford: Berg, 2002); C. M. Hann, ed., *Postsocialism: Ideals, Ideologies and Practices in Eurasia* (London: Routledge, 2002); Florian Stammler, *Reindeer Nomads Meet the Market: Culture, Property and Globalisation at the 'End of the Land'* (Münster: LIT Verlag, 2004); Yulian Konstantinov and Vladislava Vladimirova, "Changes in Property Regimes and Reindeer Herding Management in Post-Soviet Herding Collectives: The Case of the Muncipality of Lovozero (Murmansk Region, Northwest Russia)," in B. C. Forbes, et al., eds., *Reindeer Management in Northernmost Europe* (Berlin Heidelberg: Springer-Verlag, 2006), 117–133; and Jessica Allina-Pisano, *The Post-Soviet Potemkin Village: Politics and Property Rights in the Black Earth* (Cambridge: Cambridge University Press, 2008).

157 Yulian Konstantinov and Vladislava Vladimirova, "Ambiguous Transition: Agrarian Reforms, Management, and Coping Practices in Murmansk Region Reindeer Herding," Working Paper No. 35 of the Max Planck Institute for Social Anthropology

kept the basic model of mixed collective/private ownership of reindeer, post-privatization Tundra and Olenevod largely resembled the old state farms. Yulian Konstantinov and Vladislava Vladimirova call the continuation of everyday economic practices and structures associated with the state farm "sovkhoism" and argue that for Kola reindeer herders it has been "a much more stable tradition, than anything that dates before."[158]

The hundred or so herders who worked for the cooperatives in the 1990s and 2000s practiced a familiar style of large-scale reindeer herding. Sometime late in the year they went out to the tundra where they captured and slaughtered a selection of cooperative and personal reindeer. Unlike in much of Siberia, the Kola herding cooperatives were able to take advantage of their close proximity to the venison market in Scandinavia. The Swedish firm Norfrys-Polarica replaced the Murmansk Meat Combine as a monopolistic purchaser of Kola reindeer meat. This source of income, along with herders' ability to access natural resources from the tundra during crisis moments, helped sustain the villages of Lovozero and Krasnoshchel′e.[159]

But impoverishment also took a heavy toll on Kola pastoralism. First off, fewer and fewer individuals were willing to become herders. Those who did join the cooperatives often had less direct previous experience with reindeer and thus lacked the same sentient knowledge of the Kola environment as previous generations. Salaries also often went unpaid, as they did for workers throughout the country. On top of the labor shortage and missing wages, the brigades continued to reduce their interactions with reindeer. In the late 1990s pastoralists at Olenevod ceased marking calves in the spring. Instead they just killed a set of older animals and

(Halle/Saale: Max Planck Institute, 2002), 15–21; Konstantinov, "Pre-Soviet Pasts and Reindeer-Herding Collectives," *Acta Borealia* 17, no. 2 (2000): 49–50; and Yulian Konstantinov, "Memory of Lenin Ltd.: Reindeer-Herding Brigades on the Kola Peninsula," *Anthropology Today* 13, no. 3 (July 1997): 14–19.

158 Yulian Konstantinov and Vladislava Vladimirova, "The Performative Machine: Transfer of Ownership in a Northwest Russian Reindeer Herding Community (Kola Peninsula)," *Nomadic Peoples* 10, no. 2 (2006): 183.

159 Konstantinov, "Memory of Lenin Ltd.," *Anthropology Today* 13, no. 3 (July 1997): 16; Konstantinov and Vladimirova, "The Performative Machine," *Nomadic Peoples* 10, no. 2 (2006): 169–172; Dessislav Sabev, "Economic View from the Tundra Camp: Field Experience with Reindeer Herders in the Kola Peninsula," accessed June 23, 2014, www.thearctic.is/articles/cases/economicview/index.htm; and Indra Nobl Overland, "Politics and Culture among the Russian Sami: Leadership, Representation and Legitimacy" (PhD diss., University of Cambridge, 1999), 77.

left the newborns to be trampled.[160] Apparently, the herd was already too large for the herders who remained in the brigade. At Tundra the winter corral and slaughter moved later and later into the year, which in turn delayed the calving campaigns. Pastoralists seemed to have greater difficulty locating the herds in forested areas and driving them into corrals before the animals escaped to the coast for summer pasturage.[161] Over time, this decreased contact led to there being more reindeer without earmarks. It also caused the domestic herds to start behaving more like wild ones.[162]

The market reforms also brought with them the further isolation of herding communities from fishing grounds. This time, instead of the Soviet state, international companies and shady regional officials put up legal barriers to exclude the local population from waterways in the eastern part of the Kola Peninsula. While consolidation had distanced communities from fishing grounds, many continued to catch salmon in rivers and streams when the opportunity arose. In the 1990s the regional leadership agreed to lease parts of the Varzina, Ponoi, and Lumbovka rivers to foreign tourism companies such as Kola Salmon Marketing in the United States and Nature Unlimited in Finland. These companies advertised their salmon fishing expeditions by explicitly referring to the fact that Kola residents were not allowed to fish in the rivers. Inhabitants of Lovozero and Krasnoshchel′e responded with vociferous criticism of this new property regime.[163] "[W]hy must the locals fish like thieves in their own river while anything is possible for foreigners?"[164]

Just as contentious for the herders was the surge in ethnic activism. Throughout Russia, representatives of the "small peoples of the north" joined advocacy groups that focused on bolstering the status of ethnic minorities in the 1990s.[165] As they became more visible and independent,

[160] Konstantinov, "Pre-Soviet Pasts and Reindeer-Herding Collectives," *Acta Borealia* 17, no. 2 (2000): 54–56.

[161] Vladimirova, *Just Labor*, 169–225.

[162] Konstantinov and Vladimirova, "The Performative Machine," *Nomadic Peoples* 10, no. 2 (2006): 177–178.

[163] Overland and Berg-Nordlie, *Bridging Divides*, 41–43.

[164] Quoted in Overland and Berg-Nordlie, *Bridging Divides*, 43.

[165] See Patty A. Gray, *The Predicament of Chukotka's Indigenous Movement: Post-Soviet Activism in the Russian Far North* (Cambridge: Cambridge University Press, 2005); Alexia Bloch, *Red Ties and Residential Schools: Indigenous Siberians in a Post-Soviet State* (Philadelphia: University of Pennsylvania Press, 2003); and Anna M. Kerttula, *Antler on the Sea: The Yupik and Chukchi on the Russian Far East* (Ithaca: Cornell University Press, 2000).

Kola Sami activists endorsed political agendas borrowed from Western countries. Several explicitly supported "neo-traditional" alternatives to the large-scale reindeer herding of the Soviet period. According to ethnographer Alexander Pika, neo-traditionalism rejected state-driven modernization "in favor of demands for legal protection for northern peoples, freedom for independent economic and cultural development, and self-government." He continued that "a 'neo-traditionalist' economy for northern native communities presents the possibility for combining traditional native land use, natural economy (*khoziaistvo*) and market relations, on the one hand, with reliance on state help, and compensation from the processing of oil, mineral, sea, forest and other natural resources in the north, on the other."[166] This model would treat reindeer herding more as a tradition worth saving than a productive industry.

Foreign-backed campaigners for neo-traditionalist reforms to Kola reindeer pastoralism often mixed an avowed focus on using local indigenous knowledge with generalizations that poorly fit the conditions there. Some even called for developing a system of reindeer husbandry akin to the ranching practices of the Scandinavian Sami, but that had no precedent on the Kola Peninsula.[167] One internationally funded project in the 1990s sought to employ Canadian-style co-management, which intended to democratize nature use by "combining indigenous and cultural environmental wisdom about wildlife ... with scientific knowledge," to the economy of the Kola Sami.[168] Aleksei Lapin, a Sami man from Lovozero, also attempted to create a private reindeer-herding commune called Kedd'k in 2003. With financial and administrative support of the Danish non-governmental organization Infonor, Lapin's project promoted putatively traditional and ethnically-based reindeer herding.[169]

None of these endeavors bore much fruit. Instead of attracting enthusiasm from the multiethnic population actually involved in Kola reindeer pastoralism, they garnered the sharp disapproval of many herders. As reflected in the one herder's quip about the "stone age," those working with reindeer for a living often maintained an allegiance to Soviet

166 Alexander Pika, "Preface to Russian Edition," in Alexander Pika, ed., *Neotraditionalism in the Russian North: Indigenous Peoples and the Legacy of Perestroika* (Seattle: University of Washington Press, 1999), xxiii–xxiv.

167 Overland, "Politics and Culture among the Russian Sami," 157–259 and Vladimirova, *Just Labor*, 317–407.

168 Michael P. Robinson and Karim-Aly S. Kassam, *Sami Potatoes: Living with Reindeer and Perestroika* (Calgary: Bayeux Arts, 1998), 25.

169 Vladimirova, *Just Labor*, 317–390.

modernity into the 1990s and 2000s. They criticized Sami ethnic activism as a move back to primitivism and saw it as morally compromised and corrupt in part because of its newness and foreignness.[170]

Over the last decade, Kola reindeer herders have encountered new challenges and opportunities. They have started adapting to a warming climate by moving the slaughter period further into the winter and making adjustments to how and where their reindeer graze.[171] Increased poaching has also cut deeply into the now declining population of domestic reindeer kept by Kola pastoralists.[172] As Russia's government has struck back with mounting aggression against foreign non-governmental organizations, Murmansk regional authorities have begun funding a new slew of Sami reindeer-herding communes.[173] Only time will tell if this state-sponsored neo-traditionalism will be more successful than international efforts and if reindeer will remain a significant agricultural animal in the region. Perhaps the twentieth century will have been the apogee for reindeer on the Kola Peninsula, as it was for nickel manufacturing and the pollution it brought.

[170] I have depended here on the analysis, information, and interpretation of the following works: Vladimirova, *Just Labor*; Konstantinov, *Reindeer-herders*; and Overland, "Politics and Culture among the Russian Sami."

[171] Atle Staalesen, "Dramatic for Murmansk Reindeers," *Barents Observer* (March 27, 2013), accessed June 23, 2014, http://barentsobserver.com/en/nature/2013/03/dramatic-murmansk-reindeers-27-03.

[172] Philip Burgess, "Warm winters distress reindeer herders, Kola Peninsula," *Reindeer Herding* (March 24, 2010), accessed June 23, 2014, http://reindeerherding.org/blog/warm-winters-distress-reindeer-herders-kola-peninsula-france-24/#more-1173.

[173] "Kratkaia informatsiia ob obshchestvennykh organizatsiiakh, obshchinakh, natsional′nykh predpriiatiiakh," *Murmanskaia oblast′: ofitsial′nyi portal*, accessed June 25, 2014, http://gov-murman.ru/natpers/orgz/.

5

Scarring the Beautiful Surroundings

Evoking the Sami to promote an economic activity quite far removed from reindeer husbandry, Nikolai Vorontsov wrote in 1935: "Monche is a Lapp word. In Russian translation it means beautiful." It was the inspiration for naming a new town dedicated to nickel production Monchegorsk. An alumnus from the Khibiny, Vorontsov now worked as the head of construction of the Severonikel′ plant. Proving that environmental optimism outlived the Great Break, he assured newspaper readers, "This truly is a beautiful region with rugged mountain ranges and an array of beautiful lakes, streams, shores, and valleys that are covered with splendid forestland of pines, spruces, and birches. Here there is a splendid mild climate, remarkable conditions for winter skiing and skating and for sailing and rowing in the summer. Our task is to preserve this exceptional nature of the region, to create good conditions of life and work, and to create the conditions for people to relax."[1] Decades later, after the smelter rose and the country that built it had fallen apart, a much more depressing view of the area's natural surroundings dominated public discourse. "If you've ever had the notion to visit Hell," a *Lonely Planet* guide advised foreign tourists in 2000, "Monchegorsk is pretty close."[2]

How and why did this happen? Why did a town serving the nickel industry in the far north turn into an environmental tragedy despite the efforts of urban planners and city managers to maintain its beautiful nature? Setting aside the propagandistic intent of Vorontsov and

[1] N. Vorontsov, "Nikel′ na krainem severe," *PP* (May 9, 1935): 4.

[2] Richard Nebsky, et al., *Lonely Planet: Russia, Ukraine and Belarus* (Melbourne: Lonely Planet Publications, 2000), 425.

the ironic exoticism of *Lonely Planet*, these sentiments reflect a genuine contrast between the hopes for the project and its long-term results. To an even greater extent than the apatite industry, the mining and smelting of non-ferrous metals heavily polluted local water bodies and soil, decimated vegetation over large territories, and damaged human health. High concentrations of nickel, copper, sulfur dioxide, and other chemicals increased the acidity of freshwater lakes and streams and altered the chemistry of soils near the Severonikel′ combine in Monchegorsk and the Pechenganikel′ combine in Nikel′ and Zapoliarnyi.[3] This pollution turned the areas downwind of the nickel smelters into hauntingly denuded landscapes with occasional dead shrubs and trees protruding from the toxic ground. By the end of the century visible forest damage extended over approximately 39,000 square kilometers, while zones of full forest death occupied 600–1,000 square kilometers.[4] Many children in Monchegorsk and almost half of the population in Nikel′ suffered from respiratory problems.[5]

3 Ekaterina Viventsova, et al., "Changes in Soil Organic Matter Composition and Quantity with Distance to a Nickel Smelter: A Case Study on the Kola Peninsula, NW Russia," *Geoderma* 127, no. 3–4 (August 2005): 216–226; Tatjana Moiseenko, "Acidification and Critical Loads in Surface Waters: Kola, Northern Russia," *Ambio* 23, no. 7 (November 1994): 418–424; and Valery Barcan, "Nature and Origin of Multicomponent Aerial Emissions of the Copper-Nickel Smelter Complex," *Environmental International* 28, no. 6 (December 2002): 451–456. Some studies point to alternative processes besides acidification from sulfur emissions as exerting a greater impact on the Kola environment. One study emphasizes that previous papers overstated the role of sulfur dioxide and another one notes a significant under-estimation of the amount of highly toxic nickel and copper emitted from the Kola smelters. G. Kashulina, C. Reimann, and D. Banks, "Sulfur in the Arctic Environment (3): Environmental Impact," *Environmental Pollution* 124, no. 1 (July 2003): 151–171 and Rognvald Boyd, et al., "Emissions from the Copper-Nickel Industry on the Kola Peninsula and at Noril′sk, Russia," *Atmospheric Environment* 43, no. 7 (March 2009): 1474–1480. Regardless of the specific process of environmental alteration, scientific studies concur that pollution from the combines has had a major impact.

4 O. Rigina and M. V. Kozlov, "The Impact of Air Pollution on the Northern Taiga Forests of the Kola Peninsula, Russian Federation," in J. L. Innes and J. Oleksyn, eds., *Forest Dynamics in Heavily Polluted Regions* (Wallingford: CABI Publishing, 2000), 37–65.

5 V. Rautio and O. A. Andreev, *Sotsial′naia restrukturizatsiia gornodobyvaiushchei promyshlennosti Pechengskogo raiona Murmanskoi oblasti* (Murmansk: Murmanskii gumanitarnyi institut / Barents tsentr issledovanii, 2004), 56; Erik Hansen and Arnfinn Tønnessen, *Environment and Living Conditions on the Kola Peninsula* (Oslo: Fafo Institute for Applied Social Science, 1998), 121–123; and Larisa Bronder, et al., *Environmental Challenges in the Arctic – Norilsk Nickel: The Soviet Legacy of Industrial Pollution*, Bellona Report, vol. 10 (Oslo: Bellona, 2010), 43, 47. Though Hansen and Tønnessen discuss a study that could not establish a correlation between pollution and these health effects, they also mention clearer results for Monchegorsk. Rautio and Andreev cite

But what explains the trajectory of the Kola Peninsula to these inauspicious environmental and social results? Just after the Soviet collapse, Murray Feshbach and Alfred Friendly Jr. predicted, "When historians finally conduct an autopsy on the Soviet Union and Soviet Communism, they may reach the verdict of death by ecocide."[6] Were they correct? An overwhelming majority of scholars concur that the Soviet Union proved to be an especially bad environmental actor. Even those researchers who offer less damning assessments of the USSR's environmental record acknowledge the prevalence of particularly destructive practices.[7] Not just in the north, but also throughout the country, heavy industry polluted lands, air, and water so acutely that the term "ecocide" has seemed apt. Soviet attempts to manage the natural world also led to noteworthy disasters such as the Chernobyl catastrophe, the drainage of the Aral Sea, and the disruption of Lake Baikal.

Scholars have accounted for Soviet environmental deterioration in a variety of ways. Some focus on communist distortions, others on the influence of an all-encompassing capitalist world system, and a third group on the peril of authoritarian political rule. While all of these perspectives provide insights on the cause of extreme Soviet pollution, none of them fully explain the problem.

One line of thought points to intrinsic deficiencies in communist command economies. These authors argue that an orientation toward production over profits, a lack of efficiency, and inattention to market signals imperiled environmental stewardship.[8] In one rendering of this thesis, Ann-Mari Sätre Åhlander extends János Kornai's theories of the shortage economy to the environment. According to Kornai, enterprise managers' incentive to hoard, substitute inputs, and hide capacities in quota-based

evidence for the increased incidence of health ailments in Nikel′, including a claim by a Pechenga regional official, A. Ivanov, that life expectancy in 1998 for workers within the smelting sections was less than fifty years.

6 Murray Feshbach and Alfred Friendly, *Ecocide in the USSR: Health and Nature Under Siege* (New York: Basic Books, 1992), 1.

7 Jonathan D. Oldfield, *Russian Nature: Exploring the Environmental Consequences of Societal Change* (Burlington: Ashgate, 2005); Stephen Brain, "Stalin's Environmentalism," *Russian Review* 69, no. 1 (January 2010): 93–118; and Natalia Mirovitskaya and Marvin S. Soroos, "Socialism and the Tragedy of the Commons: Reflections on Environmental Practice in the Soviet Union," *The Journal of Environmental Development* 4, no. 1 (Winter 1995): 77–110.

8 See Feshbach and Friendly, *Ecocide in the USSR*; D. J. Peterson, *Troubled Lands: The Legacy of Soviet Environmental Destruction* (Boulder: Westview Press, 1993); and Joan DeBardeleben, *The Environment and Marxism-Leninism: The Soviet and East German Experience* (Boulder: Westview Press, 1985).

state-socialist economies created chronic shortages and endemic instability. Åhlander asserts that Soviet environmental regulations were a low priority in a context of hard budget constraints and disproportionally affected smaller firms with limited technological capacities. This left large polluters without effective emissions limits.[9] In another study, Fiona Hill and Clifford Gaddy concentrate on the allegedly skewed economic geography that Russia inherited from communist planning, claiming that it presents severe obstacles for the country's future development. By ignoring the costs of operating large-scale industries in the cold north, communist planners industrialized places like the Kola Peninsula that lacked economic viability. These authors also note an overlap between these improperly developed regions and the most polluted areas of the country.[10]

In direct contrast to this interpretation stands a wide spectrum of world-systems theorists, political ecologists, and green Marxists who point to the hegemony of the capitalist system in the modern world as the root cause of environmental calamities even in communist countries.[11]

[9] Ann-Mari Sätre Åhlander, *Environmental Problems in the Shortage Economy: The Legacy of Soviet Environmental Policy* (Brookfield: Edward Elgar Publishing Company, 1994), 58–79, 151–157 and János Kornai, *The Socialist System: The Political Economy of Communism* (Princeton: Princeton University Press, 1992). My understanding of Kornai's theories has been facilitated by Katherine Verdery, *What Was Socialism, and What Comes Next* (Princeton: Princeton University Press, 1996), 19–38.

[10] Fiona Hill and Clifford Gaddy, *The Siberian Curse: How Communist Economic Planners Left Russia Out in the Cold* (Washington, DC: Brookings Institution Press, 2003). A work informed by *The Siberian Curse* maintains that the lack of concern about energy consumption and pollution levels from the Soviet era still influence Kola enterprises. Vesa Rautio and John Round, "The Challenges of Going Global: Industrial Development in Remote Regions," in Vesa Rautio and Markku Tykkyläinen, eds., *Russia's Northern Regions on the Edge: Communities, Industries and Populations from Murmansk to Magadan* (Aleksanteri Institute, 2008), 117.

[11] On Soviet pollution in world-systems theory, see Immanuel Wallerstein, *Geopolitics and Geoculture: Essays on the Changing World-system* (Cambridge: Cambridge University Press, 1991), 84–97. For examples of political ecology's emphasis on the culpability of capitalism, see David Harvey, *Justice, Nature, and the Geography of Difference* (Oxford: Blackwell Publishers, 1996); Richard Peet and Michael Watts, eds., *Liberation Ecologies: Environment, Development, Social Movements* (London: Routledge, 1996); and Paul Robbins, *Political Ecology: A Critical Introduction* (Oxford: Blackwell Publishers, 2004), 45–52. Green Marxists share the conviction that capitalism has brought about the degradation of nature, but also want to reconsider the viability of some orthodox strands of Marxism in light of the Soviet environmental experience. See John Bellamy Foster, *The Vulnerable Planet: A Short Economic History of the Environment* (New York: Monthly Review Press, 1999), 96–101; James O'Connor, *Natural Causes: Essays in Ecological Marxism* (New York: The Guilford Press, 1998), 255–265; John Bellamy Foster, *Marx's Ecology: Materialism and Nature* (New York: Monthly Review Press,

From this perspective, communist economic systems too closely followed capitalism's logic of continual wealth accumulation by the elite classes and of transforming all of nature into commodities. The East-West competition of the Cold War also placed additional pressure for the Soviet Union to focus on unrelentingly increasing industrial production at the expense of environmental measures that might have been more aligned with socialist principles. Arran Gare summarizes this overall idea: the Soviet "command economy continues the domineering orientation to people and to nature of capitalism in a more extreme form."[12]

Another perspective turns to politics instead of economics. In this case, authoritarian rule in Russian and Soviet history largely explains the inability of those concerned about environmental protection to influence government policy. Two of the most prominent environmental historians of Russia, Douglas Weiner and Paul Josephson, embrace versions of this argument. In his comparative work, *Resources under Regimes*, Josephson stresses the predilection of authoritarian regimes such as the Soviet Union, Nazi Germany, communist China, and military-led Brazil for "large-scale geo-engineering projects to alter the face of the earth and its rivers" as a means of explaining their "great impact on the environment."[13] Weiner, for his part, points to deep authoritarian continuities in Russian history to account for the "treacherous patchwork quilt of poisoned lands, poisoned air and poisoned water we encounter today." He posits that the country's relationship to its natural resources has long suffered from the predatory practices of a militarized tribute-taking state that first appeared with the Muscovite tsar declaring all land his patrimony and continued into the Soviet and post-Soviet eras.[14]

The case of the Kola nickel industry suggests an alternative answer to the question of why the Soviet Union stood out as a devious destroyer

2000); and Ted Benton, ed., *The Greening of Marxism* (New York: The Guilford Press, 1996).

12 Arran Gare, "The Environmental Record of the Soviet Union," *Capitalism Nature Socialism* 13, no. 3 (September 2002): 52.

13 Paul Josephson, *Resources under Regimes: Technology, Environment, and the State* (Cambridge: Harvard University Press, 2004), 99.

14 Douglas R. Weiner, "The Genealogy of the Soviet and Post-Soviet Landscape of Risk," in Arja Rosenholm and Sari Autio-Sarasmo, eds., *Understanding Russian Nature: Representations, Values and Concepts* (Aleksanteri Papers 4/2005), 209, 209–236. A reworked version of this essay appears in Douglas R. Weiner, "The Predatory Tribute-Taking State: A Framework for Understanding Russian Environmental History," in Edmund Burke III and Kenneth Pomeranz, eds., *The Environment and World History* (Berkeley: University of California Press, 2009), 274–315.

of the natural world. Beyond communism, capitalism, or authoritarianism, the international context of the 1970s and 1980s played a decisive role in turning Severonikel′ and Pechenganikel′ from typical heavy polluters to especially egregious ones. I argue here that specific features of the late Soviet era tipped the smelters into the latter category. Until the late 1960s, Soviet nickel production harmed the environment as much as would be expected in any political economy, which is to say quite a lot. But then in the 1970s the intensifying environmental pressures of postwar industrial growth collided with major shifts in the global economy to place new stresses on the Soviet system. Still inspired by assimilationist longings to transform nature into resources whenever possible, Soviet industrialists pursued extensive growth strategies of expanding industrial production. Yet this approach started generating less economic improvement than it previously had. Thus, as nickel output hit a critical point of causing extreme environmental damage, economic strains made it harder for Soviet enterprise leaders to adopt technologies to cut emissions while continuing to prioritize production. On top of this, material properties of the natural world continued to interfere with Soviet industry's schemes for dealing with pollution.

Therefore, it was not the unchanging character of command economies, the competitive rapaciousness of capitalism, or the disempowerment of an environmentally concerned citizenry in an authoritarian regime that alone scarred the beautiful surroundings. A clash between the long-term privileging of economic expansion and the contextual troubles of a discrete historical moment more specifically helped turn the territory around the nickel smelters into a polluted hell. This all happened, of course, at a moment when the rise of environmentalism internationally brought greater attention to the effects of heavy industry on natural systems.

The following chronicle of nickel pollution traces the varying environmental relations that defined the manufacturing of non-ferrous metals on the Kola Peninsula. In each phase of its history, the Kola nickel industry interacted with disparate trends in the global economy and pursued distinctive approaches to environmental stewardship. When it first took off in the mid-1930s, the nickel sector embraced autarky along with the familiar social and ecological pathologies of Stalinism. Then, in the era around World War II, the industry shifted to making munitions out of excavated earth for the sake of assisting the Soviet military. During the first decades of the Cold War, it pursued extensive growth common in Europe and the United States; this relentless expansion of production began to cause mounting damage to the Kola ecosystem. Pollution reached critical levels in the 1970s and 1980s as the state-owned Kola nickel plants struggled to adapt to the challenges posed by economic globalization. With the Soviet collapse, Pechenganikel′ and Severonikel′ became part of a powerful multinational corporation and returned to releasing substantial, but more proportionate, emissions.

Autarky, Idealism, and Coercion

Even before the first chunk of nickel had been smelted in February 1939, newspapers touted the triumphs of the new industry in the Kola north. "In the years of the second Stalinist five-year plan the new city of Monchegorsk arose in the remote and wild tundra of the Kola Peninsula, far on the outskirts of the polar region. On account of their stubborn and persistent work, prospectors opened huge deposits of copper-nickel ore that will fully supply the combine for several decades."[15] This enthusiasm for transforming the Monche tundra echoed the chorus of praise for unleashing the productive potential of the Khibiny Mountains several years earlier. As could be expected, state economic planners maintained a Stalinist approach to the natural world while creating these northern nickel works. They again tried to simultaneously dominate and accentuate the surrounding landscape for the sake of achieving self-sufficient production of a valuable material.

Until the campaign to build "socialism in one country," Russia did not really have its own nickel industry. For a short time in the 1870s, the tsarist government mined and processed nickel in the Urals. Soon, though, the state switched to importing the metal from the French colony of New Caledonia in the south Pacific.[16] With the first five-year plan (1928–1932), the USSR returned to developing the Ufal deposit in the Urals. Knowing the metal's utility as a corrosion-resistant material for alloys, geologists also scoured likely lands for new deposits.[17] Nickel exists in comparative abundance among elements in the earth, but rarely in high enough concentrations to be efficiently extracted. Useable deposits come in two main types: laterites that appear at central latitudes near the surface and sulfides mixed with copper and cobalt that primarily occur

[15] "Dogovor," *Severnyi metalurg* (February 14, 1939): 1.

[16] Russell B. Adams, "Nickel and Platinum in the Soviet Union," in Robert G. Jensen, Theodore Shabad, and Arthur W. Wright, eds., *Soviet Natural Resources in the World Economy* (Chicago: University of Chicago Press, 1983), 536–541.

[17] V. Ia. Pozniakov, *Severonikel′ (Stranitsy istorii kombinata "Severonikel′")* (Moscow: GUP Izdatel′skii dom "Ruda i metally," 1999), 19.

deeper underground in northern regions. Those hunting for the metal ended up finding some of these latter deposits on the Kola Peninsula.

In the summer of 1929 geographer Gavriil Rikhter and botanist German Kreps went on a small expedition to the Monche tundra just west of Lake Imandra. One of their goals was to establish the borders of the new Lapland Nature Reserve, but they made a discovery that would later prove momentous for the protected territory. Rikhter took a sample of rock that caught his attention after the arrow on his compass twitched. Chemical analysis showed that this magnetic ore contained the telltale signs of a nickel deposit.[18]

Over the next few years, surveyors explored the Monche tundra. With geochemist Aleksandr Fersman again at the helm, these researchers traversed the bumpy hills to the west of Lake Imandra. They relied considerably on the hospitality and knowledge of a Sami family living there as well as on reindeer for transportation. Initial prospecting proved vexingly inconclusive about the amount of nickel and copper and technicians had trouble figuring out the best way to smelt the ore.[19] Both of these uncertainties delayed any decision to build a refinery. Leningrad party chief Sergei Kirov reportedly reacted by assuring a disheartened Fersman, "there is no land under Soviet power that cannot be changed by skillful hands for the benefit of humankind."[20] Kirov's confidence turned out to be appropriate in this case. Estimates of nickel reserves in the Niuduaivench, Sopchuaivench, and Kumuzh'ia deposits of the Monche tundra grew fivefold in 1934 and soon afterward engineers devised a process to enrich the low-grade ore from Niuduaivench and Sopchuaivench into an intermediary matte.[21] With these issues resolved, regional leaders pressed to move forward with the Severonikel' plant.[22]

18 G. D. Rikhter, "Chest' otkrytiia: vospominaniia pervoprokhodtsev," *MR* (April 7, 1977): 2 and O. I. Semenov-Tian-Shanskii, "Pamiati Rikhtera," *MR* (October 30, 1980): 4.

19 GAMO, f. 773, op. 1, d. 6, ll. 165–172, 223; GAMO, f. 773, op. 1, d. 2, l. 171; I. Brusilovskii and N. Markova, "Magnetity Kol'skogo poluostrova," *KMK*, no. 1–2 (1933): 55–58; and A. E. Fersman, *Vospominaniia o kamne* (Moscow: Izdatel'stvo "Nauka," [1940] 1969), 54–61.

20 Fersman, *Vospominaniia o kamne*, 59.

21 The total amount of confirmed metallurgic nickel there rose from 10,000 tons to 50,000 tons in 1934. GAMO, f. 773, op. 1, d. 33, ll. 130–135; GAMO, f. 773, op. 1, d. 44, ll. 11–17; and A. A. Eremeeva, "Stroitel'stvo kombinata 'Severonikel'' (period do nachala velikoi otechestvennoi voiny) v g. Monchegorske Murmanskoi oblasti," in V. P. Petrov and I. A. Razumova, eds., *Etnokul'turnye protsessy na Kol'skom Severe* (Apatity: Kol'skii nauchnyi tsentr Rossiisskoi Akademii nauk, 2004), 84–88.

22 GAMO, f. 773, op. 1, d. 51, l. 195.

Shifts in the national and international economy also influenced Soviet officials' choice to build a nickel smelter on the Kola Peninsula. At the same time that scientists discovered nickel in the Monche tundra, prospectors across the Arctic found enormous sulfide deposits of it near the future site of Noril′sk.[23] Hoping to benefit from the cost advantages of economies of scale, authorities tried to coordinate the creation of nickel plants in several different locations, including Monche, Noril′sk, and Orsk. Concerned with lowering transportation costs, they opted to first build a smelter on the Kola Peninsula instead of in Noril′sk, despite its larger deposits.[24] Soviet decision-makers also responded to an upsurge in the world nickel market, which was growing rapidly in the mid-1930s after a steep decline in the 1920s.[25] The International Nickel Company (Inco) of Canada dominated the nickel industry in this era, owning 90 percent of known reserves and holding monopoly power over competitors. It also chose to expand its mining and smelting operations abroad to the Petsamo (Pechenga) region of northern Finland in 1934 – a territory not far from the Monche tundra that had belonged to the Russian empire before World War I and would again become part of the USSR after World War II. The heads of Soviet industrial ministries saw no reason why they could not also build a plant nearby.[26]

Therefore, instead of proving the obliviousness of communist economies to the market, the creation of a nickel industry in the USSR occurred in interaction with developments in the capitalist world. Soviet leaders did not resort to economic autarky because Marxist ideology

[23] Andrew Roy Bond, "Noril′sk: Profile of a Soviet Arctic Development Project" (PhD diss., University of Wisconsin-Milwaukee, 1983), 98–118.

[24] Simon Ertz, "Building Norilsk," in Paul R. Gregory and Valery Lazarev, eds., *The Economics of Forced Labor: The Soviet Gulag* (Stanford: Hoover Institute Press, 2003), 128–137; Bond, "Noril′sk," 117–118; Pozniakov, *Severonikel′*, 19–25; and GAMO, f. 773, op. 1, d. 34, ll. 157–174, 201–206.

[25] F. B. Howard-White, *Nickel: An Historical Review* (Princeton: D. Van Nostrand Company, 1963), 157–196; GAMO, f. 773, op. 1, d. 33, ll. 41–60; GAMO, f. 773, op. 1, d. 34, l. 32; and GAMO, f. 773, op. 1, d. 59, ll. 70–79.

[26] Rautio and Andreev, *Sotsial′naia restrukturizatsiia gornodobyvaiushchei promyshlennosti Pechengskogo raiona Murmanskoi oblasti*, 12–13; Adams, "Nickel and Platinum in the Soviet Union," in Jensen, Shabad, and Wright, eds., *Soviet Natural Resources in the World Economy*, 540; and "Nickel: Industry Prospering in Peace-Time but Would Sell More Metal during a War," *The Wall Street Journal* (September 23, 1935): 5. The expansion of Canadian mining activities in the Subarctic also paralleled Soviet development. See Liza Piper, *The Industrial Transformation of Subarctic Canada* (Vancouver: University of British Columbia Press, 2009), 83–87.

demanded an equal geographic distribution of industry irrespective of costs, as Gaddy and Hill would have it.[27] As scholarship by Oscar Sanchez-Sibony and Michael Dohan demonstrates, the Stalinist state turned away from foreign trade and toward self-sufficiency in the 1930s more out of a lack of alternative paths of economic development than the pursuit of long-standing policy preferences.[28] Theorist Karl Polanyi noted as much in the 1940s: "Socialism in one country was brought about by the incapacity of market economy to provide a link between all countries; what appeared as Russian autarchy was merely the passing of capitalist internationalism."[29] Put in yet another way, autarky was the global economic context of the 1930s more generally.

The main decision to build in the Monche tundra came in the spring of 1935. Vasilii Kondrikov, who at the time led Apatit and its subsidiary Severonikel′, and Valerii Iazykov, who headed the agency overseeing nickel and tin enterprises, wrote to their boss, Sergo Ordzhonikidze, the People's Commissar of Heavy Industry, on March 26, 1935, with a proposed timetable and budget for the project.[30] Ordzhonikidze responded with an order to commence the nickel works on April 29. His directive closely resembled the initial proposal with only a slight budget cut and the appointment of another administrator from Apatit, Nikolai Vorontsov, to head the construction of the plant.[31] It stipulated that the new Severonikel′ enterprise should produce 3,000 tons of nickel and 3,000 tons of copper by the end of 1937 and 10,000 tons of each by the end of 1938.[32]

As with the Khibiny project, the planners of the Kola nickel works espoused hopeful visions of citizens living in accord with their natural surroundings. They named the new industrial city Monchegorsk and frequently pointed out that "Monche" meant "beautiful" in the Sami language.[33] One journalist explained the role of human activity in

27 Hill and Gaddy, *The Siberian Curse*.

28 Oscar Sanchez-Sibony, "Depression Stalinism: The Great Break Reconsidered," *Kritika* 15, no. 1 (Winter 2014): 23–50 and Michael R. Dohan, "The Economic Origins of Soviet Autarky 1927/8–1934," *SR* 35, no. 4 (December 1976): 603–635.

29 Karl Polanyi, *The Great Transformation: The Political and Economic Origins of Our Time* (Boston: Beacon Press, [1944] 2001), 256.

30 GAMO, f. 773, op. 1, d. 51, l. 195.

31 GAMO, f. 773, op. 1, d. 51, ll. 194, 523.

32 Ordzhonikidze's order is reprinted in Pozniakov, *Severonikel′*, 22.

33 N. Vorontsov, "Nikel′ na krainem severe," *PP* (May 9, 1935), 4; *PP* (March 14, 1936), 2; *PP* (November 7, 1936), 2; *PP* (November 18, 1936), 2; *PP* (May 12, 1938), 2; Pozniakov, *Severonikel′*, 23; and Fersman, *Vospominaniia o kamne*, 54.

beautifying the landscape to readers in November 1936. "It was wild uninhabited tundra. For centuries no one came here. High mountains surrounded the tundra and no one knew what resources they stored. But the Bolsheviks came and figured out the secrets of the mountains. And now the Monche tundra is unrecognizable. It became actually beautiful. So far this beauty consists not in constructed factory buildings and not even in avenues and squares. This beauty is in the great creative work that the Bolsheviks have begun and persistently undertake."[34] This "creative work," implied the author, would soon allow people to live there – a requirement for this wild environment to acquire worth.

In practical terms, the designers of Monchegorsk and Severonikel′ took some measures to realize their holistic vision. Claiming to have learned a lesson from his experience in the Khibiny, Kondrikov ordered that some of the old-growth forest within the city be preserved and turned into a park.[35] Monchegorsk's main architect, Sergei Brovtsev included green belts along the main boulevard and sought to maximize the views of the mountain relief.[36] Applauding these efforts, the local newspaper, *In the Fight for Nickel*, exclaimed, "In the summer the city will be engrossed in the greenery of forests. It will be a garden-city."[37] Urban planners also considered the optimal arrangement for industrial and municipal structures, transportation issues, and the means of supplying water and sewer service when picking a location for the "socialist city." In terms of water, they again wanted to protect certain bodies from pollution. Debate arose in particular around whether to use Lake Lumbolka as a water source for drinking, industry, or both.[38] City architects mulled over the question of air quality as well. So that the smoke, dust, and sulfur dioxide emissions would blow away from the residential areas, they decided to place the city upwind from the smelter. This move "to

[34] *PP* (November 18, 1936), 2.

[35] A. A. Kiselev, *Monchegorsk* (Murmansk: Murmanskoe knizhnoe izdatel′stvo, 1986), 31–32; V. A. Gladkov, *Monchegorsk* (Murmansk: Murmanskoe knizhnoe izdatel′stvo, 1961), 35–37; Pozniakov, *Severonikel′*, 23; "Boi za nikel′: Vospominaniia I. L. Kondrikovoi-Tartakovskoi," *MR* (September 11, 1986): 3–4; and GAMO, f. 773, op. 1, d. 34, l. 35.

[36] Pozniakov, *Severonikel′*, 44–46 and A. A. Eremeeva, "Formirovanie gorodskoi sredy i prostranstvennogo obraza Monchegorska," in V. P. Petrov and I. A. Razumova, eds., *Severiane: Problemy sotsiokul′turnoi adaptatsii zhitelei Kol′skogo poluostrova* (Apatity: Kol′skii nauchnyi tsentr Rossiisskoi Akademii nauk, 2006), 87–95.

[37] *V boi za nikel′* (May 1, 1937).

[38] GAMO, f. 773, op. 1, d. 34, ll. 157–174; GAMO, f. 773, op. 1, d. 55, ll. 18–19, 65–66, 126–127, 275–276; and GAMO, f. 773, op. 1, d. 62, l. 186.

protect the city from gases" succeeded in helping preserve the green spaces within Monchegorsk in later years even as pollution decimated vegetation south of the factory.[39]

Some of the higher echelons of Severonikel′ also endorsed a model of waste management that sought to reduce the factory's pollution. Fersman kept advocating for applying the "complex utilization of natural resources" to the nickel industry – a scheme designed to completely reuse industrial by-products to such an extent that enterprises would drastically cut their emissions.[40] In a 1940 discussion of "wastes and refuse of Monche," he acknowledged, "the problem of protecting the mineral substances and nature of the surrounding area of the Monche region is especially acute." The issue, above all, involved "a struggle with the loss of useful materials – nickel in lateral rock, cobalt in slag, selenium in silt and slag – but the utmost attention should be paid to the neutralization and utilization of emitted sulfur gases and the conversion of them into sulfuric acid."[41] In principle, the chief of the factory in the late 1930s and early 1940s, Mikhail Tsarevskii, agreed that, "we need to create the conditions for every waste to find its application."[42] Scientists and industry publicists also recognized the value of the sulfur-rich mineral pyrrhotite in the Monche region as a source of much-needed sulfuric acid during initial planning of the plant.[43] Shortly after Severonikel′ began production, employees of the Kola enterprises hatched plans to convert sulfur gases emitted during metal smelting into sulfuric acid – a measure that could have also helped prevent acid rain.[44]

In contrast to these sanguine visions, intractable nature, chaotic planning, and decisions to rely on forced labor once again produced abysmal conditions for those unfortunate enough to live in the new industrial settlement. Even the freely recruited workers first moved into crowded and unsanitary tents. Due in part to the destructive influence of blizzards,

39 GAMO, f. 773, op. 1, d. 34, ll. 167–169; GAMO, f. 773, op. 1, d. 53, l. 229; Pozniakov, *Severonikel′*, 44; and Eremeeva, "Formirovanie gorodskoi sredy i prostranstvennogo obraza Monchegorska," in Petrov and Razumova, eds., *Severiane*, 87–95.

40 A. E. Fersman, *Kompleksnoe ispol′zovanie iskopaemogo syr′ia* (Leningrad: Izdatel′stvo Akademii Nauk SSSR, 1932).

41 ARAN, f. 544, op. 1, d. 207, l. 2.

42 KF GAMO, f. 52, op. 1, d. 59, l. 34.

43 M. M. Kossov and B. I. Kagan, "Severnyi gorno-khimicheskii trest 'Apatit' vo 2-m piatiletii," *KMK*, no. 3–4 (1932): 19; "Pirotin est′ – budet sernaia kislota," *KhR* (October 5, 1932): 3; and ARAN, f. 544, op. 1, d. 282, ll. 1–12.

44 V. Afanas′ev, "Proizvodstvo sernoi kisloty na Kol′skom poluostrove," *PP* (February 3, 1940): 3; and Eremeeva, "Stroitel′stvo kombinata 'Severonikel′,'" in Petrov and Razumova, eds., *Etnokul′turnye protsessy na Kol′skom Severe*, 97.

snowdrifts, and flooding during spring thaws, housing construction for Monchegorsk and the mining settlements at Sopcha and Nuid languished behind schedule.[45] A party inspector offered grim details in August 1936: "in the barracks and tents 75% of all workers live cluttered in filth with children.... In rare cases workers sleep in the forest under trees because there is no room in the tents."[46] Local Murmansk historian Aleksei Kiselev also recalls how an epidemic struck his family upon their arrival in Monchegorsk in 1935.[47]

This disagreeable habitat led to a quick exodus of recruited workers and resulted in reports of widespread drunkenness and disorder.[48] Memos cited illegal deforestation and arson as common offences. One claimed as well that approximately 900 hectares of forest in the area had been burned during the previous month because of the lack of a fire fighting service.[49] The anthropogenic impact of such arson and felling at this point, however, paled in comparison to the burden that the severe surroundings posed on the people living there.

A huge portion of the new inhabitants of the Monche tundra in the mid-1930s came there as prisoners through various branches of the Gulag system. Some were "special settlers" transferred from Kirovsk and other locations, while others were part of the eighth department of the White Sea-Baltic Combine stationed in Monchegorsk or its fourteenth department, which built the tracks connecting the new town to the mainline railroad.[50] By the end of 1935, approximately 6,000 of 10,000 workers at Severonikel′ were Gulag prisoners and another 5,000 from the White Sea-Baltic Combine arrived in 1937.[51] One inmate remembered dealing with "harassment, cold, and hunger" at the construction site. Kiselev describes how "the wild and grey polar landscape, the lack of people, the

[45] GAMO, f. 773, op. 1, d. 64, ll. 207–213, 228–248 and GAMO, f. 773, op. 1, d. 53, ll. 15–16.

[46] GAMO, f. 773, op. 1, d. 64, ll. 238–239.

[47] Kiselev, *Monchegorsk*, 5. Also see "Boi za nikel′: Vospominaniia I. L. Kondrikovoi-Tartakovskoi," *MR* (September 23, 1986): 3–4.

[48] GAMO, f. 773, op. 1, d. 55, ll. 17, 696–700; GAMO, f. 773, op. 1, d. 62, l. 369; GAMO, f. 773, op. 1, d. 64, ll. 200, 238–239, 244; and GAMO, f. 773, op. 1, d. 63, l. 21.

[49] GAMO, f. 773, op. 1, d. 64, ll. 244–245.

[50] Eremeeva, "Stroitel′stvo kombinata 'Severonikel′,'" in Petrov and Razumova, eds., *Etnokul′turnye protsessy na Kol′skom Severe*, 90–92; V. Ia. Shashkov, *Spetspereselentsy v istorii Murmanskoi oblasti* (Murmansk: "Maksimum," 2004), 121–125; and A. Matveev, "GULAG na Kol′skom severe," in G. Bodrova, ed., *Murman, Khibiny do i posle...* (Apatity: Sever, 2002), 36–37.

[51] GAMO, f. 773, op. 1, d. 55, ll. 68, 711 and Pozniakov, *Severonikel′*, 54.

stunted vegetation, the cold lead-colored sky, and the perpetually stormy winds stunned some and suppressed others."[52] Forcibly sent there by a punitive carceral state, most prisoners must have experienced the Monche tundra as a forbidding place.

Combined with the elusiveness of the metals in the ground, this coercive and haphazard approach to northern development set back efforts to turn the country into a self-sufficient nickel producer. In 1936 significant delays hit the construction of the railroad line between Monchegorsk and Olen′ia. The building of industrial objects for the mines and the smelter, research on the extraction process, and the prospecting for new deposits also lagged.[53] These disruptions prevented Severonikel′ from manufacturing any metal in 1937 and 1938, as originally ordered. Contrary to what geologists and economic planners had thought, the mountains of the Monche tundra seemed to contain fewer deposits with high concentrations of nickel and copper.[54] With only stocks of poorly impregnated ore, Severonikel′ needed to mine greater quantities of rock and undertake a more expensive and energy-intensive smelting process to produce the metals.[55]

Party officials and the rank-and-file began hurling accusations about mismanagement and worse to explain any and all of these problems. In the summer of 1936 a commission of the Leningrad Regional Party filed a scathing report against the leadership of Severonikel′. It cited insufficient housing, unpaid wages, gaps in the production schedule, and the enterprise leaders' frequent absence from the worksite.[56] After this point, denunciations began piling up against the doomed ranks of Severonikel′'s

52 A. A. Kiselev, "GULAG na Murmane: Istoriia tiurem, lagerei, kolonii," *SM* (October 22, 1992): 3.

53 GAMO, f. 773, op. 1, d. 59, ll. 186–193; GAMO, f. 773, op. 1, d. 62, ll. 23–25, 138–143, 160, 163–165, 176–188, 212–216, 223–224, 366–369, 385–389; GAMO, f. 773, op. 1, d. 64, ll. 132, 191–194, 207–213, 228–248, 339; GAMO, f. 773, op. 1, d. 64, ll. 29, 261, 330–331, 344; and Eremeeva, "Stroitel′stvo kombinata 'Severonikel′,'" in Petrov and Razumova, eds., *Etnokul′turnye protsessy na Kol′skom Severe*, 86–94.

54 GAMO, f. 773, op. 1, d. 59, ll. 186–193; GAMO, f. 773, op. 1, d. 62, ll. 212–216, 223–224; GAMO, f. 773, op. 1, d. 64, ll. 212–213, 235–236; and ARAN, f. 544, op. 1, d. 186, ll. 1–7.

55 According to an estimate based on verified reserves, the enterprise would have needed to smelt 3,600,000 tons of ore from Sopchuaivench with a 0.41 percent nickel concentration, 1,500,000 tons of ore from Niuduaivench with a 0.3–0.4 percent nickel concentration, and 29,000 of rich ore from Kumuzh′ia with a 2.15 percent nickel concentration in order to meet its initial plan of 3,000 tons of nickel by the end of 1937. Pozniakov, *Severonikel′*, 39.

56 GAMO, f. 773, op. 1, d. 64, ll. 187–188, 200, 212–213, 228–248, 252, 256–258, 343 and GAMO, f. 773, op. 1, d. 65, ll. 383, 548.

management. Vorontsov, who left the Kola Peninsula after having a heart attack in November 1935, survived the terror. But shortly after Ordzhonikidze's suicide in February 1937 a slew of arrests and later executions took out many others among the enterprise's allegedly "counter-revolutionary" leaders.[57]

In the midst of this bloodbath, new geological discoveries helped push the Kola nickel industry forward. Researchers found sections of sulfide ore with over 5 percent nickel concentration on Nittis-Kumuzh'ia in 1937. Severonikel′'s new bosses hastily shifted the production plan toward extracting and processing material from this deposit. The rich ore from Nittis allowed the plant to mine sufficient material the next two years and to devise a less complex smelting scheme in order to begin production in 1939.[58] That year Severonikel′ manufactured 1,597 tons of nickel and 571 tons of copper and extracted 94,032 tons of ore.[59]

Taking stock of the influence of the nickel industry on the Kola environment in the 1930s, it is safe to say that Severonikel′ disrupted the ecosystem at an unprecedented pace and scale, but that this damage was quite minor overall compared to what came later. People in this period felt the brunt of the Soviet assault on the Monche environment, whether through exposure to the harsh elements or contamination of the worksite. Yet both production and pollution remained relatively low.[60] Certainly the nickel manufacturing on New Caledonia in this era, which belted out enough sulfur emissions to dissolve the roof of a church, inflicted greater environmental damage. So too did the massive operations in the Sudbury region of Canada, which had been occurring since the late 1880s.[61]

[57] "Nenakazannye prestupleniia," *PP* (February 27, 1937): 3; *PP* (March 30, 1937): 2; Sergei Tararaksin, *Sudeb sgorevshikh ochertan′e* (Murmansk: "Sever," 2006), 81–117; Sergei Tararaksin, "Oshibka krasnogo direktora," *KhR* (September 2, 2004): 6; GAMO, f. 773, op. 1, d. 55, ll. 223, 296; and Pozniakov, *Severonikel′*, 24–25, 29, 52–53.

[58] RGAE, f. 7793, op. 1, d. 301, ll. 2–3, 72–82; KF GAMO, f. 52, op. 1, d. 4, ll. 3–6; KF GAMO, f. 52, op. 1, d. 1, ll. 63–72; KF GAMO, f. 52, op. 1, d. 2, ll. 1–5; Pozniakov, *Severonikel′*, 69; and Eremeeva, "Stroitel′stvo kombinata 'Severonikel′,'" in Petrov and Razumova, eds., *Etnokul′turnye protsessy na Kol′skom Severe*, 93–95.

[59] RGAE, f. 9037, op. 1, d. 41, l. 9 and RGAE, f. 386, op. 1, d. 5148, l. 64.

[60] Mikhail V. Kozlov and Valery Barcan, "Environmental Contamination in the Central Part of the Kola Peninsula: History, Documentation, and Perception," *Ambio* 29, no. 8 (December 2000): 513 and Olga Rigina, et al., "Monitoring of Forest Damage in the Kola Peninsula, Northern Russia Due to Smelting Industry," *The Science of the Total Environment* 229, no. 3 (May 1999): 148.

[61] J. R. McNeill, *Something New Under the Sun: An Environmental History of the Twentieth-Century World* (New York: W. W. Norton, 2000), 34 and Gerard M. Courtin, "The Last 150 Years: A History of Environmental Degradation in Sudbury," *The Science of the Total Environment* 148, no. 2–3 (June 1994): 99–102.

Severonikel′ had begun encroaching on the conservation efforts of the Lapland Nature Reserve: first by instigating an adjustment of the reserve's borders away from the newly discovered nickel deposits in 1930 and then by surveying on the preserved Chuna tundra in 1939.[62] In neither of these instances, however, did the smelter's emissions yet impair the protected territory. This snapshot result does not reflect any sort of environmental accomplishment of the firm, but rather points to the inability of planners to introduce industrial operations as quickly as they desired. Still, Stalinist autarky by itself did not perpetrate the extensive environmental destruction of the Monche tundra.

Nickel as a Military Metal

"Although interests identified with nickel production object to the classification of their industry as one of the munitions group," prefaced *The Wall Street Journal* in 1935, "there is little question that war would greatly increase the demand for the metal."[63] Soviet leaders shared this prescient premonition of American journalists.[64] In the face of impeding wars, they incorporated the Kola nickel industry into the country's national defense complex. Henceforth, geopolitical and military concerns changed the significance of the metals taken from the ground. Instead of functioning as unleashed productive forces that could facilitate autarkic development or as wealth accruing commodities to be sold, nickel, copper, and cobalt served above all as source materials for desperately needed armaments.

Just months after Severonikel′ started smelting nickel, war began. Tensions between the Soviet Union and Germany had been high since the rise of the Nazi party to power in 1933. The Soviet government used the prospect of a war with Germany to attempt to coax Finnish authorities into a military agreement in 1938 and warned about the possibility of a preemptive strike in the case of a conflict. Geopolitical calculations changed significantly after the signing of the Soviet-German nonaggression pact in late August 1939 and the outbreak of the Second World War in Europe a few weeks later. Though the pact temporarily removed the pretext of a Nazi invasion of the Soviet Union, it also included secret

[62] V. E. Berlin, "O. I. Semyonov-Tyan-Shansky – naturalist, researcher, citizen," in *Laplandsky Zapovednik: Year-book of the Laplandsky State Nature Biosphere Zapovednik*, no. 7 (2005–2006), 4 and KF GAMO, f. 52, op. 1, d. 4, ll. 30b-4.

[63] "Nickel," *The Wall Street Journal* (September 23, 1935): 5.

[64] GAMO, f. 773, op. 1, d. 59, ll. 127–128 and P. F. Lomako, *Tsvenaia metallurgiia v gody Velikoi Otechestvennoi voiny* (Moscow: Metallurgiia, 1985).

provisions that placed Finland, along with the Baltics and parts of Poland and Romania, under a Soviet sphere of influence. The Soviet government wasted little time in exerting its newly secured power, invading Poland with Germany in September 1939 and demanding territorial concessions from Finland in October. After the refusal of the Finnish government to comply, the Soviet-Finnish Winter War broke out at the end of November 1939 and lasted until mid-March 1940. The USSR gained considerable territory near Lake Ladoga and the Salla region of Karelia from Finland, but failed to conquer the entire country. It also received the remaining portion of the Rybachi Peninsula on the Kola Peninsula.[65]

The Winter War clearly affected heavy industry on the Kola Peninsula. Concerned about leaving a borderland near Finland in civilian hands, Stalin ordered the transfer of the Severonikel′ combine from the People's Commissariat of Heavy Industry to the People's Commissariat of Internal Affairs (NKVD).[66] Soviet leaders were also responding to a decision of British companies in South Africa to stop supplying the USSR with cobalt after the Molotov-Ribbentrop pact.[67] In Noril′sk the nickel works had been under NKVD authority since their creation in 1935; thus, the reallocation of Severonikel′ also mirrored a more general Soviet strategy of placing industrial objects in difficult natural environments under secret police authority.[68]

With the switch, the industrial activities of the enterprise now constituted "crucial state tasks for the defense of the country."[69] The NKVD provided Severonikel′ with more resources to meet its output targets, including greatly expanding the enterprise's Gulag camp, Monchelag, from 3,120 prisoners to 14,735 during 1940.[70] Also boosting the supplies and equipment available to the firm, the NKVD raised its production

65 On rising international tensions and the Winter War, see H. Peter Krosby, *Finland, Germany, and the Soviet Union, 1940–1941: The Petsamo Dispute* (Madison: University of Wisconsin Press, 1968); William R. Trotter, *A Frozen Hell: The Russo-Finnish Winter War of 1939–1940* (Chapel Hill: Algonquin Books of Chapel Hill, 1991); Robert Edwards, *The Winter War: Russia's Invasion of Finland, 1939–1940* (New York: Pegasus Books, 2008); and Nick Baron, *Soviet Karelia: Politics, Planning and Terror in Stalin's Russia, 1920–1939* (London: Routledge, 2007), 223–225.

66 RGAE, f. 9037, op. 1, d. 41, l. 11–114; KF GAMO, f. 52, op. 1, d. 11, ll. 8–12; and KF GAMO, f. 52, op. 1, d. 12, l. 1.

67 Pozniakov, *Severonikel′*, 77 and *PP* (March 4, 1940), 2–4.

68 Ertz, "Building Norilsk," in Gregory and Lazarev, eds., *The Economics of Forced Labor*, 131–133.

69 KF GAMO, f. 52, op. 1, d. 12, l. 1.

70 M. B. Smirov, ed., *Sistema ispravitel′no-trudovykh lagerei v SSSR, 1923–1960* (Moscow: Zven′ia, 1998), 327.

quotas for nickel and copper for that year and added electrolytic metals manufactured from anticipated nickel-copper mattes from Noril′sk.[71] Then in the autumn, NKVD head Lavrentii Beriia demanded that Severonikel′ shift its operations to prioritize processing cobalt for the military.[72] He issued written warnings to the enterprise's leadership, Tsarevskii and Ivan Beresnev, that they faced five to eight years in prison for not following new quality standards and personally threatened to have them shot for delaying cobalt production. Severonikel′'s directors managed to satisfy their bosses sufficiently enough by the evacuation of the worksite in June 1941 to avoid these fates.[73]

But much of the situation on the ground in the Monche tundra remained disorganized under NKVD auspices. Severonikel′ continued to under-fulfill its plans, while Gulag prisoners frequently instigated work stoppages and attempted escape. NKVD authorities, furthermore, proved no more apt at controlling the environmental conditions that affected prisoner livelihoods. The fulfillment of food and housing norms vacillated wildly and the neglect of sanitary issues resulted in prisoners' dwellings being filthy, cockroach-infested, and disease-ridden. Such poor conditions lowered the productivity of the forced laborers, thereby undermining the defensive mission of the camp.[74]

While Soviet authorities introduced martial forms of organization in Monchegorsk, the Winter War militarized the nickel deposits in Pechenga/Petsamo in a more literal sense. Part of the Russian Empire until the Bolshevik government traded it for land in Karelia in 1920, Pechenga now gave independent Finland its only access to an ice-free port on the Arctic Ocean and provided the country with a valuable source of metals.[75] Finland's contract with Inco required that the company work the deposits if it deemed them profitable and return the mine and industrial objects to Finland in the event of a war. The Red Army's invasion of Pechenga

[71] KF GAMO, f. 52, op. 1, d. 11, l. 9.

[72] KF GAMO, f. 52, op. 1, d. 1, ll. 27–32; KF GAMO, f. 52, op. 1, d. 44, ll. 1–2, 8–9; KF GAMO, f. 52, op. 1, d. 63, ll. 20–31; and Pozniakov, *Severonikel′*, 78–79.

[73] KF GAMO, f. 52, op. 1, d. 11, l. 4; KF GAMO, f. 52, op. 1, d. lol, ll.11–13; and Pozniakov, *Severonikel′*, 78–79. On Tsarevskii's later stint as a NKVD camp boss in the nuclear industry in the Urals after World War II, see Kate Brown, *Plutopia: Nuclear Families, Atomic Cities, and the Great Soviet and American Plutonium Disasters* (Oxford: Oxford University Press, 2013), 107–108.

[74] KF GAMO, f. 52, op. 1, d. 101, ll. 4, 23–26; KF GAMO, f. 52, op. 1, d. 12, ll. 5–9, 42–44; KF GAMO, f. 52, op. 1, d. 59, ll. 1–4, 5–81; and KF GAMO, f. 52, op. 1, d. 41, ll. 2–15.

[75] Krosby, *Finland, Germany, and the Soviet Union, 1940–1941*, 3–4.

during the Winter War thus opened the door for reconfiguring the ownership structure of the mines. Additionally, Inco's subsidiary, the Mond Nickel Company, had not yet begun to mine the Pechenga deposits, despite geological discoveries, significant industrial construction, and demand from Europe.[76]

Military strategy influenced the behavior of the various countries toward Pechenga. At the end of the Winter War in March 1940, the Soviet Union returned most of Pechenga to Finland in order to avoid conflict with British and Canadian stakeholders, though it had sent technicians from Severonikel′ to scout out the site. Germany, which desired more nickel for munitions, had sat out this war and then quietly arranged trade agreements with Finland to take control of the nickel deposits from the Allied Powers. The Soviet government belatedly attempted to counter this move by demanding the nickel from the Pechenga deposits in late June 1940, but failed to stop the German acquisition and the initial shipments of ore through Kirkenes at the end of the year.[77] These developments set the stage for nickel from Pechenga to serve the Nazi war economy during the next several years of fighting.

German troops invaded the Soviet Union on June 22, 1941. The metal-laden land of northwest Russia again became part of a battlefield, as it had been during World War I, the Russian Civil War, and, most recently, the Winter War. Soviet officials evacuated approximately 28,000 individuals of Monchegorsk's prewar population of 33,000. Many men enlisted in the Red Army, but authorities also transferred a significant portion of workers, prisoners, and technical specialists and much of the machinery at Severonikel′ to other mining and metallurgical enterprises further from the front. Some 13,438 Gulag prisoners went to the nickel works in Noril′sk.[78] During operation "Silver Fox" in the summer of 1941, German and Finnish troops attempted to take Murmansk and bombed several cities on the Kola Peninsula before being stopped at the Zapadnaia Lista River in the autumn.[79]

[76] Rautio and Andreev, *Sotsial′naia restrukturizatsiia gornodobyvaiushchei promyshlennosti Pechengskogo raiona Murmanskoi oblasti*, 13–14 and Vesa Rautio and Markku Tykkyläinen, "Uneven Development of Economic Interaction across the Finnish-Russian Border," *Post-Soviet Geography and Economics* 42, no. 1 (2001): 39.

[77] Krosby, *Finland, Germany, and the Soviet Union, 1940–1941*.

[78] Pozniakov, *Severonikel′*, 84–85; Kiselev, *Monchegorsk*, 55–59; and KF GAMO, f. 52, op. 1, d. 101, ll. 11–13.

[79] Chris Mann and Christer Jörgensen, *Hitler's Arctic War: The German Campaign in Norway, Finland, and the USSR, 1940–1945* (New York: Thomas Dunne Books, 2003).

At first, warfare on the Kola Peninsula, like in other places in the world, influenced the environment through both physical landscape destruction and a brief reprieve from industrial manipulation. On the one hand, combat, bombings, and scorched earth tactics destroyed forests, bogs, waterways, hillsides, and land. Army troops in the area also resorted to the desperate and rapacious hunting of wildlife for sustenance.[80] On the other hand, the lapse in the mining and smelting of metals at the beginning of World War II reduced the amount of atmospheric emissions and other pollution that could despoil the Monche ecosystem, even as places like Orsk, Ufal, and Noril′sk, which increased their nickel production to compensate for the loss of Severonikel′, experienced spillover effects.[81]

The halt in industrial activities, however, was short-lived. Both sides of the polar front strongly desired nickel for armor and other military uses. The Soviet government, thus, ordered an early reconstruction of Severonikel′ in May 1942 and a Finno-German outfit accelerated nickel mining and smelting in Pechenga. With large numbers of women and children working the mines and factory, Severonikel′ managed to manufacture moderate amounts of nickel for the Red Army during the remaining years of the war. The size of Severonikel′'s workforce grew from 1,632 in January 1943 to 5,057 in the third quarter of 1944. Snowdrifts, difficulties with coordinating the production process, and occasional Nazi airstrikes (which resulted in electrical interruptions) nevertheless caused periodic disruptions in nickel manufacturing.[82]

Nickel from Pechenga went to the USSR's enemies. Having broken off its agreement with the Mond Nickel Company and taken control of Petsamo Nickel with the outbreak of World War II, the Finnish government cooperated with the German company IG Farben to supply the Nazi Army with the metal. Through late 1944, industrial operators removed 387,615 tons of nickel-copper ore, smelted 289,520 tons of ore at the settlement of Kolosioki, and shipped the vast majority, 15,661 tons, of

[80] GARF, f. A-358, op. 4, d. 1521, l. 25. Those remaining on the Kola Peninsula also faced decreased medical service during the war. GARF, f. 8009, op. 6, d. 90, ll. 1–14; GARF, f. 8009, op. 6, d. 161, ll. 1–14; GARF, f. 8009, op. 6, d. 244, ll. 1–14; GARF, f. 8009, op. 6, d. 783, ll. 1–8; GARF, f. 8009, op. 6, d. 942, ll. 1–12; GARF, f. 8009, op. 6, d. 1092, ll. 1–12; and GARF, f. 8009, op. 6, d. 1331, ll. 1–12.

[81] Adams, "Nickel and Platinum in the Soviet Union," in Jensen, Shabad, and Wright, eds., *Soviet Natural Resources in the World Economy*, 538–543 and Bond, "Noril′sk," 127–128.

[82] Pozniakov, *Severonikel′*, 86–94; Kiselev, *Monchegorsk*, 62–69; RGAE, f. 9037, op. 1, d. 81, ll. 4, 26; and RGAE, f. 9037, op. 1, d. 149, ll. 142–148, 204–210.

the processed nickel-copper matte to Germany.[83] There it served, above all, as a government-controlled materiel for manufacturing munitions.

Pechenga also played a central role in the conclusion of World War II in the far north. As the tide of the conflict turned against Germany, Finnish authorities started longing for a separate peace agreement with the Soviet Union. The armistice they signed in September 1944 returned much of the territory that the Soviet Union had won during the Winter War, but also included Petsamo/Pechenga. With ample warning of an impending agreement, the German army evacuated the territory, hauled off some of the equipment from the mines and factories, destroyed remaining infrastructure, and burned a huge area of forests. Specialists abroad believed that these actions would cost the Soviet Union at least ten years of reconstruction work.[84] The Soviet press unsurprisingly narrated these events in a different fashion. Newspapers celebrated the occupation of Pechenga by Red Army troops in October as the "liberation" of an ancient Russian territory. They also highlighted its strategic significance, noting "the Germans also needed Petsamo nickel" and "polar nickel is also fighting the war by being transformed into powerful weapons for the Red Army."[85] To honor the heroic metal the town of Kolosioki was renamed Nikel′.[86] The State Committee for the Defense of the USSR also immediately ordered the nickel works rebuilt. Workers at one of the mines even extracted enough ore to produce nickel before the end of the war in May 1945.[87]

Soviet leaders continued to view nickel as a vital military metal into peacetime. War fortified their strategic thinking about natural resources as potential sources of state power and informed their decisions to rebuild

83 Krosby, *Finland, Germany, and the Soviet Union, 1940–1941*, 186–202.

84 V. A. Matsak, ed., *Pechenga: Opyt kraevedcheskoi entsiklopedii* (Murmansk: Prosvetitel′skii tsentr "Dobrokhot," 2005), 397–409; "V osvobozhdennoi Pechenge," *PP* (October 18, 1944): 1; John McCannon, *A History of the Arctic: Nature, Exploration, and Exploitation* (London: Reaktion Books, 2012), 234; and Rautio and Andreev, *Sotsial′naia restrukturizatsiia gornodobyvaiushchei promyshlennosti Pechengskogo raiona Murmanskoi oblasti*, 13–14.

85 "Pechengskim diviziiam – slava," *PP* (October 17, 1944): 1; "V osvobozhdennoi Pechenge," *PP* (October 18, 1944): 1; "Razgrom nemtsev na Krainem Severe," *PP* (November 3, 1944): 1; "Bol′she metalla Rodine!" *PP* (November 5, 1944): 2; "Nikel′ voiuet," *PP* (November 7, 1944): 3; F. M. Ternovskii, "Bogatstva nedr Kol′skogo poluostrova na sluzhbu chetvertoi Stalinskoi piatiletki," *PP* (April 27, 1946): 2–3; "Na pechengskom zemle," *PP* (January 15, 1946): 2; and L. Potemkin, "Istoriia pechengi i ee bogatstva," *PP* (January 9, 1947): 3.

86 Matsak, ed., *Pechenga*, 397.

87 *Kombinat Pechenganikel′ OAO "Kol′skaia GMK"* (Zapoliarnyi: Kol′skaia GMK, 2005), 4–5.

and further develop the operations in Monchegorsk and Pechenga. As an even higher priority for state officials during the Cold War, the Kola nickel sector started to exert a much greater impact on the natural world than it had in the 1930s and early 1940s. Indeed, pollution from Severonikel′ had only damaged the vegetation within a six-kilometer radius of the plant by 1946.[88] While, of course, this destruction was itself regrettable, avoidable, and arguably unacceptable, it was also hundreds of times less severe than what came later.

Extensive Growth

After the war "human enterprise suddenly accelerated" to the point where people "have changed the world's ecosystems more rapidly and extensively than in any comparable period in human history." What Will Steffen, Paul Crutzen, and John McNeill call the "Great Acceleration" entailed an exponential rise in human population, economic activity, and the consumption of resources worldwide. Nickel production around the globe followed this trend, growing an average of approximately 4.4 percent annually between 1950 and 2009. These authors view the Great Acceleration as the most recent phase of the "Anthropocene" – an epoch that began with the nineteenth-century industrial revolution when humans became a dominant and global "geophysical force."[89]

The Soviet Union contributed more than its fair share to this new and environmentally perilous geological era, including by building up the Kola Peninsula into the most industrialized and populated part of the Arctic in the second half of the twentieth century. To do so it relied on a method of economic expansion that had been commonplace since the onset of the Anthropocene: increasing industrial production to stimulate the economy. The USSR was far from alone in trying to extract greater economic value from the natural world by manufacturing evermore products. For several decades after World War II, countries on both sides of the Iron Curtain embraced a similar strategy of extensive growth – one that guided the development of the Kola nickel industry.

88 Valery Berlin, "Analysis of Ambient Air at Weather Station 'Chunozero' in Lapland Biosphere Reserve," in M. V. Kozlov, E. Haukioja, and V. T. Yarmishko, eds., *Aerial Pollution in Kola Peninsula* (Apatity: Kola Scientific Center, 1993), 99.

89 Will Steffen, Paul J. Crutzen, and John R. McNeill, "The Anthropocene: Are Humans Now Overwhelming the Great Forces of Nature?" *Ambio* 36, no. 8 (December 2007): 614, 617. On global nickel production, see Gavin M. Mudd, "Global Trends and Environmental Issues in Nickel Mining: Sulfides versus Laterites," *Ore Geology Reviews* 38, no. 1–2 (October 2010): 12.

The ravages of war forced nickel producers to repeat much of the construction of the 1930s. Several historians argue that 1943 instead of 1945 should be treated as the start of this reconstruction period, and this certainly makes sense in the case of Monchegorsk.[90] Initially, Severonikel′ benefited from technology and supplies that the United States and Britain shared with their Soviet ally. By 1946 the combine reached pre-war levels of production.[91] Repair work in Pechenga began in late 1944 and likewise incorporated foreign assistance, including for the factory's new smokestack, in the immediate aftermath of the war.[92] At first restoration proceeded more quickly than initial construction had: Pechenganikel′ began mining the Kaula deposit in March 1945 and smelting some of its own ore in November 1946. The heads of the enterprise then planned to proceed incrementally to mining 420,000 tons of ore and smelting 12,000 tons of nickel matte in 1950. They exceeded the latter goal by one thousand tons and met the former one two years late.[93]

In somewhat less of a hurry than many projects of the 1930s, Pechenganikel′ also devoted considerable attention to careful geological surveying. Enterprise leaders already knew that the Kaula deposit contained drastically more metals than the ones in the Monche tundra and estimated in 1946 that, together with the less significant Kammikivi deposit, the factory could produce 11,650 tons of nickel annually for the next 200–255 years.[94] Surveyors then realized that a deposit in the nearby Pil′guiavr valley possessed a hundred times more metal than previous researchers had thought.[95] Geologists soon declared this deposit to be

[90] Jeffrey Jones makes this argument explicitly and Donald Filtzer follows this periodization. See Jeffrey W. Jones, *Everyday Life and the "Reconstruction" of Soviet Russia during and after the Great Patriotic War, 1943–1948* (Bloomington: Slavica, 2008) and Donald Filtzer, *The Hazards of Urban Life in Late Stalinist Russia: Health, Hygiene, and Living Standards, 1943–1953* (Cambridge: Cambridge University Press, 2010).

[91] Pozniakov, *Severonikel′*, 90–108 and A. A. Kiselev, *Trest "Kol′stroi" 30 let* (Murmansk: Murmanskoe knizhnoe izdatel′stvo, 1967), 18–28.

[92] GAMO, f. R-459, op, 1, d. 4, ll. 9–12.

[93] L. A. Potemkin, *U severnoi granitsy: Pechenga sovetskaia* (Murmansk: Murmanskoe knizhnoe izdatel′stvo, 1965), 185–197; Matsak, ed., *Pechenga*, 419; *Sovetskaia Pechenga* (November 21, 1946), 1; *Sovetskaia Pechenga* (November 21, 1946), 1; GAMO, f. R-459, op, 1, d. 4, ll. 29–30; and Lars Rowe, "Pechenganikel: Soviet Industry, Russian Pollution, and the Outside World" (PhD diss., University of Oslo, 2013), 108.

[94] GAMO, f. P-359, op, 1, d. 17, ll. 20–21.

[95] GAMO, f. P-359, op, 1, d. 17, ll. 38–40; GAMO, f. R-459, op, 1, d. 4, ll. 36–37; RGAE, f. 9037, op. 2, d. 175, ll. 8–14; Potemkin, *U severnoi granitsy*, 205–214; and E. A. Grigor′eva, "K istorii razvitiia nikelevoi promyshlennosti Murmanskoi oblsati," in E. Ia. Zamotkin and N. M. Egorova, eds., *Priroda i khoziaistvo Severa*, vol. 2, part 2 (Apatity: Akademiia Nauk SSSR, 1971), 313.

"the largest of the copper-nickel deposits of the Pechenga region."[96] As international tensions leading to the Cold War became more acute in 1946, the Soviet government also ordered a comprehensive search for radioactive ore that could be used for nuclear weapons. The combine's directors reported back that they found nothing significant.[97]

During reconstruction, regional party leaders also invested substantial energy in propaganda work that promoted a vision of industrial assimilation as improvement.[98] Newspaper articles again spoke of "the treasure chest of the beautiful tundra" and lauded how "the natural resources of Pechenga and the enormous scale of the planned socialist economy will provide for the quick economic development of the region. On the basis of natural resources, the full-blooded life of the Soviet population will flourish all around."[99] Officials in Monchegorsk also maintained an idea of harmony with the natural world. A sculptor erected a statue of a moose in the city center, which he described as "incarnating the nature of the polar region."[100] Kiselev, who still lived in Monchegorsk in this period, nostalgically recalled that it seemed that "the air was cleaner, the greenery more abundant, and the climate better" than in nearby Murmansk.[101]

Unsurprisingly, the situation near the nickel works was much more difficult than these portrayals.[102] With crowded housing and the lack of fully functioning sewer systems, both industrial sites possessed filthy conditions similar to what historian Donald Filtzer describes for post-war cities in the Russian heartland.[103] Pechenganikel′ struggled with snow removal, erratic shortages in hydroelectric power, and inadequate

96 GAMO, f. R-459, op, 1, d. 123, l. 79.

97 GAMO, f. R-459, op. 1, d. 28, ll. 1–3, 6, 12, 19, 22–23. Also see David Holloway, *Stalin and the Bomb: The Soviet Union and Atomic Energy, 1939–1956* (New Haven: Yale University Press, 1995).

98 GAMO, f. P-359, op, 1, d. 16, l. 10; GAMO, f. P-359, op, 1, d. 13, l. 55; GAMO, f. P-359, op, 1, d. 8, ll. 1–9; GAMO, f. R-459, op, 6, d. 3, ll. 103–111, 130–131, 142–146; GAMO, f. R-459, op, 6, d. 6, ll. 68–69; and GAMO, f. R-459, op, 6, d. 7, l. 16.

99 F. Ternovskii, "Sokrovishcha krasivoi tundry," *Severnyi metallurg* (May 22, 1947): 2 and L. Potemkin, "Istoriia pechengi i ee bogatstva," *PP* (January 12, 1947): 3.

100 Eremeeva, "Formirovanie gorodskoi sredy i prostranstvennogo obraza Monchegorska," in Petrov and Razumova, eds., *Severiane*, 92–93.

101 Kiselev, *Monchegorsk*, 6.

102 GAMO, f. P-359, op, 1, d. 17, ll. 38–40; GAMO, f. R-459, op, 6, d. 3, ll. 88, 124–125; and GAMO, f. R-459, op, 6, d. 6, ll. 3–5.

103 Filtzer, *The Hazards of Urban Life in Late Stalinist Russia* and GARF, f. A-482, op. 47, d. 7670, ll. 1–32.

safety equipment, all of which interfered with industrial operations and imperiled workers' well-being.[104] In Monchegorsk nutritional deficiencies shot up during the 1947 Soviet famine and the northern climate contributed to heightened occurrences of childhood flu.[105] And, all the while, pollution rose. Severonikel′ annually released an estimated 500–1,000 tons of nickel, 500–1,000 tons of copper and 60,000 tons of sulfur dioxide into the surrounding water, soil and air in the late 1940s.[106]

Urban sanitation inspectors at the Ministry of Public Health began filing increasingly thorough reports on the effects that this industrial pollution was having on the people living there. In 1948 they revealed that unfiltered dusts from the mines at Severonikel′ had led to twenty-six cases of silicosis and the nickel-saturated sulfur gases had caused nineteen individuals to suffer from severe forms of rhinitis, including four with nickel-based eczema and one worker whose nasal septa perforated.[107] A few years later inspectors noted that housing near Severonikel′ was situated in the "sanitary-defense zone" – the area closest to the factory that was supposed to exclude residences. They also showed that the plant already had significantly higher levels of sulfur dioxide, chlorine gas, carbon monoxide, and sulfuric acid gases than the allowable norms (see Table 5).[108] Of course, these sanitation inspectors worried mostly about human, and not ecosystem, health. In 1953 they approvingly reported that the height of Pechenganikel′'s smokestack prevented emissions from entering a "sanitary-defense zone" and that both plants only dumped into water bodies not designated for drinking.[109] These measures distributed pollution differently, but did not reduce the amount released into the air and water.

In the early 1950s Severonikel′ also encountered physical limitations to the growth of its mining sections. By 1950 geologists had failed to find new sources of nickel and copper in the mountains around Monchegorsk and the concentration of metals in the ore being processed was dropping precipitously.[110] At this time the country was in the midst of what

104 Paul R. Josephson, *The Conquest of the Russian Arctic* (Cambridge, MA: Harvard University Press, 2014), 251–253.

105 GARF, f. A-482, op. 47, d. 7670, ll. 46, 59.

106 Kozlov and Barcan, "Environmental Contamination in the Central Part of the Kola Peninsula," *Ambio* 29, no. 8 (December 2000): 514.

107 GARF, f. A-482, op. 47, d. 7670, l. 25.

108 GARF, f. A-482, op. 49, d. 3215, ll. 78–81.

109 GARF, f. A-482, op. 49, d. 7243, ll. 124–130.

110 RGAE, f. 9037, op. 1, d. 404, l. 6 and V. Ia. Pozniakov, "Razvitie tekhnologicheskoi smekhy pererabotki sul′fidnykh medno-nikelevykh rud na kombinate 'Severonikel′'"

TABLE 5. *Atmospheric Quality around Monchegorsk in 1951 According to the Murmansk Region State Sanitation Inspectorate*

Branch of Severonikel′	Toxic Substance	Quantity of Tests	Negative Results	Within Norms	Above Norms	Significantly above Norms	Average Concentration	Maximum Concentration
Smelting	SO_2	113	22	27	34	30	0.097	0.22
department	CO	78	24	20	19	15	0.058	0.12
Refining	SO_2	119	23	43	33	20	0.045	0.75–2
department	CO	58	9	26	16	7	0.08	0.21
Electrolysis	CL_2	526	454	20	14	38	0.08	0.26
department	H_2SO_4	42	–	7	10	25	0.007	0.0157
	CO	31	2	5	10	14	0.084	0.22
Cobalt	CL_2	7	6	1	–	–	0.001	0.0015
department	SO_2	34	6	15	–	13	0.08	0.26
	CO	17	4	4	5	4	0.09	0.35
	H_2SO_4	21	–	6	9	6	0.08	0.10

Note: No units were given for the concentrations.
Source: GARF, f. A-482, op. 49, d. 3215, l. 81.

historian Ethan Pollock calls the "Soviet Science Wars."[111] Ideological fervor strongly shaped professional knowledge and government policy in fields such as agronomy, economics, and physics during this period. Such internal radicalism struck geology as well.

At a meeting of the Kola section of the Academy of Sciences in July 1950, Mikhail Tsibul′chik presented an iconoclastic report replete with quotations from Stalin and references to dialectical science. In it he suggested that the inability to find new nickel reserves in the Monche tundra resulted from an incorrect theoretical approach to geological formation and proposed a new model.[112] He specifically criticized "views about the geological structure and genesis of ores rooted in existing interpretations that conclude that the Monche tundra lacks any prospects."[113] The other scientists at the meeting dismissed the ideas of this brazen newcomer to the region – with one attendee angrily exclaiming "This is a hooliganistic report!" – and highlighted the importance of empirical results above any theoretical approach for the discovery of new economical deposits.[114] Though the rise of plate tectonics would soon transform the theoretical foundation of the geological sciences, Tsibul′chik's opponents were correct on the matter of the Monche tundra: no new major discoveries occurred after this point. Severonikel′ started processing more ore from the Pechenga deposits and focusing on its smelting operations.[115]

With geological prospects contracting in the Monche region and expanding in Pechenga, Kola industry devoted more energy to reducing reusable wastes from production. The frequent exhortations in party newspapers to limit the loss of useable byproducts and the organized campaigns to collect scrap metal resembled the "metallic waste regime" that sociologist Zsuzsa Gille describes for communist Hungary in this era. In Hungary, government officials sought to maximally reuse and recycle manufactured wastes in order to obtain all possible economic value, but made the quantity of wastes that factories generated a publically taboo topic.[116] Some commentators on the Kola Peninsula took the goal of

(1938–1958)," in V. Ia. Pozniakov, ed., *Opyt raboty kombinata "Severonikel′"* (Moscow: Gosplan, 1958), 38.

111 Ethan Pollock, *Stalin and the Soviet Science Wars* (Princeton: Princeton University Press, 2006).

112 RGAE, f. 9037, op. 1, d. 404, ll. 2–130.

113 RGAE, f. 9037, op. 1, d. 404, l. 6.

114 RGAE, f. 9037, op. 1, d. 406, l. 13.

115 Adams, "Nickel and Platinum in the Soviet Union," in Jensen, Shabad, and Wright, eds., *Soviet Natural Resources in the World Economy*, 538–543.

116 C. K. Kel′manzon, "Sernaia kislota iz otkhodov metallurgicheskogo proizvodstva," *PP* (August 3, 1946): 3; *Severnyi metallurg* (May 22, 1947), 2; "Metallolom –

cutting wastes seriously enough that they fancifully predicted that new technologies would let Severonikel′ eradicate air pollution at the same time that it increased its output of metals.[117] The main engineer of the combine more soberly described the enterprise's perspective on win-win conservation measures: "the reduction of wastes to their minimum allows for an increased output of metals, a substantial lowering of the costs of production, and simultaneously the elimination of dustiness from the sections."[118]

Through improvements in processing methods and the recovery of slag, the Kola smelters did cut the concentrations of nickel, copper, and cobalt in their solid wastes by half between 1949 and 1952.[119] Pechenganickel′ gathered 2,072 tons of scrap metal in 1952, but failed to reach its target of 2,500 tons that year because of transportation difficulties (or so its directors claimed).[120] At Severonikel′ the cobalt section explored means of recapturing more metals from its liquid wastes.[121] Later on specialists developed systems for collecting and extracting metals from mining dust, which was explicitly connected to the installation of better ventilation systems in the mines, and continued to work on sulfur dioxide conversion.[122] What the plants did not do, of course, was limit their output of nickel and copper. This meant that the amount of wastes accumulating undoubtedly outpaced their efforts to recycle materials.

martenam,"*PP* (August 3, 1951): 4; "S ekonomicheskoi konferentsii na kombinate 'Severonikel′' – Reservy snizheniia serebstoimosti produktsii," *PP* (January 5, 1957): 3; "Metallolom – martenam," and "Ves metall – v delo!," *PP* (March 17, 1964): 1–2; and "Metallolom – martenam: pervyi den′ dekadnik," *PP* (March 21, 1964): 1. See Zsuzsa Gille, *From the Cult of Waste to the Trash Heap of History: The Politics of Waste in Socialist and Postsocialist Hungary* (Bloomington: Indiana University Press, 2007), 41–101.

117 Gladkov, *Monchegorsk*, 77–78.

118 Pozniakov, "Razvitie tekhnologicheskoi smekhy pererabotki sul′fidnykh medno-nikelevykh rud na kombinate 'Severonikel′' (1938–1958)," in Pozniakov, ed., *Opyt raboty kombinata "Severonikel′,"* 45.

119 RGAE, f. 9037, op. 1, d. 511, ll. 51, 24–27.

120 RGAE, f. 9037, op. 1, d. 508, l. 129.

121 GARF, f. A-482, op. 49, d. 7243, l. 130.

122 S. P. Alekhichev, "Reshenie problemy ventiliatsii rudnikov," in I. A. Turchaninov, ed., *Osvoenie mineral′nykh bogatstv Kol′skogo poluostrova* (Murmansk: Murmanskoe knizhnoe izdatel′stvo, 1974), 145–166. Mentions of these projects also appear throughout Pozniakov, ed., *Opyt raboty kombinata "Severonikel′"*; V. Ia. Pozniakov, ed., *Opyt raboty kombinata "Severonikel′" po mobilizatsii vnutrennykh reservov* (Moscow: Gosudarstvennyi nauchno-tekhnicheskii komitet Soveta ministrov SSSR, 1961); V. Ia. Pozniakov, ed., *Opyt raboty kombinata "Severonikel′" po povysheniiu kul′tury proizvodstva* (Moscow: Ministerstvo tsvetnoi metallurgii SSSR, 1971); and Kiselev, *Monchegorsk*, 95–103.

As the Kola nickel sector kept expanding, major changes hit Soviet society. The same month as Stalin's death in March 1953 state officials began releasing large numbers of prisoners toiling away in Gulag camps, including those on the Kola Peninsula. Over the next several years the new Soviet leader, Nikita Khrushchev, initiated an ambitious, but capricious, program to revive the socialist project of the country. The Thaw witnessed eased censorship and a decreased ruthlessness of the regime, but also a host of anxieties about former enemies and the deployment of new tactics for enforcing social conformity.[123] One lasting legacy of the Thaw was a dramatically different labor policy in the north. Instead of hauling off prisoners to polar cities, the government began offering migrants higher wages, longer holidays, early retirement, and access to scarce goods.[124] With improvements in the standard of living, new arrivals to the industrial worksites of the Kola Peninsula encountered less vulnerability to natural hazards than during Stalinism.[125] The USSR also witnessed a brief uptick in scientific activism around environmental issues, as Soviet legislators promulgated what ultimately turned out to be a weak and laxly enforced nature protection law in 1960.[126]

[123] The historiography of the Thaw is rapidly expanding. See Denis Kozlov and Eleonory Gilburd, eds., *The Thaw: Soviet Society and Culture during the 1950s and 1960s* (Toronto: University of Toronto Press, 2013); Polly Jones, ed., *The Dilemmas of De-Stalinization: Negotiating Social and Cultural Change in the Khrushchev Era* (London: Routledge, 2006); Miriam Dobson, *Khrushchev's Cold Summer: Gulag Returnees, Crime, and the Fate of Reform after Stalin* (Ithaca: Cornell University Press, 2009); and Oleg Kharkhordin, *The Collective and the Individual in Russia: A Study of Practices* (Berkeley: University of California Press, 1999).

[124] On the benefits for inhabitants of northern regions, see Niobe Thompson, *Settlers on the Edge: Identity and Modernization on Russia's Arctic Frontier* (Vancouver: University of British Columbia Press, 2008), 37–87; A. L. Epshtein, *L′goty dlia rabotnikov Krainego Severa* (Moscow: "Iuridicheskaia literatura," 1968); and L. Ia. Gintsburg and N. M. Smirnova, *L′goty rabotaiushchim na Krainem Severe* (Moscow: "Iuridicheskaia literatura," 1975).

[125] The concerns expressed by enterprise leaders about social issues reflect how vulnerability to natural calamities had been mitigated. R. M. Gamberg and V. P. Bindiukov, *Nauchnaia organizatsiia truda i upravleniia proizvodstvom na Zhdanovskom gorno-obogatitel′nom kombinate* (Moscow, 1969).

[126] Laurent Coumel, "A Failed Environmental Turn? Khrushchev's Thaw and Nature Protection in Soviet Russia," *The Soviet and Post-Soviet Review* 40, no. 2 (2013): 167–189. Nick Breyfogle's study of an initial moment of environmentalist concern about Lake Baikal fits with Coumel's finding about brief "environmental turn" during the Thaw. Nicholas B, Breyfogle, "At the Watershed: 1958 and the Beginnings of Lake Baikal Environmentalism," *The Slavonic and East European Review* 93, no. 1 (January 2015): 147–180.

Even with the Thaw, the Cold War continued to inspire the militarization of the Arctic in the 1950s and 1960s. With Pechenganikel′ sitting right next to Norway, the Kola Peninsula was one of the few places where the Soviet Union shared a border with a country in the North Atlantic Treaty Organization (NATO). The USSR responded to this situation by dramatically expanding the Northern Fleet of the Soviet Navy along the Murman coast and bolstering security protocols over towns in the region.[127] At the same time the United States and other NATO countries established the Distant Early Warning line of radar stations across Arctic North America and new military bases in Greenland and Iceland.[128] Far from interfering with industry, this military build-up around the circumpolar north helped propel its expansion. It thereby added greater environmental pressures as well.[129]

The time between postwar reconstruction and the stagnation of the 1970s was also when the Soviet economy grew at approximately the same rate as the capitalist West.[130] Following a program of extensive growth, Soviet authorities filled in the corridor along Lake Imandra on the Kola Peninsula with heavy industry. Along with the sustained enlargement of phosphate production in the Khibiny, two iron mining and processing plants went online in Olenegorsk and Kovdor, a rare metals facility opened in Revda near Lovozero, and, after much discussion and planning in the 1930s, authorities built an aluminum factory in Kandalaksha.[131] Job seekers and military personnel flocked to the north, which dramatically increased the population of the Kola Peninsula from 314,700

[127] Geir Hønneland and Anne-Kristin Jørgensen, *Integration vs. Autonomy: Civil-Military Relations on the Kola Peninsula* (Aldershot: Ashgate, 1999), 119–128.

[128] McCannon, *A History of the Arctic*, 238–251.

[129] Several environmental historians hypothesize that the Cold War should be seen as a potent and independent agent of environmental change in the second half of the twentieth century. See J. R. McNeill and Corinna R. Unger, eds., *Environmental Histories of the Cold War* (Cambridge: Cambridge University Press, 2010).

[130] Barry Eichengreen cites the average annual compound growth rate of gross domestic product for Western and Eastern Europe to each be 4.7 percent for the period of 1950 to 1973. Barry Eichengreen, "Economy," in Mary Fulbrook, ed., *Europe since 1945* (Oxford: Oxford University Press, 2001), 98.

[131] Overviews of these developments appear in "Vvodnyi ocherk," in A. A. Kiselev, ed., *Kol′skii entsiklopediia*, vol. 1 (Saint Petersburg/Apatity: IS/ KNTs RAN, 2008), 118; A. V. Barabanov and T. A. Kalinina, *"Apatit": vek iz veka* (Apatity: Laplandia Minerals, 2004), 95–128; and Gennady P. Luzin, Michael Pretes, and Vladimir V. Vasiliev, "The Kola Peninsula: Geography, History and Resources," *Arctic* 47, no. 1 (March 1994): 1–15.

inhabitants in 1950 to 799,500 in 1970, an average gain of over 24,000 people a year.[132]

More people also meant more production. Worldwide nickel output more than doubled from the early 1950s to 1965, which inspired the USSR to invest more in this industry and to begin marketing its nickel to foreign customers.[133] In 1956 the heads of Pechenganikel′ started setting up the Zhandovsk mine at the Pil′guiavr deposit, while architects planned the new city of Zapoliarnyi. Initially, urban planners intended to place the town in a naturally attractive valley ten kilometers from the mines, but they ended up settling on a closer location.[134] Industry leaders chose to open the Zhdanovsk mine in part as a response to the dwindling reserves of nickel in the Monche region. As they explained: "Even with the completion of the project to develop Pechenganikel′, the needed raw materials for Severonikel′ will not be met. Therefore, in order to supply Severonikel′ with raw materials and sharply increase nickel production from the raw materials of the Kola Peninsula over the next few years, we should build and bring into operation a mining and enrichment enterprise on the basis of the Zhdanovsk deposit, the largest in the USSR."[135] The Kola nickel firms indeed became more integrated with this new unit. In the early 1950s Pechenganikel′ sent about 20 percent of its mined ore and all of its smelted matte to Severonikel′, while by 1965 it shipped 80 percent of its output there.[136] To further coordinate regional production at the end of the 1960s, authorities first returned the Zhdanovsk mining and enrichment combine to Pechenganikel′ and then grouped all of Kola enterprises into the Nikel′ Association.[137]

While it grew in the 1960s, the Kola nickel industry came under more vociferous criticism for contaminating places where people lived.

[132] Iu. P. Bardileva, "Demograficheskie i sotsial′nye protsessy v Kol′skom zapoliar′e na rubezhe XX-XXI vekov," in P. V. Fedorov, Iu. P. Bardileva, and E. I. Mikhailov, eds., *Zhivushchie na Severe: Vyvoz ekstremal′noi srede* (Murmansk: MGPU, 2005), 27–35 and V. Kostiukevich, "Murmanskaia oblast′ v 60–80 gody XX veka. Istoricheskaia spravka," in V. I. Goriachkin and B. F Kostiukevich, eds., *Gody zastoinye... Gody dostoinye!* (Murmansk: NITs "Pazori," 2000), 246.

[133] Mudd, "Global Trends and Environmental Issues in Nickel Mining," *Ore Geology Reviews* 38, no. 1–2 (October 2010): 12 and Adams, "Nickel and Platinum in the Soviet Union," in Jensen, Shabad, and Wright, eds., *Soviet Natural Resources in the World Economy*, 541.

[134] Matsak, ed., *Pechenga*, 139–140.

[135] GAMO, f. R-459, op, 6, d. 508a, l. 5.

[136] RGAE, f. 9037, op. 1, d. 508, ll. 2–3 and Potemkin, *U severnoi granitsy*, 289.

[137] GAMO, f. R-1032, op, 1, d. 314, ll. 1–4, 8 and *Ob″edinenie "Nikel′"* (Murmansk: Murmanskoe knizhnoe izdatel′stvo, 1976), 3.

The company towns reacted by relocating residents away from heavily polluted areas. Though Monchegorsk proper sat at a safe distance from Severonikel′, some of the subsidiary settlements laid within the sanitary-defense zones the near the sources of pollution. The worst of these appears to have been Nizhnyi Niud, which was located only 200 meters away from the Cobalt Department of Severonikel′. According to the sanitation inspector of the Murmansk region, residents in Nizhnyi Niud lived "in particularly adverse sanitary conditions," since "its atmosphere is polluted to an extreme degree with emissions from this department (each day about two tons of chlorine, 2.4 tons of sulfur gas and 0.29 tons of sulfuric acid are released)." Unfiltered chlorine gases wafted around the settlement, making life there especially unbearable. Furthermore, Nizhnyi Niud residents suffered two-to-three times more illnesses and children experienced heightened occurrences of respiratory disorders. After the Monchegorsk Executive Committee agreed to move the population of Nizhnyi Niud in 1962 and 1963, the sanitation inspector argued that the resettlement should take place on a more expedited timeline.[138] But, instead, it languished behind schedule. Only by 1966 had authorities liquidated Nizhnyi Niud and several other highly polluted settlements, though they now lagged in relocating people away from Pechenganikel′.[139]

Whatever the social benefits of these moves, they did little to avert further ecosystem deterioration in the sacrifice zones close to the worksites. In the early 1960s Severonikel′'s Refining Department let out dusts with metal concentrations averaging up to 2 percent nickel, 5–6 percent copper, and 1 percent cobalt.[140] Despite the common interest in waste reuse, the factories could not manage to control the byproducts of mining and processing. Air and water filtration devices rarely functioned as effectively as hoped and funding for installing these technologies frequently fell short.[141] Significant fines and public censure also failed to deter the nickel combines from dumping large quantities of untreated waste into local waterways.[142] Near the end of the decade, heavy metals from the

[138] GARF, f. A-482, op. 50, d. 6178, ll. 55–56.

[139] GARF, f. A-482, op. 54, d. 350, l. 57. Such moves away from the nickel works continued to occur annually in the early 1970s. GARF, f. A-482, op. 54, d. 5009, ll. 50–52.

[140] GARF, f. A-482, op. 50, d. 6178, l. 54.

[141] GARF, f. A-482, op. 50, d. 6178, ll. 44–46, 53–56; GARF, f. A-482, op. 54, d. 350, ll. 46–54; and GARF, f. A-482, op. 54, d. 5009, l. 48.

[142] "Vtoraia sessiia oblastnogo soveta deputatov trudiashchikhsia: Okhrana prirody – delo gosudarstvennogo znacheniia," *PP* (June 18, 1961): 2.

mining and processing operations increasingly began to accumulate in surface waters, soils, and plants.[143] Forest damage related to air pollution extended to seventeen-to-twenty kilometers around the Severonikel′ plant by 1969.[144]

However, the severity of localized pollution from the nickel industry had not yet reached the aggregate environmental damage that sullied the country's reputation in its waning years. Especially because of the slow implementation of abatement technologies, pollution closely correlated with production levels. Postwar industrialization drastically increased ecosystem disruption from sulfur emissions, heavy metals, and other substances, but the amount of production and pollution remained comparable to metal firms worldwide.[145] Indeed, in terms of sulfur dioxide emissions the Kola nickel industry seemed on the cusp of improvement in the late 1960s. Severonikel′ opened a unit to convert sulfur gases into sulfuric acid in 1967 and managed to cut its emissions of sulfur dioxide from 99,000 tons in 1966 to 86,000 tons in 1968 (see Table 6).[146] The Pechenganikel′ combine likewise kept its sulfur dioxide emissions fairly stable in this period. It climbed modestly from 125,900 tons in 1966 to 128,800 tons in 1968 and then declined ever so slightly to 128,600 tons in 1970.[147] Had this trend continued, the environmental situation at the Soviet collapse would have been quite different.

The Pains of Producing

Some of the first Western scholars to examine Soviet environmental problems took a decidedly moderate tone. Even in his 1972 exposé, *The Spoils of Progress*, Marshall Goldman only warned that "there is no reason to believe that state ownership of the means of production will

[143] Kozlov and Barcan, "Environmental Contamination in the Central Part of the Kola Peninsula," *Ambio* 29, no. 8 (December 2000): 514.

[144] V. A. Alexeyev, "Air Pollution Impact on Forest Ecosystems of Kola Peninsula: History of Investigations, Progress and Shortcomings," and Berlin, "Analysis of Ambient Air at Weather Station 'Chunozero' in Lapland Biosphere Reserve," in Kozlov, Haukioja, and Yarmishko, eds., *Aerial Pollution in Kola Peninsula*, 20, 99.

[145] For information about the heavy metals industry and atmospheric pollution in the twentieth-century world, see McNeill, *Something New Under the Sun*, 84–108.

[146] Pozniakov, ed., *Opyt raboty kombinata "Severonikel′" po povysheniiu kul′tury proizvodstva*, 3–5, 24–30 and Kiselev, *Monchegorsk*, 95–103.

[147] L. A. Danilova, "Perspektivy razvitiia syr′evoi bazy sernokislotnogo proizvodstva dlia mineral′nykh udobrenii na Kol′skom poluostrove," in A. V. Galakhov, ed., *Perspektivy razvitiia i osvoeniia syr′evoi bazy apatitovoi promyshlennosti na Kol′skom poluostrove* (Moscow: Ministerstvo Geologii SSSR, 1965), 193.

TABLE 6. *Reported Sulfur Dioxide (SO_2) Emissions from the Severonikel′ Combine*

Year	SO_2 Emissions (1,000 Tons)	Year	SO_2 Emissions (1,000 Tons)	Year	SO_2 Emissions (1,000 Tons)
1966	99	1982	239	1997	140
1968	86	1983	278	1998	88
1969	94	1984	257	1999	45
1970	101	1985	236	2000	45
1971	111	1986	251	2001	44
1972	118	1987	224	2002	44
1973	215	1988	212	2003	42
1974	259	1989	212	2004	38
1975	274	1990	233	2005	41
1976	268	1991	196	2006	40
1977	246	1992	182	2007	36
1978	244	1993	137	2008	34
1979	189	1994	98	2009	34
1980	206	1995	129		
1981	187	1996	110		

Sources: The figures for 1966 and 1968 come from L. A. Danilova, "Perspektivy razvitiia syr′evoi bazy sernokislotnogo proizvodstva dlia mineral′nykh udobrenii na Kol′skom poluostrove," in A. V. Galakhov, ed., *Perspektivy razvitiia i osvoeniia syr′evoi bazy apatitovoi promyshlennosti na Kol′skom poluostrove* (Moscow: Ministerstvo Geologii SSSR, 1965), 193. The emissions figures from 1969 to 2001 appear in Valery Barcan, "Nature and Origin of Multicomponent Aerial Emissions of the Copper-Nickel Smelter Complex," *Environmental International* 28, no. 6 (December 2002): 452. Also see V. Ya. Pozniakov, "The 'Severonikel' Smelter Complex: History of Development," in M. V. Kozlov, E. Haukioja, and V. T. Yarmishko, eds., *Aerial Pollution in Kola Peninsula* (Apatity: Kola Scientific Center, 1993), 16–19. The data from 2002 to 2009 are re-printed in Larisa Bronder, et al., *Environmental Challenges in the Arctic – Norilsk Nickel: The Soviet Legacy of Industrial Pollution*, Bellona Report, vol. 10 (Oslo: Bellona, 2010), 59.

necessarily guarantee the elimination of environmental disruption" and concluded that Soviet pollution problems were "as extensive and severe" as those in the United States.[148] But by the end of the decade, Ze′ev Wolfson detailed the wholesale "destruction of nature" in an underground *samizdat* publication; after the collapse of communism, foreign observers

[148] Marshall I. Goldman, *The Spoils of Progress: Environmental Pollution in the Soviet Union* (Cambridge, MA: The MIT Press, 1972), 2, 7. Though Philip Pryde's initial assessment was even more positive than Goldman's, his evaluation was much more negative in 1991. Philip R. Pryde, *Conservation in the Soviet Union* (Cambridge: Cambridge University Press, 1972) and Philip R. Pryde, *Environmental Management in the Soviet Union* (Cambridge: Cambridge University Press, 1991).

started stressing the acutely "troubled lands" of the former USSR.[149] Such re-evaluations did not arise solely out of dissidence or Cold War triumphalism. They also reflected the significant environmental deterioration in the interim.

Despite their efforts in the late 1960s, Severonikel′ and Pechenganikel′ soon diverted from the trajectory of nickel plants elsewhere in the world. They went from inflicting considerable environmental damage locally to annihilating large swaths of vegetation that extended abroad in the 1970s and 1980s. Along with operations in Noril′sk, the Kola smelters likely became the worst despoilers of the natural world within the global nickel industry.

National and international fluctuations in pollution do not immediately make this clear. For instance, total Soviet emissions of sulfur dioxide dropped from twenty-four million tons a year in the early 1970s to twenty million tons in 1980 and then to 17.6 million tons in 1990. At each of these points the United States emitted more than the USSR: twenty-seven million tons a year in the early 1970s to 23.7 million tons in 1980 and 21.6 million tons in 1990.[150] Like sulfur, nickel and copper emissions also appear to have reached their worldwide peak during the 1970s, when approximately 42,000 and 59,000 tons, respectively, were being released each year. They then started to decline. Moreover, some nickel manufacturers in other countries such as the mines of New Caledonia also dramatically increased their pollution loads in the 1970s and 1980s.[151]

However, pollution from Kola industry grew in proportion to worldwide emissions and breached critical levels that drastically amplified ecosystem damage. Severonikel′ quickly went from emitting less than 100,000 tons of sulfur dioxide a year to over 200,000 tons a year for most of the 1970s and 1980s (see Table 6), while Pechenganikel′ rose its sulfur dioxide emissions more than threefold to close to 400,000 tons annually in the late 1970s. The plants tarnished the surrounding

[149] Boris Komarov [Ze′ev Vol′fson], *The Destruction of Nature in the Soviet Union* (White Plains: M. E. Sharpe, 1980) and Peterson, *Troubled Lands*.

[150] Charles E. Ziegler, *Environmental Policy in the USSR* (Amherst: University of Massachusetts Press, 1987), 20 and Mirovitskaya and Soroos, "Socialism and the Tragedy of the Commons," *The Journal of Environmental Development* 4, no. 1 (Winter 1995): 92. The late Soviet figure seems to align with the one reported by Feshbach and Friendly for 1988 (17,651 of sulfur dioxide), though their table does not specify that the units should be 1,000 tons. Feshbach and Friendly, *Ecocide in the USSR*, 304.

[151] McNeill, *Something New Under the Sun*, 32–35, 54.

landscapes with more metals as well. In 1977, for example, Pechenganikel′ also put 539 tons of nickel and 232 tons of copper into the atmosphere.[152] Together acid rain from sulfur emissions, accumulated metals in flora, and the frequent occurrence of extreme concentrations of pollutants in the atmosphere elevated the acidity and toxicity of the soil. The contaminated ground then inhibited the growth and survival of pines, spruces, and other forest vegetation sitting on top of it. In this way, industrial pollution almost entirely denuded the land near the factories and damaged rapidly burgeoning zones further away.[153] The area near Pechenganikel′ that was severely affected by air pollution swelled from 400 km^2 to 5,000 km^2 between 1973 and 1988.[154]

In contrast, the most infamous nickel smelter outside of the Soviet Union – the Sudbury works of Canada – turned a corner in the 1970s. Inco's and Falconbridge's mines and smelters had already created a desolate moonscape north of Lake Huron by this time. As they belted out a peak of 2.5 million tons of sulfur dioxide in 1960, the Sudbury works annihilated approximately 200 km^2 of vegetation in the area, partially destroyed an additional 800 km^2 of territory, and acidified thousands of surrounding lakes. But then the companies managed to start reducing their environmental impact by cutting sulfur and metal emissions. They installed technologies to capture sulfur gases at their smelters and Inco erected a new smokestack to disperse the fumes that it did emit more widely. Regional authorities and the companies also initiated a major campaign to reclaim some of the polluted land by first detoxifying the soil and then planting hundreds of thousands of trees.[155] These mitigation and recovery efforts coincided with both the rise of modern environmental

[152] GARF, f. A-358, op. 4, d. 1640, l. 9 and Bronder, et al., *Environmental Challenges in the Arctic – Norilsk Nickel*, 30, 33.

[153] Vasiliy Kryuchkov, "Extreme Anthropogenic Loads and the Northern Ecosystem Condition," *Ecological Applications* 3, no. 4 (November 1993): 622–630; Rigina, et al., "Monitoring of Forest Damage in the Kola Peninsula, Northern Russia Due to Smelting Industry," *The Science of the Total Environment* 229, no. 3 (May 1999): 147–163; and Barcan, "Nature and Origin of Multicomponent Aerial Emissions of the Copper-Nickel Smelter Complex," *Environmental International* 28, no. 6 (December 2002): 451–456.

[154] Geir Hønneland, *Russia and the West: Environmental Co-operation and Conflict* (London: Routledge, 2003), 36.

[155] Courtin, "The Last 150 Years: A History of Environmental Degradation in Sudbury," *The Science of the Total Environment* 148, no. 2–3 (June 1994): 99–102 and John M. Gunn, "Restoring the Smelter Damaged Landscape near Sudbury, Canada," *Restoration & Management Notes* 14, no. 2 (Winter 1996): 129–136.

awareness and the period when pollution from the Soviet nickel industry spiked.

What explains this departure? Why did sulfur emissions from the Kola smelters skyrocket out of control during the 1970s? The leadership of the enterprises understood the threat of pollution perfectly well, acknowledging in 1971 that the "products of metallurgical manufacturing – the dusts of sulfides and the oxides of nickel and copper, carbon monoxide, sulfur gas, and nickel solutions – are to varying degrees toxic."[156] But instead of curbing the release of such toxic substances, the plants began putting out even more of them. Why?

Part of the answer involves the changing properties of the ore being smelted. Around this time, Severonikel′ exhausted the supplies of ore in the Monchegorsk region with high enough concentrations of nickel. It closed the Nittis-Kumuzh′ia mine in 1969 and finished working a small deposit at Niuduaivench in 1974. Having already received large quantities of material from Pechenga, the Severonikel′ smelter now began to import and process ore from Noril′sk. Industrialists in Noril′sk were in the middle of massively expanding mining operations without raising the capacity of their smelters to keep pace.[157] In 1973 processing facilities at Severonikel′ relied almost entirely on outside ore (88.9 percent from Pechenga and 11.1 percent from Noril′sk ore).[158] The problem was that Noril′sk ore contained significantly more sulfur: one estimate notes that Kola ore averaged around 6.5 percent sulfur until the 1970s, while the rock shipped from Noril′sk contained almost 30 percent.[159] This new high sulfur ore dramatically increased sulfur dioxide emissions at Severonikel′, which nearly doubled between 1972 and 1973 as sulfuric acid conversion lagged (see Table 6). A similar phenomenon occurred in the Pechenga region where the processing units in Nikel′ and Zapoliarnyi more frequently worked ore from the Zhdanovsk deposit with lower nickel concentrations and correspondingly higher levels of

[156] Pozniakov, ed., *Opyt raboty kombinata "Severonikel′" po povysheniiu kul′tury proizvodstva*, 4–5.

[157] "Osnovnye vekhi funktsionirovaniia kombinata 'Severonikel′,'" *Sever i rynok*, no. 2 (2000): 3–9; V. A. Fedoseev and A. V. Istomin, "Ekonomicheskie predposylka osvoeniia novykh mestorozhdenii i sozdaniia pererabatyvaiushchikh proizvodstv na Kol′skom poluostrove," in Turchaninov, ed., *Osvoenie mineral′nykh bogatstv Kol′skogo poluostrova*, 224–256; Pozniakov, *Severonikel′*, 204–276; and Adams, "Nickel and Platinum in the Soviet Union," in Jensen, Shabad, and Wright, eds., *Soviet Natural Resources in the World Economy*, 541.

[158] RGAE, f. 386, op. 1, d. 5149, l. 39.

[159] Bronder, et al., *Environmental Challenges in the Arctic – Norilsk Nickel*, 30.

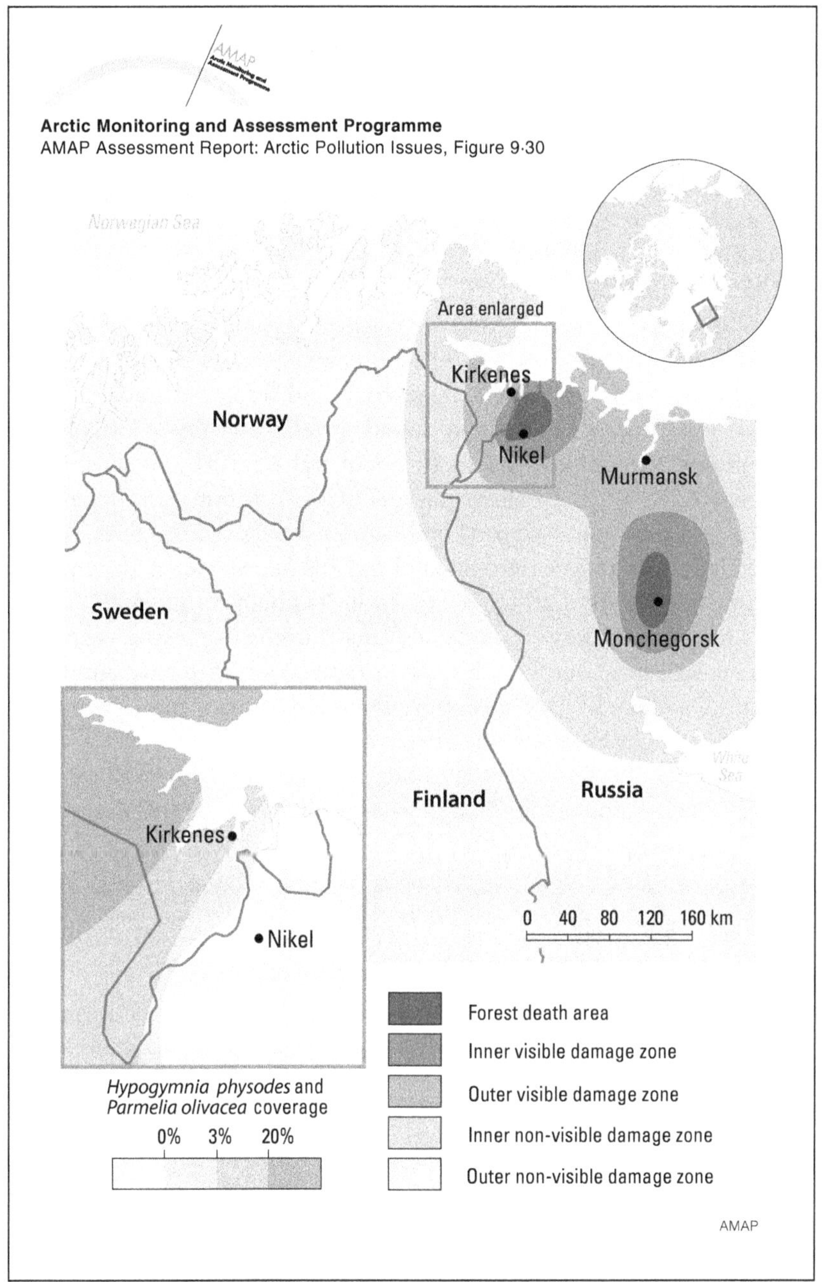

MAP 4. Forest Damage from Air Pollution in the 1990s.
Source: AMAP, *Arctic Pollution Issues: A State of the Arctic Environment Report* (Oslo: Arctic Monitoring and Assessment Programme, 1998), 647.

pollution per unit of nickel manufactured.[160] Pechenganikel′ also started smelting shipped ore from Noril′sk, which soon reached nearly one million tons annually.[161]

Shifts in the global economy also help explain the rise of extreme pollution. On both sides of the Cold War divide the economy struggled in the 1970s, but countries that responded to the slump by shifting from extensive to intensive growth strategies tended to fare better. The Soviet Union, like many but not all state-socialist countries, continued to use the capitalization of industrial development as its primary means of spawning economic growth. Many first-world capitalist countries instead pivoted toward creating wealth through new technological innovations, a shift to the service and financial sectors, and increased trade.[162] The pains of this process of Western de-industrialization and the ballooning economic inequality brought by neoliberal reforms have been well documented.[163] But the relative success of these countries in renewing their growth economies helped fund certain programs to reduce pollution, which made their environmental records appear better than many communist countries. Largely restricted in its ability to undertake such an economic reorientation, the Soviet Union instead remain focused on increasing industrial output, which, in contrast, worsened environmental problems. Production generated more pollution, but not more economic growth that might have paid for effective abatement.

Into this era of stagnation, the USSR continued to prioritize the development of heavy industry as strongly as it had in the past.[164] With the help

160 RGAE, f. 386, op. 1, d. 5147, ll. 44–49; RGAE, f. 386, op. 1, d. 5148, ll. 64–80; RGAE, f. 386, op. 1, d. 5149, ll. 10–11; and Andrew R. Bond and Richard M. Levine, "Noril′sk Nickel and Russian Platinum-Group Metals Production," *Post-Soviet Geography and Economics* 42, no. 2 (March 2001): 80–82.

161 Hønneland, *Russia and the West*, 34–35.

162 On this shift to intensive growth in the West, see Eichengreen, "Economy," in Fulbrook, ed., *Europe since 1945*, 95–145. A collection that attempts to reconceptualize the global 1970s as a period of economic promise instead of crisis is Niall Ferguson, et al., eds., *The Shock of the Global: The 1970s in Perspective* (Cambridge, MA: Harvard University Press, 2010).

163 For example, see David Harvey, *A Brief History of Neoliberalism* (Oxford: Oxford University Press, 2005).

164 Though some scholars have recently questioned whether the standard term "stagnation" appropriately captures the social and cultural life of this era, the impact of diminishing rates of economic growth on the USSR was real, significant, and multidimensional. See Christopher J. Ward, *Brezhnev's Folly: The Building of BAM and Late Soviet Socialism* (Pittsburgh: University of Pittsburgh Press, 2009) and Alexei Yurchak, *Everything Was Forever, Until It Was No More: The Last Soviet Generation* (Princeton: Princeton University Press, 2006). Stephen Kotkin offers a somewhat contrarian

of the Kola smelters, the country acquired the title of the world's largest nickel manufacturer. Industrial leaders boosted production in a period of significantly rising commodity prices and tried to minimize operating costs. Their modicum of sensitivity to international trade and efficiency only bears mentioning because scholars have typically portrayed communist command economies as completely oblivious to markets.[165] At the same time, greater output of nickel did not lead to the same levels of economic growth as it had in earlier decades. Economic historian Philip Hanson estimates that growth in Soviet gross domestic product (GDP) steadily declined from a rate of 4.8 percent during 1965–1970 to 1.8 percent during 1975–1980 and 1.7 percent during 1980–1985. All the while GDP per capita flattened after the mid-1970s.[166] Coping with these strains, the Kola nickel enterprises then started to miss their production targets for several years in the late 1970s and early 1980s. As party officials and local newspapers scorned Severonikel′ and Pechenganikel′ for these failures, the plants also lagged behind in their investments in technological upgrades and measures to mitigate pollution.[167] For instance, the repair and construction department at Severonikel′ under-fulfilled its nature protection plan in late 1979, just as "the beautiful pine saplings near the Vite Bay withered away literally before our eyes," according to an article in *Monchegorsk worker*.[168]

The comparative perspective I am offering here thus suggests that neither the inherent functioning of the centralized command economy nor

take on the Soviet economy in the Brezhnev years, but also stresses the depth of its problems. Stephen Kotkin, *Armageddon Averted: The Soviet Collapse, 1970–2000*, 2nd edn. (Oxford: Oxford University Press, 2008).

165 I am not suggesting that the Soviet economy was as attuned to price signals as capitalist economies, but simply that those running large industries were aware of and did consider costs and marketing when making decisions about output. For works that stress the communist alienation from markets, see Adams, "Nickel and Platinum in the Soviet Union," in Jensen, Shabad, and Wright, eds., *Soviet Natural Resources in the World Economy*, 536–546; Luzin, Pretes, and Vasiliev, "The Kola Peninsula," *Arctic* 47, no. 1 (March 1994): 13; and Gennadii Miroevskii, et al., "Metallurgicheskii kompleks Rossii v mirnom proizvodstve medno-nikelevoi produktsii," *Sever i rynok*, no. 2 (2000): 10–21.

166 Philip Hanson, *The Rise and Fall of the Soviet Economy: An Economic History of the USSR, 1945–1991* (New York: Longman, 2003), 244–250.

167 S. I. Osipov, ed., *"Severonikel′": uroki rekonstruktsii* (Murmansk: Murmanskoe knizhnoe izdatel′stvo, 1984); Pozniakov, *Severonikel′*, 261–276; *MR* (July 8, 1980), 1; *MR* (September 23, 1980), 3; *PP* (November 12, 1980), 1; and *PP* (November 22, 1980), 1.

168 KF GAMO, f. 52, op. 4, d. 657, ll. 31–41 and A. Bragin, "Nash vozdukh," *MR* (July 29, 1980): 3.

the competitive logic of the capitalist world-system sufficiently account for the massive environmental ruin in the Soviet Union. On the one hand, the Kola plants did not require capitalist profit motive to start generating extreme loads of industrial pollution. Sharing the broad impulse for continual economic growth for its own ideological and political reasons, the Soviet Union chose to maintain a set of development policies that proved less effective and more environmentally destructive in this period. On the other hand, the immediate results of intensive growth do not prove a clear environmental advantage of capitalism over communism in all places, eras, and contexts. For one thing, Cuba, which possesses some of the world's largest nickel deposits, experienced limited economic development under Fidel Castro. Communist rule there almost certainly, if unintentionally, preserved the island's ecosystem more robustly than had the country remained a hub for foreign tourists and business.[169] For another, Soviet economic strategies resembled the Keynesian models that had achieved high growth rates for postwar capitalist countries, but that caused non-communist countries to undergo similar strains in the 1970s. Post-colonial Zambia, for instance, embraced policies of extensive growth in its copper sector that tragically failed to remedy the country's poverty.[170]

But what of the public pressure that brought stronger pollution regulations to democratic countries? Though some have claimed that Soviet citizens knew little about environmental problems, many people participated in surprisingly wide-ranging conversations about industrial pollution in the Brezhnev era.[171] Journalists, scientists, government officials, and enterprise personnel debated environmental issues from conflicting points of view. Indeed, discussion about protecting the natural world contrasts with the portrayal of these years as closed and neo-Stalinist in comparison to the open era of the Thaw. These debates, of course,

[169] Despite a title that groups Cuba with other communist environmental perpetrators, the analysis in Sergio Díaz-Briquets and Jorge Pérez-López's account offers plenty of evidence for Cuba's superior environmental record. See Sergio Díaz-Briquets and Jorge Pérez-López, *Conquering Nature: The Environmental Legacy of Socialism in Cuba* (Pittsburgh: University of Pittsburgh Press, 2000).

[170] On Zambia, see James Ferguson, *Expectations of Modernity: Myth and Meanings of Urban Life on the Zambian Copperbelt* (Berkeley: University of California Press, 1999).

[171] This refrain appears in Komarov, *The Destruction of Nature in the Soviet Union* and Kozlov and Barcan, "Environmental Contamination in the Central Part of the Kola Peninsula," *Ambio* 29, no. 8 (December 2000): 512–517. On the environmental discussions that existed in the Brezhnev era, see DeBardeleben, *The Environment and Marxism-Leninism* and Weiner, *A Little Corner of Freedom*, 402–428.

responded to the rise of environmentalism globally and not just internal developments within the USSR.[172]

Specialists publically criticized and defended the environmental record of Kola industry in the 1970s. Fedor Terziev, the head of the Murmansk Hydrometeorological Service, declared pollution the "problem of the century" in a series of articles in *Polar Pravda* in 1973. He called out Pechenganikel′, Severonikel′, Apatit, and many other Kola enterprises as major polluters.[173] In contrast, Leonid Potemkin, a geologist who had helped open the Zhdanovsk deposit in the aftermath of World War II, argued that the limited environmental measures taken by the nickel enterprises demonstrated communism's superiority. In a 1977 book he repeatedly juxtaposed the exploitative and destructive treatment of nature in capitalism with "communist society," which "will be able to ensure the genuine harmony of technical progress and nature and the optimal combination of the development of the mining industry with the tasks of improving the environment."[174]

The most vibrant environmental attack on the Kola nickel industry came from scientists at the Lapland Nature Reserve. With their *zapovednik* sitting adjacent to the Severonikel′ plant, they had long monitored the influence of atmospheric pollution on forest cover, but began more intensive research as the smelter's emissions ballooned in the 1970s.[175]

172 On the global character of the "second wave" of environmentalism that began burgeoning in the 1960s, see Ramachandra Guha, *Environmentalism: A Global History* (New York: Longman, 2000), 63–145.

173 F. Terziev, "Zabota o prirode – eto zabota o nashem zdorov′e: pis′mo pervoe," *PP* (June 20, 1973): 2 and F. Terziev, "Zabota o prirode – eto zabota o nashem zdorov′e: pis′mo vtoroe," *PP* (June 23, 1973): 2. A few months later the newspaper printed letters of response from the enterprises under the headline, "Man is the Master of Nature." "Chelovek – khoziain prirody," *PP* (August 8, 1973): 2. For other examples of environmental discussion, see I. Beliaev, "Polezno znat′: chistota vozdukha – zabota obshchaia," *MR* (August 23, 1973): 2; A. Gladarevskii, "Kombinat sokhranit ozero," *MR* (November 12, 1977): 3; A. Khokhlov, "My i priroda – dolg pered sovest′iu," *MR* (July 3, 1980): 3; and "Zavtra – Vsemirnyi den′ okhrany okruzhaiushchei sredi," *PP* (June 4, 1982): 3.

174 L. A. Potemkin, *Okhrana nedr i okruzhaiushchei prirody* (Moscow: Nedra, 1977), 8. On Potemkin's diary and particular view of himself as a Soviet individual, see Jochen Hellbeck, *Revolution on My Mind: Writing a Diary under Stalin* (Cambridge, MA: Harvard University Press, 2006), 223–284; Veronique Garros, Natalia Korenevskaya, and Thomas Lahusen, eds., *Intimacy and Terror: Soviet Diaries in the 1930s* (New York: The New Press, 1995), 251–292; and Jochen Hellbeck, "The Last Soviet Dreamer: Encounters with Leonid Potemkin," *Cahiers du monde russe* 50, no. 1 (2009): 139–152.

175 In reserve documentation from 1966, Oleg Semenov-Tian-Shanskii gave a detailed description of the damage caused by sulfur dioxide emissions. See Berlin, "O. I.

One botanist used analysis of lichens in 1977 to demonstrate considerable disruption of flora near the nickel plant and categorized forests into zones of complete annihilation, strong damage, and deterioration.[176] In October 1980, Oleg Semenov-Tian-Shanskii, the head of the reserve, and Vasilii Kriuchkov, the director of the laboratory of nature protection of the Kola Branch of the Academy of Sciences, published an article in the national newspaper *Pravda* about the damage that Severonikel′'s pollution had done to the *zapovednik*'s forests. Not mincing words, they wrote, "a sword of smoke from the Severonikel′ combine already hung over the coniferous forests of the eastern part of the nature reserve in the 1950s. Connected to the growth in production in the 1970s the forest withered at such a tempo that the nature reserve is now at the point that it might turn into the same sort of wasteland as the outskirts of Monchegorsk."[177] Conservationists succeeded in enlarging the size of the Lapland Nature Reserve with this public protest, but did not force Severonikel′ to consistently decrease its pollution levels.[178]

Neither censorship nor ignorance prevented the Soviet public from assuaging pollution. Instead, the weakness of those voicing environmental concerns boiled down to them not possessing the power to alter the actions of industry. Even in the face of criticism, economic ministries and enterprises maintained the authority to decide to continue focusing on meeting production targets above all else. Though the Soviet conservation movement was vocal and independent, it did not constitute the seeds of a nascent civil society capable of improving environmental governance – a point that historian Douglas Weiner correctly argues.[179] While some are quick to assume that informed and concerned citizenries generally lead to better environmental outcomes, the case of pollution from the Kola nickel industry suggests the need to be cautious about that conclusion. Here a knowledge deficit mattered less than pre-existing and widespread asymmetries that gave industry disproportional influence over the treatment of the natural world.

Semyonov-Tyan-Shansky – naturalist, researcher, citizen," in *Laplandsky Zapovednik*, no. 7 (2005–2006), 8.

176 GARF, f. A-358, op. 4, d. 1640, ll. 1–86.

177 O. Semenov-Tian-Shanskii and V. Kriuchkov, "Visit dym nad zapovednikom," *Pravda* (October 10, 1980). A follow up article appeared in *Polar Pravda* several weeks later. A. Bragin, "Sledy na snegu," *PP* (November 2, 1980): 3.

178 Berlin, "O. I. Semyonov-Tyan-Shansky – naturalist, researcher, citizen," in *Laplandsky Zapovednik*, no. 7 (2005–2006), 8.

179 Weiner, *A Little Corner of Freedom*. 442–443.

Diplomacy and technology also failed to stop the escalating environmental damage from the smelters. Hoping to use environmental cooperation to improve Cold War relations with the West, the Brezhnev government signed on to the Convention on Long-Range Transboundary Air Pollution (LRTAP) in 1979. As part of this international agreement to curb transnational air pollution, Soviet politicians promised to cut the country's sulfur dioxide emissions by 30 percent in 1984. Most of this reduction was to come from converting the country's energy consumption toward natural gas and nuclear power instead of coal, but officials also slated Severonikel′ and Pechenganikel′ to reduce sulfur emissions by 56 percent and 47 percent, respectively, by 1993 (based on 1980 levels).[180] These enterprises had already undertaken new, but often ineffective, measures to try to better capture sulfur dioxide in the 1970s, including opening a sulfuric acid department at Pechenganikel′ in 1979. Both smelters also installed additional equipment to increase sulfur dioxide recovery and other upgrades after LRTAP. Additionally, almost all Kola enterprises involved in mining tried to improve the processing and reuse of wastewater.[181] But while overall Soviet sulfur emissions decreased during the 1980s, pollution from the Kola nickel industry plateaued at double or triple the amount it had been in the late 1960s.[182] Production with high sulfur ore continued to outstrip abatement.

Return to Regular Ruin

As with so much else, perestroika of the late 1980s unwittingly set off a sea change in the politics of industrial pollution. Working in the long shadow of Khrushchev, Soviet leader Mikhail Gorbachev aimed to revitalize the socialist promise of the USSR by embracing more representative institutions, more open public discourse, and more market-oriented economic policies. Among other things, these efforts ended up inadvertently

180 Robert G. Darst, *Smokestack Diplomacy: Cooperation and Conflict in East-West Environmental Politics* (Cambridge, MA: The MIT Press, 2001), 93–106.

181 KF GAMO, f. 52, op. 2, d. 619, ll. 63–68; RGAE, f. 386, op. 1, d. 5145, l. 44; F. S. Terziev, "Zapoliarnye gidrometeorlogi na sluzhbe narodnomu khoziaistvu," in Goriachkin and Kostiukevich, eds., *Gody zastoinye… Gody dostoinye!*, 215–224; *Ob″edinenie "Nikel′,"* 18–23; Kiselev, *Monchegorsk*, 104–128; Darst, *Smokestack Diplomacy*, 103–104; Potemkin, *Okhrana nedr i okruzhaiushchei prirody*, 85–87, 100–147; E. A. Shishkova, ed., *Ekologiia i kompleksnoe ispol′zovanie syr′ia v nikel′ – kobal′tovoi podostrasli: Sbornik nauchnykh statei* (Leningrad: Gipronikel′, 1990); and Vadim Dubrovskii, "Ekologicheskie problemy i ikh reshenie na kombinate 'Severonikel′,'" *Sever i rynok*, no. 2 (2000): 123–127.

182 Darst, *Smokestack Diplomacy*, 103–104.

triggering louder protests from Soviet citizens and international groups about the environmental situation. New activists in Soviet society joined professional conservation scientists and state-sponsored environmental groups to launch campaigns against industrial enterprises, including the Kola smelters.[183]

Meanwhile, Norwegians and Finns grew more alarmed about the damage that Kola industry was inflicting on their ecosystems. Smelter emissions fanned out into these foreign countries where they damaged trees and shrubs.[184] Especially in northern Norway, citizens protested these "death clouds" and began seeing the environmental situation on the Kola Peninsula as a major threat.[185] Soviet officials started negotiating with politicians, activists, and businessmen from Norway and Finland about strategies to curb emissions from the Kola plants.[186] In 1989 Nikolai Vorontsov, the head of the newly formed Soviet State Committee for Nature Protection and son of the Kola industrialist of the 1930s, agreed to cut sulfur dioxide emissions by 50 percent across all Finno-Soviet borderlands. Finland also initiated a plan to help finance and manage a massive upgrade at Pechenganikel′ that would improve the sulfur recovery rate from 35 percent to 95 percent. But when the Soviet-Finnish bartering arrangement fell apart after 1991, so too did this deal to reduce air pollution.[187] The idea that

[183] Weiner, *A Little Corner of Freedom*, 429–439; Jane Dawson, *Eco-nationalism: Anti-Nuclear Activism and National Identity in Russia, Lithuania, and Ukraine* (Durham: Duke University Press, 1996); Oleg Yanitsky, *Russian Environmentalism: Leading Figures, Facts, Opinions* (Moscow: Mezhdunarodnyje Otnoshenija Publishing House, 1993); Oleg Yanitsky, *Russian Greens in a Risk Society: A Structural Analysis*, (Helsinki: Kikimora Publications, 2000); Pozniakov, *Severonikel′*, 351–352; and Valerii Berlin, "Dlia zhizni net al′ternativy," in G. Bodrova, ed., *Murman, Khibiny do i posle...* (Apatity: Sever, 2002), 84–87.

[184] Kozlov and Barcan, "Environmental Contamination in the Central Part of the Kola Peninsula," *Ambio* 29, no. 8 (December 2000): 512–517; Barcan, "Nature and Origin of Multicomponent Aerial Emissions of the Copper-Nickel Smelter Complex," *Environmental International* 28, no. 6 (December 2002): 451–456; Kryuchkov, "Extreme Anthropogenic Loads and the Northern Ecosystem Condition," *Ecological Applications* 3, no. 4 (November 1993): 622–630; Darst, *Smokestack Diplomacy*, 121; and A. P. Kapitsa and W. Rees, eds., *Ekologiia Severa: Distantsionnye metody izucheniia narushennykh ekosistem (na primere Kol′skogo poluostrova)* (Moscow: Nauchnyi mir, 2003).

[185] Hønneland, *Russia and the West*, 113–125. Also see Geir Hønneland, *Borderland Russians: Identity, Narrative and International Relations* (New York: Palgrave Macmillan, 2010).

[186] Rowe, "Pechenganikel," 181–216.

[187] Darst, *Smokestack Diplomacy*, 106–110, 122–124.

the Nordic countries should help fund pollution abatement, however, remained.

The dizzying array of economic reforms enacted under Gorbachev, as well as the manipulation of them by well-connected individuals, ushered in the state's piecemeal retreat from responsibility over the actions of industrial enterprises. Taking advantage of a law that afforded enterprises greater autonomy from industrial ministries, Pechenganikel′, Severonikel′, and the Olenegorsk Mechanical Factory officially merged with the nickel works in Noril′sk and other assets in 1989 to create a new outfit, Noril′sk Nikel′. This reorganization of the Kola smelters set the stage for their post-communist evolution by formally integrating already interdependent operations under a corporation instead of the Ministry of Non-Ferrous Metallurgy.[188]

Perestroika, of course, failed to save the USSR. The political downfall of the Communist Party and disintegration of the country in 1991 opened the floodgates for a poorly implemented transition to capitalism. Hasty price liberalization and cuts to social benefits worsened the economic situation in Russia. One estimate indicates that Russia's GDP dropped by 40 percent between 1990 and 1995.[189] Residents of Monchegorsk, Nikel′, and Zapoliarnyi lost their life savings to rapid inflation and workers stopped receiving wages. In general, impoverishment during the communist collapse brought more significant social hardships to the people living in Kola nickel towns than pollution of the late Soviet era had.

Pollution, though, did decline with industrial production. Between 1990 and 1994, Severonikel′ dropped annual sulfur dioxide emissions from 233,000 tons to 98,000 tons, nickel emissions from 2,172 tons to 1,360 tons, and copper emissions from 1,813 tons to 726 tons. Pechenganikel′ remained the heavier polluter of sulfur dioxide but emitted significantly lighter, though steadier, loads of metals. Over the same period, the amount of sulfur dioxide released by the combine fell from 258,000 tons in 1990 and 198,000 tons in 1994. Though emissions bumped up

188 Andrew R. Bond, "The Russian Copper Industry and the Noril′sk Joint-Stock Company in the Mid-1990s," *Post-Soviet Geography and Economics* 37, no. 5 (1996): 295–297.

189 Marshall I. Goldman, *The Piratization of Russia: Russian Reform Goes Awry* (London: Routledge, 2003), 12–32; Kotkin, *Armageddon Averted*, 113–140; Rautio and Andreev, *Sotsial′naia restrukturizatsiia gornodobyvaiushchei promyshlennosti Pechengskogo raiona Murmanskoi oblasti*; Hansen and Tønnessen, *Environment and Living Conditions on the Kola Peninsula*; and Miroevskii, et al., "Metallurgicheskii kompleks Rossii v mirnom proizvodstve medno-nikelevoi produktsii," *Sever i rynok*, no. 2 (2000): 21.

again for a few years in the middle of the 1990s, the Kola smelters started returning to the status of typically destructive polluters instead of especially egregious ones.[190] De-industrialization, not enlightened policy decisions, precipitated this stage of the change.

International actors also started playing a larger role in the environmental governance of the region. Norway developed a similar proposal to earlier Finnish efforts to subsidize a technological upgrade at Pechenganikel′ – the facility that most directly polluted onto its territory. Under environmentalist Prime Minister Gro Harlem Brundtland, the country put many millions of dollars on the table to install equipment that would cut sulfur dioxide emissions at the plant by 90 percent. Researcher Lars Rowe details how divergent ideas and interests led to an impasse in this solution. Russian negotiators cared more about the economic advantages and risks of the project and saw pollution reduction primarily as a subsidiary benefit. The Norwegian side focused above all on improving the environment, but remained distrustful of Russian intentions and capabilities. Their differing perspectives came to a head, for instance, on the question of whether foreign or Russian technology would be used to upgrade Pechenganikel′. While both sides stayed ostensibly committed to the project, it stalled completely in the late 1990s until Noril′sk Nikel′ emerged as fully privatized company.[191]

After a period of limbo in the 1990s, the Kola smelters fell into the hands of individual businessmen. Wealthy banker Vladimir Potanin convinced the new Russian government to enact the notorious "Loans for Shares" privatization scheme in 1995 as an emergency measure to generate state revenue. Potanin's own bank, Interros, organized the subsequent auction of Noril′sk Nikel′ and, in a clear conflict of interest, gained a controlling stake in the company for a bid representing only a fraction of its actual value. After this corrupt privatization, Noril′sk Nikel′ established the subsidiary Kola Mining and Metallurgy Company (GMK) in 1998 to oversee Severonikel′ and Pechenganikel′. At this point Severonikel′ maintained the largest nickel refinery in Russia and Pechenganikel′ continued to mine its dwindling deposits. Noril′sk Nikel′ also globalized its assets, attentively followed trends in commodities markets, and held on to its status as the world's largest nickel producer. Under the partial

190 Bronder, et al., *Environmental Challenges in the Arctic – Norilsk Nickel*, 59–61. This data, which appear in a publication of the environmental organization Bellona, are the official figures reported by Kola GMK.

191 Rowe, "Pechenganikel," 217–253 and Darst, *Smokestack Diplomacy*, 119–127.

FIGURE 9. The Severonikel′ Smelter.
Source: Author's photograph.

management of billionaire (as well as 2012 presidential candidate and co-owner of the Brooklyn Nets basketball team) Mikhail Prokhorov in the 2000s, it became an extremely profitable multinational corporation.[192]

As the company recovered from the economic crisis of the 1990s, it revived the moribund plans to update Pechenganikel′'s facilities with Norwegian money. The managers of Noril′sk Nikel′ had previously toyed with the idea of shutting down the plant altogether, which obviously would have led to the steepest drop in pollution. But in 2001 they arranged a contract with Norwegian parties, facilitated by tax breaks from the Murmansk regional government, to move forward with technological upgrades that would extend the life of the Pechenganikel′ plant while curbing its pollution. Soon, though, new setbacks and delays hit this cooperative endeavor. The Norwegian public grew wary of paying

[192] Goldman, *The Piratization of Russia*, 1–11, 120; Bond and Levine, "Noril′sk Nickel and Russian Platinum-Group Metals Production," *Post-Soviet Geography and Economics* 42, no. 2 (2001): 77–104; and Rautio and Round, "The Challenges of Going Global," in Rautio and Tykkyläinen, eds., *Russia's Northern Regions on the Edge*, 112–142.

for a profitable company to reduce its emissions, while Noril′sk Nikel′ coyly reconsidered what would best secure its future economic profits. In 2007 it proposed that instead of updating the smelting facilities at Pechenganikel′, the company could start to simply process all of the Kola ore at an upgraded Severonikel′ smelter. Though this move would have further distanced the sulfur fumes that the company did emit from international borders, Norwegian negotiators refused to again adjust the terms of the agreement. Instead, the deadline for the upgrades passed in 2010 without Pechenganikel′ installing the new technology. In an attempt to save face while avoiding legal proceedings, Noril′sk Nikel′ secretly returned nearly eight million dollars to the Norwegian Ministry of the Environment.[193]

That is not to say that the environmental impact of the smelters again deepened. On the contrary, cuts to sulfur, nickel, and copper pollution continued. In terms of sulfur dioxide, Severonikel′ let out less than 40,000 tons a year in the late 2000s, while Pechenganikel′'s emissions hovered around 100,000 tons a year at that point – combined a somewhat lighter load than had existed in the late 1960s before pollution shot up. Nickel and copper emissions stayed steady at Pechenganikel′ (and the release of some other heavy metals might have risen), but they dropped even further at Severonikel′. A good part of this decline came from there being less sulfur in the ore itself, since the Kola smelters have cut back on shipments from Noril′sk.[194] Compared to other nickel refineries, the amount of sulfur dioxide emitted per ton of metal smelted at the Kola units was now between the rates of the Sudbury and Thompson facilities in Canada.[195] None of these changes mean that Pechenganikel′ and Severonikel′ turned into good environmental stewards, but the ruin they inflicted on landscapes became more in line with nickel smelters elsewhere in the world.

Today Noril′sk Nikel′ essentially rules over huge swaths of the Kola environment, as well as parts of northern Norway and Finland. It controls the amount and location of pollution released. The Russian government, society, and international groups take a backseat to corporate self-interest. Though the Russian Federation enacted many tough environmental protection laws in the 1990s, authorities subsequently weakened and chose to laxly enforce them. Noril′sk Nikel′, along with other Russian companies, now actively and successfully lobbies against new

[193] Rowe, "Pechenganikel," 255–279.

[194] Bronder, et al., *Environmental Challenges in the Arctic – Norilsk Nickel*, 59–61 and Rowe, "Pechenganikel," 280–285.

[195] Mudd, "Global Trends and Environmental Issues in Nickel Mining," *Ore Geology Reviews* 38, no. 1–2 (October 2010): 23.

regulations.[196] Instead of state determined output targets, profitability serves as the main arbiter for whether or not an environmental measure will be taken.

In 2005 the company summarized its environmental goals. "The adoption of nature conservation technologies is one of the most important directions of the ecological strategy of Kola GMK on the path to establishing clean production that exists in harmony with the natural environment."[197] Such a notion of forging harmony with nature in the midst of industrial growth could have been written by Soviet geologist Leonid Potemkin several decades earlier. While the transition to capitalism shifted authority from state enterprises to private corporations, the power to pollute has remained in the hands of actors dedicated to the economic exploitation of the natural world above all else. This has not only been true for the nickel industry, but for the varied enterprises of the energy sector as well.

[196] Oldfield, *Russian Nature*, 65–91.

[197] *Kombinat Pechenganikel' OAO "Kol'skaia GMK,"* 15.

6

Transforming but not Transcending

"Is the power plant something sad?" inquired a schoolteacher in the nuclear town of Poliarnye Zori in 1990. "No!" shouted back the children, perfectly playing their part with a reply guaranteed to appall a gawking foreign television audience.[1] In a sense these students were living their final days in an Arctic "plutopia" – the term historian Kate Brown uses to describe insular nuclear communities in which "residents gave up their civil and biological rights for consumer rights."[2] The country that had created this town had already lost its imperial satellites in Eastern Europe and was on the cusp of crumbling further. "Is the power plant something happy?" added the instructor. "Yes!" yelled the students in a response that would have pleased Aleksandr Andrushechko – the former head of construction at the Kola Nuclear Power Plant (Kola AES).[3]

As the Cold War offspring of horrifically destructive atomic bombs, nuclear power facilities had long been a suspicious source of energy. But the Chernobyl accident in 1986 shed a particularly ominous light on the Soviet nuclear sector, which many now saw as rife with faulty technology and inadequate safety protocols. Just the year before television crews captured these schoolchildren on film, operators at the Kola plant had chosen to keep a reactor running despite the fact that its secondary

[1] Geir Hønneland, *Russia and the West: Environmental Co-operation and Conflict* (London: Routledge, 2003), 101.

[2] Kate Brown, *Plutopia: Nuclear Families, Atomic Cities, and the Great Soviet and American Plutonium Disasters* (Oxford: Oxford University Press, 2013), 5.

[3] Hønneland, *Russia and the West*, 101.

cooling system had stopped working.[4] Indeed, observers in neighboring countries found the Murmansk region's secretive civilian and military nuclear installations especially alarming. They, along with some people on the Soviet side of the Iron Curtain, feared that invisible radioactive poison from the reactors and waste sites could infect bodies unbeknownst to the victim.

Andrushechko, unsurprisingly, did not share this bleak view of Soviet nuclear power. When the first unit of the plant went online in the summer of 1973, he expressed pride and gratitude to the workers who had accomplished a "feat of labor" by erecting the "first nuclear power station on Kola land."[5] In his later reminiscences, Andrushechko succinctly explained the primary reason for building the facility in this spot. "Having endowed the peninsula with diverse ores, nature deprived it of fuel."[6] An energy deficit had indeed plagued Kola industrialists since the construction of the Murmansk railroad, impelling them to seek varied means of meeting demand. They burned the taiga's scanty flora, forced prisoners to work, built hydroelectric dams, and shipped in fossil fuels until nuclear power finally supplied regional industry with enough energy after the 1970s.

The Kola plant was thus a solution, not a problem, to people like Andrushechko. In their minds atomic energy improved the natural world, rather than damaging it. The pioneer of an atomic north recounted how "the Kola Nuclear Power Plant lets out water that has been warmed a few degrees into Lake Imandra. Strong evidence of its absolute purity is the growth of trout, which are known only to pass through clean water, at the mouth of the tailrace canal."[7] Such defensive boosterism outlived the USSR. Like their counterparts in the West, contemporary Russian nuclear engineers insist on the safety of atomic energy and cite a lack of conclusive studies demonstrating its negative impact. Recently, the leaders of the Kola AES proposed extending operation of their outdated reactors decades into the future, confident that further accidents will not occur and that any radiation released by the plant would be harmless.

[4] Nils Bøhmer, et al., *The Arctic Nuclear Challenge*, Bellona Report, vol. 3 (Oslo: Bellona, 2001), 42.

[5] A. S. Andrushechko, "Podvig na Imandre," *PP* (July 3, 1973): 1.

[6] A. S. Andrushechko, "Rabotaet mirnyi atom," in V. I. Goriachkin and B. F. Kostiukevich, eds., *Gody zastoinye... Gody dostoinye!* (Murmansk: NITs "Pazori," 2000), 30.

[7] Andrushechko, "Rabotaet mirnyi atom," in Goriachkin and Kostiukevich, eds., *Gody zastoinye... Gody dostoinye!*, 37.

Opponents of the plant, on the contrary, continue to stress the hazards, uncertainty, and secrecy surrounding radioactive contamination. Bellona, the international environmental organization that has probably been the loudest critic of the nuclear situation on the Kola Peninsula since the Soviet collapse, argues primarily from the standpoint of unacceptable risks of a disaster. Since the Kola AES cannot meet "Western safety standards," activists there say that it should be shut down.[8] Their anxieties stem not only from an assessment of the current safety at the plant, but also from a shadowy past of Soviet vessels dumping radioactive materials into oceans and storing toxic nuclear wastes in leaky facilities along the Murman coast.

Odd as it might seem, each of these contrasting views of nuclear energy gets something right. Atomic advocates properly point to the sweeping, and sometimes positive, changes to the places people inhabit. The electricity conducted by fission has sustained urban and industrial lifestyles in this corner of the Russian Arctic. Yet critics accurately note the hidden dangers of assuming full control over the natural world. Toxins and contaminates have been given new opportunities to strike back against residents of the north by builders and operators of nuclear facilities. Abundant nuclear energy has not permanently liberated the Kola Peninsula from the strictures of the natural world, but has entangled its population with the environment in new and sometimes perilous ways.

Not only has nuclear power brought about changes both seen and unseen, but so too have all of the other means of supplying energy to the region. Converting coal, oil, wood, peat, muscles, wind, tides, and rivers into motors of industrial growth thoroughly transformed the natural world without actually separating Soviet society from it. Indeed, I argue that the energy sector succeeded only in altering the Kola environment, but not in reducing its influence. Endeavors to supply energy affected Kola lands through deforestation, physical extractions, reservoir flooding, and irradiation. Yet in each and every case the procurement of energy also created new material dependencies.

Put another way, power in a physical sense shaped the contours of Soviet power in a political sense. Vladimir Lenin's famous aphorism from 1920 – "communism equals Soviet power plus electrification of the whole country" – offered more than a simple inspirational message

[8] Bøhmer, et al., *The Arctic Nuclear Challenge*, Bellona Report, vol. 3, 43.

about the industrial agenda of Russia's new rulers.[9] His often-cited words also implied a deep connection between Bolshevik political promises and the harnessing of energy from the surrounding landscape. Perhaps Lenin subtly recognized that power in society relied in part on properties of the natural world?

Most scholars have approached Soviet power from primarily a political, social, or cultural perspective. David Priestland helpfully distinguishes between two interpretive clusters of historians with varying conceptualizations of state power in the USSR – intentionalists and structuralists.[10] The former group, on the one hand, tends to stress the decisions and motivations of Soviet leaders, the impact of Marxist-Leninist ideology on the evolution of the country, or the role of discourses in mediating peoples' experiences. Power came from plans, programs, perceptions, and personal authority, regardless of the extent or frequency with which contingent factors undermined these intentions. On the other hand, the structuralists usually emphasize the struggles of social groups, conflicts of interests among bureaucrats, and the presence of a host of extraneous and extenuating economic, social, geopolitical, and military influences. They see a complex interplay of forces shaping Soviet power and how it morphed over time. Despite their differences, both of these groups take power as something that ultimately emanates from human ideas, decisions, circumstances, or structures.

But what happens when physicists' understanding of power and energy informs historians' treatment of the subject? Is the distinction between energy as the capacity to do work and power as the rate at which energy is used helpful for understanding Soviet authorities' choices to build hydroelectric dams and nuclear power plants? A recent group of environmental historians suggests so. They advance the general idea that "all power derives from energy – it is energy put to work" and show how the control and distribution of energy can help explain power dynamics during factory conflicts in the United States and Britain in the late nineteenth century.[11] From their standpoint, the mobilization and selective release of

9 V. I. Lenin, "Our Foreign and Domestic Position and Party Tasks," (November 21, 1920), accessed July 24, 2014, www.marxists.org/archive/lenin/works/1920/nov/21.htm.

10 David Priestland, *Stalinism and the Politics of Mobilization: Ideas, Power, and Terror in Inter-war Russia* (Oxford: Oxford University Press, 2007), 1–5.

11 Edmund Russell, et al., "The Nature of Power: Synthesizing the History of Technology and Environmental History," *Technology and Culture* 52, no. 2 (April 2011): 246–259.

energy are the most basic requirements for an individual, group, or regime to be powerful. If this is the case, then Soviet power might indeed have depended on the release of energy for the sake of pursuing the country's communist agenda – a slightly revised version of Lenin's formulation.

Most promisingly, the difference between energy and power in the physical sciences points to the double-sided impact that industrial development had on relations to the Kola environment. Energy in essence is a constant; it cannot be created or destroyed but only converted. Industrialists reconfigured the distribution of energy in the region, but did not ultimately make any more of it than already existed. Bonds to the natural world, as such, remained equally strong. But the high rate at which the Soviets put this energy to work wrought far-reaching changes to the land and how people lived. Power transformed the natural and social world of this northern province, generally in proportion to the amount of energy exploited. The Soviets successfully mobilized the material world to do their work, but never escaped nature.

Burning the Landscape

Worldwide, the twentieth century witnessed a tremendous increase in the amount of energy used by human societies. According to environmental historian John McNeill's estimate, people consumed significantly more energy between 1900 and 2000 than during all of human history beforehand.[12] The Kola Peninsula, of course, shared in this trajectory with annual electricity production alone going from non-existent in 1900 to already 290 million kilowatt = hours by 1939 and on to 16,500 million kilowatt = hours in 1990.[13] This massive expenditure of Kola energy did not begin with digging for coal or striking oil, since the region lacked large stores of these subterranean carbon fuels. Instead, it involved burning huge swaths of the limited vegetation available in the Arctic. Often unusable for timber, Kola trees became fuel for desperate armies, enterprises, and individuals during the revolutionary period. The resultant deforestation visibly altered the landscape, but more for the sake of mere survival than industrial expansion.

12 J. R. McNeill, *Something New Under the Sun: An Environmental History of the Twentieth-Century World* (New York: W. W. Norton, 2000), 15.

13 "Vvodnyi ocherk," in A. A. Kiselev, ed., *Kol'skii entsiklopediia*, vol. 1 (Saint Petersburg/Apatity: IS/ KNTs RAN, 2008), 90, 118; V. M. Palumbo and G. D. Dmitriev, "Sostoianie, problemy i perspektivy gidroenergetiki Kol'skogo poluostrova," in I. R. Stepanov, ed., *Problemy energetiki zapada evropeiskogo Severa Rossii* (Apatity: KNTs AN, 1999), 15–24; and *Kolenergo, 1936–1996* (Murmashi, 1996), 18.

Kola residents had used firewood for heating and cooking for centuries before the modern era. Clergy and townspeople living in permanent settlements such as Kola, Kandalaksha, and the Pechenga Monastery chopped down nearby forests. Peripatetic groups of Sami and Pomors more selectively, but more expansively, harvested trees from seasonal encampments and along travel routes. To move around the land and the surrounding seas, these inhabitants also depended on gusts of winds and ocean currents along with the muscles of reindeer and other animals. While the burning of Kola wood obviously modified the ecosystems of the forests, it did not seem to have significantly reduced the total amount of woodland. This meant that new trees replaced felled ones about as fast as people cut them. As late as the period between 1881 and 1905, official statistics reported that the total quantity of forested land in the Aleksandrovsk and Kem districts of the Arkhangel'sk province (the Kola Peninsula and northern Karelia) stayed steady.[14] From this perspective, the energy economy of seventeenth through nineteenth centuries appears to have been less consequential than fishing in the area, which already exerted a wide and varied imprint on populations of herring, cod, salmon, and other species.[15]

Within the industrializing heartland of the Russian Empire, however, disappearing forests became a major concern. By one estimate European Russia lost up to 30 percent of its forests between 1867 and 1914.[16] Authors, artists, and scientists as diverse as playwright Anton Chekhov, painter Ivan Shishkin, poet Nikolai Nekrasov and forest specialist Dmitrii Kaigorodov mulled over the moral and ecological significance of fewer trees inhabiting the countryside. The "forest question" became yet another "painful" problem weighing on the conscience of educated Russian society.[17]

But vanishing forestland also drew timber merchants into more remote woodlands including those on the Kola Peninsula. Several small-scale

[14] The source notes that 7,623,000 *desiatin* (an old Russian unit roughly equivalent to eleven squared kilometers) of the two districts was forestland in 1881, 7,624,000 *desiatin* in 1887, and 764,200 *desiatin* in 1905. "Protokol," *IAOIRS* 2, no. 14 (July 15, 1910): 34.

[15] *"More—nashe pole": kolichestvennye dannye o rybnykh promyslakh Belogo i Barentseva morei XVII – nachale XX vv.* (Saint Petersburg: Izdatel'sstvo Evropeiskogo universiteta v Sankt-Peterburge, 2010).

[16] Brian Bonhomme, *Forests, Peasants, and Revolutionaries: Forest Conservation and Organization in Soviet Russia, 1917–1929* (Boulder: East European Monographs, 2005), 21.

[17] Jane T. Costlow, *Heart-Pine Russia: Walking and Writing the Nineteenth-Century Forest* (Ithaca: Cornell University Press, 2013).

timber companies on the southern Tersk coast began to operate intermittently around the turn of the twentieth century, including the Beliaev factory in Umba. Hired seasonal laborers primarily gathered and processed wood for construction materials instead of fuel, though they did often take free wood for their heating needs.[18] By the time of the First World War, some observers had begun lamenting the improper management of the Kola forests. Discussing Tersk timber operations, one journalist declared in January 1914, "the results of such forest predation prove yet again to be quite deplorable."[19]

The mobilization of energy resources ratcheted up dramatically with the outbreak of World War I. As tsarist officials moved ahead with building the Murmansk railroad, they solicited people, coal, and wood to do work for them. At first, much of the energy came from the metabolic conversions inside the bodies of the forced laborers building the railroad. After storing it in their muscles, humans generally convert biological and chemical energy from the plants and animals they eat into mechanical energy with approximately 18 percent efficiency. Strong individuals can maintain a maximum of around one hundred watts of power, much less than many draft animals.[20] Authorities at the Murmansk railroad treated the POWs who laid the track primarily as an energy source, thereby continuing a deep tradition of relying on the bodies of marginalized groups for economic projects. Prior to the dawn of the fossil fuel age in the early nineteenth century, a huge proportion of the energy used by human societies came from slaves, serfs, and prisoners.

Once the Murmansk railroad started operating, British coal became a main source of fuel. Engineers had designed the locomotive's combustion engines to be able to substitute 110 pounds of coal for forty-nine cubic feet of dried wood. During 1916–1917, Britain sent 30,000 tons of coal to the Murmansk railroad and continued to make shipments through

[18] I. F. Ushakov, *Izbrannye proizvedeniia: Tom 1: Kol'skaia zemlia* (Murmansk: Murmanskoe knizhnoe izdatel'stvo, 1997), 415–418, 503–531; A. A. Zhilinskii, *Krainii sever: evropeiskoi Rossii* (Petrograd: Tipo-litografiia Severo-zapadnogo okruga putei soobshcheniia, 1919), 232; D. L., "Ot Arkhangel'ska do Kandalaksha i obratno," *IAOIRS* 8, no. l1 (November 15, 1916): 456; and K. V. Regel', "'Terskii bereg' (Kratkoe fizikogeograficheskoe i estestvenno-istoricheskoe opisanie)," *IAOIRS* 9, no. 3–4 (March-April 1917): 94–95.

[19] An. Popov, "Terskii bereg," *IAOIRS* 6, no. 1 (January 1, 1914): 6.

[20] McNeill, *Something New Under the Sun*, 10–13 and Vaclav Smil, "Energy," in William H. McNeill, ed., *Berkshire Encyclopedia of World History*, vol. 2 (Great Barrington: Berkshire Publishing Group, 2006), 648–649.

much of the Russian Civil War.[21] These imports created a vulnerable dependency on the operations of coalfields abroad that proved fateful at the end of the conflict.

People in the north also began pillaging the forests for fuel. After clear-cutting for the track, workers gathered wood to help warm themselves and keep the trains running. As the new Bolshevik regime began fighting surrounding forces in 1918, their railroad managers ordered increasingly dramatic measures to supply the trains with firewood. "All possible work to procure fuel for the railroads presently possesses the utmost state significance," wrote one railroad official.[22] A. P. Shatov, the head of the Office of Forest and Peat Procurement of the Murmansk Railroad, proposed a scheme to acquire over 970,000 cubic meters of wood.[23] Assorted difficulties and, of course, the activities of anti-Bolshevik forces prevented this plan from succeeding.[24] Despite initial ambitions, the Bolshevik side ended up not gathering any forests materials on the northern parts of the railroad while the Russian Civil War raged in 1919.[25]

Foreign interventionists and White forces did, however. Kola trees helped move trains for them in 1919. An American soldier stationed there described how another exploitative use of muscle power facilitated this process. "The loading [of wood] is done by boys and girls. Some not more than twelve years of age. I can hardly bear to look at these mere children doing men's work."[26] Meanwhile, fuel shortages started to paralyze areas of the country in Red hands, precipitating the felling of more forestland during 1919 and 1920 than forestry experts had slotted for an entire decade.[27] Upon the Reds gaining control of the Kola Peninsula in early 1920, the British ceased all of their coal exports. Soviet railroad officials bemoaned "the catastrophic situation with fuel on the northern part of the Murmansk railroad" and urged "applying all strength and energy to the unconditional debarment of the fuel crisis" by intensively collecting forest materials.[28]

21 Bentley Historical Library, *Russia Route Zone A: Murman Railway and Kola Peninsula*, Copy No. 706 (Washington, DC: Government Printing Office, 1918), 26.

22 GAMO, f. R-483, op. 1, d. 2, l. 42.

23 GAMO, f. R-483, op. 1, d. 2, ll. 21–24.

24 GAMO, f. R-483, op. 1, d. 2, ll. 169–171 and GAMO, f. R-483, op. 1, d. 3, ll. 6, 31–38, 53–54, 264–265.

25 GAMO, f. R-483, op. 1, d. 100, l. 1a.

26 Bentley Historical Library, Polar Bear Collection, Harry Duink Papers, 36–39.

27 Stephen Brain, *Song of the Forest: Russian Forestry and Stalinist Environmentalism* (Pittsburgh: University of Pittsburgh Press, 2011), 66 and Bonhomme, *Forests, Peasants, and Revolutionaries*, 147–156.

28 GAMO, f. R-483, op. 1, d. 100, ll. 26, 30.

The deforestation that followed led local historian Aleksei Kiselev to declare, "all of the forest along the Murmansk railroad went into the furnaces of locomotives" in this period.[29] More precisely, the Aleksandrovsk district of the Arkhangel′sk province dropped from an estimated 3,942,000 *desiatin* (one *desiatina* is about eleven squared kilometers) of forest in 1905 to approximately 2,900,000 *desiatin* of forest in 1921. That means that the Kola Peninsula, excluding the areas around Kandalaksha that did not belong to the Aleksandrovsk district, lost over a quarter of its forest cover.[30]

As the era of war subsided, a slightly more sustainable approach to timber harvesting replaced the previous ravaging. Following a business model that substituted natural resources on the land for state subsidies, the Murmansk railroad gathered wood for fuel during the New Economic Policy. Between 1923 and 1929 it felled a total of 5,857,000 cubic meters of forest. These activities caused the greatest impact on woodlands located in Karelia, but also further depleted Kola forests.[31] Arctic trees had already reached, or in reality surpassed, their limit as a generator of industrial growth.

All Sources Possible

At the beginning of the 1930s, two staff members at the newly created Apatit trust re-evaluated the potential to use local wood as a fuel source. "In spite of the comparatively rich supplies of forests on the Kola Peninsula (a total area of 10.4 million hectares) and in the Karelian Autonomous Soviet Socialist Republic (7.4 million hectares), firewood cannot serve as a sufficient source for covering the fuel requirements." M. M. Kossov and V. I. Kagan explained, "the great majority of these forests are located at distances far from Kandalaksha, have been entirely cut down along the railroad line and floatable rivers, require considerable capital investment to organize their exploitation, etc." Such obstacles

29 A. A. Kiselev, *Kol′skoi atomnoi – 30: Stranitsy istorii* (Murmansk: Izdatel′stvo "Reklamnaia poligrafiia," 2003), 10.

30 "Protokol," *IAOIRS* 2, no. 14 (July 15, 1910): 34 and N. Ia. Ovchinnikov, "Lesa Olonetsko-Murmanskogo kraia," in *Proizvoditel′nye sily raiona Murmanskoi zheleznoi dorogi: Sbornik* (Petrozavodsk: Pravlenie Murmanskoi zheleznoi dorogi, 1923), 104–105.

31 ARAN, f. 544, op. 1, d. 115, l. 3 and A. Arnol′dov, *Zheleznodorozhnaia kolonizatsiia v Karel′sko-Murmanskom krae: Po materialam razrabotannym kolonizatsionnym otdelom pravleniia dorogi* (Leningrad: Pravlenie Murmanskoi zheleznoi dorogi, 1925), 25–28.

meant that, "the orientation of the combine toward wood fuel would be economically ineffective and would be neither possible nor expedient in any circumstances."[32] Apatit needed to look elsewhere.

The Stalinist Great Break triggered a desperate and wide-ranging search for energy resources to supply all of the new factories throughout the country. Everything that could physically do work became the potential subject of state schemes in the 1930s. As trees kept ending up in furnaces and campfires at industrial worksites, Soviet officials mobilized multiple different energy sources. They expanded coalmines and shipped this fossil fuel around the country.[33] They flirted with numerous proposals to convert everything from peat to tides into electricity. They turned again to coercion to force state enemies and criminals to carry out the labor needed to create industrial infrastructure. And they installed hydroelectric stations on rivers to provide electricity to towns and enterprises. All of these means helped generate Soviet power on the Kola Peninsula.

Apatit, Severonikel′, a special department of the Kola Production Association of Energy and Electrification (Kolenergo), and small-scale enterprises in Umba and near Kandalaksha continued to organize the collection of wood as a supplemental industrial fuel. At the end of the first five-year plan in 1932 some 319,000 cubic meters of Kola firewood were being felled annually, but by the end of the decade this had risen several times over.[34] Even with the expansion of other energy sources, the country as a whole still relied on firewood. In 1940 wood accounted for approximately 14.3 percent of the fuel used in the USSR. This national figure grew to 15.4 percent during the war, but forest collection in the Murmansk region began its decline during the conflict.[35] By this point, the territory's forest cover had gone down from about 26.5 percent of the Murmansk *okrug* (county) in 1934 to 22.7 percent of the Murmansk

[32] M. M. Kossov and B. I. Kagan, "Severnyi gorno-khimicheskii trest 'Apatit' vo 2-m piatiletii," *KMK*, no. 3–4 (1932): 20.

[33] Soviet policy focused less on expanding the use of oil and natural gas, of which the country possessed plenty, at this point. So while the Soviet production of coal rose over 4.5 times between 1928 and 1940, oil production only went up 2.7 times in these years and remained less vital to the overall energy economy of the country. Iain F. Elliot, *The Soviet Energy Balance: Natural Gas, Other Fossil Fuels and Alternative Power Sources* (New York: Praeger Publishers, 1974), 76, 130.

[34] GAMO, f. R-990, op. 1, d. 1, l. 156; GAMO, f. 773, op. 1, d. 55, ll. 65–66; GAMO, f. 773, op. 1, d. 53, ll. 260–262; RGASPI, f. 17, op. 121, d. 287, ll. 7–9; and E. V. Bunakov, "Ekonomicheskoe obosnovanie razvitiia olenevodstva Murmanskogo okruga," *SO* 4 (1934): 114.

[35] Theodore Shabad, *Basic Industrial Resources of the USSR* (New York: Columbia University Press, 1969), 6 and RGASPI, f. 17, op. 121, d. 287, ll. 7–9.

oblast' (region), which included the more heavily forested land to the southwest of Kandalaksha, in 1943.[36] Dekulakized peasants and later Gulag prisoners collected much of this wood, thereby expending calories in their bodies to provide the state with a combustible form of energy.[37]

Forced laborers also gathered peat, as workers had along the Murmansk railroad during the Russian Civil War.[38] Peat is a type of decayed vegetation that builds up in marshes and can be turned into a fuel. Collecting it often involved the difficult physical work of cutting through and digging out water soaked peat from bogs, compressing the material and allowing it to dry, and hauling it to thermal power stations. This process changed the ecology of swamps where extraction occurred by disrupting the habitat of various species. Starting in the 1920s, peat fuels supplied the USSR with a notable portion of its electricity. By one estimate, peat made up more than five percent of the fuel annually used in the Soviet Union in the 1930s.[39] It also became a much-discussed topic among artists and writers in the Stalin era. According to literary scholar Robert Bird, peat served "not merely as a source of powerful new metaphors and myths but also an important testing ground for the convergence of economic, scientific, and artistic discourses under socialist realism."[40]

Regional industry leaders on the Kola Peninsula factored peat availability into their decisions. Some of the special settlers employed by Apatit gathered the substance and early plans for the Severonikel' combine envisioned extracting up to 200,000 tons of it.[41] The comparative proximity of peat sources also figured prominently in discussions of the different

36 Bunakov, "Ekonomicheskoe obosnovanie razvitiia olenevodstva Murmanskogo okruga," *SO* 4 (1934): 113–114 and RGASPI, f. 17, op. 121, d. 287, ll. 7–9.

37 RGASPI, f. 17, op. 120, d. 26, l. 151; A. A. Kiselev, "GULAG na Murmane: Istoriia tiurem, lagerei, kolonii," *SM* (October 16, 1992): 3; and M. B. Smirov, ed., *Sistema ispravitel'no-trudovykh lagerei v SSSR, 1923–1960* (Moscow: Zven'ia, 1998), 264, 432–433. According to Lynne Viola, around 40 percent of special settlers in the USSR (565,754 of 1,427,539) worked in forestry, far more than any other industry. Lynne Viola, *The Unknown Gulag: The Lost World of Stalin's Special Settlements* (Oxford: Oxford University Press, 2007), 198.

38 GAMO, f. R-483, op. 1, d. 2, ll. 1–225; GAMO, f. R-483, op. 1, d. 3, ll. 1–226; RGASPI, f. 17, op. 120, d. 26, l. 151; and GAMO, f. 773, op. 1, d. 55, ll. 65–66.

39 Shabad, *Basic Industrial Resources of the USSR*, 6 and Elliot, *The Soviet Energy Balance*, 182.

40 Robert Bird, "The Poetics of Peat in Soviet Literary and Visual Culture, 1918–1959," *SR* 70, no. 3 (Fall 2011): 594.

41 RGASPI, f. 17, op. 120, d. 26, l. 151; Kiselev, "GULAG na Murmane: Istoriia tiurem, lagerei, kolonii," *SM* (October 16, 1992), 3; and GAMO, f. 773, op. 1, d. 55, ll. 65–66.

possible locations for an alumina factory in the region.[42] Vladimir Voshchinin, an old colleague of Gennadii Chirkin in the imperial Resettlement Administration, claimed in *Polar Pravda* in 1939 that the Kola Peninsula was rich enough in peat that up to forty million air-dried tons of it could be collected near the railroad lines.[43] In contrast to his assessments, the electrical utility Kolenergo decided around this time that peat processing only really made economic sense in Karelia and not in the Murmansk region. Kola peat supplies existed in small and isolated marshes, which prevented mechanized extraction and required a large number of laborers. The long harsh winter also limited peat gathering to a short summer season.[44] Over time the use of peat as a fuel in the Murmansk region fell to a negligible level.[45]

Speculative schemes for sources of renewable energy also found support in this period.[46] In the early 1930s a project to augment Kola electricity with wind farms began to move forward. A. F. Gudlevskii claimed in an enthusiastic report in September 1933 that a new source of energy to meet the growing need of the Apatit enterprise existed in "the possibility of maximally using wind power."[47] This option excited Alexander Fersman and Apatit's leader Vasilii Kondrikov, who called it "the energy of the future." But despite some preliminary planning work for a wind-powered electrical station, the project never came to fruition.[48] After this point Fersman continued to promote the possibility of capturing energy from other renewable resources. Seeking harmony in the midst of dominating the Arctic environment, he included both wind and tidal energy on the Murman coast as examples of how "a negative side of polar nature" could be converted into "productive forces."[49]

42 GAMO, f. 773, op. 1, d. 6, l. 6.

43 Originally from *PP* (February 11, 1939). Reprinted in S. I. Tiul'panova, ed., *Istoriia industrializatsii SSSR. Industrializatsiia Severo-zapadnogo raiona v gody vtoroi i tret'ei piatiletok (1933–1941 g.g.): Dokumenty i materialy* (Leningrad: Isdatel'stvo LGU, 1969), 117–118.

44 GAMO, f. R-990, op. 1, d. 4, ll. 2–3.

45 I. I. Kobzikov, "Toplivnyi balans Murmanskoi oblasti i voprosy ego ratsionalizatsii," in E. Ia. Zamotkin and N. M. Erogova, eds., *Priroda i khoziaistvo Severa*, vol. 2, part 2 (Apatity: Akademii Nauk SSSR, 1971), 244.

46 "Zabytye energoproekty," *ZhA*, no. 1 (September 2002): 53–55.

47 A. F. Gudlevskii, "K voprosu ob ispol'zovanie energii vetra v Khibinskom raione," in A. E. Fersman, ed., *Khibinskie Apatity: Itogi nauchno-issledovatel'skikh i poiskovykh rabot*, vol. 6 (Leningrad: NIS-NKTP Lenoblispolkom, 1933), 235.

48 V. I. Kondrikov, "Sostoianie i zadachi issledovatel'skikh rabot (Vstupitel'noe slovo)" and "Preniia i vyvody po dokladam," in Fersman, ed., *Khibinskie Apatity*, vol. 6, 17, 237.

49 ARAN, f. 544, op. 1, d. 207, l. 4.

Kola industrialists, however, more immediately concocted schemes to bring coal to the region and convert the area's rivers into wellsprings of hydroelectricity. These two sources provided most of the energy for the new factories and towns. To the chagrin of industrial planners, coal did not exist in exploitable quantities on the Kola Peninsula. Accessing it therefore required arranging networks of exchange with far-flung, but ideally still minimally distant, territories.

Such systems of importing fossil fuels and other resources have been, of course, part and parcel of industrial economies throughout the world. These networks connect remote territories to each other and unevenly distribute environmental effects among them. They create elaborate dependencies related to production and consumption that link people in different places to varied economic uses of the natural world. The decisions of states, corporations, and individuals in one region or country also can result in the polluting of a landscape on the other side of the globe. So, for instance, coal from West Virginia helps supply electricity to the Netherlands, which means that Dutch consumers rely on environmentally destructive practices such as mountaintop removal.[50] Just as significantly, the natural resource itself maintains its potency throughout every step of the commodity chain. Without this foreign coal, a Dutch factory could be forced to scale back production.

Enterprises on the Kola Peninsula and residents of its growing cities comparably depended on coal from outside the region. Early plans envisioned eventually bringing in coal from elsewhere in the Soviet Arctic, including the island of Spitsbergen and the Pechora basin.[51] Part of the Svalbard archipelago, Spitsbergen formally belonged to Norway after a 1920 treaty, but the Soviets retained economic rights over this coal-rich territory. During the Great Break, Soviet researchers also discovered large quantities of bituminous coal suitable for heating coke in the Pechora basin northwest of the Ural Mountains. As the 1930s advanced, authorities set up both a separate trust, Arktikugol′, to mine Spitsbergen coal with

50 In 2012 West Virginia exported $801 million worth of coal to the Netherlands, making it the state's main foreign consumer. *Coal Facts* (Charleston, WV: West Virginia Coal Association, 2013), 64.

51 *Murmanskaia zheleznaia doroga: Kratkii ocherk postroiki zheleznoi dorogi na Murman s opisaniem eia raiona* (Petrograd, 1916), 125–128; R. L. Samoilovich, "Znachenie Grumanta (Shpitsbergena) dlia russkogo severa," in *Proizvoditel′nye sily raiona Murmanskoi zheleznoi dorogi*, 214–224; and A. K. Portsel′, "Pervaia russkaia geologorazvedochnaia ekspeditsii na Shpitsbergen," in *Ushakovskie chteniia: Materialy pervoi nauchno-prakticheskoi mezhregional′noi kraevedcheskoi konferentsii pamiati professora I. F. Ushakova* (Murmansk: MGPU, 2004), 108–112.

prison labor and a Gulag camp in Vorkuta to start producing Pechora coke.[52] In the meantime, though, coal came to the Kola Peninsula from even farther away. Regional demand shot up nearly tenfold from 1930 to 1934. At the start of this period almost all coal arrived to the Murmansk port from abroad, but these foreign imports were subsequently replaced with shipments from Donetsk and Spitsbergen.[53] Much of this coal went to industries, but some of it served municipalities. Murmansk opened the region's first thermal electric station in 1934. Such facilities burned fossil fuels to produce steam that rotated electrical generators, warmed pipes to carry heat around town, and supplied buildings with hot water. Soon the Murmansk Thermal Electric Station produced twenty million kilowatt = hours of electricity and provided centralized heating to part of the town.[54]

In a sense the energy dearth that compelled economic planners to look toward coal from outside the region was imaginary. More than enough energy rested in the subatomic bonds of the inorganic substances present on the Kola Peninsula to fuel industrialization worldwide. The problem was that it was impossible to release and direct this energy. An alluring option arose, however, in the diversion of the regularly replenished energy from cascading water into electricity. Unlike with organic and fossil fuels, electricity was not easy to store or transport and did not provide an efficient source of heat. But the rivers of the north could conduct hydroelectricity that would move trains, refine metals, and light buildings. By regulating the flow of rivers with dams and reservoirs and capturing the energy from descending water with turbines and generators, Kola developers would be able to make the landscape itself do the work.

The middle half of the twentieth century, in many regards, was the age of "white coal" – a term that boosters frequently applied to hydroelectricity. During this time, hydropower fully infiltrated the mountainous Alps, turning them into "Europe's battery" according to historian Marc Landry, and transformed the Columbia River in North America, making

52 Demitri B. Shimkin, *The Soviet Mineral-Fuels Industries, 1928–1958: A Statistical Survey* (Washington, DC: U.S. Bureau of the Census, 1962), 65; Alan Barenberg, *Gulag Town, Company Town: Forced Labor and Its Legacy in Vorkuta* (New Haven: Yale University Press, 2014), 15–35, 278; and A. K. Portsel′, "Kak 'vragi naroda' 'sryvali' snabzhenie gorniakov na Shpitsbergene," in *Tretie Ushakovskie chteniia: Sbornik nauchnykh statei* (Murmansk: MGPU, 2006), 98–105.

53 Kiselev, *Kol′skoi atomnoi – 30*, 12.

54 L. S. Kaibysheva, *Elektricheskoe siianie severa* (Murmansk: Murmanskoe knizhnoe izdatel′stvo, 1988), 27–30 and *Fabrika tepla i sveta, 1934–2004* (Murmansk: Sever, 2004).

it an "organic machine" in historian Richard White's phrasing.[55] The installation of hydroelectric facilities also contributed to the remaking of the Nile River through the Aswan High Dam in Egypt, the Yangtze River in China with the Three Gorges Dam, and many other riparian environments.[56] Within the USSR, revolutionary leaders had promised to expand the country's electrical capacity. Following the initial State Electrification Plan (GOELRO) of 1920, Soviet authorities began a bonanza of hydroelectric construction with projects in the Leningrad region and along the Dnepr and Volga rivers. These efforts accelerated further in the Stalin period when hydroelectric power climbed from generating 4 percent of Soviet electricity in 1928 to 8 percent by 1937 and 15.2 percent by 1950.[57]

Given its lack of other sufficient energy resources, the Kola Peninsula was especially ripe for Soviet hydroelectric development. Before the promulgation of GOELRO and even before the Russian Civil War broke out in earnest, the Supreme Council of the National Economy sponsored research into the hydroelectric possibilities of the Niva River basin.[58] The GOELRO plan itself included exploratory work on an array of rivers of the Murmansk region, including the Tuloma, Kovda, Teriberka, and Niva.[59] Initial Soviet investigators extolled the plentiful electrical potential that existed in "the powerful currents of rivers and waterfalls" of the region's "white coal." One early evaluation in 1923 proposed that the Niva and Tuloma rivers, combined with a few less powerful waterways, possessed a total capacity of at least 600,000–700,000 horsepower (approximately 447,420–521,990 kilowatts) for generating electricity and insisted that more research should be done.[60]

The first project accompanied the creation of the apatite works in the Khibiny Mountains. It occurred on the Niva River. A short artery about thirty-four kilometers long in the southern portion of the Kola

55 Marc Landry, "Europe's Battery: The Making of the Alpine Energy Landscape, 1870–1955" (PhD diss., Georgetown University, 2013) and Richard White, *The Organic Machine* (New York: Hill and Wang, 1995).

56 McNeil, *Something New Under the Sun*, 149–191.

57 Paul R. Josephson, *Industrialized Nature: Brute Force Technology and the Transformation of the Natural World* (Washington, DC: Island Press, 2002), 18–27.

58 V. Ia. Shashkov, *Spetspereselentsy v istorii Murmanskoi oblasti* (Murmansk: "Maksimum," 2004), 147.

59 Kaibysheva, *Elektricheskoe siianie severa*, 8.

60 D. S. Pashentsev, "Vodnye sily Murmanskogo kraia i vozmozhnost′ ispol′zovaniia ikh v tseliakh razvitiia ekonomicheskoi zhizni," in *Proizvoditel′nye sily raiona Murmanskoi zheleznoi dorogi*, 207–213.

Peninsula, the Niva River begins its 127-meter descent at Lake Imandra and flows down to the Kandalaksha Bay of the White Sea with smaller lakes emptying out into it. At the time of its re-engineering, the Niva alternated in different places from a narrow river with a fast current and rocky banks to a wide slow-moving body surrounded by marshes.[61] Project leaders and laborers at Apatit installed a low capacity turbo-generator in the summer of 1930 to meet immediate needs, while the newly created Nivastroi firm commenced plans to build a cascade of hydroelectric stations on the river.[62]

Work began first on the middle unit – the Niva-2 Hydroelectric Station (GES) – located at Plesozero. Energy produced by the physiological processes within the bodies of victims of state repression enabled its construction. Soviet officials forcibly sent approximately 7,200 special settlers to the Niva worksite.[63] The Niva settlement's village council reported that special settlers there worked ten hours a day, lacked the proper clothing for labor in cold and marshy areas, received insufficient wages to purchase adequate quantities of food, and often fell ill, including from frostbite and workplace injuries. Their food's "caloric value is not high. Meat (almost always horse) and fish are rare and fats are almost completely absent." Most special settlers' "nourishment should not be considered sufficient in terms of quality or quantity."[64] This dietary lack predictably resulted in lower labor productivity among the special settlers, who did not obtain enough of their own energy inputs.

Among the freely recruited laborers employed by Nivastroi, many responded to the abysmal conditions at the worksite by violating their contracts and escaping the region early. The frustrated head of the dam's construction, M. K. Stepanchenko, blamed "our special climatic conditions" for the severe labor shortage that existed in November 1932. Anxious to avoid supplying provisions for more non-working women and

61 GAMO, f. 773, op. 1, d. 1, ll. 66–68 and "Semga reki Niva," *ZhA*, no. 1 (September 2002): 15.

62 GAMO, f. 773, op. 1, d. 6, l. 25; A. V. Barabanov and T. A. Kalinina, *"Apatit": vek iz veka* (Apatity: Laplandia Minerals, 2004), 26; E. F. Razin, *Kandalaksha* (Murmansk: Murmanskoe knizhnoe izdatel'stvo, 1991), 90–92; and V. I. Kondrikov, "Sostoianie i perspektivy stroitel'stva v raione Khibinskikh razrabotok," *KMK*, no. 5–6 (1931): 10.

63 V. Ia. Shashkov, *Spetspereselentsy na Murmane: Rol' spetspereselentsev v razvitii proizvoditel'nykh sil na Kol'skom poluostrove (1930–1936 gg.)* (Murmansk: Izdatel'stvo MGPU, 1993), 53 and GAMO, f. 773, op. 1, d. 15, l. 225.

64 A. Matveev, "Spetsposelok," in *Spetspereselentsy v Khibinakh: Spetspereselentsy i zakliuchennye v istorii osvoeniia Khibin (Kniga vospominanii)* (Apatity: Khibinskoe obshchestvo "Memorial," 1997), 166–168.

children, he suggested forcibly deploying "up to 1,000 Finnish deserters... On account of their small families, they would be more convenient for the construction than a new party of special settlers, since further housing construction at Nivastroi, which already has grown to a 12,000 person town, is obviously inexpedient." Stepanchenko also seemed to imply that the Finns would be less deterred by the Kola climate.[65] In the case of both hired and forced laborers the harsh northern environment taxed their bodies; significantly more calories needed to be expended on just maintaining body temperature in this cold region and this energy was then unusable for construction labor.

Along with the labor problems, flaws in the initial design, accidents at the construction site, and late freezes in the new canals delayed the completion of the station. Some of these engineering deficiencies would also later prevent the entire Niva cascade from producing optimal levels of electricity. Yet the Niva-2 GES came online in June 1934 and eventually possessed equipment that gave it a capacity of 60,000 kilowatts, almost ten times the first turbo-generators in the Khibiny and one of the highest levels in the Soviet Union at the time.[66] This unit partially electrified the Murmansk railroad and supplied the industrial and municipal facilities in the Khibiny, helping raise Apatit's productive capacities and Kirovsk's population.[67]

The installation of the Niva-2 GES also disturbed the surrounding ecosystem. Engineers reduced seasonal variation in river flow, constructed a dam along part of the riverbank, and used underground turbines to assure a comparatively stable year-round supply of energy.[68] Unlike other arteries, the Niva River had Lake Imandra and its surrounding water bodies as natural reservoirs, which limited the amount of inundated territory for the Niva-2 GES. But the hydraulic reordering of the Niva River caused the large population of salmon (*semga*) that had existed there to disappear.[69] Small communities nearby had caught a decent amount of

65 GAMO, f. 773, op. 1, d. 15, l. 225 and RGASPI, f. 17, op. 120, d. 26, ll. 195–197.

66 Shashkov, *Spetspereselentsy v istorii Murmanskoi oblasti*, 147–151; Kaibysheva, *Elektricheskoe siianie severa*, 10–18; Palumbo and Dmitriev, "Sostoianie, problemy i perspektivy gidroenergetiki Kol'skogo poluostrova," in Stepanov, ed., *Problemy energetiki zapada evropeiskogo Severa Rossii*, 19–20; Valerii Berlin, "Letopis' severnykh energoproektov," *ZhA*, no. 1 (September 2002): 20–21; and GAMO, f. 773, op. 1, d. 62, l. 24.

67 GAMO, f. 773, op. 1, d. 52, ll. 168–169 and GAMO, f. R-990, op. 1, d. 3, ll. 75–77.

68 Tiul'panova, ed., *Istoriia industrializatsii SSSR*, 119–120.

69 Kaibysheva, *Elektricheskoe siianie severa*, 104.

fish from the river, which they traded and consumed themselves. Writing in 1930 one observer correctly foresaw the impending collapse of the salmon stock: "The installation of a hydroelectric station on the Niva will totally shut off the passage up the river for salmon to their main spawning grounds and will apparently completely terminate their local population."[70]

More concerned with energy than fish, industrial planners turned to the Tuloma River in the northwest section of the Kola Peninsula next. They hoped that making a motor out of this river would supply additional electricity to Apatit, the new nickel works in the Monche tundra, the planned chemical combine in Kandalaksha, and the growing city of Murmansk. Before construction, the Tuloma River traveled approximately seventy-six kilometers from Lake Notozero and then exited into the Kola Bay of the Barents Sea at the town of Kola. It ranged from 400 to 900 meters in width and declined about fifty meters over its length.[71] The first of two planned hydroelectric stations on the Tuloma River – the Lower Tuloma Hydroelectric Station – was to be placed near Kola at the new settlement of Murmashi. Designers envisioned a stationary unit that consisted of "a strong building with chutes and tail-races and an interface between the left and right bank dams," a "mixed-type non-overflow dam" that was to be twenty-nine meters high, and a "fish-pass."[72]

Again the energy of forced laborers facilitated the project. Like the Olen'ia-Monchegorsk railroad line, the White Sea-Baltic Combine built the Lower Tuloma GES with Gulag prisoners. Poor sanitation and difficult work conditions pervaded. Upon arriving at the construction site in 1933, one Gulag prisoner recalled how they, "quickly gathered forest and peat and built more than a hundred mud-huts and barracks that were needed to endure the negative forty degree freezes." Another prisoner later described the physical demands of the labor: "Work was conducted quickly and simultaneously on the spillway, dam, and station building, although there were not enough technicians. Wheelbarrows, carts, and hand-drawn trucks were used, and in the best case draft horses." Accidental explosions that occurred during the construction of the dam killed a number of prisoners there.[73]

70 "Semga reki Niva," *ZhA*, no. 1 (September 2002): 15.

71 S. V. Grigor'ev, "Reka-Tulom – istochnik energosnabzheniia Kol'skogo poluostrova," *KMK*, no. 3–4 (1934): 37–38 and GAMO, f. R-959, op. 1, d. 1a, l. 18.

72 GAMO, f. R-959, op. 1, d. 1a, ll. 4–5.

73 A. A. Kiselev, "GULAG na Murmane: Istoriia tiurem, lagerei, kolonii," *SM* (October 16, 1992): 3 and A. A. Kiselev, "G- na Murmane: Istoriia tiurem, lagerei, kolonii," *SM*

Though the Soviet state increasingly censored information about forced labor, the Tuloma project still received official praise as an instance of socialist reforging. The public discussions of prisoner labor touched on the new relationship between people and the environment, which indicated both the ascendance of humans and the dependence of this change on interaction with nature. "The people sent to solve complex technical tasks and at the same time rehabilitate an army of former criminals will grow at Tuloma in this way," claimed one article. It continued, "Murmashi became unrecognizable. The rocks are moved aside and the shape of the shores of the mountainous Tuloma changes. But the people are transformed even more than nature."[74]

Flooding for the Lower Tuloma station physically altered the landscape and displaced people from their homes. State agencies evaluated these disruptions primarily in economic terms. "The submersion and impounding from the head of the Lower Tuloma GES did not bring any sort of noticeable damage to the national economy because of the extremely insignificant population and the complete absence of industry in the high water area," according to a government commission charged with overseeing the construction. It specified, "the overall area of the flooding of the shores is a region of 2,735 hectares, on which 1,691 hectares fall in the forested area and 712 in the marshes with undergrowth. In connection with these submersions three collective farms, which include thirty households, were transferred to locations that had not been flooded."[75] Thirty households were a drop in the bucket compared to the millions of people worldwide who were forcibly relocated to make way for hydroelectric dams in the twentieth century. But such a displacement suggests how even in the sparsely populated terrains of the Arctic, modern states usually privileged energy infrastructure over rural livelihoods.[76]

Upon its completion Soviet officials celebrated the Lower Tuloma GES as prevailing over natural constraints. They boasted that it was "the northernmost hydro-station of regional significance in the world and was accomplished in a short period (1934–1936) in the difficult natural conditions of a polar territory."[77] Like much of the industrial construction

(October 21, 1992): 3. Also see GAMO, f. R-959, op. 1, d. 1a, ll. 3–96 and GAMO, f. R-990, op. 1, d. 3, ll. 38–58.

74 S. Al′terman and Em. Germaize, "Gidrostantsiia na Tulome," *KMK*, no. 12 (1934): 50.

75 GAMO, f. R-959, op. 1, d. 1a, ll. 19–19ob.

76 Jacques Leslie, *Deep Water: The Epic Struggle of Dams, Displaced People, and the Environment* (New York: Farrar, Straus and Giroux, 2005).

77 GAMO, f. R-959, op. 1, d. 1a, l. 5.

on the Kola Peninsula, the Lower Tuloma GES in fact had been beset by unanticipated difficulties related to the natural environment, which had delayed finishing the station. The thawing of solidly frozen land, for instance, created significant structural problems for the dam.[78] As a construction manager there acknowledged in 1938, "Local polar conditions (the darkness, the snowiness, etc.) were not accounted for in the project's organizational work, which as a result led to major stoppages."[79] Despite these problems, the Lower Tuloma GES did go online in 1937 and contributed 67,400 kilowatt-hours to the Kola energy economy in 1940.[80]

In 1936 authorities also established a new unified entity to manage the hydroelectric plants and coordinate the work now being done by the Kola landscape – Kolenergo.[81] Outlining its agenda for the third five-year plan (1938–1942), Kolenergo provided a hydraulic vision of the Kola Peninsula's energy future. "One of the decisive factors influencing the character and tempo of the region's economic development is the status of its energy base." Fortunately, "in disparate areas of the region hydro-resources are rationally distributed by nature and correspond with concentrations of natural resources." The firm claimed it could eventually utilize an estimated thirteen billion kilowatt-hours of hydroelectricity available in the Karelo-Murmansk region.[82] Though its goals of constructing additional hydroelectric stations on the Tuloma and Niva rivers in the late 1930s proved overly ambitious, Kolenergo did increase the region's electrical capacity in anticipation of heightened demand from the Severonikel′ nickel combine. It also connected the Niva and Tuloma stations with high voltage transfer lines and substations in 1940.[83]

78 GAMO, f. R-959, op. 1, d. 1a, l. 8. 79 GAMO, f. R-959, op. 1, d. 5, l. 4.

80 GAMO, f. R-990, op. 1, d. 3, l. 18. I am fairly confident that this unit was one thousand kilowatt-hours, but it was not specified in the archival document.

81 The new leadership of Kolenergo soon fell prey to the violence of the Stalinist terror. Some of the allegations against them as enemies of the people involved inadequate preparation for the climate of the north. Workers also accused managers of subjecting them to excessively long work shifts and requiring pregnant women to stay on the job. GAMO, f. R-990, op. 1, d. 1, ll. 112–113, 167–169.

82 GAMO, f. R-990, op. 1, d. 4, ll. 2–4.

83 GAMO, f. R-990, op. 1, d. 3, ll. 1, 70; GAMO, f. 773, op. 1, d. 62, ll. 23–25; and *Kolenergo, 1936–1996*, 5. Given the delays in the smelting operations at Severonikel′, the electricity needs fell short of these expectations. RGAE, f. 9037, op. 1, d. 41, l. 37. One person involved with the planning of the Upper Tuloma station during the 1930s was a G. Chirkin who worked for the White Sea-Baltic Combine of the Gulag system. It seems quite likely that this individual was the same Chirkin involved with the imperial Resettlement Administration and the Murmansk railroad. GAMO, f. R-990, op. 1, d. 3, ll. 38–54.

Capacity versus Demand

"The workers looked at me with wild eyes." They had just finished assembling the final unit of the Lower Tuloma GES in the autumn of 1941 when Evgenii Shtern, the main engineer of the station, ordered them to dismantle it. Along with much of the electrical infrastructure recently installed on the Kola Peninsula, this equipment was being evacuated to Tashkent in advance of Nazi airstrikes.[84] The exodus succeeded in preserving some parts of the hydroelectric stations, but bombs still hit the Niva and Lower Tuloma units causing them to operate only intermittently and at a lower capacity. A halt in coal shipments also disrupted production at the Murmansk Thermal Electric Station. In short, the Kola Peninsula found itself in another energy crisis during the Second World War.[85]

This time around local wood poorly compensated for the shortfall. Many of the most accessible Kola forests had already been felled. Severonikel′ reported that, "despite the combine's difficult situation with supplies of firewood and industrial timber, the issue of our own forest collection cannot be resolved in a practical way during the first three quarters" of 1943; too few laborers had returned to the restored nickel plant.[86] Meanwhile, central authorities tried to unite timber firms in the Umba, Zasheek, and Kandalaksha regions into a single trust to help alleviate the fuel needs of the nearby enterprises, but this effort languished for months and does not seem to have paid off with more reliable firewood supplies reaching the factories.[87]

Having survived wartime scarcity, Kola planners quickly returned to bolstering the region's energy sources. They doubled down on waterpower by extensively expanding the network of hydroelectric stations. According to a *Polar Pravda* journalist in the mid-1950s, the USSR possessed "the richest supplies of the water energy in the world" and "the energetic value of the rivers of the Kola Peninsula is attributable to an auspicious combination of factors affecting their potential capacity."[88] The damming of more and more rivers allowed the Kola Peninsula to follow global trends of unprecedented growth in energy production. But

84 Kaibysheva, *Elektricheskoe siianie severa*, 23.

85 Berlin, "Letopis′ severnykh energoproektov," *ZhA*, no. 1 (September 2002): 28–29, 81 and Kaibysheva, *Elektricheskoe siianie severa*, 23–24, 35, 44.

86 RGAE, f. 9037, op. 1, d. 81, l. 9.

87 RGASPI, f. 17, op. 121, d. 287, ll. 7–9, 136–137.

88 P. Markov, "Gidroenergeticheskie resursy Kol′skogo poluostrova," *PP* (January 16, 1957): 3.

developers of the Soviet Arctic also remained trapped in a relentless race to find enough energy resources for the proliferating industries, cities, and military installations. Through the end of the 1960s, ballooning demand often stayed one step ahead of the capacity of the new hydroelectric and thermal stations. This competition between capacity and demand lays bare the fragility of extensive growth.

Acknowledged constraints on energy supplies also distinguished the postwar Soviet Union from the experience of the first and third world at the time. The USSR was only just beginning its oil addiction. Economic analyst Robert Campbell put it starkly: "In the early fifties the USSR was a net importer of fuel, hydropower was a more important primary energy source than natural gas, and firewood contributed more toward the total energy supply than oil."[89] Coal production boomed in this era, doubling both throughout the country and in the Pechora basin during the 1950s.[90] But neither the Soviet Union nor the Kola Peninsula had yet become territories dominated by this fossil fuel's carbon cousin.[91]

Elsewhere in the postwar world, oil undergirded "the new conception of the economy as an object that could grow without limit," according to political theorist Timothy Mitchell. Unlike the obvious "physical limits" of coal extraction and transportation, oil subverted recognition of material constraints: its price seemed to decline continuously as its abundance rose steadily and it was much cheaper to ship. Oil also served as the basis for industrializing agriculture and producing synthetic materials to replace natural resources, thereby outflanking previous Malthusian fears of limited food and mineral supplies. In Mitchell's view, this ostensible inexhaustibility of oil oriented wealthy states toward unending growth as a political imperative, which in turn forged deep dependencies

89 Robert W. Campbell, *Trends in the Soviet Oil and Gas Industry* (Baltimore: The Johns Hopkins University Press, 1976), 1. For a recent history of Soviet oil in the revolutionary period, see Sara G. Brinegar, "Baku at All Costs: The Politics of Oil in the New Soviet State" (PhD diss., University of Wisconsin-Madison, 2014).

90 Jordan A. Hodgkins, *Soviet Power: Energy Resources, Production, and Potential* (Englewood Cliffs: Prentice Hall, 1961), 44; A. B. Kovalchuk, ed., *The Coal Industry of the Former USSR: Coal Supply System and Industry Development* (New York: Taylor and Francis, 2002), 3–5; and Barenberg, *Gulag Town, Company Town*, 278.

91 Production of oil and natural gas only increased moderately in the first decade after the war before accelerating to together top 50 percent of Soviet energy in the late 1960s. But even then hydrocarbons remained a much lower portion in the Kola north. Per Högselius, *Red Gas: Russia and the Origins of European Energy Dependence* (New York: Palgrave Macmillan, 2013), 13–29; Elliot, *The Soviet Energy Balance*, 6–12; and Kobzikov, "Toplivnyi balans Murmanskoi oblasti i voprosy ego ratsionalizatsii," in Zamotkin and Erogova, eds., *Priroda i khoziaistvo Severa*, vol. 2, part 2, 244.

between the democratic political orders of the West and authoritarianism elsewhere.[92] Another theorist, Fernando Coronil, argues that control over oil allowed mid-century political leaders in Venezuela to perform seemingly spectacular and powerful deeds – ones related to development agendas and which made the state appear as some sort of magical entity.[93] From the 1940s to the early 1970s state officials on the Kola Peninsula neither operated under the political logic of Mitchell's "carbon democracy," nor were they yet able to stage a convincing performance of Coronil's "magical state" (that would come with nuclear power). Instead, they continued to strive for energy self-sufficiency in large part by making the region's water and land do work for them.

Immediately after the war, Kola industrialists sought to get the previous electrical facilities back up online. Central authorities ordered the evacuated equipment to be returned to the Niva and Tuloma stations in October 1944, though some of the turbines of these units instead stayed in Uzbekistan.[94] Kolenergo's staff reassembled the stations, but continued to encounter operational deficiencies in the Lower Tuloma's dams for years to come.[95] They then quickly turned to connecting the newly acquired nickel works in Pechenga to the Lower Tuloma GES with an electrical transfer line that traversed 154 kilometers through rugged hills and marshes.[96]

The firm also renewed a project to add two more stations along the Niva River. Believing that these new facilities could supply an extra 400 million kilowatt-hours of electricity that would help make up for an energy deficit, Kolenergo had pushed to get them operating before the war broke out.[97] The electrically rapacious Kandalaksha Aluminum Plant, which started operating in 1951, helped determine the order of the new Niva stations. The Niva-3 GES near the Kandalaksha Bay went online in 1949 and the further upstream the Niva-1 GES at Pinozero opened in 1952. Engineers submerged notable areas around Lake Pirenga and Lake Plesozero and flooded some land previously used by the Industriia state

[92] His argument aims to reverse the concept of the "resource curse" by showing the dependencies of current democratic polities on a world order organized around the access and distribution of carbon energy. See Timothy Mitchell, *Carbon Democracy: Political Power in the Age of Oil* (London: Verso, 2011), 139–141.

[93] Fernando Coronil, *The Magical State: Nature, Money, and Modernity in Venezuela* (Chicago: University of Chicago Press, 1997).

[94] Berlin, "Letopis′ severnykh energoproektov," *ZhA*, no. 1 (September 2002): 81.

[95] GAMO, f. R-959, op. 1, d. 10, ll. 4–12 and GAMO, f. R-990, op. 1, d. 290, ll. 51–54.

[96] Kaibysheva, *Elektricheskoe siianie severa*, 40–42.

[97] GAMO, f. R-990, op. 1, d. 4, ll. 6–7, 19–20.

farm.[98] Upon completion, however, Kolenergo's acting manager, Matvei Zarkhi, complained that the Niva-3 GES "works unsatisfactorily."[99] In part because of its defective operation, Kolenergo began building another set of three hydroelectric stations on the Kovda River just south of Kandalaksha – Kniazhegubskaia, Iovskaia, and Kumskaia. They were completed in 1955, 1961, and 1963, respectively, and integrated with the Niva cascade. Construction teams dammed numerous small lakes and inundated lands to create sizable reservoirs for the Kovda hydroelectric stations.[100]

Murmansk officials also promoted a slew of small-scale hydroelectric facilities to meet the needs of rural inhabitants. They viewed this option as a cheaper and more efficient means of hooking up fishing villages and collective farms than erecting poles and running lines to the often distant electrical stations.[101] One such project involved placing a small hydroelectric station in the El′iavr-Chai stream on the Lapland Nature Reserve in order to supply its small administrative settlement with electricity. Apparently less worried about the ecological effects of this unit than those from connecting the territory to Kolenergo's grid, reserve scientist Oleg Semenov-Tian-Shanskii personally assisted in launching this project. Staff at the *zapovednik* requested a year delay in 1950, which means that the station probably was not completed before the liquation of the reserve in 1951.[102] Many other such programs for creating low capacity stations and installing electrical poles to connect small municipalities encountered long delays.[103]

A higher-priority project in the aftermath of World War II was the reconstruction of a hydroelectric station on the Pasvik River that the retreating Nazi forces had destroyed. The 143-kilometer long Pasvik descends from Lake Inari in Finland. As it moves northward, the river becomes the border between Norway and Russia and flows out into the

98 RGASPI, f. 17, op. 122, d. 104, l. 173; GAMO, f. 773, op. 1, d. 55, ll. 351–356; and *Kolenergo, 1936–1996*, 17.

99 GAMO, f. R-990, op. 1, d. 290, l. 99.

100 GAMO, f. R-990, op. 1, d. 617, l. 1; *Kolenergo, 1936–1996*, 20–23, and Kaibysheva, *Elektricheskoe siianie severa*, 68–76. Planners discussed options for the Kniazhegubskaia GES before the war. GAMO, f. R-990, op. 1, d. 4, ll. 8–9 and GAMO, f. R-990, op. 1, d. 3, ll. 20, 45–47.

101 Paul R. Josephson, *The Conquest of the Russian Arctic* (Cambridge, MA: Harvard University Press, 2014), 298–299 and N. I. Lebedev, "40 let v energetike," in Goriachkin and Kostiukevich, eds., *Gody zastoinye ... Gody dostoinye!*, 167.

102 GAMO, f. A-358, op. 2, d. 853, ll. 91–160.

103 Josephson, *The Conquest of the Russian Arctic*, 298–299.

Barents Sea. After the Soviet Union captured and acquired the Pechenga region in 1944, much of the Pasvik River remained in Finland. Soviet industrialists wanted to use energy from the Pasvik's rapids to supply the revived Pechenganikel′ smelter. They knew that the restored Lower Tuloma station would be woefully inadequate to meet the enormous electrical demand of the Pechenganikel′ and Severonikel′ refineries, which both relied on an energy-intensive electrolytic smelting process. Thus, for the sake of the nickel economy, Soviet authorities bought additional upstream land along both banks of the Pasvik from Finland in 1947. This purchase gave the USSR full control over these hydroelectric resources. Officials also opted for hiring a Finnish firm Imatran Voima to rebuild the Ianiskoski Hydroelectric Station on the newly acquired sliver of the Murmansk region. Though plenty of disorder and confusion pervaded the construction site (including at least three cases of arson), this work environment was a far cry from the Gulag camps that had hitherto dominated Kola hydroelectric projects.[104]

After finishing the Ianiskoski station in 1950, Imatran Voima turned to two other stations on the Pasvik River – the Raiakoski GES and the Kaitakoski GES. Production at Pechenganikel′ was already sprinting ahead of the electrical supply during this construction. By early 1953, Pechenganikel′'s directors reported that the enterprise used over 332 million kilowatt-hours of electricity in 1952 and that smelting had become less energy efficient (averaging 860 kilowatt-hours of electricity per ton instead of 840).[105] Imatran Voima workers finished the Raiakoski GES and the Kaitakoski GES in 1955 and 1959, respectively. Subsequently, the Soviets and Norwegians exploited the hydroelectric potential from the Pasvik's waterfalls even further with four additional stations along the part of the river that they shared (Boris and Gleb, Skogfoss, Khevoskoski, and Melkefoss). Contracted Norwegian laborers built the Boris and Gleb station for the Soviet Union, though the other Soviet station (Khevoskoski) did not rely on foreign firms.[106]

Sufficiently satisfied with the results of the borderland hydroelectric stations, Soviet authorities also decided to hire Imatran Voima to build the Upper Tuloma GES further in the interior. When initially proposed in the middle of the 1930s, planners envisioned again using Gulag prisoners

104 Lars Rowe, "Pechenganikel: Soviet Industry, Russian Pollution, and the Outside World" (PhD diss., University of Oslo, 2013), 115–156; GAMO, f. R-990, op. 1, d. 290, ll. 64–68; and GAMO, f. R-459, op. 6, d. 508a, ll. 26–30.

105 RGAE, f. 9037, op. 1, d. 508, ll. 27–28.

106 Rowe, "Pechenganikel," 152, 162–167.

to install this second facility upstream on the Tuloma River. At the time the station seemed essential for meeting the anticipated energy needs for Severonikel′, but it became a less urgent postwar priority with the Soviet acquisition of the Pasvik River.[107] It came back on the agenda in the late 1950s and early 1960s. The shift from prisoner to incentivized labor that accompanied the post-Stalin reforms decreased the arduous and coercive dependence on human muscle power, though of course accidents and generally rough conditions still pervaded the worksite of the GES. Channeling the spirit of Khrushchev's Thaw, Kolenergo's engineers also gladly portrayed the collaboration with the Finnish firm as mutually beneficial. They described how Finnish experts made valuable revisions to the construction plan that allowed them to complete the station ahead of schedule, while remarking that Imatran Voima learned new techniques for erecting earthen dams from the Soviets.[108]

The Upper Tuloma GES, which went online in 1964 and 1965, transformed a huge part of the Kola Peninsula's surface. Hydraulic engineers flooded a large area to create a reservoir that would store potential energy in water that could be released to maintain desired river flow. Enormous swaths of the region's map filled in with blue. The inundation raised the level of Lake Notozero by thirty-two meters and occupied about 745 square kilometers (for the sake of comparison Lake Imandra, the largest non-artificial water body in the Kola north, takes up approximately 876 square kilometers).[109] Together the Upper and Lower Tuloma stations impaired aquatic fauna in the river ecosystem, despite efforts to build fish passes. Whitefish and perch mated in Lake Notozero, but generally preferred its shallower waters. In some years when technicians lowered the level of the Upper Tuloma reservoir, the eggs of these fish froze. Trout, loach, grayling, and salmon had difficulty traversing the altered hydrology of the Kola northwest, sometimes encountering dams and other obstructions as they attempted to find their breeding grounds. As in the case of the Niva, the salmon population in the Tuloma River dropped precipitously.[110]

This story of Kola inundation was, of course, a Soviet one more generally. During the 1960s, the total area of the USSR submerged by reservoirs doubled. Several scientists became increasingly vocal about

107 GAMO, f. R-990, op. 1, d. 3, ll. 38–49.

108 GAMO, f. R-990, op. 1, d. 840, ll. 32–47.

109 *Kolenergo, 1936–1996*, 27–28 and GAMO, f. R-990, op. 1, d. 840, ll. 32–47.

110 Kaibysheva, *Elektricheskoe siianie severa*, 104–106.

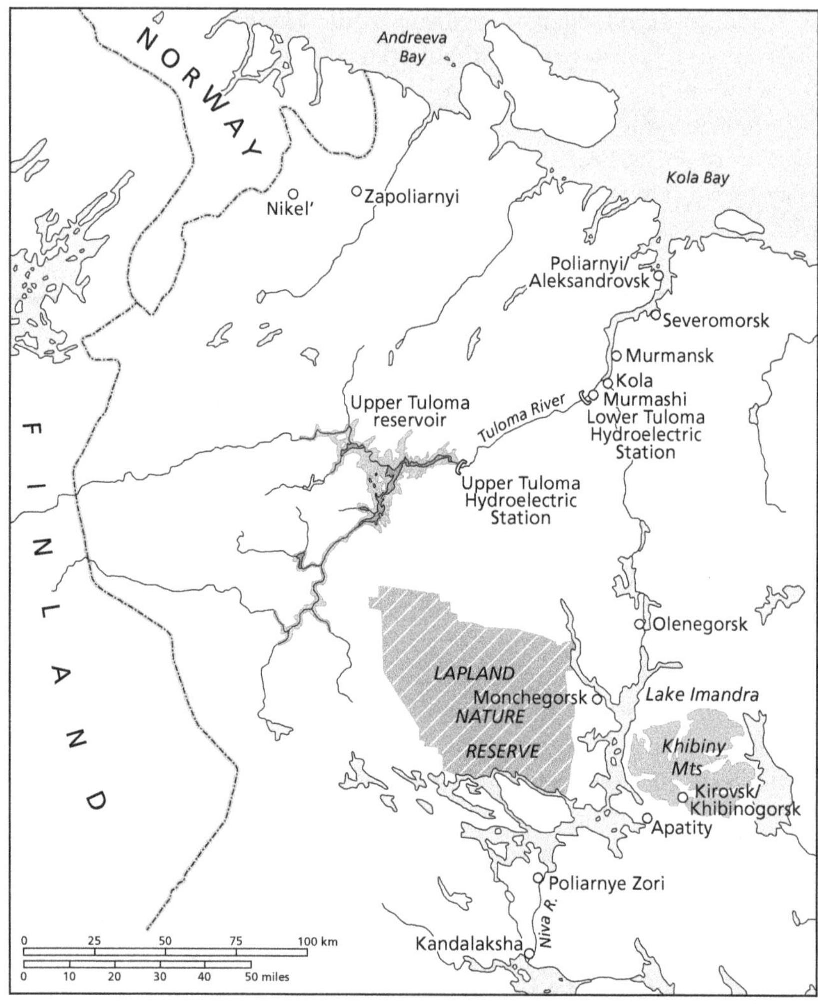

MAP 5. Inundation for the Upper Tuloma Hydroelectric Station.

the negative environmental effects of hydroelectric dams in this period, including erosion, lowered water quality, lost cropland, and disruptions to fish. This environmental pressure, along with the expansion of oil and nuclear power and bureaucratic opposition of other industrial ministries in the Soviet Union, helped crest the hydroelectric tide. Construction of new dams and stations slowed down considerably during the following decade – both union-wide and on the Kola Peninsula.[111] At this point

[111] Thane Gustafson, *Reform in Soviet Politics: Lessons of Recent Policies on Land and Water* (Cambridge: Cambridge University Press, 1981), 46–50.

80 percent of the Murmansk region's electro-energy came from hydroelectricity.[112]

Even taken together, all of these hydroelectric stations failed to keep pace with the skyrocketing amounts of energy consumed by Kola heavy industry. By one estimate apatite enrichment required a comparatively modest ninety-five kilowatt-hours of electricity per ton between 1958 and 1965, but aluminum needed 17,000 kilowatt-hours per ton and nickel 55,000 kilowatt-hours per ton.[113] And, of course, the number of tons of these substances manufactured each year, along with the small urban centers surrounding the plants, grew steadily. Within the decade after 1965, the amount of per capita fuel consumption and heat use in the Murmansk region were set to double or more.[114] Re-engineering rivers seemed to be reaching its limit.

Party leaders started to panic. Vladimir Ptitsyn, who served as First Secretary of the party apparatus of the Murmansk region in the 1970s and 1980s, recalled weather conditions straining the Kola energy network. "In the 1960s a drought struck the north. Rivers became shallow and tundra and forest burnt down. Electricity production sharply fell, which restrained the enterprises' energy consumption. We did not have replenishment from the state energy system, since electrical transmission lines still had not been built. A severe crisis ensued. The Kola north found itself on the brink of catastrophe."[115]

In order to rectify this situation, Kolenergo both expanded its network of transmission lines and turned to other sources of energy to augment the hydroelectric network. The firm quickly expanded the capacity of the recently completed Kirovsk State Regional Electric Station (GRES) fivefold and converted it to a thermal station as well. This coal powered station provided more than a third of the territory's electricity in the early 1970s.[116] Staff at the electrical utility also returned to the idea of using tidal energy by constructing an experimental station on the Kislaia

112 Kobzikov, "Toplivnyi balans Murmanskoi oblasti i voprosy ego ratsionalizatsii," in Zamotkin and Erogova, eds., *Priroda i khoziaistvo Severa*, vol. 2, part 2, 244.

113 Kiselev, *Kol'skoi atomnoi – 30*, 17.

114 Kobzikov, "Toplivnyi balans Murmanskoi oblasti i voprosy ego ratsionalizatsii," in Zamotkin and Erogova, eds., *Priroda i khoziaistvo Severa*, vol. 2, part 2, 244.

115 V. N. Ptitsyn, "Eto schast'e – sluzhit' narodu," in Goriachkin and Kostiukevich, eds., *Gody zastoinye… Gody dostoinye!*, 14–15 and GAMO, f. R-990, op. 1, d. 1242, l. 3.

116 GAMO, f. R-990, op. 1, d. 617, ll. 2–7; GAMO, f. R-990, op. 1, d. 621, l. 15; Palumbo and Dmitriev, "Sostoianie, problemy i perspektivy gidroenergetiki Kol'skogo poluostrova," in Stepanov, ed., *Problemy energetiki zapada evropeiskogo Severa Rossii*, 16–18; and Kaibysheva, *Elektricheskoe siianie severa*, 57–65.

inlet of the Barents Sea, just due north of Murmansk. It became the first and only tidal electrical station in the USSR in 1968.[117] Neither of these units overcame the dearth, however. That would come with the advent of nuclear power in the Arctic.

Steady State

In the midst of a global energy crisis, the Kola Peninsula solved its supply problems. Overlapping with the era when an embargo of the Organization of Petroleum Exporting Countries (OPEC) sparked a fourfold increase in oil prices in a matter of months, the first units of the Kola Nuclear Power Plant started generating electricity in 1973–1974. Once it became fully operational in the 1980s, the plant more than doubled the capacity and production of electricity for the region, turning it into an energy exporter after decades of relying heavily on imports. The scale of this increase was astronomical. If the capacity of the Kola Peninsula's electrical system rose by about fifty megawatts a year between 1934 and 1959 (excluding the years of World War II) and by about one hundred megawatts a year between 1959 and 1973, it now accelerated to an average of around 200 megawatts a year between 1973 and 1989.[118] Nuclear power's ascent in the Kola north was indeed even more dramatic than this trajectory indicates. Abundant atomic submarines and ships based in the region during the late Soviet period made it home to up to a fifth of the world's nuclear reactors – the most concentrated zone of nuclear power on the planet![119]

The capture of energy released during nuclear fission and conversion of it into electricity fueled a further boom in industrial production and helped attract more residents to the north. Yet the use of nuclear power also re-entangled Soviet society with the natural world in novel ways. Some theorists have argued that industrial modernity primarily involved a detachment from nature. As sociologist Anthony Giddens posits, "In

[117] "Kislogubskaia PES," *ZhA*, no. 1 (September 2002): 58–59.

[118] Palumbo and Dmitriev, "Sostoianie, problemy i perspektivy gidroenergetiki Kol′skogo poluostrova," in Stepanov, ed., *Problemy energetiki zapada evropeiskogo Severa Rossii*, 16–17.

[119] Gösta Weissglas, "Preface," in Peder Axensten and Gösta Weissglas, eds., *Nuclear Risks, Environmental, and Development Co-operation in the North of Europe: Proceedings from the Conference in Apatity, 1999* (Umeå: Cerum, 2000), 11 and James Robins, "Russian Nuclear Dustbin Threats," *BBC News* (August 14, 2000), accessed November 1, 2014, http://news.bbc.co.uk/2/hi/europe/607175.stm.

industrialised sectors of the globe – and, increasingly, elsewhere – human beings live in a *created environment*, an environment of action which is, of course, physical but no longer just natural."[120] Other scholars have countered that nature and society remain intimately, but differently, intertwined in the modern world.[121] In the words of environmental historian Liza Piper, industrial development "changed the cognitive and material links between our work and nature's work but did not separate one from the other."[122] On the Kola Peninsula relinking occurred in part through the heavy dose of secrecy and the potential threats that accompanied the rise of nuclear power. Inadequate public information about the substances, infrastructure, practices, and effects of splitting atoms and the uncertain hazards of nuclear accidents and radioactive waste bound Kola residents to their environmental surroundings just as tightly as before.

The unleashing of energy trapped in atomic bombs quite literally exploded on to the world scene with the American bombing of Hiroshima and Nagasaki at the end of the Second World War. Nuclear energy's assistance in destructive military campaigns before economic uses for it had been established and the continued prominence of atomic bombs in global security politics cast a long and a secretive shadow over the industry. The USSR took the lead in the civilian uses of atomic energy, opening the world's first experimental reactor at Obninsk in 1954. Scientists in charge of the atomic weapons program, including Igor Kurchatov and Anatolii Aleksandrov, participated in designing and promoting nuclear energy for electrical power plants, civilian and military vessels, and assorted other uses. Starting in the 1950s, the obscurely named Ministry of Medium Machine-Building oversaw both military and civilian aspects of the Soviet nuclear program. This unity of personnel and institutions placed Soviet atomic energy under an even higher level of classification than in Western countries.[123]

120 Anthony Giddens, *The Consequences of Modernity* (Stanford: Stanford University Press, 1990), 60.

121 Maria Kaika, *City of Flows: Modernity, Nature, and the City* (New York: Routledge, 2005); Gísli Pálsson, "Nature and Society in the Age of Postmodernism," in Aletta Biersack and James B. Greenberg, eds., *Reimagining Political Ecology* (Durham: Duke University Press, 2006), 70–93; and Bruno Latour, *We Have Never Been Modern*, trans. Catherine Porter (Cambridge, MA: Harvard University Press, 1993).

122 Liza Piper, *The Industrial Transformation of Subarctic Canada* (Vancouver: University of British Columbia Press, 2009), 4.

123 On the enjoined development of the military and civilian nuclear programs in the USSR, see Paul R. Josephson, *Red Atom: Russia's Nuclear Power Program from Stalin to Today* (Pittsburgh: University of Pittsburgh Press, 2000); David Holloway, *Stalin*

Sea-faring vessels first brought atomic energy to the Kola Peninsula. The Northern Fleet of the Soviet Navy had opened on the Murman coast in the mid-1930s, but it remained a comparatively small branch until the flare-up of Cold War tensions. Geopolitical imperatives now impelled the Soviet superpower to turn it into its largest and most significant naval fleet. As the Murmansk region underwent a massive militarization with numerous air bases and naval facilities clustered near the NATO border, the Northern Fleet began replacing diesel engine submarines with nuclear ones that could travel faster and go up to a year without refueling. It launched its first nuclear-powered submarine, *Leninskii Komsomol*, in 1957. The ship operated out of a base on Zapadnaia Litsa, just east of the Rybachi Peninsula on the Kola Peninsula, and suffered a major accident in 1967 that killed thirty-nine of its crew members. Not deterred, the Soviet military commissioned a slew of additional nuclear-powered submarines; the Northern Fleet eventually amassed over a hundred of these vessels. Many of the submarines also were themselves equipped with nuclear warheads. Meanwhile, the Murmansk Shipping Company started to operate nuclear-powered icebreakers for civilian shipping. Its first nuclear icebreaker, the *Lenin*, entered the northern seas in 1959, but experienced several accidents in the late 1960s that caused its reactor to be replaced. The firm continued to expand its fleet after this point, coming to maintain eight nuclear-powered icebreakers and a container ship. These civilian vessels cut through the Northern Sea Route to allow for the shipment of goods across the Soviet Arctic and would then refuel at Atomflot service base near Murmansk every three to four years.[124]

Many of the people working on these military and civilian nuclear ships lived in one of the closed cities that sprouted up on the Murman coast. These Cold War creations, which did not appear on publically available

and the Bomb: The Soviet Union and Atomic Energy, 1939–1956 (New Haven: Yale University Press, 1995); and Zhores A. Medvedev, *The Legacy of Chernobyl* (New York: W. W. Norton, 1990).

124 Bøhmer, et al., *The Arctic Nuclear Challenge*, Bellona Report, vol. 3, 1–31, Josephson, *Red Atom*, 109–145; Hønneland, *Russia and the West*, 24–28; Gary E. Weir and Walter J. Boyne, *Rising Tide: The Untold Story of the Russian Submarines That Fought the Cold War* (New York: Basic Books, 2003); Geir Hønneland and Anne-Kristin Jørgensen, *Integration vs. Autonomy: Civil-Military Relations on the Kola Peninsula* (Aldershot: Ashgate, 1999), 119–128; Erik Hansen and Arnfinn Tønnessen, *Environment and Living Conditions on the Kola Peninsula* (Oslo: Fafo Institute for Applied Social Science, 1998), 136–137; and Tomas Ries and Johnny Skorve, *Investigating Kola: A Study of Military Bases using Satellite Photography* (London: Brassey's Defence Publishers, 1987).

FIGURE 10. The Kola Nuclear Power Plant.
Source: RIA Novosti archive, image #146342/Roman Denisov/.

maps, housed Soviet military personnel, their families, and individuals employed in industries that directly served their needs. Outsiders could not enter them without special permission, while the residents of closed cities faced limited access to telephones and newspapers and prohibitions on travel. The Kola Peninsula came to possess six of these closed cities – more than any other part of the Soviet Union. Severomorsk, where the headquarters of the Northern Fleet was located, was the largest. Other closed cities included Poliarnyi in the former Ekaterina harbor, where the port town of Aleksandrovsk was established at the end of the nineteenth century, and Ostrovnoi, where the Iokanga naval base was built by the Murmansk railroad during World War I. The over 150,000 Kola residents who lived in these clandestine settlements in the late 1980s knew little about the dangers of their increasingly irradiated environment.[125]

The largest atomic energy project in northwest Russia did not involve a naval or shipping unit, however. It entailed building the Kola Nuclear Power Plant (Kola AES). Construction began in 1964 after an order from the Soviet energy and electrification ministry. Planners quickly decided to locate the power plant in a new town near the Zasheek railroad station (a former encampment for "special settlers" in the 1930s) on the southern shores of Lake Imandra. Here it could use the lake's water as a coolant

[125] Hønneland and Jørgensen, *Integration vs. Autonomy*, 91–98, 137–153. On the closed nuclear town of Ozersk, see Brown, *Plutopia*.

while also maintaining some distance from densely populated industrial centers. Authorities initially referred to the unit as the Kola State Regional Electric Station in all official documents in order to obscure its nuclear character.[126]

On November 12, 1967, journalist Evgenii Broido publically broke the news of the Kola AES. He informed readers of *Polar Pravda* that "the rapidly growing industry of the Murmansk region requires further development of energy capacity" and that it will be met with an atomic energy station already being built "somewhere on the peninsula." Part of Broido's goal in the article was to recruit workers to the project. To do so, he employed a mixed rhetoric about its natural surroundings. On the one hand, he remarked that the still unnamed town of Poliarnye Zori would include preserved forests and, on the other hand, he played on residents' self-conception as nature's conquerors. He praised those who previously "subjugated northern rivers and erected the Kirovsk GRES in the Khibiny tundra," noting that "many of them came to a new place in order devote their strength, knowledge, and experience to solve an important task for the national economy – the heroic construction of atomic energy on Kola land."[127]

The Kola press reacted with a similar emphasis on the Kola AES's combined economic and environmental value when its first VVER-230 reactor block came online in late June 1973, singlehandedly raising the region's energy capacity by 440 megawatts. One *Polar Pravda* article celebrated the Kola energy economy as the "bread of industry." It also evoked the standard Soviet theme of "a triumph of people over nature," commenting, "this huge station arose from scratch in about five years, through the conquest of the harsh northern nature of the place."[128] Alongside this militaristic rhetoric, publications conversely stressed nuclear energy as a technological solution to the environmental maladies of fossil fuels such as coal. Reporters billed the Kola plant as part of the further transcendence over environmental limitations and a means of improving nature. They posited nuclear power as "a 'clean' source of energy, which has not increased environmental pollution."[129] "On the contrary, atomic stations," another pair of journalists assured readers, "stimulate nature." They explained that the Kola station would increase the temperature of

[126] Kiselev, *Kol'skoi atomnoi – 30*, 17–26.

[127] E. Broido, "Zdes' budet Kol'skaia atomnaia," *PP* (November 12, 1967): 1.

[128] V. Belousov, "Prazdnik na Imandre. Torzhestvennoe otkrytie Kol'skoi AES," *PP* (July 5, 1973): 1.

[129] V. Berlin, "Kol'skaia AES i okruzhaiushchaia sreda," *KK* (August 20, 1976): 3.

Lake Imandra and improve the fishing stock in this body of water.[130] After construction workers completed the second 440-megawatt VVER-230 unit in late 1974, Aleksandr Volkov, the director of the Kola AES, proclaimed, "discharges, which could exert a pernicious influence on nature, have been excluded. If in the preliminary period of the AES's operation people treated it with some suspicion, the catchphrase 'nuclear power plants stimulate nature' is now generally accepted."[131]

Despite these adamant assurances, the Kola Nuclear Power Plant was far from safe and benign. It depended on manufacturing procedures that spread radiative dangers locally and throughout the country. The uranium for fuel rods came from all over the USSR, including from especially hazardous mines in Kazakhstan. Much of the spent nuclear fuel went to the Mayak waste storage facility in the southern Urals, where it exposed people living nearby to invisible contaminants with elusive potency.[132] Furthermore, the VVER-230 reactors at the Kola AES were a far cry from Volkov's insistence that the "technical equipment of the station works steadily and reliably, guaranteeing complete safety for the service personnel and local population."[133] Though better than the graphite moderated RBKM reactors at Chernobyl and other Soviet nuclear facilities, the VVER-230s suffered from technical design flaws that rendered them below international safety standards. In particular they lacked adequate containment around the reactor core and possessed insufficient cooling systems. As many scholars have observed, a lax safety culture within the Soviet nuclear industry also exacerbated the technical flaws of these reactors.[134]

130 V. Fedotov and B. Aleksandrov, "Bezvrednoe sosedstvo," *PP* (July 5, 1973): 4.

131 Quoted in Kiselev, *Kol'skoi atomnoi – 30*, 81.

132 Bøhmer, et al., *The Arctic Nuclear Challenge*, 39–43.

133 Quoted in Kiselev, *Kol'skoi atomnoi – 30*, 81.

134 Robert G. Darst, *Smokestack Diplomacy: Cooperation and Conflict in East-West Environmental Politics* (Cambridge, MA: The MIT Press, 2001), 135–197; Josephson, *Red Atom*; David R. Marples and Marylin J. Young, eds., *Nuclear Energy and Security in the Former Soviet Union* (Boulder: Westview Press, 1997); Axensten and Weissglas, eds., *Nuclear Risks, Environmental, and Development Co-operation in the North of Europe*; David R. Marples, *Chernobyl and Nuclear Power in the USSR* (New York: St. Martin's Press, 1986), 95–114; and Per Strand, Malgorzata K. Sneve, and Andrey V. Pechkurov, eds., *Radiation and Environmental Safety in North-West Russia* (Dordrecht: Springer, 2006). Some recent studies attempt to interject nuance into discussions of Chernobyl by highlighting competing conceptions of risk among Soviet nuclear power professionals. See Edward Geist, "Political Fallout: The Failure of Emergency Management at Chernobyl'," *SR* 74, no. 1 (Spring 2015): 104–126 and Sonja D. Schmid, *Producing Power: The Pre-Chernobyl History of the Soviet Nuclear Industry* (Cambridge, MA: The MIT Press, 2015).

Implicitly acknowledging the flaws of the VVER-230, atomic energy authorities opted for upgraded VVER-213 reactors when they expanded the Kola AES in the early 1980s. Construction leader Aleksandr Andrushechko also admitted that the quick building of the third reactor in 1981 occurred "not on account of a rise in labor productivity, but from a higher quantity of workers than planned." Indeed, he described the project as beset by missing supplies, wasted materials, misappropriated expenditures, and worksite accidents.[135] None of this was surprising given how the Soviet economy functioned in this era, but these deficiencies hardly matched the levels of safety and caution promised by the nuclear industry. Nevertheless, by the completion of the final reactor in 1984 the station had four functioning units, totaling a capacity of 1,760 megawatts. It produced over half of the region's electricity and significantly more than the entire network of hydroelectric stations.[136] Having solved the energy deficit, the Kola AES not only enabled continued industrial expansion, but also turned the region into an energy exporter. The plant supplied electricity to Karelia and northern Finland, connecting these territories to atomic fission occurring remotely.[137]

Kolenergo's final hydroelectric units gave the region's energy economy an additional boost in the 1970s and 1980s. In order to serve the burgeoning mining region around Revda and Lovozero, engineers looked to the Voron′ia and Teriberka rivers, which both empty directly into the Barents Sea. They installed the two hydroelectric stations of the Serebriansk cascade in the early 1970s and the Upper and Lower Teribersk GESes in the middle of the 1980s.[138] This brought Kolenergo's hydroelectric system to its pinnacle; with a total of seventeen stations it now possessed a capacity of 1,578 megawatts and annually produced between 6.1 and 7.2 billion kilowatt-hours of electricity.[139] These projects also renewed the removal of people from familiar natural surroundings. Authorities relocated

[135] Kiselev, *Kol′skoi atomnoi – 30*, 103–108.

[136] Palumbo and Dmitriev, "Sostoianie, problemy i perspektivy gidroenergetiki Kol′skogo poluostrova," and I. R. Stepanov, "Problema zameshcheniia moshchnostei rossiiskikh AES posle sniatiia ikh s ekspluatatsii," in Stepanov, ed., *Problemy energetiki zapada evropeiskogo Severa Rossii*, 18, 56–70.

[137] Hønneland, *Russia and the West*, 127–128; Darst, *Smokestack Diplomacy*, 171; and Bøhmer, et al., *The Arctic Nuclear Challenge*, 40.

[138] G. G. Kuz′min and E. F. Razin, *Kandalaksha* (Murmansk: Murmanskoe knizhnoe izdatel′stvo, 1968); GAMO, f. R-990, op. 1, d. 3, ll. 19–20; and *Kolenergo, 1936–1996*, 20–23, 42–50.

[139] Palumbo and Dmitriev, "Sostoianie, problemy i perspektivy gidroenergetiki Kol′skogo poluostrova," in Stepanov, ed., *Problemy energetiki zapada evropeiskogo Severa Rossii*, 15–18.

reindeer-herding villages on the Voron'ia and Ponoi rivers to make way for hydroelectric stations. The flooding of ancestral homelands of the Sami community for the Serebriansk cascade compelled residents to move to the growing agricultural town of Lovozero with its new, if shoddy, high-rise apartments and socialist urban design. The displacement also reduced the community's access to fishing grounds and separated them from a landscape with deep historical significance.[140]

At the same time, the steady supply of energy provided by the Kola AES and all of Kolenergo's hydroelectric and thermal stations helped draw an increasing number of migrants to the Arctic. The population of the Murmansk region more than doubled between 1959 and 1989 from 568,200 to 1,164,600.[141] Many people came and stayed because of the comparative comforts of an urbanized terrain that now possessed enough heat and light to mitigate the harshness of the polar climate. State incentives for living in the north also matured to their most generous extent in this era. This system provided Kola residents with higher wages, special bonuses, larger pensions, more vacation time, better apartments, and privileged access to consumer goods.[142]

Over time, migrants to the Murmansk region developed a "sense of place," as research by Alla Bolotova, Florian Stammler, and Geir Hønneland has shown. Industrial settlers appreciated the better provisions, but also came to value outdoor leisure activities as an attractive feature of the Kola Peninsula. Some cited a love for northern nature as a reason that they chose to remain there well beyond their intended stints of temporary work.[143] One migrant to Kovdor told Bolotova about how

140 N. N. Gutsol, S. N. Vinogradova, and A. G. Samorukova, "Istoricheskie usloviia i sotsial'no-ekonomicheskie posledstviia pereselenii Kol'skikh saamov v sovetskii period (na primere trekh saamskikh pogostov)," in V. P. Petrov and I. A. Razumova, eds., *Chelovek v sotsiokul'turnom prostranstve: Evropeiskii Sever Rossii* (Apatity: Kol'skii nauchnyi tsentr Rossiisskoi Akademii nauk, 2005), 104–108; N. N. Gutsol, S. N. Vinogradova, and A. G. Samorukova, *Pereselenie gruppy kol'skikh saamov* (Apatity: Kol'skii nauchnyi tsentr Rossiisskoi Akademii nauk, 2007), 33–37, 57; and A. V. Simanovskaia, "Chal'mny-Varre: Likvidirovanniia derevnia kak mesto pamiati," in V. P. Petrov and I. A. Razumova, eds., *Severiane: Problemy sotsiokul'turnoi adaptatsii zhitelei Kol'skogo poluostrova* (Apatity: Kol'skii nauchnyi tsentr Rossiisskoi Akademii nauk, 2006), 51–67.

141 "Vvodnyi ocherk," in Kiselev, ed., *Kol'skii entsiklopediia*, vol. 1, 70.

142 Lewis H. Siegelbaum and Leslie Page Moch, *Broad is My Native Land: Repertoires and Regimes of Migration in Russia's Twentieth Century* (Ithaca: Cornell University Press, 2014), 141–146.

143 Alla Bolotova and Florian Stammler, "How the North Became Home: Attachment to Place among Industrial Migrants in Murmansk Region," in Chris Southcott and Lee Huskey, eds., *Migration in the Circumpolar North: Issues and Contexts* (Edmonton: CCI Press, 2010), 193–220; Alla Bolotova, "Engaging with the Environment in the

her initial despair after migration changed. Upon arrival she begged her husband, "'Let me go home, I go home now.' 'Ok, wait, I get an advance [salary], and send you home'. I say 'just for a day'. 'I get my salary – I send you home'. That's how we have been living – for how long? From 1975 on. Now I don't want to go home any more. I started to like it here and don't want to go anywhere else. I wait for the winter to pass and for summer to come, in August, for mushrooms and berries . . . That's how it is. I quite like it."[144]

In Poliarnye Zori itself city architects also seem to have taken the long-standing visions of urban harmony even more seriously than in other northern towns. Though not officially closed, Poliarnye Zori needed to maintain a fairly well-educated workforce to operate the Kola AES's reactors. Ever the modernists, the Soviets promoted urban amenities as alluring features of the place. As Volkov described the town in the early 1980s: "A well-equipped, modern, urban-style settlement has been built for the energy workers of the atomic station. In our Poliarnye Zori there is a complete array of commercial enterprises, cultural establishments, and educational, health, and athletic facilities."[145]

All the while, however, the region's nuclear infrastructure, including the Kola AES, was committing a type of slow violence. According to environmental scholar Rob Nixon, slow violence is "a violence that occurs gradually and out of sight, a violence of delayed destruction that is dispersed across time and space, an attritional violence that is typically not viewed as violence at all." It is "a violence that is neither spectacular nor instantaneous, but rather incremental and accretive, its calamitous repercussions playing out across a range of temporal scales."[146] Numerous environmental maladies from exhausted water resources to invisible nuclear contamination can constitute forms of slow violence, which often disproportionally burden impoverished people.

Industrialized Russian North," *Suomen Antropologi: Journal of the Finnish Anthropological Society* 36, no. 2 (2011): 28–36; Alla Bolotova, "Loving and Conquering Nature: Shifting Perceptions of the Environment in the Industrialised Russian North," *Europe-Asia Studies* 64, no. 4 (June 2012): 645–671; and Hønneland, *Borderland Russians*, 51–79. A similar sense of attachment occurred in Chukotka, see Niobe Thompson, *Settlers on the Edge: Identity and Modernization on Russia's Arctic Frontier* (Vancouver: University of British Columbia Press, 2008).

144 Bolotova, "Engaging with the Environment in the Industrialized Russian North," *Suomen Antropologi* 36, no. 2 (2011): 24.

145 Quoted in Kiselev, *Kol'skoi atomnoi – 30*, 258–259.

146 Rob Nixon, *Slow Violence and the Environmentalism of the Poor* (Cambridge, MA: Harvard University Press, 2011), 2.

On the Kola Peninsula slow violence in part occurred through the mounting and unacknowledged threats that the taiga and tundra ecosystem, including the *Homo sapiens* living in it, faced from radiation exposure. In one egregious case, mining engineers at Apatit surreptitiously experimented with detonating underground nuclear explosions to pulverize huge chunks of ore in the Khibiny Mountains. They set off the Dnepr-1 and Dnepr-2 explosions at the Kuel'porr mine in 1972 and 1984, which released harmful levels of radiation unbeknownst to the public.[147] More systematically, however, the Northern Fleet and the Murmansk Shipping Company unloaded massive amounts of radioactive waste and spent nuclear fuel into the Barents and Kara seas of the Arctic Ocean. This dumping began in the late 1950s and increased over years, despite international agreements and public assurances to the contrary.[148] It stayed under the radar until after the Soviet collapse.

Crises and Futures

Varied crises hit Kola atoms and carbons as the Soviet Union fell into a death spiral. In their own way both fossil fuels and nuclear materials undercut late Soviet modernity, including the north's newfound status as a livable place. Putatively more environmentally friendly processes for acquiring energy wound up creating new underappreciated environmental problems, as spillover effects and clandestine contamination allowed an unforgiving material world to lash out against the Soviet behemoth.

The balance among the carbon-based fuels consumed in the region was already changing by the 1970s. Firewood and sawdust proportionally declined further, hovering around five percent of the fuel used in the Murmansk region before the Kola AES started operating and continuing a descent afterward.[149] This move away from burning the landscape seems to have helped stabilize the amount of forest cover on the territory.[150] The

147 V. V. Gushchin, *Podzemnaia razrabotka apatitovykh mestorozhdenii ot minnykh do iadernykh vzryvov* (Apatity: Kol'skii nauchnyi tsentr Rossiisskoi Akademii nauk, 2007); Bøhmer, et al., *The Arctic Nuclear Challenge*, 54; and Josephson, *Red Atom*, 247.

148 On the coexisting and likewise often duplicitous release of radioactive materials into the ocean by Britain and the United States, see Jacob Darwin Hamblin, *Poison in the Well: Radioactive Waste in the Oceans at the Dawn of the Nuclear Age* (New Brunswick: Rutgers University Press, 2008).

149 Kobzikov, "Toplivnyi balans Murmanskoi oblasti i voprosy ego ratsionalizatsii," in Zamotkin and Erogova, eds., *Priroda i khoziaistvo Severa*, vol. 2, part 2, 244.

150 Vvodnyi ocherk," in Kiselev, ed., *Kol'skii entsiklopediia*, vol. 1, 41.

Soviet Union as a whole decreased not only the proportion but also the amount of firewood used after the mid-1960s; it went from consuming 33.5 million tons of wood as fuel in 1965 to 26.6 million tons in 1971.[151] This shift, however, overlapped with the period when the Kola nickel smelters ratcheted up their evisceration of nearby vegetation.

A comparable story played out with the use of fossil fuels in the Kola north. In the still coal-dependent 1960s, sanitation inspectors and enterprise leaders alike saw the centralization of municipal heating and hot water services as a more efficient and less environmentally-damaging approach than the reliance on numerous boiler stations. One analyst at Severonikel′ encouraged measures "to implement a centralized heat supply for the city and liquidate a portion of the regional boilers," which would "free up 120 service personnel, reach a fuel economy of 10–12%, and decrease the pollution of the city by smoky gases."[152] Murmansk region sanitation officials likewise considered the steady reductions in the quantity of municipal boilers as a reflection of measures to improve urban air quality.[153] There is a deep irony in all of this, of course, since the centralization of municipal heat supplies was later criticized as a particularly wasteful Soviet practice. As the steam from the boilers traveled through pipes to locations all the way across town, a significant portion of the energy was lost, thus requiring excess fuels to be burnt in order to produce the same amount of heat.[154]

The Soviet oil boom also sparked an ambiguous transition away from coal as the main source of thermal energy. Into the 1960s, the thermal electric stations in Murmansk and outside Kirovsk and the heating units at the enterprises relied almost exclusively on coal and coke ash. But as Soviet petroleum production more than doubled during this decade and would do so again in the 1970s (making the USSR the world's largest oil producer with over 600 million tons of crude oil sucked out of the earth almost every year in the 1980s), industry leaders started turning away from coal.[155] Kolenergo and individual enterprises retooled their heating

[151] Elliot, *The Soviet Energy Balance*, 273.

[152] A. P. Skibin, "Energosnabzhenie kombinata 'Severonikel′,'" in V. Ia. Pozniakov, ed., *Opyt raboty kombinata "Severonikel′" po mobilizatsii vnutrennykh reservov* (Moscow: Gosudarstvennyi nauchno-tekhnicheskii komitet Soveta ministrov SSSR, 1961), 140.

[153] GARF, f. A-482, op. 54, d. 350, l. 58 and GARF, f. A-482, op. 54, d. 5009, l. 49.

[154] Iu. G. Dunin and S. F. Salina, "Analiz teplosnabzheniia severnykh gorodov," in Stepanov, ed., *Problemy energetiki zapada evropeiskogo Severa Rossii*, 31–35.

[155] Marshall I. Goldman, *Petrostate: Putin, Power, and the New Russia* (Oxford: Oxford University Press, 2008), 4–6, 35–37.

facilities to use a low-grade oil product akin to unprocessed diesel called mazut (sometimes referred to as residual fuel oil). Instead of arriving from the Komi Republic or Spitsbergen like coal did, mazut came to the Kola enterprises from refineries near Kirishi and Iaroslavl′. By late 1973 Pechenganikel′ kept a greater quantity (by tonnage) of mazut in reserve than coal, while Severonikel′ seemed to be burning its mazut supply more quickly than its stored coal.[156] The Murmansk Thermal Electric Station also converted to primarily using mazut in the mid-1970s.[157] For the time being this left the Kirovsk GRES as the main primarily coal-based electrical plant on the Kola Peninsula.[158]

Authorities billed this switch from coal to mazut as part of the Soviet effort to protect the environment. As typical for coal-powered electrical plants in the era, the Kola stations belched out massive quantities of smoke, carbon dioxide, and sulfur dioxide, causing standard ailments such as smog, climate change, and acid rain.[159] An article in *Polar Pravda* warned about deteriorating air quality in the region and noted that Murmansk now had sulfur dioxide levels comparable to the much larger city of Leningrad. It also included some of the coal-based power plants in a list of enterprises that "emit a considerable amount of toxic and harmful substances into the air everyday."[160] Indeed, the Kirovsk GRES released 19.4 tons of ash and 110.3 tons of sulfur dioxide a day in the mid-1970s. Around this time managers and engineers at Kolenergo promised that the transition of the Murmansk Thermal Electric Station to mazut, the construction of a new smokestack, and the opening of an environmental monitoring lab would reduce pollution in Murmansk. They more tepidly reported that repairs to one of the boiler units at the Kirovsk GRES should cut daily emissions of harmful substances.[161] The switch to mazut at the Murmansk Thermal Electric Station did cut coal consumption by 62,400 tons between 1975 and 1984 and successfully curbed some forms of air pollution in Murmansk.[162] By the mid-1990s, the thermal electric

[156] RGAE, f. 386, op. 1, d. 5145, l. 43.

[157] Kaibysheva, *Elektricheskoe siianie severa*, 34.

[158] GAMO, f. R-990, op. 1, d. 1633, ll. 95–97.

[159] McNeill, *Something New Under the Sun*, 50–117 and Dunin and Salina, "Analiz teplosnabzheniia severnykh gorodov," in Stepanov, ed., *Problemy energetiki zapada evropeiskogo Severa Rossii*, 30–38.

[160] F. Terziev, "Zabota o prirode – eto zabota o nashem zdorov′e: pis′mo pervoe," *PP* (June 20, 1973): 2.

[161] GAMO, f. R-990, op. 1, d. 1633, ll. 95–97, 175–176.

[162] Kaibysheva, *Elektricheskoe siianie severa*, 34.

facilities and remaining local boilers on the Kola Peninsula were burning 1,600,000 tons of mazut and just 700 tons of coal a year.[163]

Though the transition from coal to an oil product reduced air pollution at the site of consumption, it did not prevent environmental consequences from accumulating nearby and elsewhere in the country. For one thing mazut itself, though less polluting than coal, still released significantly higher quantities of sulfur fumes than natural gas or other further refined hydrocarbon products.[164] More to the point, fuel importation had long caused significant spillover effects on the remote environments where coal and oil were extracted. In the case of coal, mining operations in the Pechora basin annually generated approximately 90,600 tons of harmful materials, including 28,000 tons discharged into the atmosphere, and dumped some thirty-three million cubic meters of contaminated water into surface streams at the end of the Soviet era.[165] Kola coal consumption still contributed its part to this despoilment even as the region had reduced its demand. Furthermore, mazut originated in oilfields that became toxic terrains themselves. Ze′ev Wolfson vividly described the scene at one such area on the Caspian Sea: "Along 200 kilometers of beach it is difficult to find a place where there are no black gobs of mazut on the sand or rainbow-colored films on the water."[166] Again, economic activities on the Kola Peninsula bore intimate ties to this far-flung pollution.

Deeper, more de-stabilizing problems shook the newly massive Soviet oil industry in the 1980s, which had profound reverberations on the far north and the fate of the country as a whole. Global oil prices started to decline after Soviet leader Leonid Brezhnev left the scene and then plummeted quickly during the reign of reformer Mikhail Gorbachev. A major source of the USSR's economic stability had vanished just as Gorbachev initiated ambitious adjustments to make the Soviet system more market oriented. In the view of some analysts, this loss of oil revenue was a significant factor in the downfall of Soviet communism and the disintegration of the USSR into fifteen successor states.[167] Yet on the Kola

163 Dunin and Salina, "Analiz teplosnabzheniia severnykh gorodov," in Stepanov, ed., *Problemy energetiki zapada evropeiskogo Severa Rossii*, 31.

164 David Wilson, *The Demand for Energy in the Soviet Union* (London: Croom Helm, 1983), 191–193.

165 Kovalchuk, ed., *The Coal Industry of the Former USSR*, 31.

166 Boris Komarov [Ze′ev Vol′fson], *The Destruction of Nature in the Soviet Union* (White Plains: M. E. Sharpe, 1980), 37.

167 On the significance of the oil industry for late Soviet political developments, see Thane Gustafson, *Crisis amid Plenty: The Politics of Soviet Energy under Brezhnev and Gorbachev* (Princeton: Princeton University Press, 1989); Goldman, *Petrostate*; Stephen

Peninsula another energetic substance was also haunting the landscape of perestroika and the Soviet collapse.

On April 26, 1986, one of the reactors at the Chernobyl Nuclear Power Plant in Soviet Ukraine exploded, releasing massive amounts of toxic radiation into the atmosphere. The Soviet government initially tried to keep the disaster a secret before fessing up to its scale and seeking international assistance from external agencies.[168] For his part Gorbachev seized the opportunity presented by Chernobyl to try to end the nuclear arms race. Speaking in Murmansk in October 1987, he outlined an idea for a demilitarized Arctic free of nuclear weapons and united in international cooperation on development, science, and environmental protection.[169]

For their part many residents of the Kola Peninsula, like people living elsewhere in the country, reacted to Chernobyl with heightened suspicion toward nuclear power.[170] An article in the local press that appeared about two years after the accident reported that people thought of the Kola AES as a "dangerous neighbor." The author excoriated the previous public silence about the plant's operations, but also tried to reassure readers of its safety.[171] In contrast to urbanites' fears about atomic energy, Kola reindeer herders did not appear to share the anxieties about radioactive fallout from Chernobyl entering the food chain through lichen absorption, reindeer forging, and venison consumption that existed among the Scandinavian Sami.[172]

Yet, even after Chernobyl, oceanic dumping of nuclear wastes in the Arctic Ocean continued; indeed it increased during perestroika.[173]

Kotkin, *Armageddon Averted: The Soviet Collapse, 1970–2000*, 2nd edn. (Oxford: Oxford University Press, 2008), 10–30; and Thane Gustafson, *Wheel of Fortune: The Battle for Oil and Power in Russia* (Cambridge, MA: Belknap Press, 2012).

168 Darst, *Smokestack Diplomacy*, 149–159. Also see David R. Marples, *The Social Impact of the Chernobyl Disaster* (New York: St. Martin's Press, 1988).

169 Kristian Åtland, "Mikhail Gorbachev, the Murmansk Initiative, and the Desecuritization of Interstate Relations in the Arctic," *Cooperation and Conflict* 43, no. 3 (September 2008): 289–311.

170 On anti-nuclear activism in the aftermath of Chernobyl, see Jane Dawson, *Eco-nationalism: Anti-Nuclear Activism and National Identity in Russia, Lithuania, and Ukraine* (Durham: Duke University Press, 1996).

171 V. Vishniakov, "AES: prezhde vsego-nadezhnost′," *PP* (April 19, 1988): 2.

172 Hugh Beach, "Reindeer Herding on the Kola Peninsula – Report of a Visit with Saami Herders of Sovkhoz Tundra," in Roger Kvist, ed., *Readings in Saami History, Culture and Language III* (Umeå: University of Umeå, 1992), 125; Hansen and Tønnessen, *Environment and Living Conditions on the Kola Peninsula*, 149; and Jenny Leigh Smith, "Radioactive Reindeer in Sweden and Russia" (paper presented at the World Congress of Environmental History, Copenhagen/Malmö, August 2009).

173 Darst, *Smokestack Diplomacy*, 184.

Information about this secretive practice only came to the fore as the Russian Federation had replaced the Soviet Union as the country ruling the Murmansk region. In response to allegations and public confessions, Aleksei Iablokov – an advisor to president Boris Yeltsin and a leading Russian environmentalist – released a report in 1993 that detailed the decades of dumping and unsafe storage of radioactive wastes.[174]

The results were astonishing. Since mid-century, the Northern Fleet and the Murmansk Shipping Company had released wastes amounting to about 38,450 terabecquerel (38,450 trillion nuclei decaying per second) of radioactivity. It included not only contaminated liquids but also sixteen retired nuclear reactors, several with spent nuclear fuel still in them. Authorities also stored much of the remaining nuclear materials in leaky facilities in the Murmansk region itself. These storage sites included a number of retired ships that remained docked in the Kola Bay and land containers near the closed military cities. The refueling vessel *Lepse* at one point held on board about 30 percent of the amount of long-living isotopes released during the Chernobyl meltdown and a dilapidated storage unit in the Andreeva Bay came to possess over twenty-seven million curies (close to one billion terabecquerel) of radioactivity.[175] For its part, the Kola AES produced more solid nuclear wastes than naval and transportation bodies and kept much of it on site. By one estimate its on-site wastes were to total around 47,700 terabecquerel in 2010.[176]

In contrast to the unquestionably large amount of radioactive waste that the Soviets accumulated on or near the Kola Peninsula (some of it with significantly long half-lives), the health and environmental effects of these poisonous materials have been much more elusive. Only those exposed to harmful doses of radiation in extremely close proximity to a nuclear installation would have experienced illnesses with a clear linear causality. Of course, the classified operations of so many of these facilities left it unclear if such exposures had ever happened and to whom. Many more people may also have suffered from stochastic effects, which can only be assessed in terms of aggregate probabilities of harmful outcomes and would not have been directly proportional or obviously assignable

[174] A. V. Iablokov, *Facts and Problems Related to the Dumping of Radioactive Waste in the Seas Surrounding the Territory of the Russian Federation* (Moscow: Office of the President of the Russian Federation, 1993).

[175] Darst, *Smokestack Diplomacy*, 184–190 and Bøhmer, et al., *The Arctic Nuclear Challenge*, 13–14.

[176] Bøhmer, et al., *The Arctic Nuclear Challenge*, 43–45 and Hansen and Tønnessen, *Environment and Living Conditions on the Kola Peninsula*, 139.

in individual cases. In such circumstances a person would not be able to know whether radiation exposure caused a particular ailment such as thyroid cancer. Lichens or birds or other species would often end up in an even more ambiguous position in which genetic mutations over the long haul might or might not be attributable to long-term contact with low doses of radioactive isotopes.

This undetectable essence of a nuclear impact has borne its own influence, enmeshing human bodies with unknowable natural processes. Governmental and industry representatives also have been able to evoke the imprecision of radioactive contamination opportunistically. Describing the "Soviet and post-Soviet responses to Chernobyl," medical anthropologist Adriana Petryna writes: "state power is as concerned with making bodies and behaviors ever more predictable and knowable as it is with creating – both intentionally and inadvertently – spaces of nonknowledge and unpredictability. The biology of the population is held in question; the government of life is unmoored. Where Soviet officials generate medical statistics, they designate them state secrets. People become uncertain as to what medical categories they belong to, how sick or healthy they are."[177] Those living in irradiated zone have often been forced to place more, not less, trust in the authorities responsible for threatening their health.

Danger also came from the heightened probability of a radiological emergency. The presence of large amounts of radioactive waste, the surfeit of nuclear reactors, and the structural vulnerabilities of operating in Arctic conditions already posed considerable risks at the time of the Soviet collapse. But the chance of a nuclear disaster on the Kola Peninsula became even more likely with the economic and social crisis of the 1990s. Like everywhere else in post-Soviet Russia, the region found itself in dire straits. Workers' salaries went unpaid, life expectancy plummeted, residents lost their savings, and subsidies for living in the far north vanished. Ending decades of an expanding population, the Murmansk region lost over a quarter of its residents between 1989 and 2006.[178] The Kola nuclear sector's perilous instability became apparent in a string of accidents and near accidents. In 1993 the oldest reactor at the Kola AES experienced a coolant failure during a storm that knocked out power at

177 Adriana Petryna, *Life Exposed: Biological Citizens after Chernobyl* (Princeton: Princeton University Press, 2002), 13.

178 Timothy Heleniak, "Growth Poles and Ghost Towns in the Russian Far North," in Elana Wilson Rowe, ed. *Russia and the North* (Ottawa: University of Ottawa Press, 2009), 129–159.

the facility. This incident nearly caused a meltdown and exposed plant workers to harmful levels of radioactive contamination.[179] A decision by Kolenegro in 1995 to cut off electricity to naval bases because of unpaid bills led to similar cooling system failures on decommissioned nuclear submarines. This close call only ended when armed soldiers forced the company to turn the power back on.[180] Leaks at the waste storage unit in the Andreeva Bay also continued to pollute the immediate vicinity with highly toxic cesium-137 and long lasting plutonium-239.[181] Finally, one of the Navy's nuclear submarines, the *Kursk*, sank in August 2000 after an explosion during a practice exercise. The vessel's entire crew died in the tragedy.[182]

While desperation and poverty increased nuclear threats in the Kola north, international efforts to improve nuclear safety pushed in the opposite direction. Funds from Norway and the United States flowed into the Russian government for the decommissioning of a large portion of the Northern Fleet's nuclear submarines and for safety upgrades at the Kola AES. The defueling of the vessels resulted in further nuclear wastes that required safe handling and attracted additional international support. Though these projects significantly curbed some of the risks of radioactive contamination, they also encountered significant setbacks.[183] For instance, in the late 1990s Russian prosecutors pursued an espionage case against Aleksandr Nikitin – a former naval officer who became a whistleblower for the environmental group Bellona. Only after several years of trials and public outcry was Nikitin acquitted on these trumped up charges.[184] On the top of that, many of the projects seen as a priority for foreign environmentalists, such as the clean up of the Andreeva Bay, the docking and defueling of the *Lepse*, and the closure of the old units

[179] Darst, *Smokestack Diplomacy*, 165, 169–170 and Kiselev, *Kol'skoi atomnoi – 30*, 171–172.

[180] Hansen and Tønnessen, *Environment and Living Conditions on the Kola Peninsula*, 126.

[181] Thomas Nilsen, "Naval Nuclear Waste Management in Northwest Russia: Nuclear Safety, Environmental Challenges and Economic Impact," in Axensten and Weissglas, eds., *Nuclear Risks, Environmental, and Development Co-operation in the North of Europe*, 37.

[182] Kiselev, *Kol'skoi atomnoi – 30*. 171–174; Darst, *Smokestack Diplomacy*, 165; and Weir and Boyne, *Rising Tide*, 217–252.

[183] Darst, *Smokestack Diplomacy*, 186–193; Hønneland, *Russia and the West*, 31–33; and Bøhmer, et al., *The Arctic Nuclear Challenge*, 57–66.

[184] Aleksandr Nikitin and Nina Katerli, *Delo Nikitina: Strategiia pobedy* (Saint Petersburg: Izdatel'stvo zhurnala "Zvezda," 2001).

of the Kola Nuclear Power Plant, have languished if not outright been abandoned by Russian officials.[185]

Those living in a nuclearized north frequently saw the place as a landscape of risk. Some shared the alarm of outsiders about the likelihood of a major accident, while others viewed one as improbable. Most seem to have worried less about the effects of radiation exposure or the chance of a nuclear disaster than other economic, social, and environmental dangers.[186] As one woman told political scientist Geir Hønneland, "I'm not afraid of radiation because wherever you look you can find something that's not quite right. Gas emissions, polluted water. You can die of anything." A more upbeat man commented, "There are neither earthquakes nor all manner of tornados and tsunamis in the north. The nuclear fleet and nuclear power plant – we can put up with them."[187]

Of course, another environmental hazard beyond earthquakes or nuclear pollution has recently come to the Arctic, altering the Kola Peninsula's energy future as well. Climate change has conspired with geological discoveries and technological advances in hydrocarbon drilling to open up the possibility of harvesting natural gas deposits under the Barents Sea. In something of a perverse feedback loop, two centuries of burning carbon-based fossil fuels has triggered climatic warming through the greenhouse effect, thus rendering the fossil fuels under the Arctic Ocean more accessible and easier to transport. For a long time the Russian energy company Gazprom promoted its plans to develop the Shtokman field, some

185 The toxic refueling vessel *Lepse*, for instance, was only removed from the waters of the Kola Bay in October 2014. Anna Kireeva, "Murmansk's Biggest Floating Radiological Threat Finally Taken off Water," The Bellona Foundation (October 29, 2014), accessed November 26, 2014, http://bellona.org/news/nuclear-issues/2014–10-murmansks-biggest-floating-radiological-threat-finally-taken-water. Yet that same month Russia's Federal Service for Environmental, Technological, and Nuclear Oversight granted the Kola AES authority to operate its fourth reactor for another quarter century, almost doubling its initial thirty-year lifespan. See Anna Kireeva and Charles Digges, "Kola Nuclear Plant Gets Go-ahead to Run its No 4 Reactor for a Record Breaking 25 More Years," The Bellona Foundation (October 13, 2014), accessed November 26, 2014, http://bellona.org/news/nuclear-issues/2014–10-kola-nuclear-plant-gets-go-ahead-run-4-reactor-record-breaking-25-years and "Vtoraia ochered′ Kol′skoi AES," *Sever promyshlennoi*, no. 5 (2006): 14. On the activities of the state nuclear energy corporation, Rosatom, since the Soviet collapse, see Paul R. Josephson, *Would Trotsky Wear a Bluetooth?: Technological Utopianism under Socialism, 1917–1989* (Baltimore: The Johns Hopkins University Press, 2010), 163–192.

186 For an analysis of a survey of Kola residents, see Hansen and Tønnessen, *Environment and Living Conditions on the Kola Peninsula*, 175–226.

187 Quoted in Hønneland, *Borderland Russians*, 114.

650 kilometers to the northeast of Murmansk. Potential projects included a new facility to liquefy natural gas for shipment near the village of Teriberka, a pipeline running through the Kola Peninsula, and an expansion of the Murmansk port.[188] Primarily responding to the rise in hydraulic fracturing to acquire natural gas in the United States, which has made offshore drilling much less cost effective, Gazprom decided to shelve the project indefinitely.[189] In the meantime, another Russian energy company, Rosneft, has started flirting with the development of the Murmanskoe field, even closer to the Murman coast of the Kola Peninsula.[190] Whatever the future of energy in the Russian northwest, at least one thing is certain. Russian industrialists, like their Soviet predecessors, will never fully eclipse the influence of the natural environment, regardless of how sweeping and ambitious their schemes end up being.

188 Charles Emmerson, *The Future History of the Arctic* (New York: PublicAffairs 2010), 211–216; Hønneland, *Borderland Russians*, 32–37; and Arlid Moe and Elana Wilson Rowe, "Northern Offshore Oil and Gas Resources: Policy Challenges and Approaches," in Rowe, ed. *Russia and the North*, 107–127

189 Atle Staalesen, "The Shtokman Field is Unlikely to be Launched before after 2030, Information from Gazprom Indicates," *Barents Observer* (February 12, 2013), accessed May 10, 2013, http://barentsobserver.com/en/energy/2013/02/shtokman-moves-further-out-sight-12-0 and Christopher Helman, "Gazprom Bows to Shale Boom, Cancels Shtokman Plans," *Forbes* (August 30, 2012), accessed May 10, 2013, www.forbes.com/sites/christopherhelman/2012/08/30/bowing-to-shale-gas-boom-gazprom-cancels-shtokman-plans/.

190 Atle Staalesen, "The State Oil Company is Considering to Develop the Murmanskoye, a Gas Field Located in Waters Near the Kola Peninsula," *Barents Observer* (April 23, 2014), accessed November 26, 2014, http://barentsobserver.com/en/energy/2014/04/rosneft-looks-murmansk-gas-field-23-04.

7

The Life of the Soviet Environment

Inna Tartakovskaia lived a Soviet life. Born in Odessa as the 1905 revolution shook the Russian Empire to its core, she found herself in the recently renamed city of Leningrad in the 1920s. There she pursued her dreams of becoming a ballerina while working at a bank, where she met her soon-to-be husband, Vasilii Kondrikov. In previous eras his Old Believer background might have clashed with her Jewish ancestry, but they now resided in an anti-religious state committed to socialist transformation – a project they both believed in. Tartakovskaia's career ambitions were interrupted, however, when the prominent Bolshevik Sergei Kirov hired her husband to manage a new industrial enterprise in the Khibiny Mountains. She even followed Kirov's advice and enrolled in a technical school in order to help bolster her husband's shaky knowledge of phosphate mining and enrichment. During Kondrikov's meteoric rise as a captain of Kola industry in the 1930s, Tartakovskaia spent more and more time in the far north working as a much-needed technical specialist.

Terror then threw this unanticipated life into disarray. Not only was her husband arrested and shot, but Tartakovskaia herself ended up in the Gulag. Torn away from her young child, Dmitrii, she endured stints in Siberian prison camps, first in Tomsk and then in Kolyma. Reviving an earlier interest, she performed in a carceral dance troupe during this time. Reunited with her son after the war, they lived in Magadan where she worked at a theater. During the Thaw era, she returned to a technical institute in Leningrad and even made several business trips back to the Kola Peninsula. She also started recording her recollections as a "veteran" of the north, including in an extended series of interviews published by a Monchegorsk newspaper a few years before her death in 1990.[1]

In crafting these reflections, Tartakovskaia dwelt more on triumph than trauma. As historian Polly Jones suggests, this victim of Stalinist repression was hardly alone in opting for bland and mostly celebratory commemoration over gloomy retrospection. Even into the perestroika period, many Soviet citizens preferred to indulge in a more limited public memory of the Stalin era than to open old wounds.[2] It is telling all the same that Tartakovskaia's deliberate reminiscences featured nature as prominently as they did. The "memory work" she was willing to engage in about her Soviet past necessitated recalling interactions with the Kola environment. She seemed to recognize that the natural world played an active role in her biography.

Like many of the supposed "conquerors of the north," Tartakovskaia possessed both an aesthetic and scientific appreciation for Kola nature. She described first seeing the Monche tundra from Lake Imandra in 1934. "It was a marvelous morning of the northern summer. The smooth surface of the wide lake disappeared in the distance, merging with the blue sky in a misty haze. Clothed in the green attire of the shore, the steep promontories that jut out into the lake gave way, opening a vast expanse. Mountain peaks soared as far as the eye could see. In every direction there was forest, forest. The sun, not having touched the horizon, rose, shining light all around. In a dreamy silence the panoramic scenes passed by, one more

1 These biographical details have been pieced together from "Boi za nikel′: Vospominaniia I. L. Kondrikovoi-Tartakovskoi," *MR* (September 9, 1986), 3–4; "Boi za nikel′: Vospominaniia I. L. Kondrikovoi-Tartakovskoi," *MR* (September 11, 1986), 3–4; "Boi za nikel′: Vospominaniia I. L. Kondrikovoi-Tartakovskoi," *MR* (September 13, 1986), 3–4; "Boi za nikel′: Vospominaniia I. L. Kondrikovoi-Tartakovskoi," *MR* (September 16, 1986), 3–4; "Boi za nikel′: Vospominaniia I. L. Kondrikovoi-Tartakovskoi," *MR* (September 18, 1986), 3–4; "Boi za nikel′: Vospominaniia I. L. Kondrikovoi-Tartakovskoi," *MR* (September 20, 1986), 3–4; "Boi za nikel′: Vospominaniia I. L. Kondrikovoi-Tartakovskoi," *MR* (September 23, 1986), 3–4; "Boi za nikel′: Vospominaniia I. L. Kondrikovoi-Tartakovskoi," *MR* (September 25, 1986), 3–4; "Boi za nikel′: Vospominaniia I. L. Kondrikovoi-Tartakovskoi," *MR* (September 27, 1986), 3–4; I. L. Tartakovskaia, "Fersman i Kondrikov," *ZhA*, no. 1 (October 2001): 34–37; Tat′iana Shishkina, "Pamiat′o nem khranitsia zdes,′" *KhR* (September 16, 2004), 6; Sergei Tararaksin, *Sudeb sgorevshikh ochertan′e* (Murmansk: "Sever," 2006), 81–90; Arkadii Arsh, "Ia liubliu tebia, Magadan!" accessed December 10, 2014, http://neisri.narod.ru/academnet/1school/15-1951/arsh/index.htm; and "Zhertvy politicheskogo terror SSSR," Memorial, accessed December 10, 2014, http://lists.memo.ru/d32/f109.htm.

2 Polly Jones, *Myth, Memory, Trauma: Rethinking the Stalinist Past in the Soviet Union, 1953–1970* (New Haven: Yale University Press, 2103).

splendid than the next. The sun warmed up everything and a wonderful day began." Valuing the sun's assistance in this field expedition, she then describes how the trip set off further prospecting and planning for the future nickel works there.[3] Decades later in retirement she maintained an attachment to the Arctic landscape. Tartakovskaia wrote to mineralogist Igor Bel'kov requesting a watercolor painting depicting the Khibiny's geology. Bittersweet nostalgia combined with a fondness for scientific portrayals in her explanation. "For me and for my son this region is very dear," she wrote, adding, "after all since youth my life has been happily and unhappily bound to the Khibiny."[4]

Tartakovskaia also recalled northern nature as an obstinate presence. Some complications for Kola industrial projects "rested in the harsh and unlivable character of the north."[5] She once called the provision of decent living conditions to new migrants "the hardest issue. The worker did not come to us here out of a love for the northern lights, but in order to labor and live in human conditions." One time, "a worker did not arrive at work because he could not leave from the cold, wet lodging in which he could neither sleep nor rest."[6] In her writings such disruptions of Kola nature also intruded into experiments with the flotation reagents used during apatite enrichment and the catastrophic avalanches that hit Kirovsk in the second half of the 1930s.[7] By acknowledging these frequent setbacks, Tartakovskaia herself seems to have understood that the conquest of nature was much more of an aspiration than an accurate portrayal of the Soviets' relationship to the environment – a contention I have insisted upon in this book.

Indeed, power in the Soviet Union existed as an assemblage in which the varied elements of non-human nature also exerted their own influence on the project of forging a socialist society. Sometimes they enabled Soviet efforts to economically transform the north, such as when nickel and apatite under the ground created the possibilities for thriving heavy industries. Other times they stymied communist ambitions, such as when reindeer refused to stay within specific areas or when re-engineered rivers failed to generate enough hydroelectricity. In each of these cases and

3 "Boi za nikel'," *MR* (September 11, 1986): 3.

4 Printed in Iu. L. Voitekhovskii, "Neizvestnoe pis'mo I. L. Kondrikovoi I. V. Bel'kovu," *Tietta*, no. 5 (2008): 48–49.

5 "Boi za nikel'," *MR* (September 18, 1986): 4.

6 "Boi za nikel'," *MR* (September 23, 1986): 3–4.

7 I. L. Tartakovskaia, "Nachalo," in G. I. Rakov, ed., *Khibinskie Klady: Vospominaniia veteranov osvoeniia Severa* (Leningrad: Lenizdat, 1972), 64–65.

plenty of others the material world participated actively in the Soviet experiment. Appreciating its involvement in what often has been viewed solely as a human story should compel scholars to see key episodes in Soviet history in a new light.

The era of the Russian Revolution and Russian Civil War, for example, witnessed divergent reactions to the natural environment. Planners effused about the promise of an enlivened Kola north until the harsh realities of building and operating a railroad in the swampy taiga took hold. Material features of the landscape sparked different rhetoric about nature and divergent experiences of trying to economically harness remote terrains, which in turn influenced the approaches to development taken during the periods of the New Economic Policy and the Stalinist Great Break. Concerning the latter era, recalcitrant nature contributed to the chaos and the unintended consequences that defined the push for rapid industrialization. Snowdrifts, mountain slopes, and strong winds disrupted work in the Khibiny with particular potency, but also wreaked havoc at other Stalinist industrial sites. Meddlesome matter even played a part in the violent frenzy of the terror. Nickel's concentration in a less prospected mountain of the Monche tundra served as fodder in the case against Kondrikov and harmful epizootics that spread among collectivized reindeer became evidence for a Sami nationalist plot. The point here is not that the terror overall required this involvement, but that elements of the natural world helped shape its outcomes.

After Stalin, the physical environment took on a volatile role in the economic life of the country. Copper, phosphates, venison, and descending water in the Kola north buttressed successful extensive growth in the first postwar decades. They provided value to the state that could be redirected toward various policy agendas, including the further provision of consumer goods during and after the Thaw. In a sense they helped enable reforms to make the USSR a more humane place by affording a sounder economic base for experimentation. But the materials harvested from the Kola landscape started to reverse course in the 1970s and 1980s. The exploitation of evermore tonnages of natural resources ceased to yield the same monetary value in a period of global economic transition. At the same time accumulated pollution increasingly reared its ugly head. Sulfur dioxide, nepheline tailings, and radioactive wastes disturbed the Kola environment to the point of undermining the economic utility of industrial production. In the process they helped destabilize the Soviet system more generally, contributing at least indirectly to the collapse of communism.

This grounding of Soviet power within the confines of an active material world was, of course, only one side of the Kola Peninsula's story during the twentieth century, albeit the more frequently neglected one. Equally significant was the Soviets' ability to radically alter human relations with the surrounding environment in the far north. Planners and prisoners, managers and migrants, scientists and Sami accomplished an impressive feat of changing a sparsely populated periphery into an extensively industrialized landscape. How was the USSR able to achieve this transformation and why did it invest so much energy into doing so?

My main answer to these questions has been to treat the Soviet Union as participating in a global project of economic modernization. Soviet leaders attempted to launch a distinctive industrial economy that would be deserving of the name socialism and eventually communism. But the methods they used and their ideas about the natural environment bore many overarching and defining similarities to modernizing states under capitalist regimes. As political theorist Susan Buck-Morss writes, "By adopting the capitalist heavy-industry definition of economic modernization, however, Soviet socialism had no alternative but to try to produce a utopia out of the production process itself. In making this choice, the Soviets missed the opportunity to transform the very idea of economic 'development,' and of the ecological preconditions through which it might be realized."[8]

So, on the one hand, the Soviet Union environmentally belonged to a continuum with the preceding and proceeding political regimes that ruled Russia. In each period authorities prioritized treating the northern environment as an object of industrial exploitation. This utilitarian view of nature as primarily a source of economic value appeared early on in development schemes in late imperial Russia, continued as an essential element of the Soviet project to build socialism, and later shaped the sweeping market reforms of the 1990s. More chronologically bounded links united the USSR with the imperial and post-Soviet eras as well, including the use of forced laborers to industrialize severe environments during the first half of the twentieth century and the abiding faith that technical fixes could overcome any contradictions between environment and economy in the latter part of it.

The Soviet Union, on the other hand, also joined many other countries that delved deeper into the Anthropocene. Anthropogenic ecological

[8] Susan Buck-Morss, *Dreamworld and Catastrophe: The Passing of Mass Utopia in East and West* (Cambridge, MA: The MIT Press, 2000), 115.

changes, shifts in human livelihoods, and new perceptions of nature in the Soviet Union followed worldwide patterns, including the rise of heavy industry and the forms of pollution it engendered, the move away from rural villages and toward dense cities, and the increasingly common view of earth's materials as simply commodities. By contributing to the intertwined ballooning of human population, economic activity, and energy use throughout the planet, the USSR helped place unprecedented pressures not only on specific ecosystems, but on the global geosphere as well. This common trajectory does not mean that Soviet leaders stumbled into hyper-development by accident or happenstance. No, they made conscious political choices to modernize their economy – choices shared by empowered state representatives and businesspeople elsewhere in the world, choices that relentlessly sought to grow economies, and choices to degrade the natural environment habitually.

But what led the Soviet state to develop this section of the Arctic in particular? Why did it not just leave the Kola Peninsula as a remote and isolated outpost? Here motivation in part came from the general impulse to overcome backwardness wherever it seemed to reside, as well as from a desire to take advantage of the specific industrial opportunities afforded by Kola nature itself. Laying railroads, mining apatite, industrializing reindeer, smelting nickel, and installing hydroelectric dams seemed a way to help the polar region advance in time on the basis of its own preexisting resources. Ideological concerns also enhanced the attractiveness of large projects in far-flung places. New factory towns in the tundra had the appeal of demonstrating the capacity of the Soviet Union's alternative political system.

Geopolitical and military concerns certainly prompted state officials to pay extra attention to this part of the Arctic as well. Authorities decided to erect a railroad connection to the Murman coast and place the Northern Fleet of the Soviet Navy there because the territory possessed strategically significant harbors that did not freeze in the winter. With a border touching a NATO country during the Cold War, the Murmansk region became an obvious hub for the proliferating Soviet military establishment. In these geopolitical circumstances, almost any powerful government would have built up this parcel of land. Modernization of the Kola north thus dovetailed with its militarization.

In many ways the most distinctive force driving Kola development was the dualistic conception of nature that ripened during the twentieth century. Deriving from technocratic imperialism and wartime conquest of the tsarist era, this interpretation of the industrializing process as simultaneously about dominance and harmony became a defining feature of Soviet socialism in the Stalin era. Economic planners, scientists, and enterprise personnel in this period touted their desires to subdue the environment while finding accord with it. Inspired by Alexander Fersman's concept of the complex utilization of natural resources, Kola industrialists argued that they could minimize, if not eliminate, pollution through maximally exploiting the natural world. Though such ideas were less exclusively antagonistic toward the environment than many scholars have noted, they all the same gave rise to varied patterns of destructive nature use. Under Stalin the reckless and hasty treatment of the natural world often exposed human beings to acutely hazardous conditions. In the later Soviet era the exponential exploitation of resources instead generated extreme pollution that placed entire Arctic ecosystems in grave peril.

Environmental anomalies of the Soviet system came from other realms as well. The country's leaders proved willing to extend some of the practices of total war into peacetime. Whereas the reliance on forced laborers and exposure of them to extreme threats during the construction of the Murmansk railroad occurred in part because World War I was raging, the Stalinist state did not face such pressing imperatives when it opted to brutalize former kulaks and Gulag prisoners in order to industrialize the north. The centrally planned command economy that abided until the Soviet collapse also functioned differently. Significantly, it did not adapt well to shifts in the global economy in the 1970 and 1980s: changes that caused service and finance to play a larger role in generating growth than production. Accelerated production combined with economic stagnation to create even higher levels of unaddressed environmental pollution than existed in many capitalist countries. Finally, Soviet communism placed especially robust confidence in the ability of public policy and government regulations to resolve any conflict that emerged between economic activity and the environment. Though a similar conviction exists in strands of capitalist thinking, it has often been subordinate to another fanciful belief – that the market itself will optimally distribute environmental goods and bads.

But, ultimately, the uniqueness of the Soviet relationship to the environment was quite narrow. A final story of a father and a son can illustrate its limited extent. In the late 1960s, Nikolai Vorontsov, who like Tartakovskaia's husband was a former industrialist in the Khibiny Mountains and the Monche tundra, maintained his enthusiasm for the characteristically Soviet mix of mastering and caring for the natural world. Echoing his buoyant sentiments from the 1930s, he told a reporter, "Monchegorsk is beautiful... especially its metallurgical combine, wide prospect, new streets, park and greenery. There is a lot of greenery... I am very happy that the tradition of our construction pioneers – to preserve the green resources of Monchegorsk – lives on."[9] In his mind the splendor of the nickel smelter enhanced the aesthetics of the foliage instead of detracting from it. And he felt this despite the fact that emissions from that very smelter were already destroying "green resources" on adjacent lands.

Vorontsov's son – also named Nikolai – took a very different path than his father, but an equally Soviet one. After pursuing a career in science, he became a well-known and outspoken environmentalist in the 1980s. He even came to serve as the Minister of the Environment of the Soviet Union as the country was splitting apart. Shortly after the collapse, the son offered some tentative and cautious optimism: "It can only be hoped that the former constituent states of the Soviet Union as well as the world at large will develop a new set of guiding principles to stem the further impoverishment of biological diversity on our common planet."[10] This wish certainly resonates more strongly with common environmentalist tenets than the father's utterances, but it also now sounds unfortunately premature. Almost a quarter of a century has already past since the USSR disappeared from the map. What perhaps is most striking today about the elder Vorontsov's desire to combine industry and conservation without contradiction is how widespread such sentiments still are in mainstream policy toward the natural environment.

Therefore, the lessons I take from the environmental experience of Soviet communism for the twenty-first century rest less in a negative example of what went wrong than in a general warning about the difficulty of finding sustainable modes of land use in the context of continual economic growth. The case of the Soviet north helps show how market capitalism has neither been the exclusive cause of, nor a good solution to, modern environmental problems. Something that transcended the distinctions between capitalist and communist political-economic systems has led to similar environmental trajectories: the relentless impulse to modernize society and the natural world. As mass species extinction and

[9] L. Doronina, "I tundra pokorilas′," *MR* (September 23, 1967): 3.

[10] Nikolai Nikolaevich Vorontsov, "Nature Protection and Government in the USSR," *Journal of the History of Biology* 25, no. 3 (Fall 1992): 383.

global climate change promise to further remake the planet in tumultuous ways, people worldwide may need to rethink economic expansion as a non-negotiable criterion in policymaking. And even if they do, there is nothing to prevent the natural world from responding to human actions again in new, potent, and unforeseeable ways.

Index

Printed in the USA
CPSIA information can be obtained
at www.ICGtesting.com
LVHW091655211223
767102LV00001B/132